WOMEN'S DANCE TRADITIONS OF UZBEKISTAN

SERIES: DANCE IN THE 21ST CENTURY

Dance in the 21st Century features books by leading scholars offering concise and accessibly written introductions to contemporary dance styles circulating in the world today that reflect the critical insights of dance studies in the 21st century. Together, they offer introductory texts on dance practices that resist over-simplification and focus on complexity. Varied approaches of discovery allow readers to look into differences, including historicity, intersectionality, and transcultural dimensions of dance practices. A major goal of this series is to increase the accessibility of decolonizing and anti-racist epistemologies in the global contemporary dance landscape. These include critiques of outdated binaries such as "dance history" and "world dance," as well as problematic orientalist, nationalist, and elitist conceptions of dance that often persist in public discourses, structures of higher education and funding schemes, and cultural programming for dance around the world. By making these critical approaches available to wider audiences, this series forwards a socially engaged public humanities agenda and aims to spark contemporary dialogue among stake-holders in dance communities.

Series Editors:

Emily Wilcox
Thomas F. DeFrantz
Hanna Järvinen

WOMEN'S DANCE TRADITIONS OF UZBEKISTAN

Legacy of the Silk Road

Laurel Victoria Gray

methuen | drama

LONDON · NEW YORK · OXFORD · NEW DELHI · SYDNEY

METHUEN DRAMA
Bloomsbury Publishing Plc
50 Bedford Square, London, WC1B 3DP, UK
1385 Broadway, New York, NY 10018, USA
29 Earlsfort Terrace, Dublin 2, Ireland

BLOOMSBURY, METHUEN DRAMA and the Methuen Drama logo are
trademarks of Bloomsbury Publishing Plc

First published in Great Britain 2024

Series design: Ben Anslow
Cover image © People's Artist of Uzbekistan, Kizlarkhon Dusmukhamedova

Library of Congress Cataloging-in-Publication Data
Names: Gray, Laurel Victoria, author.
Title: Women's dance traditions of Uzbekistan : legacy of the Silk Road / Laurel Victoria Gray.
Description: London ; New York : Methuen Drama 2024. |
Series: Dance in the 21st century | Includes bibliographical references and index.
Identifiers: LCCN 2023033736 (print) | LCCN 2023033737 (ebook) |
ISBN 9781350249479 (paperback) | ISBN 9781350249516 (hardback) |
ISBN 9781350249486 (pdf) | ISBN 9781350249493 (epub)
Subjects: LCSH: Folk dancing, Uzbek–History. | Dance–Uzbekistan–History. |
Choreography–Uzbekistan–History. | Women dancers–Uzbekistan–History. |
Uzbekistan–Social life and customs.
Classification: LCC GV1700.7 .G73 2024 (print) | LCC GV1700.7 (ebook) |
DDC 793.3/19587–dc23/eng/20230828
LC record available at https://lccn.loc.gov/2023033736
LC ebook record available at https://lccn.loc.gov/2023033737

ISBN: HB: 978-1-3502-4951-6
          PB: 978-1-3502-4947-9
          ePDF: 978-1-3502-4948-6
          eBook: 978-1-3502-4949-3

Series: Dance in the 21st Century

Typeset by Integra Software Services Pvt. Ltd.
Printed and bound in Great Britain

To find out more about our authors and books visit www.bloomsbury.com
and sign up for our newsletters.

This book is dedicated to my first Ustoz,
People's Artist of Uzbekistan, Kizlarkhon Dusmukhamedova,
who opened the way for me.

To those who gifted me with their dances
Tamara Khanum, Galia Izmailova, Viloyat Akilova,
But who left too soon.

To Rozia Karimova, Tuhfakhon Pinkhazova, Oliyaxon Hasanova,
and Gul'sum Khamraeva
who shared their knowledge with me.

To Gavkhar Matyokubova, Kadir Muminov and Shanazar Boltaev
who continue to teach me.

To those pioneers of Uzbek dance I never met—
Yusufjon-Kyzyk Shakarjanov, Usta Olim Komilov,
Mukarram Turgunbaeva, and Isaqar Aqilov.

And to the Unnamed dancers,
who carried this Art in their resilient bodies
through countless generations.

CONTENTS

A full filmography and additional images are available at https://www.bloomsburyonlineresources.com/women's-dance-traditions-of-uzbekistan.

ILLUSTRATIONS

FOREWORD

Dana Tai Soon Burgess

W*omen's Dance Traditions of Uzbekistan: Legacy of the Silk Road* is a much anticipated publication that freshly illuminates the depth and breadth of the history of an Asian dance tradition that is little known in the West. Laurel Victoria Gray, Doctor of Humane Letters (*honoris causa*), draws poignant connections between the factors that have shaped these dances, including Central Asia's diverse physical landscape, religious traditions, women's history, and the impact of major sociopolitical events. *Women's Dance Traditions of Uzbekistan* is recuperative and in many instances overcomes previous Western scholars' outsider perceptions. It honors Central Asia's rich culture and histories, thus highlighting the resilience of its population while keeping sight of the beauty of the dances themselves. With a special focus on women dance pioneers, *Women's Dance Traditions of Uzbekistan* takes the reader on an exploratory journey from antiquity to modernity, touching upon Eastern history and literature from the *Shahnameh* and the *Bāburnāmah* to contemporary Uzbek authors. It clarifies the origins of steps, gestures, rhythms, and costumes through both historical references and anecdotes, while illustrating how the vibrant dances of Central Asia continue to evolve and to thrive.

Gray's quality research is informed by over forty years of scholarship that includes academic training as a historian, complemented by embodied knowledge as a dancer, choreographer, and educator. Her dedication to Central Asian dance and cultural diplomacy enable her to seamlessly share a unique insider's perspective of the origins and the development of the region's dances. She first visited Uzbekistan in 1973 when it was under Soviet rule. This initial introduction to Uzbek culture led her to return over a dozen more times. Gray lived in Uzbekistan for two years at the invitation of Tashkent's State Academic Bolshoi Theater of Opera and Ballet. Even before Uzbek independence, she was involved in active cultural exchanges and led delegations of artists to and from Central Asia. In 1979, Gray met celebrated dancer and People's Artist of Uzbekistan Kizlarkhon Dusmuhamedova, who became her mentor, thus bestowing her with a direct link to the Uzbek dance legacy.

Called "our treasure in the U.S." by Uzbek ambassador Javlon Vakhabov, Gray continues to travel to research and study with the dance specialists of Central Asia. She also hosts guest teachers through the Central Asian Dance Camp here in the United States. Her renowned Silk Road Dance Company, which she founded in 1995, has presented its impressive repertoire of Central Asian, Persian, Arab, and Turkic dances across America, from the State of Washington to the White House in Washington, DC, and around the world. Gray has served as a juror at the invitation of the Uzbek government for multiple international performing arts festivals. Gray is the recipient of the 2009 Selma Jeanne Cohen Fulbright Dance Lecture Award, and in 2021, she received the prestigious *Xalqlar Do'stligi* Medal from the Ministry of Culture of the Republic of Uzbekistan in recognition of her contribution to the preservation and promulgation of Uzbek culture.

The engaging prose of *Women's Dance Traditions of Uzbekistan: Legacy of the Silk Road* will satiate the seasoned dance scholar, motivate the professional dance artist, and inspire the novice dancer.

PREFACE

The opportunity to write about a dance form that first captivated me in 1979 allowed me to focus my decades of studying, performing, and teaching Uzbek and Central Asian dance. Here was the chance to share my research, as well as my embodied performance experience, to impart the information that I wish I had from the very beginning of my Silk Road dance adventure. Initially, the structure for this book seemed quite straightforward: provide some background, give descriptions of regional styles, discuss the development during the Soviet era and, finally, examine new trends that emerged after Uzbekistan achieved independence. But as I worked on the material, ancient patterns emerged. As an artist, I had been actively involved in weaving my own small portion of the tapestry of Uzbek dance. When I stepped back from my own involvement, a more complex picture emerged.

Although the invitation to write this book came during the outbreak of COVID-19, making travel impossible, library access in Washington, DC was still possible, as well as a wealth of online resources. More importantly, my own personal library on Central Asian dance and culture, collected over forty years, was right at hand. Some books were very limited editions. One costume book came from the 1957 World Festival of Youth and Students. As I opened these books with a new purpose in mind, I often saw handwritten dedications from those who had gifted the volumes, sometimes from the authors themselves, many of whom were no longer living. The sense that they had bequeathed their knowledge with the intention that their gift could be useful felt devastating. How could I possibly fulfill their expectations? And why had it taken me so long to write more about this dance than my past encyclopedia passages, short articles, anthology chapters, and conference papers?

As I gathered information, I gradually realized that the experience afforded by the years of travel, performance, teaching, choreographing, and directing my own dance company contributed to form a deeper knowledge of the dance. Even the design and construction of costumes made me aware of adaptations made for stage dance. At times, performing some of the "classics" of Uzbek stage choreography, I had literally danced in the footsteps of those past pioneers. My years of teaching university courses in non-Western dance forms helped me discern commonalities in the traditions and experiences of other peoples, especially those of the Turkic and Persianate world.

One of the lessons learned in my studies of history at Occidental College, the University of Waterloo, and the University of Washington was that all writers have bias and each generation writes history anew. My own perspective was shaped by my earliest trip to the USSR, while still a teenager. This study tour, which included Uzbekistan, was followed by subsequent journeys during the Soviet era as well as living for two years in independent Uzbekistan, and continued with many subsequent visits, including performances, as well as participation in official delegations. At this writing, I have returned from my fourteenth trip, having served as a member of the jury for the first Lazgi International Dance Festival in Khiva. For more than forty years, I have witnessed and participated in both change and continuity in Uzbekistan's performing arts, as reflected in the nation's society in general.

My goal is to examine the development of women's stage dance in Uzbekistan without trying to promote any particular social theory or political model, although I clearly sympathize with the artists themselves. My conclusions seem to most align with "ethnosymbolism," which, as succinctly described by Marlene Laruelle, views nations as a "modern construct" that are "built upon some preexisting cultural and ethnic roots that are reinterpreted in new contexts."[1] But what may be most important in viewing the construction of stage dance in Uzbekistan is that it was primarily created by women who risked their lives to perform in public. And all this took place at the same time when other women, like Katherine Dunham, were changing and reshaping their dance heritage on the world stage.

Soviet scholarship on Uzbek dance reflected the political ideology and the moral values of the USSR. We owe much to the respected researcher Liubov Avdeeva, who wrote numerous books on Uzbek dance and dancers, enriched by her personal familiarity with them. She provides great insight into the creative process of the choreographers and performers, poetically describing in detail their special dance gifts with admiration and accuracy. Avdeeva rarely mentions the famed—and infamous—dancing boys known as *bachas*, who were the only dancers permitted to perform publicly in pre-Revolutionary Turkestan. With their connections to wealthy and powerful men, as well as links to homosexual practices deemed immoral, the boys were a vestige of a past that the Soviets hoped to expunge from their new society. Rather than ignoring the *bachas*, I have chosen to write about their dances, including my research on "dancing boys"— first published in 1986—with descriptions from various parts of the Islamic world.

---

[1]Marlene Laruelle, "The Nation Narrated: Uzbekistan's Political and Cultural Nationalism," in *Constructing the Uzbek State*, Lanham, MD: Lexington Books, 2017, p. 261.

These children deserve recognition for their contributions as artists and carriers of tradition. While their "effeminate" performances most often caught the attention of the European and American men who witnessed their presentations, I have noticed that only certain portions of their program included imitations of female dance. The descriptions of these dances provide a useful glimpse into what the hidden women's dances of the *ichkari* were like because, as young boys, the *bachas* would have been raised in the women's quarters and would have had in their early childhood first-hand experience of female dance styles.

This work does not include the dance traditions of the Surkhondarya region, or the Tajiks, which truly deserve their own detailed study. Lurking within their vestigial rituals and dances, historical links with ancient Sogdiana and China await discovery. Likewise, I have not discussed in depth the Sufi *zikr*, in which I have participated, because it is not stage dance, but ancient ritual.

My personal experiences with Uzbekistan, its people, and its dance will remain, for the most part, in the footnotes; those are tales for another time. This story belongs to the people of Uzbekistan themselves, so I will endeavor to place them center stage. But before I step back behind the curtain, I will reveal my own very personal bias.

At an international conference in Khiva in April 2022, Hulkar Hamroeva of the Uzbekistan State Academy of Dance brought to my attention a poem, written in 1987, by People's Poet of Uzbekistan Anwar Obidjon. She discovered it was one of only a handful of Uzbek-language poems written about dance.[2] To my great astonishment, the poem was written about me, "Greyhonim," as I am known in Uzbekistan. The full text is included in the index of the companion web page of this book, but in the last line the poet recognized something I had, even back then, intuitively embodied in my dance and which I now understand is woven throughout this book—*Uzbekning dardini tinglaguvchi kam*—"there are few people who listen to the pain of Uzbeks." While the joy of Uzbek dance may be more evident, it is from the resilient endurance of the pain that the magnificent, many-faceted gem of women's dance has emerged.

---

[2]Khulkar Khamroeva, *Gavkhar Matyokubova Izhod va Ilm Integratsiyasi*. Tashkent: Monografiya, 2022, p. 204.

ACKNOWLEDGMENTS

Yaxshi so'z—ko'ngil podshosi
(A good word is the king of the soul.)

UZBEK PROVERB

Many good words are owed to many "kings" and "queens" who generously shared their time and encouragement. First, I thank Emily Wilcox, whose interest in my work launched this project and brought me to the attention of Bloomsbury Academic Press. And special thanks to my diligent editors at Bloomsbury who helped in this process.

Deep gratitude goes to my dance colleague Dana Tai Soon Burgess, Professor Emeritus of Dance at the George Washington University, whose continuous chant of "write the book" helped manifest this reality. I thank him for his unflagging willingness to read chapters, always providing insightful comments and suggestions.

Special thanks to my long-time Seattle friends, Delilah Flynn and Joanne Young, who both accompanied me at different times on my travels to Uzbekistan, and actively participated in hosting Uzbeks in Seattle, invigorating the cultural exchange; and to Barbara Endicott Popovsky, who hosted in her Seattle home in 1982 the first Uzbek dance workshop, taught by Kizlarkhon Dusmukhamedova. The Seattle–Tashkent Sister City Committee, under the leadership of Rosanne Royer, in 1979 sustained a remarkable relationship that enabled me to continue and deepen my contact with Uzbekistan during the Soviet years and into Independence.

My heartfelt thanks go to Nilufar Rakhmanova, native of Bukhara, who blesses Silk Road Dance Company with her readiness to discuss nuances of Uzbek language and customs, and to Sepideh Farshadi who greatly assisted with Persian language questions. And to all the members of Silk Road Dance Company for sharing my enthusiasm for Uzbek dance.

Several individuals behind the photographs in this book generously shared their talents. Uzbek photographer Rustambek Shapirov granted permission to publish his images of dancers taken over the decades. Special thanks to Andrew Hale of Anahita Gallery for the vintage photo of dancing boys at a gathering in Khiva.

More photos appear on the companion website for this book. The brilliant male dancer Nosirjon Dekhkanov shared his color photos of the newly revived Bakhor Ensemble. Jon K. Chang and Larisa Valentinovna Kim graciously provided historic photographs of the Koryo-Saram dance groups, which appear in the supplemental website to this book, as well as detailed information about the community. Todd Harris used his skill to format the photographs I took of the Bakhor Ensemble at Tashkent's State Academic Bolshoi Theatre of Opera and Ballet. Todd and his bride Kathy Papienski shared some cautious holiday celebrations during the isolation of quarantine. My cat-loving neighbor in Tashkent, Laura Osifyan, created the charming map of Uzbekistan for this book.

My deep love and appreciation go to my parents, Ann and Leo, my brother Frederick Cooper Gray and my sisters Diana and Carolee Gray for providing emotional and material support in this process. And to my late brother Jack, who was a wonderful role model of a professor who always taught with humor and energy.

Friends and colleagues in and from Uzbekistan and the CIS: Elena Kari-Yakubova, Hulkar Hamroeva, Hamid Kakhramonov, Leonid Kudryavtsev, Yulduz Gaybullaeva, Afag Huseynova, Yuldosh Juraboev, Anaxon Otajonova, Dilorom Amanullaeva, Malika Khaidarova, Alagez Salakhova, Fazliddin Shamsiev, Azizdjan Karimov, Rakhim Karimov, Rafael Nektalov, Yulya Semchenko, Sashar Zarif, Gulnara Musaeva, and Rustam Ilyasov.

Over many decades, Tamara Khanum, her daughter Vanzetta, and her granddaughter Alagez Salakhova have all shown me generous hospitality and kindness. What an astounding privilege to have known these three women, and what a loss that they are no longer among us.

Friends from college and graduate school: Don Van Atta and Janet Evans Houser, also helped with this project.

Travis Fontaine Jarrell shared two Uzbek trips with me along with her insights. Theodore Levin helped with several research questions, as did Sahra C. Kent.

James Pickett and Saidolimkhon Gaziev both generously shared information they found about dance in Turkestan. Special appreciation goes to Jon K. Chang, who shared his research on the Koryo-Saram. My gratitude also goes to He Zhang, for sharing her conference paper on the Sogdian Whirl and Shamanism.

In Uzbekistan, the staff at the House Museum of Tamara Khanum, Shoista Alieva and Shaxlo Sharipova, shared photographs and information.

Over the years, the continuous support of the diplomatic staff at the Embassy of the Republic of Uzbekistan in Washington, DC, including Akhror Burkhanov and Ambassador Javlon Vakhabov.

And a final—and perhaps most surprising— acknowledgment belongs to the remarkable Korean artists of BTS, whose energizing music and astonishing choreography provided endless, bright inspiration throughout the years when I worked in the isolation caused by the COVID-19 pandemic. 고맙습니다!

NOTES ON TRANSLATION, TRANSLITERATION, AND HONORIFICS

Russian translations of text, unless otherwise indicated, are my own and rendered according to the Library of Congress system. Of course, exceptions are made for people and places already embedded in English, such as Tchaikovsky and Moscow.

Uzbek translations are also properly attributed if they are not my own, but transliterations are not entirely consistent. Just as the dance traditions of Uzbekistan are layered with the movement vocabulary of different cultures and ethnicities, so too have many various alphabets been used for writing Uzbek names, places, and terms. At present in Uzbekistan, one difference is that the letters "q" and "x" have been used in place of the "k" and "kh" from Soviet-era transliterations of Russian spelling. While I have a great personal fondness for the letters "q" and "x," they can become bumps in the path of otherwise smooth prose, causing an English-speaking reader to stumble for a moment wondering whether an "x" is pronounced as it is in "xylophone" or how they can possibly be expected to wrestle with the formidable "qyrq qyz." English-language spelling rules require that the letter "q" should always be accompanied by "u," and it may seem peculiar to English-speakers when "q" appears "unchaperoned" in Uzbek words.

And then there is the habit of familiarity of acquaintance made with people and places first encountered during the Soviet era. Thus, my beloved *ustoz* Kizlarkhon Dusmukhamedova will remain as I first encountered her, and not as Qizlarxon Do'stmuhamedova, as her name is rendered in current Uzbek orthography.

While specialists may recoil from my transgressions, please be indulgent. If the past one hundred years have shown anything, it is that orthography is transient. Who knows? We may yet return to Turkic runes.

Concerning Honorifics

In Uzbekistan, as in many Asian cultures, special honorifics are traditionally used to denote respect and status. When addressing a person, the suffix "opa" (elder sister) and "aka" (elder brother) can be added to the first name of an individual as a sign of respect and acknowledgment of seniority.

Other honorifics, indicating a particular profession, were sometimes embedded within a name. "Usta" indicates a master, "kari" a reciter of the Quran, and "kyzyk" denotes a comedian or comic. "Khanum" is a polite form of address somewhat comparable in English to "madam" or "lady." (In the case of Tamara Khanum, some foreigners have mistaken this honorific for her family name.) Consequently, my references to both Tamara Khanum and Mukarram Turgunbaeva are often given with only their first names, and without the honorific of "khanum" or "opa." No disrespect is intended, only an attempt at clarity for the English-speaker wrestling with unfamiliar names.

TIMELINE OF UZBEK DANCE AND CULTURE

1869	Birth of Yusufjon-Kyzyk Shakarjanov in Margilan.
1879	Russian victory over Kokand.
1973	Birth of Kamolxon Muxammajanov in Kokand.
1875	Birth of Usta Olim Kamilov in Margilan.
1885	Adolxon "Tanovarxon" born in Margilan.
1888	Railway reaches Samarkand via Bukhara.
1889	Birth of Hamza Hakimzade Niyazi in Kokand.
1896	Birth of Mukhitdin Kari-Yakubov in Fergana.
1898	Railway extended to Tashkent and Andijan.
1906	Birth of Tamara Khanum in Margilan.
1909	Birth of Kamil Yashin in Andijan.
1911	Birth of Tursunoi Saidazimova in Tashkent.
1912	Birth of composer Mukhtar Ashrafi in Bukhara.
1913	Birth of Mukarram Turgunbaeva in Fergana.
	Birth of Nurkhon Yuldashkhojayeva in Margilan.
1914	Creation of amateur theater group *Turon* by Uzbek Jadids.
	Birth of Isaqar Aqilov in Samarkand.
1916	Birth of Rozia Karimova in Kazan, later placed in Margilan orphanage.
1917	Bolshevik Revolution.
	Beginning of Civil War.
1918	Hamza and Kari-Yakubov create Drama Troupe of Muslim Youth.

1919	AgitProp Brigade of Turkestan Front led by Hamza.
1920	Emir of Bukhara flees. Bukharan Emir Alim Khan flees to Dushanbe, then Kabul.
1921	Tamara Khanum joins Uzbek Soviet Theater troupe.
1922	Young Pioneer organization founded in USSR.
	Kari-Yakubov begins vocal studies in Moscow.
1923	Vera Maya opens "plastique" Duncan-style dance studio in Moscow.
1924	Republic of Uzbekistan in USSR established with capital in Samarkand.
	Tamara Khanum and Mukhitdin Kari-Yakubov study in Moscow.
1925	Paris hosts the World Exhibition of Decorative Arts.
	Tamara Khanum and Mukhitdin Kari-Yakubov perform.
	Karakalpak Autonomous Oblast established.
1926	Mukhitdin Kari-Yakubov founds the Ethnographic Concert Ensemble.
1927	*Hujum* (Attack) Soviet unveiling campaign launched on March 8.
	Daughter Vanzetta born to Tamara Khanum and Mukhitdin Kari-Yakubov.
1928	Murder of "Uzbek Nightingale" Tursunoi Saidazimova by her husband.
1929	Nurkhon Yuldashkhojayeva murdered by her brother in honor killing.
	Hamza stoned to death in Shohimardon.
	Mukarram Turgunbaeva leaves family to join the first Uzbekistan State Musical Theater in Samarkand.
	Arsin Mal Alan operetta with group dances choreographed by Tamara Khanum.
	Katta O'yin, Usomina, Sadr, Ufari Sahta, and *Dilhoroj* staged.
1930	*Olympiada* of Folk Creativity in Moscow.
	Tamara Khanum performs *Sadr* to *usuls* played by Usta Olim Kamilov.
	Sakhta Ufari staged by Gavkhar Rakhimova and Usta Olim Kamilov.

1932	*Red Caravan.*
	Tamara Khanum organizes Urgench theater with Pulat Rakhimov and Z. Kabulov.
1933	*Farhad and Shirin* musical drama, based on poem by Alisher Navoi, staged.
	Leily and Majnun musical drama created, based on poem by Alisher Navoi.
	Pakhta (Cotton) first staged by Uzbek Musical theater.
	Langston Hughes and Si-Lan Chen visit Uzbekistan, meet Tamara Khanum.
	Tamara Khanum opens first dance school in Tashkent.
1934	Kari-Yakubov organizes the Uzbek Opera Studio at the Moscow Conservatory, the basis of the Uzbek National Opera and Ballet Theatre.
1935	London hosts First International Folk Dance Festival. Uzbekistan sends Tamara Khanum and Usta Olim, winning gold medals.
1937	Ancient dance *Katta O'yin* restaged by Yusufjon-kyzyk Shakarjanov, Usta Olim, and Tamara Khanum. Presented as a solemn arrival of Farhad into the palace.
	Gul O'yin staged by Tamara Khanum with Usta Olim for the production of *Farkhad and Shirin,* to depict Shirin and her handmaidens bringing flowers to look at canal built by Farhad.
1938	Khwarezmian Archeological-Ethnological Expedition, led by Sergei Tolstov, encounters ancient fortress of Topraq Qala.
	Faizulla Khodzhaev executed by firing squad.
1939	Great Ferghana Canal constructed.
	Korean population of the Soviet Far East forcibly relocated to Central Asia, including Uzbekistan.
	Shakhida with Mukarram Turgunbaeva and Usta Olim Kamilov.
1940	First Uzbek Ballet *Gulyandom* with Tamara Khanum and Mukarram Turgunbaeva.
	Theater director Vsevolod Meyerhold executed.
1941	Germany invades USSR.

1942	*Ulugbek* opera premieres, featuring dance solo *Munojat*.
	Uzbek dance artists tour Iran.
	Mukarram Turgunbaeva brings *Tanovar* to stage.
1943	*Ak Bilyak* ballet premieres.
	Choreographer Pavel Yorkin creates Tashkent ballet studio.
	Rozia Karimova and other Uzbek artists perform at Tehran Conference.
1944	Stalin forcibly deports Crimean Tatar population; many sent to Uzbekistan.
1945	*Fountain of Bakhchisaray* with Mukarram Turgunbaeva as *Zarema*.
	Japanese POWs arrive in Tashkent; many work on construction of Opera House.
1947	Tashkent Choreographic School reopens as Tashkent Conservatory.
1949	*Ballerina* (Dancer) staged at Navoi Theatre.
1950	Dance artists tour of People's Republic of China.
1951	*Dekada* of Uzbek Literature and Art in Moscow.
	Elizaveta Petrosova invited to create Karakalpak stage dance.
1952	Mukhitdin Kari-Yakubov arrested and "repressed" as an Enemy of the People.
	Mukarram Turgunbaeva creates a new variant of *Pilla* as a *massovyi* stage dance.
1954	Mukarram creates solo Indian dance, stages *massovyi* Mongolian dance.
1955	Uzbek artists tour India, North Korea, Albania, Italy, Austria, Afghanistan.
	Korean solo dance added to repertoire.
	Kari-Yakubov released. Returns to family in Tashkent.
1956	*Secrets of the Paranjah* based on play by Hamza.
	Bakhor Ensemble tours Cambodia, Thailand, North Korea, Afghanistan.
	Khrushchev "Secret Speech" at 20th Congress of CPSU.
	Tamara Khanum awarded "People's Artist of the USSR."

1957	Mukhitdin Kari-Yakubov passes away after accidental injury.
	Moscow hosts *World Festival of Youth and Students*, with participation of artists from Uzbekistan, including Bakhor Ensemble.
	Crimean Tatar population receives permission to form Khaytarma Ensemble.
1960	Bakhor Ensemble awarded title of Uzbek State Folk Ensemble of UzbekSSR.
1964	Bakhor Ensemble performs in Moscow, Kiev, Kazakhstan, Karakalpakia, Khorezm, and Ferghana Valley.
	Shodlik (Joy) choreographed by Rozia Karimova with *usuls* by Sh. Niyazov.
	Kaldiroch (Swallow) choreographed by Rozia Karimova, *usuls* by R. Icakhozhaev.
1965	Bakhor Ensemble tours Libya, Sudan, Morocco, Egypt, and Tunisia.
1966	Earthquake devastates Tashkent.
	Kamiljon Otanyazov performs with verses to Lazgi at Navoi Theater.
1967	Statue of dance martyr Nurkhon, created by Valentin Klevantsov, erected in Margilan.
1968	Kizlarkhon Dusmukhamedova premiers *Gozel* solo on Uzbek television.
	Uzbek artists perform in Cairo and Alexandria.
	Gavkhar Rakhimova brings Khorezm artists to Tashkent, creating Lazgi Ensemble.
1969	Kayagum, the first semiprofessional Korean song and dance ensemble, created by the Uzbek Philharmonic.
1973	Seattle–Tashkent Sister City relationship established.
1978	*Blue Maqom* by Mukarram Turgunbaeva stage at Navoi Theater.
	Bakhor Ensemble performs at Tchaikovsky Concert Hall in Moscow.
	Death of People's Artist of Uzbekistan Mukarram Turgunbaeva.
1979	Members of Bakhor Ensemble and guest artists tour the USA.

1984	Premier of *Tomyrys* ballet, based on legendary queen of the Massagetae.
1987	Release of film *Smysl Zhizni* (The Meaning of Life) with a re-enactment of the building of the Ferghana Canal, with dancer Alagez Salakhova playing the role of her grandmother Tamara Khanum. Also performing, Dilyafruz Djabbarova.
1989	Uzbek artists perform in Washington, DC *Timur and the Princely Vision* Smithsonian exhibit.
1991	Uzbekistan declares independence from USSR.
1992	Crimean Tatar Ensemble "Khaytarma" departs Uzbekistan to return to Crimea.
	First *Mustaqillik Bayram* celebration held in Tashkent.
1993	Statue in Margilan dedicated to the martyred Nurkhon removed.
1995	First Central Asian Dance Camp held in Santa Fe, New Mexico.
1997	Tashkent State Higher School of Folk Dance and Choreography reorganized.
	Sharq Taronalari Festival inaugurated in Samarkand.
	Presidential decree establishes *UzbekRaqs,* combining professional dance groups.
2000	5th Central Asian Dance Camp held in DC at Uzbek Embassy.
2001	Kizlarkhon Dusmukhamedova's *Ensemble Munojat* performs at Kennedy Center.
2015	*Silk and Spices Festival* inaugurated in Bukhara.
2016	Death of Uzbek President Islam Karimov.
2018	Inaugural *Maqom Festival* held in Shahrisabz.
	Raqs Sehri (Magic of Dance) *Festival* inaugurated in Khiva in 2018.
	15th Central Asian Dance Camp held at Embassy of Uzbekistan in Washington, DC.
2019	*House of Korean Culture* opens in Tashkent.
	International Festival of Handicrafts hosted in Kokand.
	Raqs Sehri Festival held in Khiva 2019.

16th Central Asian Dance Camp held at Embassy of Uzbekistan in Washington, DC.

2020 February 4, Uzbek President Shavkat Mirziyoyev issues proclamation on dance art which reconstitutes Bakhor Ensemble.

Choreography Institute becomes Uzbekistan State Academy of Choreography.

2021 Premiere of *Lazgi: Dance of Love and Soul* ballet at Navoi Theatre.

2022 Death of People's Artist of Uzbekistan Viktoria (Viloyat) Aqilova.

1st Lazgi International Dance Festival and Scientific Conference held in Khiva.

Evening gala honoring People's Artist of Uzbekistan, Mukhitdin Kari-Yakubov.

The revived Bakhor Ensemble performs in Moscow, Leningrad.

2023 Bakhor Ensemble performs in Dubai, Spain, and Russia.

Death of People's Artist of Uzbekistan Kizlarkhon Dusmukhamedova.

Concert and conference in celebration of 110th anniversary of the birth of Mukarram Turgunbaeva.

50th anniversary of the Seattle–Tashkent Sister City Association.

Death of People's Artist of Uzbekistan Sherali Jo'rayev, traditional singer who performed with leading Uzbek dance artists on stage and television specials.

Death of film actress and artist, Alagez Salakhova, grand-daughter of Tamara Khanum and Mukhitdin Kari-Yakubov.

PART ONE

HIDDEN ROOTS

1 THE GODDESS AND THE DANCING BOYS

Invisible roots feed the visible tree.[1]

Of all art forms, dance remains the most difficult to document because it is so ephemeral. As Saidolimkhon Gaziev observed, the history of Central Asia, for the most part, "remains a domain of elite history" focusing on "men who were privileged by birth, wealth, or education."[2] Dancers were far from elite, of low social status because of the opprobrium linked with such entertainment in traditional Islamic society.[3] They occasionally stepped into the orbit of the rich and powerful in their role as performers, sometimes appearing for foreign guests, but these were *male* dancers, the famous dancing boys known as *bachas*. With only a few notable exceptions, the travelers' accounts of their performances were written by men, cultural outsiders and non-dancers, often with a Eurocentric bias, who were forbidden the precincts of the harem, the *ichkari* of Central Asian homes. Women's lives went largely unrecorded—unless they ran afoul of the law—making attempts to trace women's dance in Turkestan's[4] highly gendered Islamic society an even greater challenge. Clues can be gleaned from studying the *bachas* because their repertoire sometimes included purposeful imitations of women's appearance and dance. Although frequently attributed to the Muslim practice of secluding women, the presence of dancing boys in Turkestan, and the custom of dressing youths in female garb, pre-dates Islam. Much more ancient roots exist, connected

---

Sections in this chapter come from Laurel Victoria Gray, "Dancing Boys." *Arabesque*, Vol. XII, no. 1, May–June 1986, pp. 8–11.
[1] "*Nevidimyye korni kormyat vidimoye derevoI*," folk saying cited by Usman Karabaev in *Ethnokultura: traditsionnaya narodnaya kul'tura*. Tashkent: Shark Publishing, 2005, p. 130.
[2] Saidolimkhon Gaziev, "Regulating the Intimate: Prostitution in Russian Turkestan," Humboldt University, https://nomadit.co.uk/conference/cess2018/paper/43874.
[3] Laurel Victoria Gray, "Music and Dance within the Islamic Context." *Arabesque*, Vol. X, no. 1 (May–June 1984): 24–25, 34–35.
[4] Turkestan is one of the historical names for most of the region of present-day Uzbekistan.

both to the once widespread goddess cults of the region as well as the militarization of male society. The enduring tension between masculine and feminine spheres of power and influence still existed after the acceptance of Islam and surfaced in dance performances.

Ancient Goddess Cults and Gender Roles

Goddess cults abounded in the Near East, Caucasus, and Central Asia. The cult of Anahita was deeply established as evidenced at archeological sites such as Topraq Qala in Uzbekistan and Penjikent in Tajikistan. Burnt remnants of her sanctuaries and temples bear witness to the destructive fury with which they were attacked. But even after centuries, her lingering presence remains. Today, on the territory of present-day Uzbekistan, "most of the female gatherings in that area relate to the system of celebrations based on a solar/lunar calendar or on different religious beliefs (predominantly Islam, but also other pre-Islamic beliefs, such as that of the female goddess from Manichaeism, Tengri cults, and Zoroastrianism)."[5] The deity was female, source of human fertility and by this association, the feminine was closer to divine. In the lands touched by Zoroastrianism, the Goddess was "an Indo-Iranian cosmological figure, Anahita"[6] of the life-giving waters. "Associated with fertility, healing, and wisdom, she looked after the well-being of women, promoting fertility, safe childbirth, and making the life of women a little easier."[7] In the Khorezm region, "Anahita became Ambar-Ona, whose power comes from the Amu-Darya River. Female shamans still invoke her name for the success of healing rituals. At Navruz (the pre-Islamic New Year celebration), songs in her honour are still sung during the preparation of the sacred meal sumalyak."[8] The goddess *Bibi-Seshanbe* (Lady Tuesday) is still revered today in the Boysun region of Uzbekistan, where she "is believed to be the protector of all women in the world. She is praised and her help is invoked whenever women gather together."[9] In present-day Ferghana Valley, male shamans "have been compelled to put on female attire and to perform particularly female duties imitating women in everything."[10] One shaman, Tashmat, living "in the village Gova of the Chust district of the Fergana

---

[5]Razia Sultanova, "Female Celebrations in Uzbekistan and Afghanistan: The Power of Cosmology in Musical Rites." *Yearbook for Traditional Music*, 40 (2008): 8.

[6]"Anahita was known as Aredvi Sura Anahita in the Avestan language." Sultanova, "Female Celebrations," p. 9.

[7]Ibid.

[8]Ibid.

[9]Ibid.

[10]Adkham Ashirov, "Traces of Shamanistic Beliefs in Life Patterns of the Uzbeks in the Fergana Valley," p. 5. www.Academia.Edu/9761920/Traces_Of_Shamanistic_Beliefs_In_Life_Patterns_Of_The_Uzbeks_In_The_Fergana_Valley.

Valley, was compelled to modify his sex, donning female dress because men's clothing was forbidden by the spirits-patrons."[11]

Much farther to the East in Kyŏngju, capital of the ancient Silla kingdom, a silver bowl engraved with the image of Anahita was discovered in one of the royal tombs of Korea's Silla Dynasty dating back to the fifth or sixth century CE.[12] The widespread cult of Anahita also existed in the Caucasus where she was celebrated in dance. In Georgia, she was known as Nana. The Georgian dance *Samaya* takes its name from the word *sami*, meaning "three," and was always danced in groups of three women, echoing the sacred trinity of Mother, Maiden, and Crone. Dedicated to the moon goddess Nana, the dance was done to honor her upon the birth of the first female child born into a family.[13] Dances were also dedicated to another goddess of the Caucasus, the golden-haired Dali, but, according to Georgian dance scholar Avtandil Tataradze, were later "reassigned" to her son Amirani, signaling the transition from matriarchy to patriarchy.[14]

The worship of female deities extended into the Arabian Peninsula. Prior to the advent of Islam, statues of goddesses were among the many idols housed in the Kaaba at Mecca, which pilgrims visited to worship the female deities *al-Lat, al-'Uzza, Manat*, and others. In one alleged incident, the Prophet Muhammad mistook for divine revelation the so-called "Satanic verses" that praised these three Meccan goddesses. Profoundly controversial, scholars still debate the authenticity of such an occasion because it opened the door to polytheism that the monotheistic nature of Islam had soundly shut.[15]

Some vestiges of goddess worship remained on the Arabian Peninsula as recently as the first half of the twentieth century, according to Wilfred Thesiger, who traveled[16] extensively among the Bedouins and witnessed their customs. In the 1940s, he attended one ceremony that was performed on pubescent boys who were dressed up as girls for the occasion,[17] apparently an imitation of menarche, the onset of menstruation that signals sexual maturation and fertility for girls.

---

[11]Ibid.

[12]"Assuming that the tomb was constructed in the fifth or sixth centuries, it is safe to say that Persian merchandise had already found its way into Korea and was being used by Koreans." Lee Hee Soo, "Evaluation of Kūshnāma as a Historical Source in Regard to Descriptions of Basīlā." *Acta Koreana* 21, no. 1 (2018): 19–20. Muse.Jhu.Edu/Article/756449.

[13]Avtanidil Tataradze, personal interview arranged 1989 by Guliko Abashmadze of the Georgian Friendship Society, who also served as translator. See Laurel Victoria Gray, "The Goddess Dances: Women's Dance of Georgia." *Habibi* 14, no. 4 (Fall 1995): 17, 39. thebestofhabibi.net/vol-14-no-4-fall-1995/the-goddess-dancing/.

[14]Gray, "The Goddess Dances," p. 17.

[15]For detailed references on the so-called "Satanic verses" and the connection with the pre-Islamic Meccan goddesses al-Lat, al-'Uzza, and Manat, see Sam Shamoun, "Muhammad and the Daughters of Allah: A Summation of the Evidence for the Satanic Verses," www.answering-islam.org/Shamoun/satanic_verses.htm.

[16]Wilfred Thesiger, *Arabian Sands*. New York: E.P. Dutton and Company, Inc., 1959, p. 91.

[17]Ibid.

Thesiger believed it to be "the modified form of a rite older than Islam" and one which Ibn Saud[18] had forbade as a pagan custom.[19] Music and dance played an integral role in the ritual.

> For a fortnight the young men who were to be circumcised had danced each evening and late into the night, waiting for the day when the old men would announce the positions of the moon and stars were favorable. The initiated wore short tight-sleeved red jackets and baggy white drawers, tight in the ankles, the only time in their lives when they wore drawers, which were women's dress.[20]

The operation entailed a particularly extreme form of circumcision. When completed, the lad, whose drawers had been removed for the rite, "sprang forward and, to the compelling rhythm of the drums, danced frenetically before the eager, craning crowd, leaping and capering while the blood splashed down his legs."[21]

The effeminate dress, red colors of the initiate's garb, importance of the position of the moon all suggest links to menarche and the pagan culture of the Great Mother that once flourishes in the Middle East. "Castration as a means of acquiring feminine powers was still evident among priesthoods of the Great Mother, along with other female-imitative devices such as transvestism."[22] Circumcision seems to have originated as a "modified form of earlier, female-imitative castrations."[23]

The Muslim conquest of Persia that began in 633 CE and had extended into Central Asia by the 680s brought Islam in its wake, although adoption of the new religion was not immediate. With the collapse of the Sasanian Empire, Peroz III, the son of the last king, Yazdegard III, retreated to China and served as a Tang general.[24] Some Zoroastrians fled Persia, finding refuge in India and elsewhere, where they became known as Parsees.

The eventual acceptance of Islam and the adoption of customs of veiling and the seclusion of women created a void in society, one which may have been filled

---

[18]Abdulaziz bin Abdul Rahman (1876–1953), the first king of Saudi Arabia.

[19]Thesiger, *Arabian Sands*, p. 91.

[20]Ibid.

[21]Ibid.

[22]Theodore Gaster, *Myth, Legend, and Custom in the Old Testament*. New York: Harper and Row, 1969, p. 317, cited in *The Woman's Encyclopedia of Myths and Secrets* (San Francisco: Harper and Row Publishers, 1983), p. 145. For a discussion of the Great Mother of Arabia, see Robert Briffault, *The Mothers: A Study of the Origins of Sentiments and Institutions*. New York: The MacMillan Co., 1927, Vol. III, pp. 79–81.

[23]*The Woman's Encyclopedia*, p. 145. For further discussion on the topic, see Francis Huxley, *The Way of the Sacred*. New York: Doubleday and Company, 1974. See also the chapter "Castration, Circumcision, and the Great Mother" in Bruno Beelheim's work *Symbolic Wounds* (Glencoe, IL: The Free Press, 1954). G. A. Barton suggests that originally all Semitic circumcision was a sacrifice to the goddess of fertility. See his essay, "Semitic Circumcision," in *Encyclopedia of Religion of Ethics*. New York: Charles Scribner's Sons, 1911, Volume III, p. 680.

[24]M. Compareti, "The Last Sasanians in China." *Eurasian Studies*, 2, no. 2 (2003): 197–213.

all the easier because of the existence of ancient rituals in which initiates mimicked women. In the Arab world, these connections continued. The musician Tuwais ("the little peacock"), dubbed the "father of song in Islam," not only wore women's clothing, but dyed his hands with henna, earning him—and those who followed him—the title of *mukhannath*, "effeminate."[25] He was driven from the holy city of Medina because of his vocation; perhaps his dress and manner were uncomfortable reminders of the rituals of pre-Islamic cults.

Intriguingly, performances by young boys in female attire continued to be associated with circumcisions in Muslim society into the nineteenth century. The British Orientalist Edward Lane noted that dancing boys were "often employed, in preference to the Ghawazee [professional female dancers], to dance before a house, or in its courtyard, on the occasion of a marriage-fete, or the birth of a child or a circumcision; and frequently perform at public festivals."[26] Lane attributed their popularity to the Islamic prohibition against public display by women:

> Many people of Cairo, affecting, or persuading themselves to consider that there is nothing improper in the dances of the Ghawazee but the fact of it being performed by females, who ought not to thus expose themselves, employ men to dance in the same manner, but the number of these male performers, who are mostly young men, and who are called "Khawals," is very small.[27]

The *Khawals* were Muslim and natives of Egypt. Lane characterized their dancing as "exactly of the same description as that of the Ghawazee" and also accompanied by "castanets."[28] The dress of these dancing boys combined masculine and feminine elements and consisted of "a tight vest, a girdle, and a kind of petticoat."[29]

> Their general appearance, however, is more feminine than masculine: they suffer the hair of the head to grow long, and generally braid it, in the manner of women; the hair of the face when it begins to grow, they pluck out; and they imitate the women also in applying kohl and henna to their eyes and hands.[30]

Some dancers went so far as to veil themselves when venturing out in public "not from shame, but merely to affect the manners of women."[31]

---

[25]Philip K. Hitti, *History of the Arabs*. New York: St. Martin's Press, 1953, p. 18.
[26]Edward Lane, *The Manners and Customs of the Modern Egyptians*. New York: E. P. Dutton and Co., Ltd., 1908, p. 389.
[27]Ibid., pp. 388–89.
[28]Probably *sagat*, i.e., finger cymbals.
[29]Lane, *Manners and Customs*, p. 389.
[30]Ibid.
[31]Ibid.

In addition to the *Khawal*, there existed another class of male dancers, "whose performances, dress, and general appearance" resembled the *Khawal*, "but was known by a different name 'gink,' a term which is Turkish, and has a vulgar signification which aptly expresses their character. They are generally Jews, Armenians, Greeks, and Turks."[32]

Among Turks, both the dancing boys and girls were known as *çengi*, a term from which "gink" may have derived.[33] The origin of the word is unclear, but it has been linked to the *çenk* (mouth harp or so-called "Jew's harp") that sometimes accompanied their dancing.[34] "Another explanation of the origin of the word derives from çingene meaning gypsy and it will be remembered that the majority of dancing boys and girls were, in fact gypsies ... "[35] Unfortunately, early Turkish sources offer little on the subject because, as was so often the case in Islamic society, "dancing was considered a wicked sport, especially when indulged in by professional women and boys."[36] Other terms for dancing boys were *köçek* ("baby camel") and *tavşan* ("rabbit").

The dancing boys often accompanied their performances with finger-snapping, clappers, finger cymbals, or the *cengane* ("Jingling Johnie").[37] They cultivated an effeminate appearance, often growing their hair long and dressing like girls. As for their style of dance, travel accounts by foreigners paid particular attention to this and "although they emphasized the slack morality and obscene character of their dancing, they could not hide in their descriptions the breathless interest that they took in these performances."[38] One nineteenth-century traveler, J. L. S. Bartholdy, determined that there were perhaps as many as six hundred dancing boys in the taverns of Constantinople, some of whom were performers of great virtuosity.[39] The *köçek* enjoyed such popularity among the Janissaries that they were often the cause of discord among the troops, and Sultan Mahmud forbade their appearances in an attempt to preserve order in the army.[40] Many of the dancing boys fled to Egypt, where they found employment under the Khedive Mehmet Ali Pasha. "Finally, so as to put an end to riots, there was a law passed in 1857 which outlawed köçek, prohibiting their performances."[41] To the east, another analog existed in Korea, first mentioned in the *Samguk Sagi* (*The History of the Three Kingdoms*) compiled in the twelfth century. It tells of the *hwarang*, the "flower boys," a unique

---

[32]Ibid.
[33]Metin And, *A Pictorial History of Turkish Dancing*. Ankara: Dost Yaymlari, 1976, p. 138.
[34]Ibid.
[35]Ibid.
[36]Ibid.
[37]Ibid., p. 139. The Jingling Johnny is a percussion instrument consisting of a staff ornamented with bells.
[38]Ibid., p. 138.
[39]Ibid., p. 140.
[40]Ibid., p. 141.
[41]Ibid.

society of warriors that received "ethical, artistic, and military training" during the reign of Kim Jinheung of Silla (540–576 CE). The group "was composed of young lads (starting from 13–15 years of age) in large numbers with a story that they replaced women who had fulfilled the same functions before them." The *hwarang* "were chosen from the nobility for their beauty and arrayed in cosmetics, fine clothes, and jeweled shoes … "[42]

> They encouraged one another morally, and delighted one another with singing and music, playing (dancing?) among the hills and streams. They visited 'celebrated' (i.e., sacred) mountains and rivers where they sang and danced, praying for national peace and progress. Good ministers and loyal subjects arose from among them, and they produced great generals and brave soldiers … They softened an age of barbaric splendor with their adolescent gentleness as much as they ennobled it with their courage.[43]

The ancient struggle between masculine and feminine spheres for power and dominance emerged in different cultures. Just as the Korean *hwarang* had association with the military training of youth who assumed some of the entertainment roles previously held by women, so too did Central Asian society develop male institutions. Special "men's houses" became "the main centers in the struggle of men for the predominant influence in the community … which arose during the patriarchy in connection with the separation of the sexes."[44] These houses "were home to unmarried youths who had reached puberty and were initiated. They were a gathering place for men of the community where they spent their free time in the transition period from the matriarchy to patriarchy" and became a sort of "men's union" that "acquired a qualitative new social meaning … *oriented toward eliminating the influence of women*"[45] (Italics mine).

As a sort of "ancient club," the men's unions brought together youth with the primary purpose of preparing young men for an independent life, teaching skills such as food preparation and ritual traditions.[46] They also served a cultural and creative function; the evenings were accompanied by dancing, singing, and dramatized scenes. The men's houses "also served as a place for singers and storytellers to perform these functions," becoming a sort of "folk art house" that passed on the traditions of ethnic culture.[47] The "constant interaction of the elders and the younger" helped

---

[42]Alan Heyman, ed., *The Traditional Music and Dance of Korea*. Seoul: Song Lim Printing Co., Ltd., 1993, p. 10.
[43]Ibid., pp. 10–11.
[44]Usman Karabaev, *Etnokul'tura: traditsionnaya narodnaya kul'tura*, Tashkent: Shark Publishing, 2005, p. 203.
[45]Ibid.
[46]Ibid., p. 111.
[47]Ibid., p. 203.

to solidify cultural values. They transmitted traditional rules of men's behavior in various games and competitions such as "horse races, archery competitions, and fist fights" that were part of the complex of spectacles that had accompanied the circumcision and wedding celebrations.[48] Special occasions and games linked to initiations "resembled similar masquerades of secret societies in the early stages of historical development. They also performed a defensive military function" and "in some places the youth houses looked very much like a small military detachment."[49] The traditional competitions provided "a way of systematic training and education of strong courageous warriors. In general youth associations with their militarized coloring go back to that era."[50] In a region beleaguered by almost constant invasions and war, early military training and the inculcation of camaraderie and loyalty were central to creating warriors who could protect their homeland. These deeply rooted, pre-Islamic social structures created traditions where males gathered and entertained themselves in spheres removed from women.

Male dancers from Bukhara and Ferghana—or at least the Ferghana Valley region—had historic connections where Central Asian warriors served in the military of foreign nations. During the Tang Dynasty, there was a military dance known as the Castle Dance or *An Yueh*, with "An" signifying Bukhara. It was "a symbol of strong military power which could keep the peace for ever … In the dance, there were eighty people wearing leather hats and fierce wooden masks decorated with metal and thready wigs, marching in a square floor pattern (a battle array in the ancient time) to the Bokhara music."[51] Far to the West, at the Abbasid Courts, there was "a description by Abū al-Fara al-Ifahānī of a group of dancing *farāġina* in al-Muʿtaṣim's (r. 218–227/833–842) court."[52] Male dancers called faragina—of Ferghana—appeared in connection with caliphal *Nawrūz*[53] celebrations at popular *Samāġa* performances that were characterized by masked entertainers and "semi-theatrical and semi-carnivalesque"[54] antics, very similar to the Central Asian *masqaraboz*.[55] "The *farāġina* corps were an elite troop of the Caliphal army"[56] and may have brought their traditions of farcical masquerade with them.

[48]Ibid., p. 113.
[49]Ibid., p. 204.
[50]Ibid.
[51]Peter Kim-Hung Wong, "Cultural influences on dance in the T'ang dynasty and the movement characteristics of a dance of the period" (PhD diss., University of Wisconsin, Madison, 1989), p. 72.
[52]Massimiliano Borroni, "Samāġa Performances in Third/Ninth-Century Abbasid Courts." *Bulletin of the School of Oriental and African Studies*, 82, no. 2 (2019): 289. doi:10.1017/S0041977X19000351. Although "Faragina" indicates a connection with the Ferghana region, it may have been a general term for troops from Central Asia.
[53]*Nawrūz* is an alternate spelling of Nowruz or Navruz, the pre-Islamic celebration of the New Year at the Spring Equinox.
[54]Borroni, "Samāġa Performances," pp. 289–90.
[55]The *masqaraboz* are traditional masked comic actors and jesters that existed—and still exist—in Central Asia.
[56]Borroni, "Samāġa Performances," ft. 41, p. 300.

The *Bachas*—Dancing Boys of Central Asia

Although performances by young boys in imitation of girls and women were known throughout Asia for centuries and in a variety of cultures, the topic was avoided in Soviet scholarship on Uzbek dance. The Central Asian dancing boys, known as *bachas*,[57] were often associated with pre-Revolutionary activities deemed unacceptable for the new Socialist society, such as homosexuality, slavery, and the abuse of children. In her discussion of the famous *Katta O'yin* dance suite of the *bachas*, Liubov Avdeeva, respected writer on Uzbek dance, mentioned in an oblique manner that, in addition to characteristic movements and rhythms, the dance was filled "with erotic overtones or unhealthy nervous tension" (*eroticheskim podtekstom ili nezdorovym nervnym napryazheniyem*), which was "brought to pathological ecstasy" (*patologicheskogo ekstaza*).[58]

To continue this Soviet-era reticence on the topic of the *bacha* and ignore their existence altogether would subject these boys to another kind of abuse, that of historical erasure. They were, after all, professional artists. An analysis of their presentations reveals their contribution to the development of Central Asian dance art, especially because descriptions of performances by girls and women during the pre-revolutionary period are almost completely non-existent. Although dancing boys were known throughout the East before Islam, the *bachas* occupied the void left by females in the highly gendered space of Central Asian societies. Despite the often difficult circumstances of their early lives, the *bachas* were able to not only survive but attain a level of artistic achievement that won admiration from local audiences and foreign observers alike. Their dance inspired some of the early choreographies of Uzbek women's stage dance and, for their artistic gifts, these young boys deserve recognition.

In Central Asia, the dancers encountered by foreign male travelers were also young boys, like those in Egypt and Turkey. Their performances were often outdoors, sometimes arranged especially for the entertainment of esteemed guests, although they also appeared in *chaikhonas* (teahouses) and within the walls of private homes. Their entertainment was found throughout Turkestan and beyond, with seemingly little regional variation, unlike the folk dances of the women which, isolated from outside influence in the *ichkari*, tended to remain local in nature.

---

[57]The term *bacha* is derived from the Persian word for child. For an examination of the difficult subject of bacha-bazi, or "boy play," see Ali Abdi, "The Afghan Bachah and its Discontents: An Introductory History." *Iranian Studies*, 56, no. 1 (2023): 161–80. doi:10.1017/irn.2022.42.

[58]Avdeeva, L. Tantseval'Noe Iskusstvo Uzbekistana. Tashkent: Gosudarstvennoe Izdatel'stvo Khudozhestvennoi Literatury, 1963, p. 104.

Bachas performed at parties, festivals, and at teahouses, with female dancing being limited to the women's quarters.[59] "The dance as a social entertainment is quite unknown, it is spectacle, and as women are forbidden by the Emir (of Bukhara) to dance, at any rate in public, and as in the opinion of the Sunni Mussalman it is improper for women to dance in public or private, boys are trained for it."[60]

A syncretic tradition, Central Asian entertainment merged several kinds of performance genres and included circus elements associated with acrobatics, "strong man" demonstrations, tight-rope walking, puppetry, masked entertainment—i.e., *masqaraboz*—and wrestling, as well as displays of horsemanship. They were accompanied by live music, especially piercingly loud "outdoor instruments"—the *nagora* drum, *karnai* trumpet, *surnai* wind instrument—all historically used in military music with sound that would carry across a noisy battlefield.[61]

Keeping a troupe of dancing boys imparted status to the patron. Nobles and wealthy men maintained male dancers in various numbers.[62] One traveler noticed among the court of the Khan of Khiva "a number of good-looking boys of effeminate appearance, with long hair streaming down their shoulders, and dressed a little like women." The youths "lounged about and seemed to have nothing in particular to do."[63] Indeed, it was rumored that the Emir of Bukhara and others had "both female and male harems" and that even the spiritual mullahs were known to patronize them: "For instance, Muhammad Hisari wrote that upon his appointment the new governor of a Bukharan province sent two dancing boys (shatir, lit. 'one who teases') as a gift."[64] The "raging desire for dancing boys" went so far that those who could not support a troupe themselves pooled their resources with others in order to keep *bachas*, "or they plunder or murder to be able to procure a dancing boy. Parents often sell their boys to become batchas, then their future is secure for many a favorite batcha obtains a good public office when he gets old."[65]

---

[59]Mary Grace Swift, *The Art of Dance in the U.S.S.R.* Notre Dame, IN: University of Notre Dame Press, 1968, p. 180.

[60]O. Olufsen, *The Emir of Bukhara and his Country.* London: William Heinemann, 1911, p. 436.

[61]For a detailed analysis of various battle drums, see Valerii P. Nikonorov, "The Use of Musical Percussion Instruments in Ancient Eastern Warfare: the Parthian and Middle Asian Evidence," in Ellen Hickmann, Ingo Laufs, and R. Eichmann, *Music Archaeology of Early Metal Ages: Papers from the 1st Symposium of the International Study Group on Music Archaeology at Monastery Michaelstein,* May 18–24, 1998 (Blankenburg, Germany); *Orient-ArchŠologie, 7; Studien zur MusikarchŠologie II,* Rahden/Westf: Verlag Marie Leidorfe, 2000, pp. 71–82.

[62]Olufsen, *Emir of Bukhara,* p. 436.

[63]Fred Burnaby, *A Ride to Khiva.* New York: Harper and Brothers, 1877, p. 255.

[64]James Pickett, *Polymaths of Islam: Power and Networks of Knowledge in Central Asia.* Ithaca, NY: Cornell University Press, 2020, p. 183.

[65]Olufsen, *Emir of Bukhara,* p. 436.

Performance Elements

The pattern of these performances became an important consideration when these dances moved to the Western proscenium stage in the twentieth century, because Central Asian entertainment was done traditionally "in the round," with the audience seated or standing all around the performance space and the musicians located in one section of this circle. So popular were the public performances of *bachas* that those unable to crowd within the immediate circle would climb trees to get a view. If the performance was held in the courtyard of a home, onlookers would stand or sit on the roofs of adjacent buildings, the flat roofs of Uzbek homes being convenient for this.

Travelers' accounts mention a similar presentational structure. The entertainment usually began with one or more boys sedately tracing a circular path on the carpets that marked the dance floor, with the performance gradually becoming more animated "by degrees to wild dances and antics" intermixed with singing and shouting.[66] One observer noted "a sort of stomach dance," seemingly connecting it to the *danse du ventre* of the Arab world, also noticing "sexual gestures illustrating a love-scene."[67] Gradually, dance movements were added and, as the music became more "excited," so too did the audience and the musicians. After the climax of the performance, there would be a break, and the dance was repeated by one or more different dancers.

Eyewitness accounts of dancers with one arm or both arms raised during the dance resemble postures in vintage photographs of the *bachas*. The descriptions of their dances as "sensuous contortions of the body" labeled the dance at times as of a sexual or even obscene nature—a less than systematic analysis of actual dance movements. One account describes a *bacha* rocking his hips while "playing castanets" (undoubtedly *kairoki*, as can be seen in the old photographs) and mentions "hands raised in a trembling movement," which aptly describes *titramish*—a vibratory trembling of the hands characteristic of Khorezm dance.[68]

Not all of the dances of the *bacha* were truly in imitation of the women. A well-known Central Asian entertainment known as *Katta O'yin*—literally "grand or great entertainment" or "great game"[69]—consisted of several elements of performance. Some accounts note acrobatic elements,[70] such as tumbling; a few

---

[66]Ibid., p. 438.
[67]Ibid., p. 438.
[68]Ibid., p. 438 and Count K. K. Pahlen, *Mission to Turkestan*, translated by N. J. Couriss, London: Oxford University Press, 1964, p. 170. Both men noted the trembling element in some of the dances.
[69]Uzbek writer Hamid Ismailov used *katta o'yin* in the Uzbek title of his book *Jinlar basmi yoxud katta o'yin* (rendered in English as *The Devil's Dance*) playing on the political meaning of the term "The Great Game," the nineteenth-century rivalry between the Russian and British empires seeking control of Central Asia.
[70]Pahlen noted the acrobatic elements in the account of his visit to Khiva, *Mission to Turkestan*, p. 170.

vintage photographs show a boy doing a movement called a "bridge." There were also performances by *masqaraboz*, the often-itinerant performers of a clowning tradition who, dressed in ragged, patched cloaks, presented humorous skits that often mocked the wealthy and powerful.

Musicians provided the accompaniment for *bacha* performances. The most important element was the Central Asian frame drum, known as a *doira*. Other percussion instruments like the *nagora* drums, played with sticks, were also used, with the boys themselves playing *kairoki*. Labeled as "castanets" by foreign travelers, they were two elongated, flat, smooth river stones played as pairs, a set in each hand, emphasizing the dancers' rhythmic movements.

One foreigner remarked that the first dance of the *bachas* was called *Katta O'yin* and it was distinct from regional specialty dances. A favorite dance seemed one where the dancing boy "is dressed as a girl, with long braids of false hair and tinkling anklets and bracelets. Usually but one or two in the troop can dance the women's dance and the female attire once donned remains for the remainder of the feast and the batcha is besought here and there to sit among the spectators to receive their caresses."[71] Other dances were known by special names such as Afghan, Shirazi, and Kashgari, all linked to different regions and ethnicities. (The inclusion of dances from other nationalities in dancers' repertoires would be continued in Soviet times.) "The younger boys usually perform those dances which have more of a gymnastic character, with many summersaults [*sic*] and hand-springs; while the elder and taller ones devote themselves more to posturing."[72]

Braids, Jewelry, Makeup, and Henna

The *bacha* were not always dressed as girls with braids and makeup and henna. A beardless appearance was required, but fine hair on the upper lip was acceptable. The front of the head was shaved, with the hair left to grow long in the back. Traditional Central Asian male and female garments generally have similar lines, but with the woman's *chapan* (robe) gathered beneath the arms. The shape of the *dupi* (skullcap) can also be similar, but the most distinguishing signals of gender are the braids, jewelry, makeup, and henna.

Bachas sometimes wore bells around their ankles, a practice with links to Sasanian images of Anahita as well as a connection with Bukharan female dancers. Whatever the origin, it enraptured one poet to write "from the sound of the bells on their feet [even] the nightingales of beautiful voice forgot how to lament."[73]

---

[71]Eugene Schuyler, *Turkistan; Notes of a Journey in Russian Turkistan, Khokand, Bukhara, and Kuldja.* 2nd ed. London: S. Low, Marston, Searle & Rivington, 1876, p. 134.
[72]Ibid.
[73]Cited by James Pickett in *Polymaths of Islam*, p. 185.

The *bacha*s also sang. At times, theatrical vignettes would be part of the presentation, with one boy playing the feminine role. This provided the opportunity for a *lapar*, a kind of playful and witty conversation in song. Poetic lyrics of songs focused on the theme of love and longing. One observer characterized the dance of the *bacha*s as frequently risqué, "a mixture of dance, gymnastics and song, beating of castanets, all mixed up and always of an obscene character."[74]

The entertainment, at least as seen in Khiva, included acrobatic elements associated with circus performances as well as wrestling. In addition to the rhythm provided by musicians, the boys added percussive ingredients such as rhythmic clapping and the playing of *kairoki*. However, a special part of the performance seemed to be dedicated to purposeful female impersonation.[75] The American journalist J. A. MacGahan witnessed a lengthy performance of the *bacha*s in Khiva in 1874. While seated outdoors on a grassy plot, he watched as about eight to ten young boys entered the performing area and "made a respectful salaam." They wore "the long loose khalat of the Khivans, which reached almost to the heels. Their heads were shaven with the exception of two long black locks, which were behind their ears, and fell over their shoulders." As it grew dark, torches were brought out to illuminate the dance area and stuck into the ground or fastened to trees. "The prettier of the boys now dressed himself up as a girl, with little bells to his wrists and feet, and a very elaborate and pretty cap, covered with bells and ornaments of silver, and with a veil hanging down behind." This dance was of a different nature, "more quiet and modest than that he had gone through as a boy." He initially performed as a soloist but then another boy joined him, and "dancing together, the two enacted a love scene very prettily."[76] MacGahan noted that "all this was done very gracefully and with much seeming intelligence. The actions of the one who was playing the girl were very pretty and coquettish. The torches casting a fitful light on the nodding branches of the tree overhead, the wild faces around, and these two children enacting a love scene, made-up a very strange and picturesque tableau."[77]

Bachas were most often observed dancing on carpets with bare feet. At a party in Bukhara, dancing boys "wore red, loose caftans, wide trousers, all were bare-footed, and their longish hair was hanging down their backs."[78] More than once *bachas* are described wearing red clothing, perhaps echoing the lyrics of Uzbek wedding songs in which the "red color is a symbol of a girl, a white color is a

---

[74]Olufsen, *Emir of Bukhara*, p. 436.
[75]J. A. MacGahan, *Campaigning on the Oxus and the Fall of Khiva* [correspondent of the *New York Herald*]. New York: Harper & Brothers, 1874, p. 320.
[76]MacGahan, *Campaigning on the Oxus*, p. 322.
[77]Ibid.
[78]Olufsen, *Emir of Bukhara*, p. 438.

symbol of a boy."[79] An observer of a *bacha* troupe in Khiva noted the nails of their hands and feet painted red, suggesting they had been painted with henna, a clear imitation of women's practice. Eyebrows were "jet black" and connected to meet "over the bridge of the nose,"[80] a sign of feminine beauty in Turkestan and Persia. In one performance, "servants ran about with lamps and candles which they held up before the faces of the batchas, that they and their mimics could be admired …"[81] Facial expressions, the eyes, and even movements of the eyebrows are all specific to traditional women's dance, an element that became somewhat lost in the transition from the intimate surrounding of the *ichkari* to the concert stage.

The writer Sadriddin Aini described an event in 1888 in Bukhara:

> A multitude of onlookers had gathered in a small square in the middle of which burned a bonfire. A row of tambourine players sat by the fire, and about twenty lovely dancing boys with false braids sung and danced nearby. All about were earthen vessels filled with oil in which rags were burning like torches. Guards armed with sticks shooed the onlookers away so they would not press too close.[82]

Recalling this event that he witnessed on his first night in Bukhara, Aini commented that "there was something about that feast I didn't like."[83]

The Russian painter Vassily V. Vereshchagin, whose detailed paintings depict iconic Central Asian scenes, turned his artist's eye for observation to a description of the *bachas*. He explained that the "usually pretty boys" become *bachas* from the age of eight or older, but the boys were "playing some strange" and "not normal role" that was "uncomfortable to explain." The boys were given up by their parents for money, then trained by older, retired dancers and singers, who "groomed" them for the profession.[84]

Vereshchagin, who had often attended these performances which were known as *tomasha*, requested a special one. Upon his arrival, he noticed that there were people already gathered for the entertainment and the courtyard was packed with onlookers. The only seated spectators were in a circle around the performance area. Others watched from doorways and on the rooftops. The guests were placed next to the *doira* players and musicians, with the entire scene illuminated by a huge oil torch with a red flame, creating a dramatic contrast against a dark evening sky.

---

[79]Mohichehra Ro'ziyeva, "Color Symbolism in Uzbek Folklore." *International Scientific Journal Theoretical & Applied Science*, 85, no. 5 (2020): 278.
[80]Count Pahlen, *Mission to Turkestan*, p. 170.
[81]Olufsen, *Emir of Bukhara*, pp. 438–39.
[82]Sadriddin Aini, *Bukhara: Reminiscences*. Moscow: Raduga Publishers, 1986, p. 133.
[83]Ibid.
[84]V. V. Vershchagin, *Povesti, Ocherki, Vosnominaniya*. Moscow: Sovetskaya Rossia, 1990, p. 140. Vershchagin was a famous Russian painter.

One acquaintance at the event approached Vereshchagin and whispered, "come here." It was an invitation to see something special, the preparation of "how the bacha is dressed."[85] The painter was led to a closed room with only "a few chosen ones"—mostly high-status locals—surrounding a "beautiful boy" who was being dressed for the performance.

> He was transformed into a girl; long hair was tied into several finely braided plaits, his head was covered with a large light-colored silk scarf tied above the forehead, tied with another, narrowly folded, bright red. A mirror was held in front of the batcha, in which he always looked flirtatiously.[86]

Vereshchagin noted that the heavy-set man who held up a candle to provide light throughout the process was so excited that he could barely breathe, causing the author to assure the reader that this description was "no exaggeration." The eyebrows and eyelashes of the boy were darkened, and a few beauty marks were added. Through this process "he was really transformed into a girl and greeted with loud cries of approval when he appeared before the audience."[87]

The performance of this *bacha* followed the same pattern described elsewhere, with the boy quietly walking in circles. The audience clapped along with the *doira*, with the dancer "gracefully bending his body, playing with his hands and moving his head." The artist noticed that the boy's eyes, "large, beautiful, black, and his handsome mouth had some defiant expressions, at times too immodest." The boy's "meaningful glances and smiles" so impacted the viewers that they "melted with pleasure" and behaved obsequiously toward the child, addressing the boy with expressions like "my joy, my heart" and even pleading, "take my life, it is nothing before your smile." As the music became louder, the boy's dance grew livelier and increasingly dexterous as his arms "snaked" around his body. The *doira* rhythms grew faster and louder and the barefoot dancer "turned even faster, so the hundreds of eyes barely had time to follow his movements"—a description which echoes the words of Chinese poets writing about the Sogdian Whirl. Finally, with the desperate crackle of music and the frantic exclamation of the audience, the final figure followed, after which the "male dancer (*tantsor*) or female dancer (*tantsovshchitsa*)"—and here the author underscores the gender ambiguity—paused to drink tea served to him, then again quietly walked across the stage, undulating his arms, "throwing to the right and left, tender, languid, crafty glances."[88]

---

[85]Ibid.
[86]Ibid., p. 141.
[87]Ibid.
[88]Ibid.

Vereshchagin noted that the musicians themselves became even more enthusiastic than the audience and in the "strongest places" they even jumped from their usual squatting position to their knees, violenting pounding on their already loud instruments.[89] The "girl bacha" (*batchudevke*) was then "replaced by a boy batcha, the general nature of whose dances differs little from the first." The dance was followed by singing, which Vereshchagin found monotonous—a term used by many other Europeans, perhaps because of the absence of harmony—and noted the lyrics were characterized by "longing and sadness," expressions of depressed, unsatisfied "but ecstatic love," and very rarely happy love. Such were "the typical themes of these songs, listening to which the native will hunch over and sometimes will cry."[90]

Other observers noticed a similar structure and content to *bacha* performances, noting that, as they continued, the music grew faster and the lyrics of the songs, reflected in the movements of the dancers, focused on the "love and the beauty of women."[91] One observer characterized the increasing tempo of the music as "representing passionate over-excitement."

> The musicians drummed and fluted a regular devilish music, the spectators chimed in and applauded, servants ran about with lamps and candles which they held up before the faces of the batchas, that they and their mimics could be admired …[92]

The pace quickened and "swifter and swifter moved the dancers till they finally sank, seemingly exhausted and enchanted by love."[93]

When the American poet and author Langston Hughes visited Uzbekistan in 1933, he learned about the *bacha* tradition and was told that *bachas*, after retirement, sometimes created their own dance troupes, while others opened teahouses. One informant told him that "at certain times of the year there would be a sort of dancer's fair, when prospective buyers of boy-dancers would gather to select entertainers. At these colorful dance-markets,[94] the best and most handsome of the youthful performers would display their steps before a vast gathering seated around an enormous space in the open air." Hughes learned of one gathering

---

[89]All behavior similar to the physiological reactions described by Neher.
[90]Vereshchagin, *Povesti, Ocherki, Vosnominaniya*, p. 141.
[91]Pahlen, *Mission to Turkestan*, p. 170.
[92]Olufsen, *Emir of Bukhara*, pp. 438–39.
[93]Pahlen, *Mission to Turkestan*, p. 170.
[94]Langston Hughes, "Tamara Khanum, Soviet Asia's Greatest Dancer." *Theatre Arts Monthly*, 1934, p. 832.

attended by four thousand men, "including many rich *beys* who had come for miles around to the dance market. In their turbans and silk gowns, the rich men bargained for the dancers"[95] (Figure 1.1).

After watching traditional Uzbek dances, Hughes concluded that they differed from folk dances of the West.

> Nor are they artificially acrobatic in the manner of the ballet and the theatre. Uzbek dances, typical of the dances of the East, are delicately patterned, graceful body-rhythms, often weaving a subtle story in plastics that the uninitiated would not understand. Each of the old dances had its own traditional beginning, middle and end - the strict forms, always respected and observed, being a mold for the grace of the individual performer.[96]

The traditional dances had been "handed down for generations of dance-makers of the past" with variation depending on the skill of the performer, but

FIGURE 1.1 Dancing boys playing *kairoki* at an all-male gathering in Khiva. Their hair is shaved above the forehead and worn long in back over their shoulders. Musicians, playing *doiras* and *surnai*, are seated directly behind them in the circle of spectators.
Photo source: Anahita Gallery.

[95]Ibid.
[96]Ibid.

the "famous boy-dancers originated marvelous variations. Extremely subtle and extremely delicate movements of the wrists and of the hands, the fingers and the head, the mouth and the eyes might come into play." As an improvisational dance form, the individual artists had liberty to create new movements of their own. (Ironically, the innovations in dance created by Central Asian women in the twentieth century would be labeled as "made up" and an "invented tradition" by a few Western scholars who were unaware that the music, costumes, themes, and gestures they used were deeply rooted in tradition.)

Hughes described a specific eyebrow undulation, with one moving up and the other down, that purportedly originated "from the way in which a rice-mill is propelled by a flowing stream." As a result, he reported that all over Uzbekistan people said, "How good it is that we have rice-mills, because from them we have been given a dance."[97] A very similar movement was described by a Western woman who visited a Persian harem who did not find it charming, and even Chinese annals from more than a thousand years earlier commented on a Tashkent dancing boy who moved his eyebrows.

Even under Islam, some found a way to circumvent the rules of gender separation. In Bukhara, known to be particularly strict about religious convention, a Sufi "gathered with his acolytes in a mosque. During the evenings, women with no licit relationship to any of the males present would mingle with them to sing, dance, and play musical instruments. Those present became so enraptured by the music that they lost themselves in it and carried on for three days straight."[98]

However, two foreign men did see female dances. One was Swedish explorer Sven Hedin, who viewed a private performance of women in the "unsavory quarter" of Samarkand. The other, Eugune Schuyler (1840–1890)—the impressive writer and diplomat who had gone hunting with Leo Tolstoy—stated with authority that "it is not only boys who dance in Central Asia, girls and women do so as well: but their exhibitions are in general confined to the women's court." While in Kokand, Schuyler was invited by Asudullah Bek to see "a splendid tomasha, or spectacle—a dance of women—a thing looked on with orthodox horror by most Mussulmen."[99] Schuyler recalled when the performance began, the sound of drums and instruments drew such a crowd that the Cossacks had to be called to keep them away. The entertainment started around sunset.

---

[97]Ibid., p. 833. Hughes' discussion of Uzbek rhythms and the drummer Usta Olim Kamilov is more thoroughly described in chapter 2 on Uzbek rhythms.
[98]Pickett, *Polymaths of Islam*, p. 185.
[99]Schuyler, *Turkistan; Notes of a Journey*, p. 136.

After a while a girl of thirteen, with a pretty dark face and bright black eyes, though her beauty was spoiled by an indiscreet use of cosmetics—for her eyebrows were turned into a dark line, and the rouge was very prominent on her cheeks—came out to dance. Her dress was a loose bright red silk robe, and her hair hung about her neck in a dozen small braids. Her head was covered with a long silken scarf hanging behind like a veil, fastened with ornaments of silver, and she wore earrings filled with turquoise and colored glass. Her feet were bare.[100]

Her performance followed a pattern similar to descriptions of the dancing boys, in that "she slowly circled on the carpet, bowing first to one and then another, and as the beats of the tambourine became faster her motions became more rapid, and after whirling round a dozen times she sank to the ground, much to the delight of the spectators. Then rising again she commenced a slowly swaying movement, and with arms swinging in cadence completed the circle of the carpet three or four times, again whirled about, and once more sat upon the ground. "[101]

Schuyler noted that "she was succeeded by others and the dances were very similar to those danced by boys, though less vigorous and less graceful; and there was little variety in style until a little girl of eleven—for the most of them were very young, a girl of eighteen being already an old woman."[102]

At intervals she would kneel before one of the spectators, swing her arms as if invitation, and, as it were, make motion of enchantment, each time leaning nearer and nearer to him, until finally, when the enchantment was supposed to be at its height, he was expected to give a kiss, and the dance was ended. Though the enchantment might be practised upon many the kiss was reserved for only one, for the girl would extricate herself like a snake from the proposed embrace and immediately be on her knees before another.[103]

Although rare, there was another occasion when female dancers performed in public, offending local sensibilities. "Such a dance was once before arranged on a public festivity when the Governor-General was present, but he was deceived by the story that the women who danced were the wives of chief natives, who did this in his honour, and he even presented them with some silver cups and souvenirs, which were found the next day in various brothels."[104]

---

[100]Ibid., pp. 136–37.
[101]Ibid., p. 137.
[102]Ibid.
[103]Ibid.
[104]Ibid., p. 140.

Bearded Ladies

Ethnomusicologist Theodore Levin noted in his seminal work on Central Asian music, *A Hundred Thousand Fools of God*,[105] that while travelers' accounts wrote about cross-dressing by dancing boys, another phenomenon "less conspicuous … but far more prevalent in Bukharan society itself (as well as elsewhere in Central Asia) has been male role-playing by women." While the *bachas* were public performers, women had their own forms of entertainment with dance, song, and theatrical vignettes, all presented in the privacy of the *ichkari*. In Bukhara, these entertainers were known as *sozanda*, small groups of three to four women, who could be invited to perform at all-female gatherings. Until the 1950s and 1960s, about ninety per cent of *sozanda* were Jewish, the remaining percentage made up by Tajik and Uzbek women.[106] The *sozanda* sang and danced without instrumental music, accompanying themselves by playing *doira*. Their multifaceted performances consisted of songs, dances, poetic recitations, and playful skits.

And here may be the root of the widely stated impression by Westerners that women did not dance: Central Asian dance has two major genres. One category of dance was *Katta O'yin*, consisting of the "grand entertainment" for large public gatherings, i.e., "male only" events, while *khona bazam* designated the dances performed indoors—chamber dances presented in small, intimate settings. Presented in the smaller indoor space, the *khona bazam* dances are restrained, more psychological, more lyrical, more intimate.[107] The circumscribed space mirrored the circumscribed lives of the women themselves. Like the miniature paintings of Central Asian artists, every tiny detail added to the charm of the picture, from the delicate hand movement, the pliant upper body sways, a directed gaze, a movement of an eyebrow—all these minutiae were part of the dance, unseen by outsiders. The big, grand dances of male dancers used bold gestures but the intimate dances of the *khona bazam* were more personal and delicate with subtle movements, even the fluttering of eyelashes.[108]

These *khona bazam* entertainments took place in the *ichkari*, the women's quarters of the Central Asian home. While the "four walls" were condemned as a sort of prison for women, they also served to preserve certain traditions, as the very same walls that kept things in also served to keep things out. In a region characterized by endless centuries of invasion, these households protected the most treasured possession—one's own family—from the prying eyes of passersby.

---

[105]Theodore Levin, *The Hundred Thousand Fools of God: Musical Travels in Central Asia (and Queens, New York)*. Bloomington: Indiana University Press, 1996, p. 120.
[106]Tuhfakhon Pinkhasova, in Levin, *The Hundred Thousand Fools*, p. 119.
[107]Avdeeva, *Tantseval'noe Iskusstvo Uzbekistana*, p. 16.
[108]Ibid., p. 17.

Women also created their own domestic theater, performing for other women, creating their own scripts, and wearing male robes when portraying masculine roles.[109] *Sozanda* cross-dressed on occasion, putting on men's clothing and donning false beards.[110] The beloved Bukharan *sozanda* Tuhfakhon Pinkhasova (1928–2010) recalled performing at *tois* where she, along with the celebrated *sozandas* Chrivanzan, Karkigi, and Mashkati, dressed in men's robes, hats, and belts, and also wore false beards. They completed the role by carrying a long staff used by wandering mendicants known as *qalandars* and dervishes.[111]

Among the comics were women comics, the girls' comic theater operated independently, and its audience and performers consisted only of women. The role of a man was also skillfully played by women, dressed as men, with beards and mustaches. The names of such professional comedians as Zulfi Suidieva from Samarkand, Kuydiniso Rasulmatova from Pishkent, Salomat Mutalova from Tashkent were very popular among our people.[112]

This practice of cross-dressing for performances also occurred in the Ferghana Valley, among the female *yallachi*, professional entertainers who fulfilled a role similar to that of the *sozanda* and "dressed in men's clothes, performing for wealthy people, covering their hair under a hat, and putting on boots and caftans girdled with a sash belt."[113] According to an interview with Akutkhan Isakova, the grand-daughter of Gavharkhon Uzakova, "this was how her grandmother performed during religious ceremonies, festivals, holidays, and weddings."[114] In a literary source, *Mehrobdan Chayon* ("Scorpion from the Altar") by Abdullah Qodiriyi, the author describes "a number of episodes about the lifestyle of court women in the Kokand Khanate" including one when forty girls relaxed in a garden after sundown, sitting on a tapchan, and "sang yalla and danced. Performers were brought to the palace from different cities of the country as gifts to the khan."[115]

The *sozanda* sometimes re-enacted weddings as part of the entertainment they provided for women in the *ichkari*. Weddings, after all, were and still are often the most important event in a woman's life, lively occasions for feasting, music,

---

[109]Usman Karabaev, *Etnokul'tura: traditsionnaya narodnaya kul'tura*. Tashkent: Shark Publishing, 2005, p. 120.
[110]Pinkhasova, quoted in Levin, *Fools of God*, p. 120.
[111]Ibid.
[112]Ilkhom Yuldashev, "National Features of Estrada Acting Skills (On the example of People's Artist of Uzbekistan Yusuf Qiziq Shakarjanov)." *International Journal for Innovative Engineering and Management Research*, 10, no. 5 (May 2021): 43. DOI: 10.48047/IJIEMR/V10/I05/10.
[113]"Iskusstvo yalla v zhizni zhenshhin ferganskoi doliny." *San'at, Journal of the Academy of Arts of Uzbekistan*. 10/11/2015, no. 3, 2015. https://san'at.orexca.com/2013-rus/2013-3-2/iskusstvo-yalla-v-zhizni-zhenshhin-ferganskoj-doliny/
[114]Ibid., pp. 220–21.
[115]Ibid.

and dance, making them pleasant to recall. Enacting "pretend" weddings provided amusement for women in the *ichkari*. The *sozanda* would dress one of the guests like a bridegroom and, drawing a mustache on her face, would then "marry" her to the girl selected to play the role of the bride. Other aspects of the wedding ritual followed, including serving *sharbat* and reading prayers. This practice continued up until the 1970s, but "then it was prohibited."[116]

This playful practice appears in Abdullah Qadriy's famous novel *O'tkan Kunlar* (Bygone Days) with a tender description of a *qizlar majlisi*—a party where an anxious young bride, surrounded by her friends, nervously awaits her wedding night with a man she has never met. The author takes the reader behind the "four walls" where lovely young girls in their most beautiful dresses gathered to mark their friend's transition from girlhood to womanhood. All performed— poets, dancers, artists, and musicians.[117] Her friends began to play the dutar and *childrima*,[118] singing, clapping, and dancing in response to the lyrics. But the fearful bride could not be comforted: her friends "sought to lighten her heart and distract her," moving on to "the most interesting part of the bridal shower: *lapar*."[119] The *lapar* is a witty conversation sung between a man and woman. One girl played the role of the bridegroom while another pretended to be the bride.[120] A film version of *O'tkan Kunlar* beautifully depicts this episode.[121]

While the *bacha* performances sometimes imitated girls—based in part on their early years as very young boys still allowed in the *ichkari*—the women in turn imitated elements of *bacha* performances when, after the Bolshevik revolution, they emerged to step onto the concert stage. They now faced the challenge of adapting their traditional dances to a much larger space. The *bachas* provided the most immediate model of how this could be done. As Mukarram Turgunbaeva, who became the director of Uzbekistan's Bakhor Ensemble, recalled, "I saw the dances of the bachas once in early childhood, but simple men's dance I almost did not have a chance to see, because youths and men danced in the men's half of the house, the *tashkari*."[122] She learned of the high level of performance techniques achieved by some of the *bachas* who could pass in *charkhs*—sagittal axis spins— while traveling in a circular path, making several circles at a very fast pace. Their bodies leaned sharply into the center of the circle, but "to count how many *charkh* turns was impossible."[123] Yusufjon-Kyzyk Shakarjanov (1869–1959) said that he

---

[116]Pinkhasova, quoted in Levin, *Fools of God*, p. 120.
[117]Abdullah Qodiriy, trans. Mark Reese, *Bygone Days: O'tkan Kunlar*. Nashville, TN, 2018, p. 116.
[118]A *childrima* is another term for *doira*.
[119]Qodiriy, *Bygone Days*, p. 120. The lapar genre would later be developed into the signature genre of Tamara Khanum.
[120]Ibid.
[121]Film version of *O'tgan Kunlar*, www.youtube.com/watch?v=L13l4aVTxo8.
[122]Mukarram Turgunbaeva, quoted in Avdeeva, L. *Tanets Mukarram Turganbaevoi*. Tashkent: Gafur Gulyam, 1989, p. 57.
[123]Ibid.

himself could make three hundred and sixty turns around his axis, passing up to ten wide circles.[124] A performer from a very early age, Shakarjanov embodied the Central Asian tradition of entertainers who blended theatrical elements of comedy, clowning, improvisational humor, acrobatics, theater, and dance. His ability won him the title of "*kyzyk*," which, as an honorific, became connected with his birth name, just as "*usta*" (master or teacher) and "*kari*" (reciter of the Koran) were linked to the names of others.

In the twentieth century, during the Soviet period, the syncretic nature of Central Asian performing arts began to be separated into different areas of specialization, such as circus arts, theater, and dance. But in the early days immediately after the Bolshevik Revolution, instances of cross-dressing continued, combining theater and dance. Mukarram Turgunbaeva blossomed with this new-found freedom. Avdeeva noted that dance "polished" Mukarram, "stretched her up, straightened her shoulders, raised her head, she became a slender teenager," so it was "not surprising" that she was cast as a male extra in early roles.[125] Tamara Khanum, as an adult woman, sometimes playfully placed the Uzbek man's characteristic black and white *dupi* at a rakish angle on her head, tied a man's *belbok* scarf around her waist and, making her hands into fists, coiled her arms into rotations toward her body in imitation of masculine dance.

Of the numerous dances that Mukarram Turgunbaeva choreographed, now considered classics of Uzbek stage dance, three are inspired by men's dances. *Andijon Polka* depicts the fierce energy of young *jigits*—horsemen—with their exuberant games and horse races. In *Zang*, dancers wore bells on wrists and ankles, using postures, gestures, and costumes evoking the legendary *kyrk kyz* - forty female warriors – and Queen Tomyris.[126] In creating dances like *Andijon Polka*, she asserted that she did not use men's movements, but instead adopted a masculine manner that was more energetic, more active, more powerful.[127] Turgunbaeva's setting of *Katta O'yin*, created in collaboration with the master doirist Usta Olim Kamilov, was founded on the basis of the famous suite of dances and songs performed by the *bacha*, using some of their well-known rhythms and steps.

In this way, Mukarram created a turnabout, boldly invading the performance space long dominated by boys and youths. If some of the *bachas'* performances copied the feminine attire, mannerisms, and dances performed in the women's quarters, the former inmates of the *ichkari* now seized on some movements and performance techniques from the *bacha* repertoire. Women's dances would continue to evolve and expand as they came to dominate the concert stage.

---

[124]Ibid.

[125]Avdeeva, *Tanets Mukarram Turganbaevoi*, p. 57.

[126]L. Avdeeva, introduction to Roziakhanum Karimova, *Tantsy Ansambl'a Bakhor v Postanovke Mukarram Turgunbaevoi*. Tashkent: Literatura i Isskustvo, 1979, p. 17.

[127]Ibid., p. 58.

2 THE PRIMACY OF RHYTHM

The *doira*,[1] a hand-held Central Asian frame drum, provides the heartbeat of Uzbek dance, creating the rhythms that accompany movements and gestures. There is a deep relationship between dance, melodies, and poetic lyrics, but vocal and instrumental accompaniment are not the most essential ingredients for dance—only rhythm—and the *doira* is the most common percussion instrument for this purpose.

Ethnomusicologist Jean During noted that the musical identity of Central Asians was shaped by their nomadic origin. As a result, "the attachment to territory is less powerful: they adapt, they make do, they borrow from others. For them it is more important to preserve the sense of rhythm, musical space, organization of performances, context, and rapport with the public than the content, form and canons."[2]

Nomadic roots may explain the connection to the sounds inspired by the natural world, especially the nomads' constant companion, the horse, with its two-beat, three-beat, and four-beat gaits, as well as the domesticated and wild animals central to survival. As the British ethnographer Annette Meakin observed in the twentieth century, "everybody rides in Turkestan, even beggars in the street are frequently mounted."[3] Hoofbeats were part of the soundscape and considering that the "brain-to-brain communication between horses and riders is an intricate neural dance,"[4] equine rhythm patterns may have become deeply embedded in humans. Among the Kazakhs and Tuvans, percussion instruments created from the hooves of horses, respectively known as *tai tuyak* and *duyuglar*, quite accurately reproduce the sound of galloping horses to accompany folk music.

---

[1] Also known as *childrima*.

[2] Jean During, "Power, Authority and Music in the Cultures of Inner Asia." *Ethnomusicology Forum*, 14, no. 2 (2005): 160.

[3] Annette M. B. Meakin, *In Russian Turkestan: A Garden of Asia and Its People*. London: G. Allen, 1903, p. 242.

[4] Janet Jones, "Becoming a Centaur." *Aeon* Newsletter, January 14, 2022. https://aeon.co/essays/horse-human-cooperation-is-a-neurobiological-miracle.

Rhythm patterns are known as *usul*. Just as Arabic rhythms are expressed by the sounds *dum*, *tak*, and *ess*, Uzbek rhythms, too, can be "spoken" with onomatopoeia corresponding to the actual sound made when playing the *doira* in different ways. Strong beats, created by striking the center of the drum skin, are expressed as *bum*, while tapping near the wooden rim of the drum creates the *bak* and *baka* sound. Finally, the silence of a rest can be spoken as the sibilant *ist*.[5]

A large frame drum, the *doira* rests in the left hand and is played with both hands. Animal skin covers one side of the drum and large metal rings—between forty and one hundred—are attached at regular intervals to the inside of the wooden drum frame. A doirist—or *doiradast* as they are called in Uzbek—sometimes shakes the frame to make the rings produce a metallic shivering sound that can crescendo into a loud rattling. The *doira* is often mentioned in accounts by foreign travelers who invariably referred to it as a tambourine, or called it a *baraban*, the Russian word for drum. This seemingly simple instrument can create an impressive variety of distinct sounds and textures, from soft thuds to loud thunder, and Uzbek doirists will claim with pride that they can imitate the sound of any kind of drum.

Another percussion instrument, the *nagora*, is a pair of drums created from clay pots with animal skin drawn tightly over the top of each, held in place by leather thongs. A kind of kettle drum, the *nagora* comes in different sizes and is played with sticks. It has ancient associations with military music used in battle, found in depictions at archeological sites such as Topraq Qala and Penjikent.[6] *Nagora* were in regular use in the late nineteenth century, "widely employed by the troops, retinues and police forces of the emirs of Bukhara as well as the khans of Khiva and Kokand." Eyewitness accounts by visitors to Bukhara and Tashkent mentioned a huge *nagora* "set up at prominent places and played by two men" using sticks. At first the drum "emitted a hollow sound," but then created "thunder-like peals that were heard over a distance of several kilometers."[7] The drums had association with military signaling used by nomadic populations. According to an account by Marco Polo, Mongols "never joined battle until the '*nakar*' of their leader gave a signal."[8]

Used for outdoor performances in combination with the *karnai* (a long trumpet) and the *surnai* (a reed instrument), the *nagora* announces celebrations or accompanies circus entertainment, such as tightrope walkers, or men's acrobatic

---

[5]Johanna Spector, "Musical Tradition and Innovation," in *Central Asia; 120 Years of Russian Rule*, edited by Edward Allworth. Durham, NC: Duke University Press, 1989, p. 455.

[6]For a detailed discussion, as well as drawing of images, see Valerii P. Nikonorov (1998), "The Use of Musical Percussions in Ancient Eastern Warfare: Parthian and Central Asian Evidence," in Ellen Hickmann, Ingo Laufs,and R. Eichmann, *Music Archaeology of Early Metal Ages: Papers from the 1st Symposium of the International Study Group on Music Archaeology at Monastery Michaelstein*, May 18–24, 1998 (Blankenburg, Germany); *Orient-ArchŠologie, 7; Studien zur MusikarchŠologie II*, Rahden/ Westf: Verlag Marie Leidorfe, 2000, pp. 71–82.

[7]Nikonorov, *The Use of Musical Percussions*, p. 72.

[8]Nikonorov, *The Use of Musical Percussions*, p. 75.

dances. They were also used in entertainment featuring dancing boys. A visiting Russian dignitary, commenting on an outdoor *bacha* performance in Khiva hosted in his honor by the Khan's heir, observed an "orchestra mainly composed of twin flutes, kettle drums, and a half a dozen man-sized silver trumpets."[9]

Men and women both play *doira*, but archeological evidence indicates that it was originally a woman's instrument, often linked to goddess images. "The ancient frame drum of trans-Mediterranean cultures" recalled the shaped of the grain sieve; both were "symbolic of the feminine, fertility, grain, moon, the sun, and the primordial first body of water,"[10] echoing connections with the goddess Anahita who was worshiped widely throughout Central Asia. In the ruins of the ancient fortress of Topraq Qala, a room dubbed the "Hall of the Dancing Masks" featured murals of men and women dancing together in couples. One scene depicted a woman playing a frame drum raised a bit above the level of her head and slightly leaning back, with one foot behind, as if caught in a moment of dance.[11]

Traditionally in Central Asia and other parts of the East, musical training was transmitted orally from *ustoz* (master) to *shagird* (disciple) through repetition and memorization.[12] Doirists passed rhythms to each other, connected to movements. Before the revolution, the doirist was recognized as the "ballet master," i.e., the dance creator or choreographer. Pre-Revolutionary practices mirrored the tradition in Indian classical dance of a performer naming one's guru and lineage before dancing. Thus, it was not announced that "such and such dancer danced," but instead announced that "danced the dancer of the doirist" (*tantseval tantsor duarista*) and only then gave the name of the dancer (*a potom uzhe nazvali imya tantsora*).[13]

For most stage performances today, males play to accompany dance. Professional doirists are usually male, perhaps reflecting a past when women could not perform publicly. The years of constant playing shape the men's fingers into calloused mallets, a single digit seemingly "strong enough to lift an elephant," as one observer quipped. During the autumnal wedding season, when musicians are most in demand, doirists tape their fingers to protect them from damage caused by constant playing. Mamurjon Mirdadayev, doirist with the Uzbekistan's Bakhor Ensemble, recalled that his crowning number—"solo on three doiras"—always

---

[9]Count K. K. Pahlen, *Mission to Turkestan*, edited by Richard Pierce, translated by N. J. Couriss. London: Oxford University Press, 1964, p. 170.

[10]Layne Redmond, *When the Drummers Were Women: A Spiritual History of Rhythm*, 1st ed. New York: Three Rivers Press, 1997, p. 19.

[11]Reconstructed diagram in Iu. A. Rapoport, "The Palaces of Topraq-Qal'a." *Bulletin of the Asia Institute*, 8 (1994): 169. www.jstor.org/stable/24048773.

[12]A system of notation came in the nineteenth century, between 1873 and 1874, when Khorezm music was transcribed by Palwan Niyaz Mirza Bashi, ordered by the Khan of Khiva, Muhammad Rahim. Spector, "Musical Tradition and Innovation," pp. 470–71.

[13]Avdeeva, *Tantseval'noe Iskusstvo Uzbekistana*, p. 36.

won tumultuous applause from audiences, fascinated by the sounds and his fast, virtuoso playing.[14] And in the group *massovyi* dances, the energy of the rhythms always raised the spirits of the audience.

Women usually performed within the licit boundaries of the *ichkari* and not in front of men. However, in November 1890, Swedish explorer Sven Hedin witnessed female performers of music and dance in Samarkand. He recalled that, "in the company of a Frenchman, I took a nocturnal walk to Pai-Kabak, the not-too-savory quarter of the women dancers. We were ushered into perfumed rooms, carpeted with rugs, and with divans along the walls." He noted that "beautiful women" played the *setara* and the *chetara*, "manipulating the strings with dainty little fingers. Others with like skill and grace, played the tambourine. In order to keep the drumhead tight, they would now and again hold the instrument over a *mangal*, or glowing brazier,"[15] just as doirists today heat the drumhead before performances.

> As the music rose in the night, the dancers appeared in light, floating garments, with movements full of grace. Some of them were Persians or Afghans, others had Tatar blood in their veins. And to the rhythmic sounds of music from the stringed instruments, they danced in undulating measure, like fairies in a dream—messengers from Bihasht and the joys of Paradise.[16]

In "respectable" homes, women drummed to accompany each other's songs or dances but, when no *doira* was available, they kept time by clapping their hands. They could also take up household items to provide percussion, tapping out rhythms with metal thimbles on a saucer or clicking the porcelain lid on a teapot, sometimes incorporating these elements into their dances. In Samarkand, women used "metal trays, kettle lids, washtubs, and buckets" to create a domestic rhythm section.[17] In the Surkhandarya region, a pair of wooden spoons called *qoshiq* are held in each hand—a sort of improvised set of "kitchen castanets"—and are incorporated into the movements of the dance.[18] In the Samarkand region,

---

[14]Mumurjon Mirdadyev quoted in the article by Olga Fazylova on the 60th anniversary of the Bakhor Ensemble, *Legendarnomu Ansamblyu Bakhor—60 Let*. https://darakchi.uz/ru/34075.

[15]Sven Hedin, *My Life as an Explorer*. Translated by Alfhild Huebsch. New York: Kodansha International, 1996, p. 9.

[16]On February 19, 2015, a dance concert, *An Edwardian Evening on the Silk Road*, in commemoration of the 150th anniversary of Sven Hedin's birth, took place at the Arts Club of Washington (Washington, DC). Actor Sean Coe, playing the role of the explorer, read from Hedin's descriptions of his Silk Road travels, including his comments on the dancers of Samarkand. https://svenhedinfoundation.org/theatrical-event-to-highlight-silk-road-explorations-of-sven-hedin/.

[17]Mentioned by Begimov, p. 1, cited in David MacFadyen, *One Language in the Middle of Nowhere*. New York: Routledge, 2006, p. 54. This practice is also mentioned by Gulsum Khamraeva in *Obshchie zakony stsenicheskoy choreographii natsionalnaya obraz tantsa*. Tashkent: Institute of Art Studies (PhD Diss., 1986).

[18]In 2003, Kadir Muminov taught his *Surkhan Darya* choreography based on this tradition featuring wooden spoons to the Silk Road Dance Company in Washington, DC.

rhythm combines with song and dance in a special folk tradition known as *qarsak*, from the word for "hand clapping." Most typically it is performed by women who rhythmically clap special *usuls*—in particular the *beshqarsak*, or "five claps"—while singing couplets that are folk poetry. The songs have connections to Zoroastrian practice.[19] *Qarsak* can also be accompanied by *doira*.

In Khorezm and Bukhara, dancers sometimes accompany themselves by playing the *kairoki*, a pair of long, flat river stones held in each hand. Occasionally a flat, elongated piece of iron is used in place of a second stone, creating a more metallic sound. From these rudimentary instruments a musician or dancer can coax many distinct rhythms, from the pattering sound of raindrops to the hoofbeats of galloping horses. Vintage photographs sometimes show dancing boys holding *kairoki* and they are still played in Khorezm dances such as *Lazgi* and *Narim Narim*, as well as in Bukharan *sozanda* dances. A miniature painting from 1538, from the Bukhara school, depicts a female dancer with uplifted arms, holding instruments that appear to be *kairoki*.[20]

Even within their own homes, women had to be cautious about playing too loudly, especially in Bukhara where, at times, stringent prohibitions were enforced because music was considered sinful.[21] In the Ferghana region, women took measures to muffle sound and "before they started singing and dancing to the sound of *doira* and *dutar*, put water in a porcelain vessel on the windowsill to block the sound."[22]

The Mysterious Rhythms of *Katta O'yin*

Credited with having a phenomenal memory, Yusufjon-Kyzyk Shakarjanov (1869–1859)[23] carried within him ancient oral traditions, a hundred *usuls*, and dozens of folk dances that have become "classics" of Uzbek stage dance, such as *Katta O'yin*. His performance of the latter was thought to be his best. People's Artist of Uzbekistan Ganijan Tashmatov commented that to see the complex and serious work performed by Yusufjon-Kyzyk "was an unforgettable sight," because this difficult piece was not one that every dancer attempts to perform. "It's a pity this dance

---

[19]Audio recordings and a description of *Qarsak* can be accessed at http://ich.uz/en/materials/audio-materials/486-qarsak.

[20]Bukhara miniature painting, *Couple Entertained in a Pavilion* from the *Haft Manzar of Hatifi*, collection of the Smithsonian National Museum of Asian Art.

[21]The word for "music" does not appear in the Quran. As a result, the propriety of music has long been a subject of debate among Muslim theologians. See Gray, "Music and Dance within the Islamic Context." *Arabesque*, X, no. 1 (May–June 1984): 24–25, 34–35.

[22]Nasiba Turgunova, "The Traditions of the Women's Art 'Yalla' of Central Asia." *Journal of Literature and Art Studies*, 5, no. 3 (March 2015): 220. doi: 10.17265/2159-5836/2015.03.008.

[23]Yusufjon-Kyzyk Shakarjanov, also known as Yusuf-Kyzyk, will be more fully introduced in Chapter 6: Mentors and Martyrs.

disappeared from history along with Usta Yusufjan."[24] A compelling performer, rhythmically precise, he "proudly raised his head" and with an eagle-like gaze, opened wide his arms, "embraced everything around him," lifted his palm and began to spin.[25] His performance of the energetic Khorezm dance *Lazgi* could challenge even a young dancer and in it he embodied "masculine courage, human victory, and the rhythm of joy" (*muzhskoy otvagi, pobedy cheloveka, ritm radosti*).[26]

Yusuf-Kyzyk asserted that *Katta O'yin* went back to the time of Alexander the Great's invasion of the territory of present-day Uzbekistan (328–329 BCE) and was originally accompanied by the military *nagora* drums pounding out the marching cadence for the conqueror's *Iskanderi* troupes. It is not too difficult to imagine the tramping boots of marching armies in the opening *usuls* and steps of *Katta O'yin* echoing the rhythmic stride of soldiers.

Based on sources known to her, Avdeeva posited a connection between the *usuls* comprising the suite of dances contained in *Katta O'yin* and the tale of the handsome Prince Siyavash, whose story is found in the *Shahnameh*.[27] In the tale, Sudabeh—the stepmother of the young warrior—tries to seduce Siyavash and accuses him of rape when he rejects her. (The tale of Potiphar's wife and the "beautiful Joseph" from the Old Testament book of Genesis 39:1–20 contains similar plot points, specifically the false accusation of rape made against an attractive young man who rebuffed sexual overtures made toward him.) In the *Shahnameh* version, Siyavash proved his innocence by riding through flames unscathed. But even this feat did not quell gossip, so he crossed the Amu Darya and went into exile in Turon. There he found refuge with the ruler of Afrasiab—a region near Samarkand—whose daughter he married. Siyavash founded the city of Bukhara, but Afrasiab suspected him of plotting a rebellion and ordered the beheading of Siyavash, burying his head beneath one of the walls of the Ark fortress of Bukhara. When Kai Khosrow, the son of Siyavash, grew to manhood, he sent the legendary hero Rustam to lead an army to besiege Afrasiab near Bukhara. After two years, Rustam captured and killed him. The tomb of Afrasiab is located near one of the historic gates of Bukhara.[28]

Much of this familiar story of Siyavash, known throughout the Persianate world and beyond, unfolds on the territory of present-day Uzbekistan. Al-Narshiki in his *History of Bukhara* (943 CE) writes that in Bukhara "there are special songs of the

---

[24]People's Artist of Uzbekistan Ganijan Tashmatov, quoted in Mukhtar Ganiev, "Shut Margilanskiy." *Pis'ma o Tashkente*, Dec. 31, 2020. https://mytashkent.uz/2020/12/31/shut-margilanskij/.
[25]Tashmatov quoted by Ganiev, ibid.
[26]Ibid.
[27]The *Shahnameh* is the revered Persian language epic poem of Ferdowsi, written between the years of 977 and 1010 CE, containing the legends and history of the Persian people.
[28]Abu Bakr Muhammad Narshakhi, referred to as Al-Narshaki, *The History of Bukhara*, translated by Richard N. Frye. Princeton, NJ: Markus Wiener Publishers, 2007, p. 17. "Siyavush" is an alternate spelling.

people on the killing of Siyavush. The musicians called these songs Kin-e Siyavush. Muhammad ibn Ja'far says that from his time it was three thousand years ago"[29] (Figure 2.1).

The ancient legend of Siyavash is preserved in dance as well. In Avdeeva's analysis of *Katta O'yin*, she sees a pattern in the *usuls* of the piece that retells this ancient story. The opening *usul* is *rez* or *dildir*—"splashing water"—followed by trembling, quivering *titratma*. The *usul qashqar* depicts clapping hands while performing a swift turn when the dancer moves his arms as if he had collected a handful of water in his palm, and throws it upwards. This is the famous "*shokh*'" turn, always done in place and to the left,[30] and is a core movement in Uzbek dance

FIGURE 2.1 Uzbek rhythms, known as *usul*, commonly used in dance, transcribed by Cynthia Connelly Ryan.

[29]Al-Narshakhi, *The History of Bukhara*, p. 17. Note that this attribution by Al-Narshakhi predates the *Shahnameh*, suggesting an ancient, widespread knowledge of the Siyavash legend.
[30]The *shokh* turn exists in Tajik dance as well and also is done only to the left. F. Ayubdjanova, *Traditsionnyi tadzhikskiye tantsy*. Khudzhand: Fakul'tet iskusstva, 2000, p. 28.

with connections to the Sogdian Whirl. *Sarbozi* connotes a warrior and *charkh*, that deeply embedded term given to a special spin, conveys the movement of the spinning wheel and marks "rotations in a circle or on the spot."[31] The *usul* called *Iurga* mirrors the hoof beats of horses.

Avdeeva notes that of the forty-seven *usuls* still known, many names are lost, or the meanings are incomprehensible to the current generation. (And here it should be noted that many of the names are of Persian origin.[32]) Only a small portion are truly illustrative while most seem most connected to the character or behavior of a person, such as *khakkoni* (honor), *oram* (rest), and *zhilvoni* (coquetry).[33] But one *usul—sadra*—would play an important role in the survival of the *usuls* and the fate of Uzbek dance.

Linked to funeral rituals, *sadra* embodies the emotions of mourning, with the dancer lowering his head, walking slowly, "waving" his arms side to side, but wearily, as if there is no strength left in the body. A similar funeral dance known as *poyamol* exists among the Tajiks, which includes arms swinging side to side but never rising above shoulder level.[34] The arms rise again and collapse again, as if weighed down by grief. Avdeeva noted that rhythms grow in intensity as the dancer leans increasingly forward, attempting to overcome the overwhelming sadness, and the movements increase in speed. In these various *usuls*, Avdeeva found a choreographic parallel to Eastern poetic forms, such as the ghazal, where each verse contains special ideas or feelings.

Usta Olim Kamilov

In the development of Uzbek professional stage dance, the fundamental role of Usta Olim Kamilov looms large. In 1875, he was born in Margilan, like Yusuf-Kyzyk Shakarjanov. Similar to many musicians in pre-Revolutionary Turkestan, Usta Olim had a non-musical primary profession, going to work at age 10 as a craftsman of the Central Asian *arba*, the wooden cart with two huge wheels as tall as a man and drawn by a donkey or horse. Music was an avocation.[35] In the evenings, the young Kamilov went to the teahouse—the *chaikhona*—that all-male gathering place in pre-Revolutionary Turkestan, which served as a nexus of Central Asian cultural traditions of music, poetry, humor, storytelling, and dance. Usta Olim

---

[31] Avdeeva, *Tantseval'noye iskusstvo Uzbekistana*, p. 3.
[32] Special thanks to Sepideh Farshadi for verifying these terms.
[33] Avdeeva, *Tantseval'noe Iskusstvo Uzbekistana*, p. 4.
[34] This information initially came from a personal conversation with a Tajik man who explained the dance and has been confirmed by Lola Ulugova, who consulted with Tajik dance specialist Amon Musoev on February 14, 2023. *Poyamol* is identified as a ritual dance for the dead in Ayubdjanova, *Traditsionnyye tadzhikskiye tantsy*, p. 6.
[35] Avdeeva, *Tantseval'noe Iskusstvo Uzbekistana*, p. 33.

spent time there in his childhood, watching, listening, and picking up the different *usuls* to play on the *doira*. He heard folk singers and absorbed rhythms, learning to play *doira* and *nagora*. The boy caught the attention of Salomat-khola, a female performer known as a *yallachi*[36] who performed only at women's gatherings. She began taking the young Kamilov along with her to women's celebrations known as *tois* when he was still young enough to be admitted to the *ichkari*. Working with Salomat, he gained experience of the communication between dancer and doirist. When he was no longer considered a boy, and too old to be allowed entrance to the women's quarters, he attended the men's *gap* sessions[37] where his skills soon earned him recognition as an *usta*, "master." He began to train dancers (undoubtedly male) for competitions, which they usually won.[38]

The beginnings of Kamilov's lifetime collaboration with Tamara Khanum began around 1916, when she first heard him play at a *sayil* (folk festival). The young girl could not see over the heads of the crowd to identify the source of the rhythms, but she could discern all kinds of sounds, from the trill of a nightingale to the roll of thunder, to the rush of water streaming over boulders, to the whisper of flowing grains of sands. She recalled that, "solemn sounds poured, expanded; it seems that my wings had grown behind me and I had soared higher and higher." She edged forward to the first rows of the audience but, instead of seeing an entire orchestra, discovered only one drum and "a small, dry little man."[39] Usta Olim was over forty years old when Tamara met him. He is usually pictured holding a *doira*, but because he is frequently cited as a choreographer, he may have been a dancer in his youth. He collaborated with Tamara Khanum, both as her *ustoz* and as a co-creator; he also trained several of the young dancers who followed her courageous lead to perform in public.[40] His deep understanding of the relationship between movement and rhythm proved valuable because rhythms frequently shift in Uzbek dance, requiring the performer to perfectly match the beats of the *doira*. One of the earliest pieces created by Usta Olim and Tamara Khanum, *Pilla* ("Silkworm"), reflects the various tasks associated with sericulture, from feeding mulberry leaves to the silkworms, to unspooling the silken threads of the cocoon, to weaving and embroidering with silken threads. It is performed solely to constantly shifting *doira* rhythms. This creation was one of the dances that Tamara Khanum performed

---

[36]Hamza Hakimzade Niyazi's 1922 play *Paranji sirlaridan bir lavha Yoki yallachilar ishi* (One Episode from the Secrets of the Veil or the Case of Yalla Singers) paints an unflattering portrait of the Yallachi and their involvement in a tragic situation in which a young girl is ensnared into prostitution by a man who disguises himself wearing a paranjah to enter the women's quarters.

[37]Traditionally, a *gap* is a gendered social event where people regularly gather to talk about common concerns.

[38]Avdeeva, *Tantseval'noe Iskusstvo Uzbekistana*, p. 36. Langston Hughes learned of these pre-Revolutionary dance contests when he met with Uzbek musicians in 1933, described in Chapter 1.

[39]Avdeeva, *Tantseval'noe Iskusstvo Uzbekistana*, p. 35. Kamilov was about forty-one years old at this time.

[40]For example, Mukarram Turgunbaeva, Rozia Karimova, Galia Izmailova, and many others.

at the historic 1939 mass labor project, the construction of the Ferghana Canal. In a legendary episode that reflected Tamara Khanum's improvisational skill, the dancer went down to the bottom of the canal to rinse her hands in the "sacred waters," a gesture that recalled the ancient goddess of the waters, Anahita, as well as the Uzbek saying *suv hayot*—"water is life." At that iconic moment, someone flung an Uzbek men's scarf, a *belbak*, toward her. Tamara Khanum caught the scarf and began to pantomime the act of embroidering it. When she finished the impromptu scene, she tossed the scarf back up the slope to a group of young men. After that incident, the embroidery pantomime sequence with an actual scarf became embedded in the dance, all to the rhythm of the *doira*.[41]

Originally a solo piece with two sections, the first of which protested forced labor, it was later reimagined in 1943 by Mukarram Turgunbaeva to portray the various tasks involved with sericulture. It evolved once again in 1958 as a *massovyi* choreography for the Bakhor Ensemble.[42] Notation for this version, also performed to *doira* only, shows thirty-four shifts in rhythm, alternating between 2/4, 4/8, 4/4, and 6/8 time signatures.

Together, Tamara Khanum and Usta Olim also created the *Doira Dars*—"doira lesson"—a drill with commonly used dance movements performed to typical rhythms, a sort of primer for training dancers. Still used today at the Uzbekistan State Academy of Dance (formerly known as the Choreographic Institute), this kinesthetic drill exists in different variations, teaching dancers to embody certain movements with the appropriate rhythms. Because Uzbek dance is traditionally improvisational, a skilled artist can respond to rhythm cues in a live performance just as the doirist can likewise follow the movement cues of the dancer.

The *Doira Dars* originated from the *Katta O'yin* dance suite of the *bacha* dancing boys. Originally, *Katta O'yin* (from *katta* meaning "grand or great" and *o'yin* meaning "play, game, entertainment")[43] consisted of a performance featuring a variety of dances and musical offerings that lasted for hours. At certain moments within the suite, *bachas* would perform solos. In other sections, several boys would dance at the same time, apparently not in unison, but simply improvising as individuals within a shared space.

When traveling in Soviet Central Asia in 1933, the African American poet and writer Langston Hughes was introduced to Usta Olim in Tashkent by Tamara Khanum. From him, Hughes learned that the master doirist knew "sixty sets of traditional folk rhythms" and had "developed from them more than two hundred

---

[41]Avdeeva, *Tantseval'noe Iskusstvo Uzbekistana*.

[42]Rozia Karimova, *Tantsy Ansambl'a Bakhor*. Tashkent: Literatura i Isskustvo, 1979. Choreography and musical notation for *Pilla*, pp. 145–70.

[43]Hamid Ismailov played with the meaning of *Katta O'yin* as a reference to "The Great Game" of European powers in Asia. The Uzbek name for his book, *The Devils' Dance*, is *Jinlar basmi yoxud katta o'yin* ("Demons Entertainment or The Great Game").

variants," but added that Kamilov said of his own teacher that he "knows all the rhythms."[44] Hughes also wrote that Tamara Khanum "had studied in Samarkand the now forbidden dances of the dervishes with their four basic rhythms" and from them had created some patterns of her own.[45]

Another visiting foreigner, Si-Lan Chen, a dancer of Trinidadian French Creole and Chinese descent, had become acquainted with Langston Hughes in Moscow, but their paths seemingly did not cross again when she also went to Tashkent in 1933. Tamara Khanum arranged for her to study Uzbek dance with Usta Olim during that summer. Chen wrote of Kamilov's mastery of rhythms and commented that "he could beat out a sixty-five rhythm beat, and the young dancer had to be very skillful to follow his intricate beats."[46]

The connection between dancer and doirist is not a one-sided conversation, but a duet of shared energy. The best doirists attentively watch the dancer, accenting her movements, like the subtle lift of a chin, or highlighting a series of spins by speeding up the tempo and dramatizing the climactic moment when she unfurls from a spin into a final pose. In set choreographies, this is also an essential skill, because the doirist must maintain the proper tempo for each movement sequence.

Virtuoso players present astounding solos on the *doira*, showcasing these different sounds while executing a number of seemingly impossible ways by which to play the drum. Beginning with basic rhythms, the presentation becomes increasingly complicated, such as spinning one *doira* balanced on a fingertip while playing a second one lodged between the knees, then adding another *doira* to play in inventive ways. The *doiradast* can set one drum on the floor to spin around the chair where he is seated, holding several *doiras* with one hand while playing them with another, and tossing a drum in the air. This pyrotechnic display typically holds the penultimate place in a concert of Uzbek music and dance.

The Struggle against the *Doira*

Despite the central role that the *doira* held in Uzbek dance tradition, it came under attack during the Soviet era when attempts were made to exclude it from

---

[44]Langston Hughes, "Dances and Music of Uzbekistan," A Negro Looks at Soviet Central Asia. Moscow-Leningrad; Co-operative Publishing Society of Foreign Workers in the U.S.S.R, 1934. p. 36. Reprint by Red Star Publishing. https://www.redstarpublishers.org/HughesSovietCentralAsia.pdf.

[45]Although difficult to determine the meaning of this and the specific rhythms she learned, a common rhythm used in Sufi rituals, such as the *zikr*, is the Arabic *ayub*. The dervishes with their connections to Islam and Sufism were repressed under the Soviets.

[46]Si-Lan Chen Leyda, *Footnote to History*, p. 170. For more about the career of this dancer, see Jennifer Wilson, "Overlooked No More: Si-Lan Chen, Whose Dances Encompassed Worlds." *New York Times*, May 27, 2021. www.nytimes.com/2021/05/27/Obituaries/Si-Lan-Chen-Overlooked.Html.

performances because of its connection with shamanism, which was antithetical to the atheist state.[47] The shaman's large frame drum, essential to ritual, resembles a *doira*; for this reason, the Commissariat of Education launched a *borba* (struggle) against the frame drum as a shamanic tool. Although shamanism was not a religion but a spiritual practice, it was deemed primitive and backward, a superstitious custom condemned as unsuitable for the new Soviet society.[48]

Shamanism has deep roots in Central Asia. In pre-Soviet Turkestan, shamanism existed—and still exists—alongside Islam, sometimes becoming intertwined, and this Islamic form is widespread throughout Transoxiana. Suppressed by the Soviets, male shamans were more easily singled out because local traditions denied strangers access to women's rituals, so females could continue their practice unobserved by outside authorities. The inviolability of the *ichkari* provided them protection, even after the Soviet revolution, and may explain why today most shamanic ritualists (*bakshi*) are women.[49]

People turned to the shaman to cure illness. Shamans were also sought out to solve issues of infertility by women who wished to fulfill the primary duty of a wife—to produce a son for her husband.[50] Pregnant women also sought out the shaman to ensure a safe delivery. One account of a woman seeking treatment from a *bakshi* describes the role of drumming and dancing in the ritual. "He played upon a drum and chanted some incoherent gibberish, the woman meanwhile holding a rope that hung from the roof, and dancing round it until giddiness ensued."[51]

The Communist Party, in its zeal to eliminate shamanism as well as Sufism, altered "the musical heritage. Certain epics from nomadic cultures with historical themes influenced by animism were prohibited. Sufi and shamanic elements were also expurgated from both popular and classical songs."[52] While shamanism was more prevalent in the Siberian north, it still existed in Central Asia alongside Islam, but Soviet officials condemned it:

---

[47] Avdeeva, *Tantseval'noe Iskusstvo Uzbekistana*, p. 59.

[48] Quote from article about the campaign against shamanism.

[49] Transoxania (in Arabic *Māwarā' al-Nahr*) means "beyond the Oxus river," and refers to the territory of contemporary Uzbekistan and Tajikistan. The term is widely used in these countries. "Shamanism, which in an Islamic form is widespread in Transoxania, was suppressed by the Soviets. Male ritualists suffered the most because local custom, which was stronger than the Soviet revolution, kept strangers away from female circles. Thus today most shamanic ritualists (*bakshi*) are women." During, "Power, Authority and Music in the Cultures of Inner Asia," p. 161.

[50] In her autobiography, *The Dancer from Khiva*, Bibish—no other name—explains that her grandfather was often sought out to cure infertility. Men would bring their barren wives to live with him for several days "to be cured." Bibish, *The Dancer from Khiva*. New York: Grove/Atlantic, Inc., 2008, p. 15.

[51] Ella C. Sykes and Sir Percy Sykes, *Through Deserts and Oases of Central Asia*, London, Macmillan and Co., limited, 1920, p. 314. Her painful word choice—"incoherent gibberish"—dismisses the possibility that the words were comprehensible to both the shaman and his patient.

[52] During, "Power, Authority and Music in the Cultures of Inner Asia," p. 144.

Shamanism is and will be an obstacle to socialist construction. The struggle against shamanism cannot and must not be conducted in isolation from the general construction. The struggle against shamanism is a part of the socialist construction itself.

Innontii Mikhailovich Suslov (1931: 128)[53]

The *doira*, with connections to both Sufism and shamanism, came under attack. This official animosity was so entrenched that even the pleas from master artists that "without the *doira* Uzbek dance would die" did not help.[54] Facing this challenge, Usta Olim Kamilov and Tamara Khanum decided to take bold measures and to present choreographies performed solely to *doira* rhythms for the All-Union Olympiad of Folk Art, which was held in Moscow in 1930. They adapted *Katta O'yin*, the historic dance suite of the *bachas*, shortening the rhythm sections and making a *massovy* dance for girls which they renamed *gul o'yin*, or "the dance of flowers." This piece was preceded with a solo by Tamara Khanum, *Sadra*, based on burial rituals, and part of the ancient version of *Katta O'yin*. *Sadra* was also performed only to *doira* rhythms. The mournful grieving changed as rhythms grew increasingly impassioned and tempestuous, symbolizing the awakening of the human forces and of energy—all in harmony[55] with the theme of building a new socialist society.

Tamara Khanum and Usta Olim hid their daring plan from directors of the Olympiad. Tamara's solo *Sadra* opened the Uzbek presentation, followed by the group dance *gul o'yin*, both choreographies with only *doira* accompaniment—a considerable and defiant risk. But the Moscow audience enthusiastically responded, demanding a curtain call with their applause, so the number was repeated. As dance historian Liubov Avdeeva succinctly observed, "this is how the doira won the right to live" (*Tak doyra bylo zavoyevala pravo na zhizn*).[56]

---

[53] Tatiana Bulgakova and Olle Sundström, "Repression of Shamans and Shamanism in Khabarovsk Krai. 1920s to the early 1950s," chapter 9 in *Ethnic and Religious Minorities in Stalin's Soviet Union; New Dimension of Research*, edited by Andrej Kotljarchuk and Olle Sundström, 2017, Huddinge: Södertörns högskola Södertörn Academic Studies, p. 225.
[54] Avdeeva, *Tantseval'noe Iskusstvo Uzbekistana*, p. 59.
[55] Ibid.
[56] Ibid.

PART TWO

THE DANCE ZONES

3 FERGHANA DANCE

Introduction to the Dance Zones

Dance grows from place. Uzbek dance traditions reflect the nuances of natural, historical, and social geographies. While over many centuries the territory of current-day Uzbekistan has worn different names, connected with different populations, the land itself remained fundamentally unchanged. *Sogdiana* came with its connection as the homeland of the famed Silk Road traders. With the Arab conquest (673–751) came the name *Mawarannahr*—from the Arabic *mawara' un-nahr*—"the land beyond the river." Persian poet Ferdowsi's monumental work, the *Shahnameh*, or The Book of Kings, chronicled the age-old conflict between the Persian Empire and the often-nomadic Turkic populations of *Turan*. This association with Turkic peoples also led to the name Turkestan—"land of the Turks"—not to be confused with modern-day Turkmenistan, although some areas are shared. And most confusingly, the ancient Latin name for the Amu Darya, Oxus, resulted in both Transoxiana *and* Transoxania.

Or, as the American journalist Anna Louise Strong (1985–1970) noted, citing Russian revolutionary and writer Karl Radek, "social and economic factors change, but geography remains."[1]

From the verdant Ferghana Valley in the northeast corner to the Kyzyl-Kum ("red sand") desert west of Khorezm, these divergent environments developed different ways of life and unique customs, resulting in characteristic ways of moving. Caught in the amber of time, the gestures of everyday life—the curvilinear strokes of a rice harvester, the bent knees of a horseman, the pliant wrists of a silk weaver—all embedded themselves in dance. Even the soundscape of the land made its way into the folk music that accompanies dance and the varied rhythms of the Uzbek frame drum, the *doira*, provides the fundamental heartbeat of Uzbek

---

[1] Anna Louise Strong, "Red Rule in Golden Samarkand." *The North American Review*, 228 (1929): 309.

dance. As the musician Akhmadjan Aka Uzmozaif told Langston Hughes during the American writer's visit to Uzbekistan, "in the silence of the steppes, there are a thousand sounds. Our instruments know them all."[2]

The region's central location at the heart of the Silk Road nurtured trade acumen as well as gracious hospitality, a virtue deeply embedded in the people. More than merchants' wares moved along these routes; humans traveled these lands, taking with them their distinct embodied movement styles. Some, like the Sogdians, were merchants who traveled of their own volition, while others were captives and slaves "gifted" to foreign rulers. Tang dynasty annals make intriguing references to the "mulberry branch" dance of Tashkent and the famed Sogdian whirling dance. Enslaved Persian women were popular dancers in Chang'an wine taverns. Troupes of traveling performers also traversed the lands along the Silk Road. Artists, after all, are cosmopolitan, always seeking new inspiration, a bigger stage, and the security of patronage. Occasionally, a clue of cross-cultural sharing surfaces in Uzbek dances such as gestures similar to Indian *mudra*, the ankle bracelets of Sasanian dancing goddesses, and the costumes of Mughal court dancers.

The Uzbeks themselves distinguish three major and separate "schools"—or *maktabs*—of dance, i.e., Ferghana, Bukhara, and Khorezm, which align with the former political entities of the Khanate of Kokand, the Emirate of Bukhara, and the Khanate of Khiva. They are distinguished by unique elements of posture, movement vocabulary, music, genres, costumes, and jewelry, as well as some linguistic differences. The Uzbek *maktabs* may be seen as somewhat analogous to the *guranas* of Kathak dance, with distinct forms that evolved in the cities of Lucknow, Banaras, and Jaipur. However, the Uzbek genres extend beyond specific cities and reflect widely varied geography and separate historical traditions that pre-date the political delineation established by the Soviets as Uzbekistan in 1924, and which became an independent nation in 1991. For this reason, the designation of "dance zones," a concept developed by ethnochoreologist Elsie Dunin,[3] provides a more nuanced way of understanding the unique aspects of these dance traditions.

The Ferghana Zone

The Ferghana Dance Zone encompasses the fertile Ferghana Valley region where the Uzbek language is considered to be purest. This zone includes Kokand, once the capital of a Khanate, as well as the cities of Ferghana, Margilan, Namangan, and Andijan (Figure 3.1). Kokand was the birthplace of the female

---

[2]Quoted by Langston Hughes in "Tamara Khanum, Soviet Asia's Greatest Dancer." *Theatre Arts Monthly* (November, 1934): 833.
[3]Special thanks to ethnochoreologist Sahra C. Kent, who suggested using Dunin's system of "dance zones."

FIGURE 3.1 Map of Uzbekistan created by Laura Osifyan Goldman.

poet and de-facto ruler of Kokand, Nodira Begim[4] (1792–1842), and the conqueror Zahir ud-Din Muhammad (1483–1530), founder of India's Mughal Dynasty and better known to history as Babur, was a native of Andijan. (He was so greatly dissatisfied with the local melons and fruits he found in India[5] after conquering it that he sent to his homeland for a gardener to cultivate the fruit in his new empire.) For modern Uzbekistan, some of the nation's most gifted dancers, musicians, and poets—and the earliest pioneers of Uzbek stage dance—were born and raised in the Ferghana Valley.

Elements from nature, along with traditional activities, all left traces in the dance movements of this zone, the region located closest to China. The roads are often lined with mulberry trees, a reminder that the Ferghana Valley is the sericulture center of Uzbekistan. Silkworms, traditionally raised in homes, feed exclusively on the leaves of this tree. A visiting dancer, Si-Lan Chen (1905–1996),[6] who traveled in Uzbekistan and elsewhere in the USSR in the early 1930s, noted gestures with connections to work when she studied Uzbek dance in the summer of 1933, asserting that "most of the movements are stylized grape picking,

---

[4]Nargiza Hasanova, "Ladies of Andijan Receive a Dignified Place in the History of State and Public Governance." *Eurasian Journal of History, Geography and Economics*, 7 (April, 2022): 66.

[5]Babur. *Babur Nama*. Translated by Annette Susannah Beveridge. London: Penguin Books, 2006, p. 275. He complained there were "no grapes, musk melons, or first-rate fruits …"

[6]See her autobiography, Si-Lan Chen Leyda, *Footnote to History*. Edited by Sally Banes. New York: Dance Horizons, 1984.

silk-weaving, harvesting. These movements ornament simple patterns of grace and allurement."[7]

The strong divide between masculine and feminine worlds meant that girls were brought up in a different way and "special attention was paid to the cultivation of such female traits as tenderness, femininity, modesty, shyness, sensitivity, foresight, responsibility, devotion … " and unlike boys, "they were taught not to openly appear in public places, to be less noticeable, not to look at men, to talk with lowered eyes."[8] This clear difference between men and women was felt not only in clothing, manners, and behavior, but also in the main spheres of life—in everyday life, daily tasks, leisure activities, and household tasks, certain activities were clearly relegated to the female sphere, including special folklore rituals.[9] Uzbek scholar Usman Karabaev suggested that the temperament and psychological character of the people was shaped in part by climate. As a result, the traditional culture of the peoples of the East, especially the peoples of Central Asia, can be divided into two parts—masculine, constituting an "external open" culture, and feminine, constituting an "internal closed" culture.

For females, there were three general stages of life: young girls, married women, and, finally, elderly women.[10] Each stage had certain activities and responsibilities. Young girls enjoyed special games contributing to the development of musicality and the ability to dance, often gathering to play in the garden of one of the girls. From about the ages of nine to thirteen, they began to play separately from the boys. Girls who deviated from this rule were shamed[11] and it was around this age that they were given their first *paranjah*. On the eve of holidays or weddings, girls gathered for "secret" rites, dressing up and putting on makeup, painting eyebrows with herbal juices like *usma*, all accompanied by ritual folklore songs and poetry.

The abundance of nature in the Ferghana region appears in girls' spring rituals such as gathering wild mint, hyacinths, or tulips. Girls would crown their heads with willow branches, also weaving them into their braids and competing to see who had the longest and most luxurious braids. This tradition became the inspiration for the stage dance *Majnuntal*—literally "Majnun's hair," the name for the willow because its long, leafy branches are reminiscent of the unkempt hair of the legendary and love-sick Majnun who wandered in the wilderness.

In the Ferghana Valley they had special women's *gap* sessions where they gathered together and talked with *gap* serving as a cooperative consisting of mutual education and support. Women also had amateur associations that gathered for different activities such as writing and reciting poetry and performing *lapar*, a

---

[7]Ibid., pp. 169–70.
[8]Usman Karabaev, *Etnokul'tura: traditsionnaya narodnaya kul'tura*. Tashkent: Shark Publishing, 2005, p. 116.
[9]Ibid., p. 116.
[10]Ibid., p. 117.
[11]Ibid., p. 117.

genre that combines singing and dancing. Poetic creativity was widespread among women in the period of the late Middle Ages with the names of about 300 female poets known. Poetry contests and amateur theater provided creative outlets for women who entertained each other with *tomasha* (entertainments) in their leisure moments. These amateur performances would blossom and develop on the public stage once women were freed from the restraints of life in the *ichkari*. Unfortunately, many forms of folk entertainment came under attack during the Soviet political campaign of the "struggle against the old," which characterized folk art as vestiges of ancient feudal and reactionary systems, inappropriate for a new socialist world.[12] Traditional storytellers, comic performers like the *masqaraboz* and *kyzykchi*, even tightrope walkers came under ideological attack. Even *Askia*, the humor competition between sharp-wits, was considered a negative phenomenon.[13] Yet, somehow, certain dance traditions embedded in dance managed to survive, embodied in gesture.

The "Lost" Boat Dance—to China and Back?

The choreographic creativity of dancers from Fergana Valley included a curious dance that may have traveled from Central Asia to China and back again. Tang Dynasty annals mention a dance performed by girls on boats or rafts.[14] Intriguingly, a traveler to Kokand in 1871 wrote about witnessing dancing boys in small boats.

> He asked the Sultan's brother, the Sultan Mu-rad, "How did the people of Kokand adopt this dance in boats, which is unknown elsewhere in Central Asia?" In reply, he was told that "this occurred at the order of Khudayar Khan, in imitation of a Chinese dance, only replacing the [female] dancers with boys."[15]

Avdeeva describes a boat dance called *kema o'yin* in which a light-weight faux boat is hung from the dancer's belt, with fabric attached from the bottom of the vessel to cover the feet and create the illusion of being in water. Usually performed at night and in large groups, the performers were lit by burning torches attached fore and aft to their artificial boats. The watery illusion was achieved with movements

---

[12]Ibid., p. 122.

[13]Ibid.

[14]One episode of the 2018 Chinese television series, *Legend of Ruyi*, evokes this tradition when concubines dance and sing on rafts for the entertainment of the emperor.

[15]From *Turkestanskie Vedomosti*, nos. 29–30, 1872; no. 9, 1873. *Turkestanskie vedomosti*, no. 95, 1871. Cited in the section on Kokand, *Fergana Valley*, edited by Frederick Starr, p. 160.

like rocking side to side, or spinning as if caught in a whirlpool, rushing through rapids, running aground, then finally resting on gentle waves.[16] While working in Kari-Yakubov's Ethnographic, the boat dance was revived and staged by Yusufjon-Kyzyk Shakarjanov, sometime between 1926 and 1928.[17]

Tanovar

Mukarram Turgunbaeva declared that the "roots of our dance tradition are very deep. Their origins go back several thousand years."[18] One of the most famous of traditional women's dances, *Tanovar*, originated in the Ferghana zone and exists in over a dozen variations, with the lyrics of many telling of unrequited love, some quite tragic.[19] Some of the most beloved are *Adolat Tanovar, Kora Sochim, Yevvoyi Tanovar*, and *Hino Tanovar*, into which singers and dancers could pour the pain of their personal lives. The most popular version is a melody known by all. Several possible etymologies exist for *tanovar*,[20] but the quality of the dance expresses sadness and longing, a yearning that matched the poetry to which it was performed. The stage version created in 1942 by Mukarram Turgunbaeva became best known, but in actuality *Tanovar* was the legacy of dancers who grew up in the traditions of women's improvisational dance in the *ichkari* as a deeply personal form of self-expression. European and American travelers to Turkestan, who wrote often provocative accounts about the *bacha* dancing boys, remained silent about women dancers because they could not enter the women's quarters of traditional Uzbek homes.[21] As a result, some recent scholars have asserted that women did not have their own dance culture and Uzbek women's stage dance is

---

[16]Avdeeva, *Tantseval'noe Iskusstvo Uzbekistana*, pp. 17–18.
[17]Ilkhom Yuldashev, "National features of estrada acting skills (On the example of People's Artist of Uzbekistan Yusuf Qiziq Shakarjanov)." *International Journal of Innovative Engineering and Management Research*, 10, no. 5 (2021): 44. https://ijiemr.org/downloads/Volume-10/Issue-5 DOI: 10.48047/IJIEMR/V10/I05/10.
[18]Mukarram Turgunbaeva, quoted in Rakhimov, *Mukarramkhonim "Tanovar"i*, p. 40.
[19]Ibid., p. 43.
[20]Television director Hamid Kakhramanov collected over a dozen variants of Tanovar. He suggested one possible etymology was related to the word for tree trunk. Sepideh Farshadi confirmed that TanAvar (تن‌آور) is used in the *Shahnameh*, "for instance describing a strong army and it's also used to describe large trees." The term is related to "*tanoomand*" and signifies someone who is strong, sturdy, big, and thick (like a tree trunk), with the root *tan* (body) and *avar* (to bring) indicating someone who has or is in possession of a large body. Although Uzbek is a Turkic language, it has a large percentage of vocabulary of Persian origin. In pre-Islamic times, certain trees were believed to have magical properties. It was thought that hugging a tree would bring fertility to childless women. See Zaynab Abidova, "Worship of Trees in Cultural Practice of the Uzbeks of the Khorezm Oasis." *EPRA International Journal of Socio-Economic and Environmental Outlook (SEEO)*, 10, no. 3 (March 2023): 11.
[21]Notable exceptions were Swedish explorer Sven Hedin and the American Eugene Schuyler, who did view professional female dancers.

an "invented tradition."[22] Like the proverbial question of whether a tree falling in a forest makes a sound with no one around to hear it, the very existence of women's dances in pre-Revolutionary times was brought into question because male European travelers, who did not see it, could not write about it. Yet a few foreign men and women actually did see it and more more viewed it during the early Soviet years, recognizing a form that was already clearly developed. Si-Lan Chen compared Uzbek dance to the styles she observed in the Caucasus: "While the Georgian dance is primarily a man's dance, the Uzbek dance is a woman's."[23] Uzbek dance scholar Lyobov Avdeeva addressed this more directly: "how could a highly professional dance culture be born and developed if there were no foundation— no folk dance?"[24] She argues that only the isolation of women brought about by Islam, and attitudes about the sinfulness of dance, shaped its development, discouraging mingling of the sexes and *massovy* i.e., communal dances, except somewhat among men.

No less an authority than Tamara Khanum, the first woman to appear onstage with an "open face," learned the dances of women in the *kishlak* (village) in the Ferghana Valley region where she grew up during pre-Revolutionary times. She described three different dancers from pre-Revolutionary times—Adolxon, Kamolxon, and Nazirxon—who were known for the performances of *Tanovar*, each of whom interpreted it in a different way. As a young child, Tamara saw these "master dancers" (*ustoz rakkosalarimiz*) at big folk festivals known as *sayil*, held in Margilan and Kokand in 1915–1916. She attributed to them her inspiration to become a performer of *laparchi*, an Uzbek folk genre that combined song and dance. These "queens of their profession" were both talented singers and dancers, but with unique style and they did not copy each other. "It is as if they created their own three separate islands."[25]

Adolxon—also known as Tanovarxon[26]—was born in Margilan in 1885. Both Usta Olim Kamilov and Yusuf-Kyzyk Shakarjanov recalled that Adolxon knew the famous *ghazals* of the female poets Uvaysi and Nodira Begim, reinforcing the deep philosophical link between dance and poetry that remains central to Uzbek performing arts. Combined with music, these three elements give dance a special captivating power to the performer. When, in 1932, Tamara Khanum learned that Adolxon had passed away, she took Mukarram Turgunbaeva with her to Kokand to pay their respects, "a visit that was both a debt and an obligation." Mukarram had been too young to see any of Adolxon's performances, but Tamara Khanum

---

[22]For example, Mary Masayo Doi, Anthony Shay, and Grigor Ubrira.
[23]Leyda, *Footnote to History*, p. 169.
[24]Avdeeva, *Tantseval'noe Iskusstvo Uzbekistana*, p. 6.
[25]Tamara Khanum in *Uzbekistan adabiyoti va san'ati*, no. 1. Newspaper, 1982. Saodat magazine 1982, no. 12, cited by Rakhimov, *Mukarramkhonim "Tanovar"i*, pp. 46–47.
[26]Literally, "Queen of Tanovar."

remembered the dancer as graceful and beautiful. Adolxon "created a new world of her own when she danced and sang ... intoxicating her audience in a magical (*sekhrli*) world of dance."[27]

Nazirxon was another famous dancer of *Tanovar*. She was born in Fergana in the early 1880s and died in 1930. When Tamara Khanum saw her perform, the dancer wore no jewelry or ornaments on her dress but "her jewel-like eyes replaced any jewelry." Dance artists from India, Iraq, and Iran came to see her skills. Nazirxon sought to "alleviate the dreams and pains of contemporary women," not to win the sympathy of the audience, but to show the "delicate, mysterious feelings and the sublime qualities hidden in the heart of a woman."[28]

Another Tanovar dancer from the Fergana region, Kamolxon Mukhammajanova, was born in Kokand in 1873 and passed away sometime around 1948–49. She was completely different from the others. Tamara Khanum characterized her style as *chapani*[29]—unrefined yet powerful—"as if the ground were shaking when she danced." Tamara Khanum emulated her style when she performed *tanovar* in the 1930s. Kamolxon's teacher was a man—the famous male dancer, Ota Haji. He taught his student "all the secrets of dance" and, unconventionally, took her with him to men's gatherings.[30] In Komalxon, the young Tamara Khanum noticed some of her own qualities. "I dreamed of being like this dancer." She was greatly impressed by her traveling spins—*ailanish charkh*—performed in the *maidona* (open square). Echoing the impressions that the Sogdian Whirl made on Tang Dynasty poets over a thousand years earlier, Tamara Khanum described the turns as "ten times stronger than any storm" and sadly observed that "today our dancers cannot continue the work of these teachers ... because we are not dervishes. Mukarram Turgunbaeva was a dervish. Probably she took that *dervishness to that world* ... "[31]

Munojat

Another treasure of women's cultural heritage is *Munojat*. The word itself comes from Arabic, meaning a prayer, a supplication with roots in Islam and Arab traditions.[32]

---

[27]Tamara Khanum quoted by Rakhimov, *Mukarramkhonim "Tanovar"i*, p. 47.
[28]Ibid.
[29]From the word "chapan"—a man's coat—suggesting a masculine flavor to the dance. Tamara Khanum quoted in Rakhimov, *Mukarramkhonim "Tanovar"i*, p. 48.
[30]Tamara Khanum quoted by Rakhimov, *Mukarramkhonim "Tanovar"i*, p. 49.
[31]Ibid.
[32]Adelya Shagiduliina, "Tatar Folk Music and Its Influence in the First National Ballet" (PhD Diss., Temple University), 2019, p. 43.

By its musical style, the munadjat was a hybrid of musical folklore, Quran recitation, and "book singing." The genre of munadjat in a way brought a sophisticated art of Quran recitation that derived from Arabic culture to the masses. That music, one way or another, was rooted in a religious act of praying. Whether it is the Quran recited by one designated person, an imam, or a personal prayer such as munadjat, the music is most often interpreted as a "monologue."[33]

This folk song, deeply rooted in Uzbek women's tradition, would, in Soviet times, became part of the repertoire of the Bakhor Ensemble, as well as a memorable solo piece choreographed by Isaqar Aqilov for People's Artist of Uzbekistan, Kizlarkhon Dusmukhamedova. Through her interpretation of the piece, Kizlarkhon "was able to show the thoughts of the Eastern woman."[34] Musical performances of *Munojat* by esteemed vocalists Berta Davidova and Munojat Yulchieva hold a special place in Uzbek culture.

Professor Xamidulla Ikromov, theatrical scholar and son of the master composer Imomjon Ikromov, recalled hearing his grandmother often singing a sad song to herself but never knew its meaning until, one day, he asked his father about it. He was told that it was *Munojat*, "a love song for women, their mysterious voice." He grew up with this melody and through it "entered the world of mysterious melodies and magical music. Before your grandmother sang this song, your great-grandmother also sang it." This music, these "three- to four-minute melancholy songs were imprinted on my heart when I was young."

The melody of *Munojat* has been connected to the *ghazal* of Alisher Navoi, *Ul sarvi gulru kelmdi*, when, in 1943, it was first performed by Berta Davidova, People's Artist of Uzbekistan. It is also linked to the poetry of Alisher Navoi. Mukarram Turgunbaeva started working on a stage version of *Munojat* as early 1942 for a dramatic scene in the opera *Ulugbek*. However, the version of *Munojat* choreographed by Isaqar Aqilov for Kizlarkhon Dusmukhamedova remains closer to the original, private pain of the piece. Kizlarkhon has described the piece as "an internal monologue" embodying the hopeless situation of a young woman separated from her beloved. In her deep depression she scarcely moves, gently swaying from side to side as only her head turns slowly in denial. Gradually, both of her arms reach upward, beseechingly, in prayer. She tentatively takes a few steps forward and then turns follow, as one arm reaches low then sweeps up into a sagittal turn, characteristic of the *charkh* spin lyrically unfolding into a series of *ailanish* spins. The dancer sinks down to one knee when the music unexpectedly changes, becoming brighter and faster. Imagining her beloved before her, she

---

[33]Ibid., p. 43.
[34]Rahkimov, *Mukarramkhonim "Tanovar"i*, p. 98.

joyfully reaches toward him, traveling laterally across the front of the stage, her hand stroking beneath her chin with the *baqbaqa silash* gesture. The dancer travels around the entire parameter of the stage with the *ailanish* traveling spin, then travels backwards in a zigzag herringbone pattern as both arms lift upward as she moves in one direction, then downward when she again changes directionality. Emotions build to a point where she spins quickly in place until again, and just as unexpectedly, the music changes, and she suddenly realizes the entire interlude was a hallucination. Her beloved is not there. She has no escape. Submitting to her fate, she exits, perhaps to her death.

Remembering the deeper, poetic, and philosophical nature of *Munojat* as a prayer, the dance resonates on a deeper level, mirroring the soul's yearning for union with the Divine. Without deep understanding by the dancer "it is just a collection of subtle, beautiful, and mournful dance moves."[35] In Sufi thought, the "wedding day" is the day of death, the moment when the ultimate union with the Beloved is achieved. These layers of understanding allow the dance to be interpreted on different levels, as a tragic love story or as a representation of the human spiritual journey. The power of music and dance of this "divine miracle" makes us "we feel as if we have stepped into heavenly paradise."[36]

Traditional Costuming

Located in a silk manufacturing center, the women's clothing of the Ferghana Zone features this magical fabric in many variations, weights, and blends. Unlike men who, in Islamic practice, were forbidden to wear pure silk, women were permitted to wear silk next to their skin. Long-sleeved shifts made of silk were layered with jackets and coats, sometimes made of brocade. The distinctive striped *bekasam* fabric worn by both men and women is a regional signature of the Ferghana area. Most famous, the Uzbek *khan atlas* patterns appear in dresses and jackets, and also as the lining of paranjahs, which are usually sewn with exteriors of inconspicuous fabric, with the exception of some truly splendid garments for wealthy and aristocratic women. During the Soviet era, production of *khan atlas* moved to factories, favoring bright colors. Now, with the restoration of the art of hand-woven fabric, older designs have been revived, as well as other color palettes, including pastels. Professional dance ensembles have begun to use these hand-woven textiles in their costumes. They have also started to incorporate more traditional lines of dresses and coats that are much closer to historic garments depicted in Eastern miniature paintings, especially the works associated with Kamoliddin Bekhzod.

---

[35]Rakhimov, discussion of performers of Munojat, *Mukarramkhonim "Tanovar"i*, p. 98.
[36]Ergash Ochilov, quoted by Rakhimov, *Mukarramkhonim "Tanovar"i*, p. 99.

Delicate and even musical, Uzbek women's jewelry includes the magnificent crown known as *tillakosh* ("golden eyebrows"), which, when worn properly, mirrors the shape of a woman's eyebrows. The chest ornament called *zebigardon* attaches at the shoulder seams, then drops in tiers to the heart area and below. Earrings with fanciful shapes like paisleys and peacock's tail are embellished with small pearls. Amulets shaped like triangles or tubes are called "*tumor*" (pronounced like "too-more") and can hold a written prayer or even a useful sewing needle. Coral, carnelian, and turquoise appear in rings and earrings. In addition to these, women wear necklaces that are strings of pearls or coral. Ornaments with tassels and tiny beads can be woven into braids. The *popak* imitates braids with braided cords attached to a fabric strip that can be placed across the back of a coat at shoulder level.

Dance Characteristics

The posture for women's dance from the Ferghana zone has a modest demeanor with a slight forward inclination of the upper torso, bringing to mind the admiration of humility as expressed in the Uzbek proverb that "only a barren tree stands straight" *(mevasiz daraxt egilmas)*, because the branches of a tree bend under the weight of the fruit. The movements of the head can be deeply expressive, with the eyes following the motions of the hands, the head does normally not tip upward unless expressing a prayerful reaching to the heavens or following the path of the hands.

> The greatest characteristic ... is the fluid transition of arms from one position to another, accompanied by gentle, rotating movements of the hands. The alternation of soft, undulating movements from high to low levels, the curved movements of one or two arms—all these are difficult to describe but are, nonetheless, expressive movements.[37]

Torso mobility demonstrates both grace and fluidity in Ferghana dance as "the body can easily shift position, turn right, left, bend forward or to the side. Some movements are performed by a girl on her knees, and in these movements, the torso is especially pliant—it sways forward, bends deeply to the side and to the back, almost touching the floor."[38]

Wrist circles ornament hand movements as they travel from one position to the next. The circles can rotate outward, away from the body column, or inward, toward it, but for dances with a more introverted demeanor, the wrists turn

---

[37]T. Tkachenko, *Narodnyi Tanets*. Moscow: Gosudarstvennoe Izdatel'stvo, 1954, p. 159.
[38]Ibid.

inward. Hands can also undulate, pulsing as the energy moves extending through to the fingertips, then relaxes momentarily. Wrist bells are sometimes worn for girls' dances, but not as frequently as they are in Khorezm and Bukharan dances.

The ubiquitous *kigiir buyin* head slide often occurs at the end of a phrase, an accent that serves as a sort of a physical punctuation mark. Sometimes there is an almost imperceptible chin lift combined with a glance and a lifting of eyebrows. Gestures often illustrate song lyrics that describe a girl's hair, brows, and eyes. Motions that mimic the brushing or braiding of hair also embellish the dance.

Level changes are common in Ferghana dance, with the dancer often kneeling on the floor in part of the dance for pantomime sequences, such as crushing leaves to make *usma* with which to darken the eyebrows.

Footwork is simple, with a light 1-2-3 traveling step often maintained under the flowing movements of the upper body, arms, and hands. The *kaichi* (scissor) step can be used to glide smoothly across the stage while the arms move in graceful pathways or rotate in place. At times in choreography, a dancer will rise up on the balls of her feet to run for a few steps, as if to express an emotion of anticipation or excitement.

The fluid upper torso swaying from side to side adds an emotional quality to the dance, as if the dancer is unable to contain an inner emotion. Shoulders are relaxed. Deep backbends, often done slowly, can allow the dancer's braids to touch the floor. As with other Uzbek styles, the face can be highly animated and is often framed by gestures such as "*lola*" (tulip), with hands held under the chin and arched wrists. Hands often lightly touch one or both sides of the waist. During gestures done in imitation of applying eye makeup, one hand anchors at the waist while the other draws the brow, then the wrist rotates as the hand travels beyond the face.

All of these graceful and lyrical elements create the character of dances from the Ferghana region, distinct from the genres from the Bukharan and Khorezm dance zones. In the words of Yusuf-Kyzyk Shakarjanov, "*Ferganskiy tanets—eto devich'i ulybki*" (Ferghana dance is the smiles young young maidens).[39]

---

[39]Yusuf-Kyzyk Shakarjanov, quoted by Avdeevain *Galia Izmailova*. Tashkent: Gafur Gulyam, 1975, p. 65.

4 BUKHARA AND SAMARKAND

Teacher at pre-Revolutionary Boys School:
"Who can tell me which nationalities live in Bukhara?"
Student #1: Uzbek!
Student #2: Tajik!
Student #3: Uyghur!
Then all the students begin shouting out different
nationalities at once.

SCENE FROM UZBEK FILM *"ЗАВЕЩАНИЕ*
СМАРОГО МАСМЕРА," 1962[1]

These preceding lines come from *Zaveshchaniye starogo mastera* (Testament of the Old Master), the 1962 four-part Soviet Uzbek film series based on a book by Kamil Ikramov. It tells the story of a mysterious notebook written by a master blacksmith in the era of the Emir of Bukhara, discovered by a few Young Pioneers in the ruins of an old building as it is being demolished. Through flashbacks, the story depicts life in old, pre-Revolutionary Bukhara. In one scene, a young Jadist teacher at the "New School"—not a madrasah—shows students a world globe and points out different countries, then asks about the population of Bukhara. The children's vociferous response underscores the diverse origins of the city's inhabitants.

Any exploration into the histories of Bukhara and Samarkand similarly uncovers multiple ethnic legacies, layered one over another, blending and surviving to create a remarkable art dance of the twenty-first century.[2] In October 1997, the city of Bukhara celebrated the 2,500th anniversary of its founding. As an important city on the Great Silk Road, Bukhara felt the influences of Greek,

---

[1] *Zaveshchaniye starogo mastera* (1962). The scene described begins at 1:43:49 and can be accessed here: https://youtu.be/k5pZqcyx954?t=6229
[2] Laurel Victoria Gray, "The Splendor of Uzbek Dance Part Three: Bukhara." *Habibi*, 16, no. 3 (Fall 1997).

Chinese, Indian, Arabic, and Persian cultures. Shamanism, Zoroastrianism, Buddhism, Manicheism, Judaism, Nestorian Christianity, and Islam have all been practiced here. In Samarkand, at the ancient site of the Afrasiab palace, vividly painted murals depict diplomatic emissaries, possibly from Korea's Silla Dynasty dating from the seventh century.[3] Sogdian merchants from Bukhara and Samarkand traded with Tang dynasty China, some even settling there.

Theories about the origin of the name Bukhara bear testimony to the various peoples who have left their traces here. One suggestion links the city with the term *vihara*, which means Buddhist monastery. Another term, the Zoroastrian word *bukhar*, meaning "source of knowledge," was mentioned by Hafizi Tanish in the sixteenth century as the root of the city's name.[4] Another tradition credits Siyavash, the handsome prince from Ferdowsi's epic poem the *Shahnameh*, as the legendary founder of the city.

During the pre-Islamic period, there were images of dancers depicted at the archeological site of Varakhsha, the ancient capital of Sogdian kings in the Bukhara oasis near the delta of the Zarafshan River. Professor M. Kodirov contends that in pre-Islamic times at the Varakhsha's Palace of Governors, there were musicians and singers and "among them were also famous dancers." Excavations confirmed this, uncovering a sculpture of a dancer holding a scarf that dates from the eighth century CE.[5]

According to Uzbek dance scholar Liubov Avdeeva, the "Bukaharan dance school unites dances of the current oblasts of Uzbekistan—Bukhara and Samarkand."[6] Using the concept of dance zones, the Bukharan "school" includes Samarkand. They are located about 150 miles apart, a distance which a camel could traverse in about a week, an important consideration before the Trans-Caspian railway connected Samarkand and Bukhara in 1888. At different times, these cities each served as political centers. For Emir Timur and his descendants, the capital was Samarkand. In the mid-sixteenth century, the Uzbek Shaybanids made Bukhara their capital and, in 1785, when the Manghit dynasty took control, it became the capital of their emirate. For centuries both cities were part of the same Persian- (and Persianate-) speaking empire, vital cultural centers where scholars, poets, musicians, and artisans all sought court patronage.

When the Scottish explorer and diplomat Captain Alexander Burnes (1805–1841) was sent to Bukhara in 1834, he noted the astounding ethnic diversity of its population:

---

[3]Diplomats from Silla (ancient Korea) have been identified in a mural at Afrasiab, the historic site near Samarkand.
[4]Gray, "Splendor of Uzbek Dance: Bukhara."
[5]M. Kodirov from his 1997 work, *Holidays and Festivals*, p. 131, cited by G. M. Khudoev in "Peering into Culture of Ancient Bukhara." *Journal of Literature and Art Studies*, 5, no. 8 (August 2015): 630–31. doi:10.17265/2159-5836/2015.08.007
[6]Avdeeva, Introduction to Roza Karimova, *Bukharskii Tanets*. Literatura i Isskustvo, 1977. Tashkent: Gafur Gulyam, p. 5.

A stranger has only to seat himself on a bench of the Registan, to know Uzbeks and the people of Bokhara. He may converse with the natives of Persia, Turkey, Russia, Tartary, China, India and Cabool. He will meet with Toorkmans, Calmuks and Cossacks from the surrounding deserts, as well as the natives of more favoured lands.[7]

The heritage of these complex, interwoven, multi-ethnic connections emerge in some of the most memorable—and most analyzed—lines of Persian poetry.[8]

Agar ān tork-e shirāzi be dast ārad del-e mā rā
Beh khāl-e hendoyash bakhsham Samarqand-o Bokhārā rā.
Should that Turk from Shiraz take our heart into his hands,
I'd give up, for his Indian mole, all Samarkand and Bukhara.[9]

These opening lines of *Shirazi Turk*, the famous ghazal of beloved Persian poet Hafez (1315–1390), provide a poetic introduction to the ethnic, social, mythic, and historical complexity of Bukhara and Samarkand, all of which surface in the dance traditions of those two cities. The verse begins with linguistic ambiguity because of the ungendered third person singular pronoun[10]—assigned a male pronoun in this translation—makes it unclear whether the object of desire is male or female. Shiraz is a Persian city, so where did the Turkic person come from?[11] But "Turk" was sometimes used to designate a slave, and Bukhara was a notorious slave trading center. The black mole is described with the word *hendoyash*, a term linked to Hindu India and its black "Indian ink."

Subsequent lines of the poem continue with a dizzying array of people, places, and things.

Feghān kin luliyān-e shukh-e shirinkār-e shahrāshub
Chonān bordand sabr az del ke torkān khwān-e yaghmā rā.
Alas! Those jesting gypsies, so gracefully have cast the city in turmoil
and robbed my heart of patience as Turks plunder the feast.[12]

This third verse mentions the chaos caused by the "gypsies" or, more precisely and less pejoratively, *Luli*, the Central Asian Romani people mentioned in Babur's

---

[7]Alexander Burnes, *Travels into Bokhara*, 1834, cited by Kathleen Hopkirk in *Central Asia through Writers' Eyes*. London: Eland, 1993, p. 52.

[8]Translation and transliteration from the Persian by Domenico Ingenito (2018): "Hafez's 'Shirāzi Turk': A Geopoetical Approach." *Iranian Studies*, DOI: 10.1080/00210862.2018.1511507. I am indebted to Ingenito for his remarkable analysis of this famous poem.

[9]Ibid.

[10]Ibid.

[11]Ibid.

[12]Ibid.

memoirs as performers at his victory celebration.[13] Turkic invaders also show up in this verse, a grim reality at the time when the poem was written; Tamerlane, who made his capital in Samarkand, began his conquest of Persia in 1383.

In the fifth verse, Hafez references the Quranic story of Yusuf and Zuleikha—rendered here as Joseph and Zoleykha—which echoes the Old Testament story of Potiphar's wife, her attempted seduction of the beautiful young Joseph, and her rape accusation against him.

> *Man az ān hosn-e ruzafzun keh Yusof dāsht dānestam*
> *keh 'eshq az pardeh-ye 'esmat borun ārad Zoleykhā rā.*
> From that daily-growing beauty that was Joseph's, I knew that love
> would bring Zoleykhā out from behind the veil of chastity.[14]

The story of Joseph and Potiphar's wife from the Hebrew Pentateuch, specifically Genesis (39:7–20), pre-dates the Yusuf and Zuleikha story, providing a reminder of another significant community of culture bearers, the Bukharan Jews, who greatly contributed to the legacy of Central Asian dance. "According to legend, migrations of descendants of the Babylonian Jews from Iran and Afghanistan began in the first century CE."[15] By the early Middle Ages they had begun to settle in Merv, Balkh, Bukhara, and Samarkand. Central Asian Jews were mentioned by historians and geographers such as Narshaki, Tabari, Biruni, and others "from the ninth to the sixteenth centuries."[16] As musicians and dancers, Bukharan Jews performed in the court of the Emir, continuing vital and ancient traditions. "Bukharan Jews were renowned for their skills as musicians, singers and manufacturers of musical instruments. Jewish musicians played at every Tajik or Uzbek wedding."[17]

The Yusuf and Zuleikha story also shares resonance with the Persian speakers through a story in Ferdowsi's *Shahnameh*, which related Sudabeh's attempts to seduce the handsome Siyavash, the very same Siyavash known as the legendary founder of Bukhara.

In the layered and nuanced lines of this Hafez poem, almost everyone and everything tied up in the cultural legacy of Bukhara and Samarkand makes an appearance. There is the Persian poet himself, Hafez, who references the Persian city of Shiraz, and presents an ambiguous Turk—a conqueror or an enslaved dancer?—for whom the poet will trade the magnificence of the cities of Samarkand and Bukhara. The word "*hendoyosh*" hints at an Indian connection,

---

[13] *Babur Nama: Journal of Emperor Babur*. Translated by Annette Susannah Beveridge. London: Penguin Books, 2006, p. 324.
[14] Ibid.
[15] Ibid., p. 33.
[16] Ibid.
[17] Ibid., p. 64.

perhaps indicating the black mole on the face of the beloved, or the black color of Indian ink, and Indian merchants long had ties with Bukhara. Mischievous Luli people—who still live in Bukhara and were known to have performed for Emperor Babur himself—also appear. Unruly Turkic invaders plunder a banquet, *motreb* entertainers turn up in verse seven, and Zuleikha comes out from behind a veil, suggesting the "lifting of a veil" gesture typical of Bukharan women's dance. Subsequent to all this, Tamerlane himself makes an appearance in an apocryphal story of an encounter with Hafez himself, in which the ruler expresses his anger with the poet for devaluing his treasure cities of Bukhara and Samarkand.[18]

Although the presence of the Persians themselves is implied through the reference of Shiraz as well as the ethnicity of the poet himself, the Tajiks— among the most ancient inhabitants of the region—are not mentioned by name because the ethnonym "Tajik" that currently distinguishes them only gained widespread currency much later.[19] The Tajiks were "the dominant population of Bukhara, Samarkand and Shakhrisabz."[20]

Also unmentioned are the Sogdians, that ancient and significant Persianate speaking population of Bukhara and Samarkand whose vibrant civilization declined after the Islamic conquest in 712 of Samarkand, one of their primary cultural centers. However, the Sogdian legacy in dance remains.

Heirs to the Sogdian Whirl

In dance, the highly significant commercial and cultural connection between Bukhara and Samarkand dates to their significance as major cities of Sogdiana, an ancient Iranian civilization existing from about 600 BCE to 1100 CE. While the Sogdians traded throughout regions traversed by the caravan routes associated with the Silk Road, those who settled in China's Tang Dynasty capital of Chang'an built Zoroastrian temples there and sometimes married Chinese women. As outsiders, the "Sogdians were called Hu (胡), meaning barbarian, in medieval

---

[18]This apocryphal story first appears in *Anis al-Nas* by Shoja' Shirazi (1426). In it, Timur upbraided Hafez for this verse and said, "By the blows of my well tempered sword I have conquered the greater part of the world to enlarge Samarkand and Bukhara, my capitals and residences; and you, pitiful creature, would exchange these two cities for a mole." Hafez, undaunted, replied, "It is by similar generosity that I have been reduced, as you see, to my present state of poverty." It is reported that the King was pleased by the witty answer and the poet departed with magnificent gifts. Cited by Ingenito, "Hafez's 'Shirāzi Turk,'" p.11.

[19]"Tajik," the "Ethnonym: Origin and Application," in *Encyclopedia Iranica* online. www.iranicaonline. org/articles/tajik-i-the-ethnonym-origins-and-application.

[20]Tatjana Emelyanenko, *Facing West. Oriental Jews of Central Asia and the Caucasus*, edited by Hetty Berg. Zwolle, Netherlands: Waanders Publishers, 1999, p. 34.

China."[21] Individual Sogdian traders in Chang'an were also given surnames by the Chinese that linked them to their specific Sogdian cities of origin, such as "An" for Bukhara, "Kang" for Samarkand, and "Chash" for Tashkent.[22]

Sogdians catered to the Tang fascination with the exotic "West"—Central Asia was considered the West for China—trading many items such as silk, spices, furs, gems, amber, weapons, horses, medicinal herbs, along with slaves and dancers. It was the Sogdians' unique spinning dance that captivated even the Chinese court, creating a genuine dance craze and perhaps enabling a political rebellion. Depictions of Sogdians feasting, drinking, and dancing appear in Chinese art, as well as on Sogdian funerary objects. The dance of Sogdian Westerners—the *huxuan wu*[23]—fascinated Chinese poets, who wrote awe-struck verses about performances, often linked to drinking the grape wine of the West.

> The Iranian from Tashkent appears young.
> He dances to the music holding the wine goblet, as rapid as a bird.
> He wears a cloth cap of foreign make, empty and pointed at the top,
> His Iranian robe of fine felt has tight sleeves.
>
> —Liu Yanshi (d. 812)[24]

One of China's generals, An Lushan—known to be of "Western" Sogdian and Turkic ancestry—excelled at this spinning dance, even though he reportedly weighed 330 catties[25] (over 436 pounds) and needed to put his arms around his advisors in order to walk. But when he came before the emperor, he quite astoundingly performed the "Dance of the Barbarian Whirl" and moved "as swiftly as the wind."[26] His mother was a Turkic shamaness, "who told fortunes for a living"—a possible connection between shamanic ritual and the whirling

---

[21]Joo-Yup Lee, "The Sogdian Descendants in Mongol and post-Mongol Central Asia: The Tajiks and Sarts" (PDF). *Acta Via Serica*, 5, no 1 (June 2020): 189. [The moniker of "Hu," the repetitive first syllable of the three pillars of the Sogdian's Zoroastrian faith—*Humata, Hukhta, Huvarsha* (Good Thoughts, Good Words, Good Deeds), may have caught the ear of Chinese speakers, who then associated it with these foreigners. "Hu" dates from the Han dynasty (206 BCE–220 CE), so the contact would have been very early.]

[22]Sogdian surnames created by Chinese may be seen here: https://sogdians.si.edu/sidebars/the-nine-sogdian-surnames/

[23]Professor Zhang Qingje draws a distinction between the male *huteng wu* dancers from Tashkent and the *huxuan* dancers from Samarkand, who could be male or female. See Zhang Qingje. "Studies of Sogdian Dancing Images in China." *Circle of Inner Asia Art*, Issue 17 (June, 2003): 3–9.

[24]Cited on the Smithsonian website on the Sogdians, https://sogdians.si.edu/sogdian-dancer/. Ishida Mikinosuke, "Études sino-iraniennes, I. Apropos du *Hou-siuan-wou.*" *Memoirs of the Research Department of the Toyo Bunko* 6. Tokyo: The Oriental Library, 1932, pp. 61–76, cited in Edward H. Schafer, *The Golden Peaches of Samarkand: A Study of T'ang Exotics*. Berkeley, Los Angeles, and London: University of California Press, p. 293, n. 141.

[25]A *catty* is a Chinese unit of weight.

[26]Tang Annals cited in *Biography of An Lu-shan*, translated and annotated by Howard S. Levy, Berkeley and Los Angeles: University of California Press, 1960, p. 34.

dance practice that surfaces elsewhere. After his father died, "he accompanied his mother among the Turks," which may explain why he would later claim to understand six "barbarian" (i.e., non-Chinese) languages.[27] An Lushan developed a close relationship with the 27-year-old imperial concubine Yang Guifei, who adopted him as her son, a practice in the Tang era to create political support and one which would benefit the non-Chinese general. An Lushan taught her the spinning technique that helped her catch the eye of Emperor Xuanzong. Her dance entranced him. She became his favorite and—as described by the poet Bai Juyi in his *Song of Everlasting Sorrow (Chang Hen Ge*, 長恨歌)—an unhealthy obsession that led to political chaos.

It was this same dancing general An Lushan, with his Sogdian surname of *An* linking him to Bukhara, who in 755 CE led a bloody and destructive rebellion against this Tang emperor. By the end of the revolt, all three of the central characters in this tragedy were dead, along with an estimated 36 million people.[28] After this devastation, the formerly cosmopolitan Tang Dynasty grew increasingly xenophobic. That development, together with the Arab invasion of Sogdian lands to the West, lessened Sogdian influence as commerce fell to conquest.

The so-called "Sogdian Whirl" still exists in the dances of Central Asia and beyond. Eyewitness accounts from nineteenth-century travelers to Russian Turkestan, expressing the same amazement that dazzled Chinese poets, wrote of the whirling turns of the dancing boys. This spin seems preserved in Bukharan dance; it is distinct from the Western ballet technique of "spotting" during spins and turns that was introduced under the Soviets. This unique spin is still practiced today in men's ritual physical training centers known as *zurkhaneh*, "houses of strength," in Iran and Azerbaijan, and has origins as a martial arts technique as the men train to acquire the strength of the legendary heroes known as *pahlavan*.[29] "Pahlavans with their whirling movement increase their coordination, balance and overall fitness. The movement was used in battle to repel multiple surrounding assailants."[30] This technique also occurs in Asian martial arts. When performed with blades in each hand, the fast movement "blinds" opponents and makes the warrior a deadly whirlwind. This military connection might explain why General An Lushan excelled at it in spite of his size, if it had been a technique he had learned and mastered at an early age.

---

[27]Ibid., p. 31. It is possible that he acquired the An surname from his mother's second husband and that his birth father's name was Kang, but "Kang" would connect him to Samarkand, another Sogdian city.
[28]For an analysis of ethnic conflict connected with the An Lushan rebellion, see Lee Chamney, 'The An Shi Rebellion and Rejection of the Other in Tang China, 618–763' (MA thesis, University of Alberta), 2012.
[29]Quote from documentary film about the zurkhaneh practices in Iran, *History of the Zurkhaneh and the story of Hossein e Golzar Kermanshahi*, www.youtube.com/watch?v=mOmY2ljQ_Ws
[30]Ibid.

This Sogdian style turn is still part of Bukharan dance and known as *charkh*,[31] the Persian word for wheel. (*Charkh* is also the term for both the Uzbek water wheel and spinning wheel.) The Uyghurs, with close linguistic and historical ties to the Uzbeks—as well as military involvement in putting down the rebellion of An Lushan—have a tradition containing some elements reminiscent of the Sogdian Whirl. In a men's ritual known as *zikr*, participants travel in a counterclockwise circle.[32] At times, individuals turn around themselves in the center of the circle, rotating to the left, over the heart, as is done with the Mevlana dervishes. Other shared characteristics of the Sogdian Whirl appear in dance forms with connections to Zoroastrianism, as well as Persian-born Shia Islam. In the Pamirs, there is *Rapo*, a mesmerizing dance with turns that continually shift directionality, then build to a continuous spin. The "whirling dervishes" of Turkey—members of the Mevlana Order founded by the Persian-speaking refugee from Balkh, Jaladdin Rumi[33]—call their turn *çark*, as do the Shia Alevi sect, who include the turn in rituals in which both men and women participate.[34] The Afghan *Attan*, originally a war dance performed in a long line that travels along a circular path, gradually builds in speed and intensity until participants execute a series of fast spins that also include quick head circles.

Connections to Indian Dance—Bells, *Mudras*, and Spins

Not only were Bukhara and Samarkand important Silk Road trade centers, but so was the ancient Sogdian city of Penjikent. Located in the Sughd region of what is today Tajikistan, the town of Penjikent was mentioned in Achaemenid times, dating from the sixth century BCE. It fell to Arabs of the Abbasid caliphate in 722 CE. Among the burned remains of the structure is a caryatid carved from wood, depicting a dancer standing in the familiar *tribhanga* "thrice bent" pose evocative of Indian classical dance, with a bend at the knees, waist, and neck, to

---

[31]An Iranian linguist has asserted that the term used to be "chakhr," but it has evolved to be "charkh" beacuse it rolls easier on the tongue. If so, then "chakhr" has an even closer connection to the Indian dance term "chakkar." https://youtu.be/peZY0w9n8v4 (comment made at about 30:50). Special thanks to Sepideh Farshadi for finding this video.

[32]Tursun Gabitov, Zukhra Ismagambetova, Aliya Karabayeva, Saltanat Aubakirova and Zarina Mukanova, "Circle Dance as a Symbolic Form of Culture." *International Journal of Advanced Research*, 4, no. 5 (2016): 75–84.

[33]Jalaleddin Rumi, also called "Balkhi," 1207–1273 CE.

[34]"This ritual dance must not be considered as an ordinary dance or even as folklore with a cultural–historical background." It is performed by both men and women, bare-footed. "Every religious song that is sung and every recited poem is internalized by the dancers, and brings them to ecstasy. Literally they fly towards the sky like cranes." Remzi Kaptan, *Alevi Teaching*. Stuttgart, pp. 44–45. www.alevitentum.de.

create a sensuous curve of the body. At Penjikent, archeologists excavated images of Lord Shiva as well as the Zoroastrian goddess Anahita, framed by a pair of lions. Buddhist and Christian artifacts also surfaced, evidence of a diverse cosmopolitan civilization.

Other traces of historic connections with India appear in Bukharan dance, reminders of the well-documented and long-standing contact between Bukhara and India that occurred significantly through trade, religion, and conquest. The ancient Central Asian Bactrian kingdom, founded in 256 BCE, at times extended into India; the Indian goddesses Lakshmi and Sarasvati turn up on Bactrian coinage. Indian traders brought textiles such as calico and brocade into Central Asia, along with spices like nutmeg, cloves, and ginger. Naqshbandi Sufism, originating in Bukhara, traveled into Mughal India in the late sixteenth and seventeenth centuries. Indian merchants were also documented as living "in special *caravanserais*, Saroi-Hindi being the largest in Bukhara."[35]

In 1526, under the Turkic conqueror Babur, the cultures of Central Asia, Persia, and North India began to commingle, eventually flowering in the arts of the Moghul Dynasty. In architecture, the iconic Taj Mahal symbolizes this cultural confluence; in dance, it is Kathak that embodies these legacies. Intriguingly, Bukharan dance shares with Kathak dance three striking elements: *mudra*, specific hand gestures; *ghungroo*, ankle bells, and *chakkar*, fast spins done in place, with a technique and name similar to *charkh*. While the spins seem to have evolved from Sogdian sources and the ankle bells may share common Sasanian and Indian links, the *mudra* appear most clearly connected to India. Ancient and symbolic, the hand gestures known as *mudra* are a characteristic of several Indian classical dance forms, adding to the story-telling aspects of these dances.

At least two Indian *mudras* surface in Bukharan dance. They fall into the category of *samyukta hastas*, or "double hand" gestures. In one, the pinkie of the right hand connects with the pinkie of the left hand, which hangs below the right. The gesture turns up in Bukharan dance, including the choreographies of Isaqar Aqilov, founder of Uzbekistan's Bukharan stage dance. It is also commonly used by the historic female performers known as *sozanda*. In both Kathak and Bharatanatyam classical dance, this gesture is a specific *mudra* called *kaleeka*, meaning friendship, love, or even the intimate union between divinities. In another gesture, called *ustanga*, the arms are held out from the shoulder, bent at the elbow, with the fingertips of each hand hovering above the shoulders; this is found in Kathak dance, but not Bharatanatyam. *Ustanga* indicates a touch, an embrace. A similar pose occurs in Bukharan dance, but the hand position is more relaxed. It can also be seen in Tajik dance, hinting at a mutual, early Sogdian origin.

---

[35]Andrei G. Nedvetsky, *Bukhara: Caught in Time: Great Photographic Archives*, Edited by Vitaly Naumkin. Garnet Publishing Limited, 1993, p. 59.

The ankle bells, or *ghungroos*, of Indian dancers are worn in Kathak dance and other classical Indian dance styles. Until quite recently, ankle bells were also worn in Bukharan dance, but it is difficult to determine whether this came into practice as a result of contact with Indian dancers through the Moghul Court, or even earlier through Persian or Sogdian traditions.

Pre-eminent scholar of Uzbek dance Liubov Avdeeva noted that descriptions in "Eastern poetry" about Central Asian dancers "not once" mentioned bells or jewelry. The specific verses to which she refers are not clearly identified, but earlier in the same work, a famous poem by Bai Juyi is given in Russian translation, but without citation.[36] This previously cited Tang Dynasty poem describes a performance of the Sogdian Whirl. Many existing images of the *huxuan wu* commonly show the male dancers wearing boots, although, as mentioned earlier, Zhang Qingje identified this masculine dance with Tashkent. Female dancers, probably performing *huxuan* of Samarkand, appear more in the garb of *bodhisattvas*, swirling amidst fabric streamers. None of these depictions shows ankle bells.

The Sasanian connection comes from objects dating from the third to fifth centuries. One depicts a dancer with bells or, more correctly, a large single half-bell on each ankle and a corresponding half-bell held in each hand. These curious anklets are not the more familiar ankle bells of Indian dance, but they indicate that, at least in the Sasanian empire, a dancer could provide a rhythmic accompaniment to her performance. Some Sasanian plates depict a dancing woman, often identified as the Goddess Anahita, wearing tubular anklets. Bracelets that look similar to these on the anklets are seen in the bracelets worn by Baluchi women in dance. The hollow tubes are filled with tiny beads that make a rattling sound, like the so-called "rain stick," perhaps an auditory reference to Anahita's role as the Lady of Waters.

Avdeeva describes another Persian connection with dancers providing their own percussive elements. She notes that in Bukhara and nearby cities, populations also performed "*irani raqs*" in which dancers played *chak-chaka* or finger cymbals.[37] Photographs of People's Artist of Uzbekistan Tamara Khanum[38] show her playing *chak-chaka* while also wearing wrist bells. There is a mention from the 1940s of Iranian girls in Tehran wearing ankle bells in a dance performance.[39] One possible avenue of this transmission from Persian dance comes from Bukhara's historic slave trade. Persian girls and women fetched high prices, but once purchased disappeared into households and harems. Some were even taken as far as China, where they were sold into wine houses as desirable entertainers; others were sent

---

[36]Avdeeva, Introduction to Karimova, *Bukharskii Tanets*, p. 6.

[37]Ibid., p. 15.

[38]A photograph by Max Penson shows Tamara Khanum wearing distinctive Khorezm pectoral and wrist bells while wearing finger cymbals that are not used in Uzbek dance.

[39]Nesta Ramazani, *The Rose and the Nightingale*. Syracuse, New York: Syracuse University Press, 2002, p. xiv.

as gifts and found their way into royal harems.[40] Still, the "invisibility" of these often-nameless captured girls and women does not mean they had no significant impact on local dance culture, it simply makes their contribution difficult to trace. An analog may be found in the example of enslaved Africans whose resilient dance traditions endured and have powerfully shaped dance in America and throughout the world.

Although it is difficult to determine from these tantalizing clues when Bukharan dancers began wearing ankle bells, the practice continued well into the mid-twentieth century. In his novel *The Life Story of a Naughty Boy from Bukhara*, Timur Pulatov (b. 1939) describes a professional dance performance by "Oliya" that took place in a courtyard during a wedding celebration. It was the cause for excited conversation by neighbors.

> They spoke of the famous ruby bracelets, each the width of four fingers, which Oliya wore on her wrists and ankles—they were gifts from her admirers. They jangled with every movement of her lovely body.[41]

It is possible that the dancer in the story was Oliyaxon Hasanova (Figure 4.1), one of Bukhara's famous female performers known as *sozanda*. These dancers traditionally wore ankle bells, as evidenced in a 1957 photograph of the Bukharan *sozandas* Tuhfakhon Pinkhasova and Asiyakhon Ilyasova, taken at a Navruz celebration. A photograph of People's Artist of the USSR Galia Izmailova (1923–2010), dressed in a Bukharan dance costume, also shows her wearing ankle bells.

When People's Artist of Uzbekistan Kizlarkhon Dusmukhamedova toured the United States in the 1980s, she wore ankle bells in addition to wrist bells in her solo, *Star of Bukhara*. Kizlarkhon was mentored by Isaqar Aqilov of the legendary Bukharan Jewish cultural dynasty of the Aqilov family; this solo dance was choreographed by him. Kizlarkhon confirms that wearing ankle bells for Bukharan dance was traditional at the time of her performance. Now, in contemporary performances, Bukharan dancers wear only wrist bells, not ankle bells. The reasons for discontinuing the tradition of wearing ankle bells is unclear. One possibility may be that fast costume changes in contemporary performances require that dancers quickly shift from one regional dance style to the next; removing or putting on ankle bells would add more time to the transition. A different style of pants might also tend to mute the sound. But the use of ankle bells surely would have made

---

[40]Maria Marinova in "Status of Women in Ancient Sogdian Society." 古代粟特社会中女性的地位. (2021), p. 8, doi:10.13140/RG.2.2.31477.29922.
[41]Timur Pulatov, *The Life Story of a Naughty Boy from Bukhara*. Moscow: Raduga Publishers, 1983, p. 162.

FIGURE 4.1 Bukhara 1992, with *sozanda* Oliyaxon Hasanova (center), Travis Fontaine
Jarrell (left), and Laurel Victoria Gray (right).
Photo source: Author's personal archive.

a significant difference in the "soundscape" of Bukharan dance, amplifying the
accented stomp that sometimes occurs in the dance.[42]

Sozanda—Legacy of Ancient Goddess Rites?

While foreign visitors wrote about the *bachas* who danced for them, the women of
Bukhara and Samarkand had their own artists, the *sozanda*. As with other forms
of entertainment in Turkestan, several elements were combined during their
syncretic performances—song, dance, rhythm, poetry, and theater. By confinement
to their homes, to the *ichkari*, women were able to continue ancient traditions
that had helped the rituals survive for generations. *Sozanda* entertained at private
parties known as *tois*, in celebration of important events such as weddings and
circumcisions, as well as the *beshek toi*, the ritual held when an infant is placed in
a cradle, marking the first 40 days of its life.

The Sozanda dance tradition contains eight primary characteristics. First,
the dance possesses distinct postures, gestures, and hand positions; second, the
dance is performed to special rhythms accompanied by *doira, kairoki, zang,* and

---

[42]Nizam Nurdzhanov, *Traditsionnyi Teatr Tadzhikov*, Volume 1, p.283, mentions stamping the foot in
Bukharan dance.

even thimbles tapping on saucers. The third distinction comes from the loose-fitting dress worn by women for the dance, with long, wide sleeves and a veil, or shawl, attached to the *peshanaband*. All these costume parts could be grasped or manipulated at different times in the dance. A fourth characteristic, shared in other Central Asian forms, is the apprenticeship system, which emphasized dance lineage. A fifth element comes from the Sogdian, Indian, and Persian gestures or movements that surface in the dance. Links to pre-Islamic rites and shamanism form a sixth distinction, and the seventh trait consists of the incorporation of theatrical vignettes and cross-dressing in the performances.[43] Finally, an eighth consideration as proof of their professionalism, in a purely monetary sense, the *sozanda* were registered and were required to pay into their emir's treasury.[44]

Sozanda performed solely for the female audiences of the home, "completely isolated from the male eye," so, unlike the dancing boys, there were no male European accounts of their dance. This may also explain why several Western scholars—with no knowledge of the *sozanda*—have insisted that prior to the Soviet era, women in Uzbekistan had no dance traditions. In reality, "no celebration went without the presence of a sozanda performer, be it an engagement, a wedding, the birth of a first child, circumcision, celebrations and performances that would last 2–3 days."[45]

Annette Meakin wrote of her experiences in Russian Turkestan at the turn of the last century, before she returned to England in March of 1902. She did not specifically identify the location of the event in the following passage, but she mentions "the schoolmistress at Samarkand" a few sentences later. Several characteristic elements such as the purple velvet tunics, the elongated sleeves, the dancers' spins, and the similarity in color and style of the dancers' clothing all suggest that they were *sozanda*. Note, too, the presence of little boys watching and interacting with the dancers, a reminder that young boys witnessed women's dances in their childhood.

> Outside in the courtyard there would be a row of female musicians seated on mattresses, and dancing-girls performed to the tambourine music. The girls wore red cloths tied over their foreheads, strings of coral round their necks, and purple velvet tunics over robes with sleeves half a yard longer than their arms, which flapped about like fins. Round and round they twirled, the centre of an

---

[43]Laurel Victoria Gray, "Sozanda: Women's Professional Dance Traditions in Bukhara before the Soviets." Conference presentation, Middle Eastern North African Central Asian (MENACA) Dance Symposium, Pomona College, April 13–16, 2023.

[44]Avdeeva, Introduction to Karimova, *Bukharskii Tanets*, p. 15.

[45]Gulmira Rakhminova,*Tuhfakhon, The Greatest Sozanda*, published by Gulmira Rakhminova, p. 38. Djumaev, in his discussion of the practices of the Sozanda in "Musical Traditions and Ceremonies of Bukhara." *Anthropology of the Middle East*, 3, no. 1 (2008): 52–66.

admiring crowd, singing as they danced, and presently the little boys, without waiting for a pause, threw them coins, which they dexterously caught in their mouths.[46]

Unique to Bukhara and Samarkand, *sozanda* originally consisted of small groups, or *dasta*, of perhaps only three or four women, under a single leader known as *a sozanda bozinga*. She led her ensemble in song and dance, accompanied with percussion on the *doira* and *kairoki*, occasionally using thimbles to tap on saucers. In this regard, they skirted the boundaries of acceptable behavior because according to most *hadith*,[47] "clapping of the hands along with the playing of the frame drum *daf* is allowed for women at celebrations."[48] Their traditions mirrored other forms of Central Asian entertainment, which was never strictly dance but a combination of various elements of performing arts and sometimes rituals linked to pre-Islamic practices. Poetry and special blessings, all recited by heart, formed part of their presentations, which could last for hours. *Sozanda* sometimes included playful theatrical skits for the entertainment of the women who hired them. At different moments in the performance, the *sozanda* pretended to be men, dressing like *qalandars* or dervishes, and moving among the guests asking for "alms" to earn tips for their performance. In these skits, they imitated the appearance of the wandering ascetics, putting on false beards and patched coats, and carrying walking sticks and begging gourds.[49]

Sozanda transmitted their tradition through the *ustoz–shogird* (master–disciple) system, with the student learning from a teacher the many facets of their art including the memorization of countless *rubais*, the celebrated quatrains of beloved poets. The *ustad* guided her student, taking her along to performances. When the pupil was deemed ready, often after years of apprenticeship, there was a special ceremony to solemnize her new status. In this ritual, the teacher presented her student with a special belt.[50]

Strict observance of Islam in Bukhara could spell death for anyone stepping outside the bounds of proper behavior. Tajik dance scholar Nizam Nurdzhanov tells of a woman named Maidakhon who, together with her daughter, came to Bukhara around the beginning of the twentieth century to learn the art of the

---

[46]Annette Meakin, *In Russian Turkestan: A Garden of Asia and Its People*. London: G. Allen, 1903, p. 142.

[47]*Hadith* are traditions of sayings and actions attributed to the Prophet Muhammad, providing a guide for righteous behavior.

[48]William O. Beeman, "Music at The Margins: Performance and Ideology in the Persianate World," in *Music and Conflict*, edited by John Morgan O'Connell and Salwa El-Shawan Castelo-Branco, 2010, p. 144.

[49]Rakhimova, *Tuhfakhon, The Greatest Sozanda*.

[50]A. Djumaev, in his interview with Tuhfakhon discusses the ritual significance of the *kamarband* belt, "Musical Traditions and Ceremonies of Bukhara." Anthropology of the Middle East, 3, no.1 (2008): 52–66. doi:10.3167/ame.2008.030106.

sozanda. Known for her "delicate figure and elegance" she earned the nickname Maida, meaning "tiny," but her success seems to have provoked some jealousy when, through deception, "she was brought to a gathering of rich young men … "[51] To perform before men was strictly forbidden and Maidakhon was arrested and taken to jail before she could even enter the house. That same night she was executed by firing squad. They even killed her while she was wearing the chachvan (*Dazhe ubivali yeyo pod chachvanom*) At the moment of death, her face still could not be seen.[52]

While the sozanda entertained at women-only performances, they also appeared in the court of the Emir of Bukhara, performing for the women of his harem. Miniature paintings of the Bukharan school depict female dancers and musicians entertaining in courtly settings. One woman, Khalilirkhon—nicknamed Kirkigi—was "a famous singer and dancer in the court of the Emir of Bukhara himself."[53] Her costumes were distinguished by "luxury and beauty. In fact, dancers of the court wore as many as ten different outfits throughout their performances," changing their dress in consideration of "the character of their dance movements, for Bukharian dances are a constant flow of innovative movements."[54] These robes were made from "expensive fabrics, brocade, silk, and velvet, and were adorned with precious jewelry, gold necklaces, rings, earrings, and bracelets."[55] In the 1955 Soviet Uzbek film *The Collapse of the Bukharan Emirate*, a brief scene choreographed by People's Artist of Uzbekistan Isaqar Aqilov depicted these court dancers performing at the whim of the Emir, and dispersed by whip-wielding male attendants. While this last detail may have been artistic license, the profession of the *sozanda* required stamina because the artist "had to be ready to perform healthy and ill, and even pregnant, almost to the final day." The aforementioned *sozanda* Mikhali Karkigi, who was one of the teachers of Isaqar Aqilov, said that she gave birth to her oldest daughter only thirty minutes after performing at the Emir's palace for an event that lasted three days and nights. She resumed her performances after only about two weeks.[56]

The sheltered women of the royal harem experienced a shocking fate when Emir Said Mir Muhammad Olimxon fled from Bukhara on August 30, 1920, taking his group of dancing boys but leaving behind the women—perhaps a practical consideration, because arrangements for traveling with women would have complicated escape. The aftermath of the harem's abandonment was described

---

[51]This episode from Nizam Nurzhanov is cited by Gulmira Rakhimova, in *Tuhfakhon, the Greatest Sozanda*, p.207.

[52]Ibid., p. 207.

[53]Rakhimova, *Tuhfakhon, The Greatest Sozanda*, p. 43.

[54]Mariam Yakubova, "How I became an Actress," p. 13, cited by Gulmira Rakhimova in *Tuhfakhon, the Greatest Sozanda*, p. 44

[55]Rakhimova, *Tuhfakhon, The Greatest Sozanda*.

[56]Nurdzhanov story cited by Rakhimova, *Tuhfakhon, The Greatest Sozanda*, p. 207.

by Indian revolutionary M. N. Roy (1887–1954), who actively participated in the Communist movement in Russian Turkestan and later became a member of the presidium of the Comintern.[57] In his memoirs, Roy mentioned that when the ruler departed, the Emir's harem of about four hundred women "were orphaned" and "they had no other place to go. Nor were they very anxious to leave the comfortable asylum voluntarily."[58] The support of these women presented a financial dilemma for the new Revolutionary Government of Bukhara headed by Faizullah Khojaev (1896–1938). Roy, referring to the women as "parasites" accustomed to living "in a luxurious fashion,"[59] suggested that Faizullah issue a proclamation that "the Emir's harem was disbanded and its inmates set at liberty," with the women free to remarry should they so desire. An additional incentive "declared that any soldier who would take a former inmate of the Emir's harem for a wife and settle down in peaceful domestic life, would receive a grant of land and some cash to cultivate it."[60] However, "the deserted Begums would not leave their cells of comfort and luxury."[61] Roy then advised "a storming of the harem" in which "the soldiers who had responded to the proclamation were allowed to enter the harem and each choose his wife, provided that there would be no violence nor any rowdyism." In a prurient commentary, Roy noted that the women "behaved like scared rabbits,"

> but the sight of the husky young men scrambling for them must have made some impression on them. Able-bodied young men seeking their favour was a new experience to women whose erotic life naturally could not be satisfied by a senile old man. [Author's note: The emir was 40 years old at the time he left Bukhara and Roy himself was 33.] At the end, it was a pleasing sight—the secluded females happily allowing themselves to be carried away by proud men. Russian soldiers also took part in the scramble and carried the lion's share of the booty.[62]

Roy congratulated himself on his "solution" and accepted as a reward from Faizullah a robe of the Emir that had caught his eye.[63] There seems to have been no attempt to reunite the women with members of their original families, nor an understanding that for Muslim women, the Russian soldiers were foreign infidels.

Clues to the subsequent fate of these women and girls may exist in Bukharan archives, but at least one survivor, Zevar Razikova, ended up working at a "red

---

[57]"Comintern," i.e., the Communist International, founded in 1919.
[58]M. N. Roy, *Roy's Memoirs*. New York: Allied Publishers, 1964, p. 452.
[59]Ibid.
[60]Ibid.
[61]Ibid., p. 453.
[62]Ibid.
[63]Ibid.

chaikhona"[64] where she was visited by Langston Hughes during his travels in Central Asia. His article about their encounter appeared in a 1934 issue of *Woman's Home Companion* magazine,[65] illustrated with a stereotypical caravan drawing depicting the travelers attired in Arab, not Central Asian, clothing. The story begins with a titillating account of the Emir ordering his young harem inmates to disrobe and bathe in a pool for his entertainment. Shifting away from this Orientalist fantasy, Hughes introduces Comrade Razikova who, at age 12, had been forcibly removed from her parental home and brought into the Emir's harem. She was called to his chambers only once[66] and about five years later she had been given away to a 75-year-old man, one of the Emir's ministers. Zevar's conversation with Hughes took place about a dozen years after the fall of the Emir in 1920. At the time of their meeting, she was free, had learned to read and write at age 26, had married and divorced, and was living independently. She related that life in the harem had been tedious and far from luxurious, with the women frequently underfed.[67] (When Roy himself took a look at the inside of the Emir's palace, he found that the rooms "had only one entrance and no windows."[68]) Zevar made no mention of dance, but other accounts establish that it was one form of entertainment allowed to the inmates of the harem. While celebrating Zevar's new life and newfound freedom, Hughes does not consider that in traditional Central Asian society, with its communal family structure, a woman alone was both pitiable and vulnerable. The "liberation" of the Emir's harem proved one of the first Soviet attempts to emancipate women in Uzbekistan, but seemingly without any serious planning beyond handing them off to strange men, like the discarded robes of the Emir.

Beyond the gaze of male European eyes, the dance art of the *sozanda* has only recently received attention. One American dancer, Travis Fontaine Jarrell, traveled to Bukhara in 1992, working with the *sozanda* Oliyaxon Hasanova and her ensemble. Travis later studied with the celebrated Bukhara *sozanda* Tuhfakhon Pinkhasova after she emigrated to the United States. Jarrell felt that the antiquity of Tuhfakhon's "songs, poems, and simple dances were the sounds and colors of old cultures, weaving together families, generations, traditions, even different religions and secular life."[69] Jarrell realized that Tuhfakhon embodied an ancient women's tradition, describing "her vast repertoire of songs and *muhammas* (blessing poems), many ancient, and many composed herself" as a "treasure

---

[64]The "Red Chaikhona" was an early Soviet-era teahouse that disseminated propaganda about the new regime.

[65]Langston Hughes, "In an Emir's Harem." *Woman's Home Companion*, September 1934, p. 91.

[66]An alarming rumor told to foreign visitors to the palace was that the Emir believed that syphilis could be cured by sexual intercourse with a virgin. This could explain his continual search for new, young girls for his harem.

[67]Langston Hughes, "In an Emir's Harem," pp. 12, 91–92.

[68]Roy, *Roy's Memoirs*.

[69]Jarrell, quoted by Gulmira Rakhimova, in *Tuhfakhon, The Great Sozanda*, p. 167.

chest of blessing, encouragement, delight, gentle admonishment, flirtation, and cultural wisdom."[70] The opportunity of performing with Tuhfakhon on many occasions allowed Jarrell to understand the nuances of the tradition from an artist's perspective, noting that even though the order of the songs and dances was planned in advance, during the actual show "the unexpected was inevitable."[71] These improvisational roots, fundamental to Central Asian music and dance, were at the heart of performances because Tuhfakhon, as a "true *Sozanda*," was "reading the energy of the audience and creating the event in the present moment, to bring not just entertainment and culture, but blessing and true joy." Her many years of experience in directing her own group of *sozanda* "had given her a real freedom and creativity in a performance setting."[72]

> As an experienced *Sozanda* at wedding parties, she was quick to determine the ethnic heritage and emotional state of the individuals, and could bring forth for them the perfect poem, song, or saying to bless and delight them. Her work was to knot together the community through music and tradition, charging children and parents to be respectful and loving of each other, comforting and encouraging tired spirits, ennobling young romantic hearts.[73]

One essential role of the *sozanda* echoes not only shamanism with its role in healing, but also the ancient connection to the goddess of fertility, especially "the custom of the *sozanda* offering prayers and blessings on behalf of a woman desiring to have a baby. Tuhfakhon's many 'babies' were a source of matronly pride and pleasure for her, and the impromptu informal ceremonies of women gathered round her, hands gestured in prayer and touching the belt of her *kurta* or dress, after she danced, a testament to the special regard proffered a Sozanda of her stature."[74, 75]

Sozanda were honored when hosts showered them with beautiful gifts. Tuhfakhon recalled in childhood being taken to a performance by her aunt Miriam who was herself a *sozanda*. The guests were so entranced that they placed gold coins on the dancer's forehead after first moistening them. (This custom exists elsewhere in the East.) "With her high mastery, Miriam Khola would take everyone to another world into the ancient world of song and dance."[76]

Esteemed scholar of Uzbek dance Liubov Avdeeva acknowledged that "because of the *sozanda*, the dances, rhythmic melodies and dance compositions have

---

[70]Ibid.
[71]Ibid.
[72]Ibid., pp. 167–68.
[73]Ibid., p. 169.
[74]Ibid, p. 168.
[75]Ibid.
[76]Ibid., p. 51. Miriam Khola was also known as Miriam Karaeva.

been preserved, and because of the *sozanda*, the traditions, the foundations of traditional dance of the Bukharian school, famous in the East for over centuries, have also been preserved."[77]

The Aqilov Dynasty

The person primarily responsible for bringing this precious legacy of Bukharan dance to the concert stage was People's Artist of Uzbekistan Isaqar Aqilov. Born in Samarkand in 1914 to a family of Bukharan Jews, his mother was Davora-khanum, a dancer in the women's quarters of the court of the Emir of Bukhara, and his grandmother also performed at the court of the Emir.[78] As a boy, he joined the performance group, established in Samarkand in 1927, known as *Kuk Kuylak* ("Blue Blouse")[79] under the direction of choreographer Ali Ardobus. Part of a nation-wide phenomenon that existed from 1923 to 1928—and known in Russian as *Siniaya Bluza*—these groups numbered as many as five thousand and gave theatrical presentations with sociopolitical content that incorporated acting, music, acrobatics, and dance in their performances. Some were influenced by the biomechanics of Meyerhold[80] and performed to jazz music, creating skits imitating factory machinery. "Collective dance based on the movement of machines—for example, the movement of a pump or a turning wheel—was the 'dance of the machine.' Purely physical exercises and gymnastic numbers (individual or collective) were also presented."[81] American Louise Strong happened to attend one of these performances when she was in Samarkand, possibly viewing a concert that included the Isaqar.

The *Kuk Kuylak* gave young Isaqar public stage experience. With talent evident at an early age, Isaqar was already choreographing dances when only 15. Still a teenager, he participated in the 1930 All-Union Olympiada of Theater and Art in Moscow.[82] Aqilov is credited with mastering the knee spin known as *charkh do zona* after seeing it in 1932, when a female dancer from Bukhara[83] visited the home of one of his teachers, Isroil Tolmasov. At 16, he was invited to tour with Tamara

---

[77] Avdeeva, cited by Rakhimova in *Tuhfakhon*, p. 77.

[78] "K 100-letiyu vydayushchegosya khoreografa i tantsora Isakhara Akilova." *The Bukharian Times*, No. 649 (July 18–24, 2014), pp. 26–272, 2014.

[79] The "Blue Blouses" were theatrical groups founded throughout the young Soviet Union. Deák, František. "'Blue Blouse' (1923–1928)." *The Drama Review: TDR*. 17, no. 1 (1973): 35–46, p. 37. https://doi.org/10.2307/1144790. See also Robert F. Crane, "From Kamchatka to Georgia, The Blue Blouse Movement and Early Soviet Spatial Practice." PhD diss. University of Pittsburgh, 2013, p. 268.

[80] Ibid., p. 43.

[81] Ibid., p. 37.

[82] A. Rybnik, in introduction to R. Karimova, *Uzbekskie Tantsyi v Postanovke Isakhara Akilova*. Tashkent: Gafur Gulyam, 1977, p.8.

[83] According to Nurdzhanov, when Sozanda performed at formal receptions in the large "sozxona" at the palace of the Emir of Bukhara, they had enough space to perform to knee spins. p. 298. Nizam Nurdzhanov. *Traditsionnyi teatr tadzhikov. Vol 1.*, Published with the support of the Aga Khan Humanities Project in Dushanbe, Tajikistan, 2003.

Khanum and at 24, he was appointed the director of the Leninabad (Dushanbe) opera house. There Isaqar met, in 1935, and married a young dancer, Margarita, who self-identified as Persian, also tracing her lineage to a dancer at the court of the Emir of Bukhara. The couple became a vital and active team in the development of Uzbek dance and Margarita appeared in several dance dramas created by her husband. They raised a family of artists, including three dancers—Zulya, Viloyat, and Lola. Known affectionately as "Vika" (from her legal name Viktoria) Viloyat followed in her father's footsteps as a choreographer (Figure 4.2). She studied dance in Moscow, working with Igor Moiseyev and staging a choreography for his ensemble. In 1987–88, she was sent to Kabul, Afghanistan, founding two ensembles there, Nargis and Shukufa. Upon returning to Tashkent in 1989, she became the director of the Zarafshan Ensemble composed of both male and female dancers and specializing in Bukharan, Samarkand, and Tajik dance. And, in 1990, she came to the United States with the Uzbekistan Folklore Ensemble delegation for the Goodwill Games.

Isaqar Aqilov excelled at creating *massovyi* dances. Perhaps the best remembered is his Mavrigi choreography for the 1937 *Dekada* of Uzbek Art and Literature, featuring 90 performers in bright-colored Bukharan costumes all with gold embroidery.[84] Using original folklore rhythms and characteristic Bukharan

FIGURE 4.2 People's Artist of Uzbekistan Viloyat Aqilova (right), daughter of Isaqar Aqilov, passing on the hallmarks of "Aqilov style" to her *shagird*, Rushana Sultanova (left). Rushana was also awarded the status of People's Artist of Uzbekistan in 1998. Photo credit: Rustambek Sharipov.

[84]Avdeeva, *Tantseval'noe Iskusstvo Uzbekistana*, p. 124.

elements, Aqilov did "not create new movements" but instead designed staging patterns and original dance transitions using traditional folklore rhythms.[85] His dynamic, memorable choreographies, as well as those of his daughter Viloyat, continue to be performed by professional ensembles in Uzbekistan, as well as dance companies in the United States and Japan.

Costuming and Movement

The shape of traditional Bukharan women's dresses differ from those of other dance zones. "Bukharan women normally wore two or three dresses over each other" with "the top one being the most exquisite ... to give the impression of a sturdy build, which was a sign of prosperity and therefore the standard of beauty of the day."[86] Characterized as "bright, colorful and magnificent," traditional costumes "in general, were exclusively made from a red or purple velvet" embellished with gold-thread embroidery called *zardozi*. Under their voluminous dress, dancers wore brocade or velvet pants decorated around the hem with *zardozi*. Each woman had her own special jewelry but "in general, they would wear ruby beads on their neck or golden beads *kadmala*, on their chests a gold pendant, *tapish* with a red stone in the middle, with metal work and miniature pearls."[87] For one *sozanda*, Asiyakhon Ilyasova, a favorite jewelry piece was "a coral necklace with golden plated beads— *kadmala*."[88] "As one woman recalled the dances of our ancient Bukhara are full of sundrenched energy, saturated with an extraordinary radiant passion. As I remember today, during all the female celebrations, a theater-like performance took place, as each performer would exhibit her mastery in singing, dance or poetry."[89]

Both Bukhara and Samarkand shared a legacy of fabulous clothing. According to Ruy González de Clavijo, who in 1403–06, visited the court of Emir Timur (1336–1405) as an ambassador from Henry III of Castile, the ruler's favorite wife Saray Mulk Khanum wore a headdress so tall and elaborate that she needed to be accompanied by two handmaidens to steady it for her. Known to the West as Tamerlane, Emir Timur presented "robes of honor" as gifts to visiting dignitaries. Later accounts tell of other emirs who gave robes as rewards for vanquishing their enemies, the quality ascertained by the number of heads presented to the ruler. The more heads, the more splendid the robe, suggesting a morbid and literal meaning of the term "headcount."[90] Sumptuary laws enforced a social code that

---

[85]Ibid., p. 126.
[86]Tatjana Emelyanenko, "Central Asian Jewish Costume." In Hetty Berg, ed., *Facing West: Oriental Jews of Central Asia and the Caucasus*. Zwolle: Waanders Publishers, 2nd ed., 1999, p. 56.
[87]Rakhimova, *Tuhfakhon*, p. 40.
[88]Ibid., p. 49.
[89]Ibid., p. 39.
[90]Andy Hale and Kate Fitz Gibbon, Introduction. *Ikats, Woven Silks from Central Asia: The Rau Collection*. Oxford: Basil Blackwell, 1988, p. 10.

linked status with clothing.[91] In Bukhara, "every group had a costume established over the centuries. The cuts were more or less similar for all Bukharis, but the colors and materials strictly reflected a particular social estate."[92]

Known for their conspicuous display of wealth and power, the elite of Bukhara wore sumptuous clothing as strong visual markers of status. In his work, *Bukhara: Reminiscences*, the Tajik poet and writer Sadriddin Aini (1878–1954) evoked this sartorial splendor in a description of a crowd of important men—*bais* and Muslim clergy—walking through the streets of Bukhara after a celebratory banquet. He noted that "they wore outer robes of the finest silk with luxurious braid borders over inner robes of colorful satin. On their heads were turbans of the softest muslin topped by old-fashioned hats of gold-thread brocade. Their *ichigi* boots were covered by overshoes of new patent leather … " Walking "with the flaps of their robes tucked up … it was difficult to ignore the fact that even the linings of their robes were made of the finest silk."[93]

Bukhara was famed for the art of gold-thread embroidery[94] known as *zardozi*, which involves a technique known as "couching," where a cardboard design is placed on the "face" of the fabric to be embellished—usually velvet or brocade but, in earlier times, leather. The metallic thread is repeatedly drawn across the surface of the design, but with each "pass," the metallic thread is securely anchored in place by cotton threads. This keeps the valuable golden thread on top of the fabric so it is not wasted on the underside where it would not show and where the metallic thread could gradually cut through the fibers of the garment's fabric. Traditional dresses ornamented with *zardozi* embroidery become heavy, which impacts the dance style. Significantly, the terms for *zardozi* designs and techniques are often Persian words.

Dance Characteristics

Bukharan women's dance reveals the region's unique cultural and historical legacy. The posture is lifted and confident as if the sun is touching the solar plexus.[95] Many of the movements of the head and shoulders require isolation, during which one portion of the body is moved while the rest remains still. Shoulder movements are sharp, making them discernible even when the dancer is attired in heavy velvet and brocade robes. The wide sleeves sometimes become part of the dance, grasped at the bottom of the sleeve opening in a manner to hide the face or held in place

---

[91]Ibid.

[92]*Bukhara, Caught in Time: Great Photographic Archives*, edited by Vitaly Naumkin. Garnet, 1993, p. 15.

[93]Sadriddin Aini, *Bukhara: Reminiscences*. Moscow: Raduga Publishers, 1986, pp. 351–52.

[94]The threads are not pure gold but blended with another fiber.

[95]Avdeeva, Introduction to Karimova. *Bukharskii Tanets*, p. 7.

while the arms are pulled out to the sides to reveal the full dimensions of the dress, showing the richness of the costume. At other moments, the side of the dress is held in one hand to bring attention to it, a reminder of the great emphasis placed on clothing and status.

The most typical dance rhythm is a moderate 6/8, becoming faster as the dance progresses and builds toward a finale. The movements alternate between quick, sharp gestures of the hands and shoulders and soft, lyrical rocking of the torso, head, and arms.

Movements include head slides, with the head sliding horizontally above the shoulders, which remain stationary. The chin can also trace a crescent shape. Another movement is a small, quick chin lift. These are done as an ornament at the end of a phrase or during a pose, when the rest of the body is still. In keeping with the proud carriage, the style includes "slightly thrown back head"[96] and "small tremors of the upper part of the body." The unique dance turns, harkening back to the Sogdian Whirl, involve a series of complex rotations in a circle performed with simultaneous rotation of the body on a sagittal plane. Avdeeva characterizes the style as "stately" and saturated with a "deep restrained passion."[97]

The head is lifted, tilted majestically back[98] creating a proud and regal impression, amplified by the Bukharan tall, cylindrical headdress known as the peshanaband, about twelve centimeters in width,[99] although this can vary. All the characteristic head movements—head slides, tilts, chin lifts—are amplified by the peshanaband. A fringed shawl or a veil—sometimes more than one veil—is attached to the back of the headdress, also necessitating the need to keep the head up, because the veil falls forward when the head is tipped down. A light-weight veil of about two meters in length is attached to the back of the headdress, but folded in half to create an upper portion that is somewhat shorter than the back. At the top of the fold, the veil is gathered and made into a fan shape of about twelve centimeters in height, then the entire scarf is attached to the back of the peshanaband. The upper layer of the veil is often initially pulled over the top of the head and down in front to hide the dancer's face, in the manner of a Western bridal veil. This piece is long enough to cover the upper portion of the dancer's torso and wide enough to be delicately held out in front at shoulder level width. At times the dancer can play with the veil, teasingly revealing, then concealing, her face momentarily before finally tossing the veil up and back where it falls into place over the longer portion hanging down the back. At times during the dance, the veil or shawl can also be grasped with one hand and "shaken." This motion is

---

[96]Ibid., p.20.

[97]Ibid.

[98]Karimova, *Uzbekskie Tantsyi v Postanovke Isakhara Akilova*, 1987, p. 11.

[99]Costume note in Roziakhanum Karimova, *Tantsy Ansambl'a Bakhor v Postanovke Mukarram Turgunbaevoi*. Tashkent: Literatura i Iskustvo, 1979, p. 245.

so characteristic that Bukharans, when asking if someone is going to dance, they will pantomime the gesture of holding and shaking a veil held with one hand.[100] During sagittal spins, the veil can be held to create a dramatic delayed line.

Shoulder movements known as *yolka kokish* emphasize strong, precise rhythmic accents. Because Bukharan dance costumes are typically sewn from velvet and brocade, and often ornamented with golden embroidery, the movements are strong enough to be evident beneath heavy fabric. Shoulders alternate between pushing one shoulder forward while the other shoulder pushes to the back. At times, the ribcage is lifted and quickly "dropped" as a sharp accent. The upper torso can sway gently from side to side during the dance, and the hands often move in a horizontal figure-of-eight path in front of the upper body.

Indian and Sogdian Connections?

The closest living relative of Bukharan dance is the classical Indian style known as *Kathak*. The genres share many similarities in the characteristic poses with only a slight variation of the level of an extended arm to mark the difference. In both dance forms these poses often mark the climatic end of a dramatic movement phrase and are held for several moments before the dance continues. In both *Kathak* and traditional Bukharan dance, sections of the dance are performed seated on the floor, embellished with pantomimic elements and facial expressions that are known in Kathak as *Angika-abhinaya*, the gestural section of dance that conveys emotional, story-telling content. Both genres share a historical connection through the Mughals, a dynasty founded by the Central Asian Timurid prince Zahir ud-Dīn Muhammad (1483–1530). Another relationship may be found in the dance of the *Luli*, whose performance was mentioned by Babur and who are found today in Bukhara.[101]

Bukharan dance uses several specific hand gestures and movements; several are identical to *mudras* used in classical Indian dance. These are integral parts of the dance. Most characteristic is the flattened palm stretched energetically with fingers and thumb all held tightly together. The hands in this position can frame the sides of the head next to the *peshanaband*. At times, one flattened palm may be brought to rest upon another, but with fingers in opposite directions. The hands when held in the flat palm position can make a cutting movement, briskly "slicing" diagonally across the upper torso, starting at the upper left shoulder, as

---

[100]As noticed by Travis Fontaine Jarrell, who studied with the *sozanda* in Bukhara in 1992.

[101]"The very first scholar of Central Asian Gypsies, Alexander Vilkins, had expressed doubts about the reasonability of linking Luli with Gypsies and preferred to designated them as Борема (in analogy with Bohémiens, which is what the Gypsies were called in medieval France), or Gypsy-like (Вилькинс 1882)." Cited in Elena Marushiakova and Vesselin Popov, Gypsies of Central Asia and the Caucasus, London: Palgrave Macmillan, 2016, p. 20. doi:10.1007/978-3-319-41057-9.

if opening the chest above the heart. The same flattened palm can "cut" across the lower and upper arm with quick, sharp movements. A similar movement can be seen in Rajasthani Roma folk dances, perhaps reflecting a legacy of historical contact with Moghul court dancers during the dynasty established by Uzbek conqueror Babur.

Another fascinating connection with both Rajasthani dance and historical performances surfaces in costuming depicted in paintings of Mughal court dancers. As noted by Avdeeva, the dresses show long-sleeved garments tightly fitted through the waist, with skirts sewn from as many as twelve, twenty-four, and even thirty-six wedges or "gores." These flared skirts resemble historic costumes of Kathak dancers. Avdeeva noted that dancers historically performed bare-footed, with henna-stained feet, and wore bells on their wrists and ankles.[102] Two photographs of the *sozanda* Tuhfakhon Pinkhasova, one dating from 1958, show her wearing costumes cut in this style.

Another characteristic hand position is when the two pinkie fingers interlock, with the right hand held higher and the left hand hanging below. This is the same as the *keelaka mudra* in Kathak dance. In another characteristic position, the forearms are lifted to bring elbows to shoulder level, the hands hang above each respective shoulder, fingers pointing downward, but not actually touching the shoulder. This is similar to the *utsanga* mudra in Kathak dance.

The flattened palm position can also be used to imitate a mirror, with one hand held up at head level with the palm turned to face the dancer, as if holding a mirror. This can be done with either the right or the left hand. The gesture brings to mind the association of the mirror with the Zoroastrian goddess Anahita. Pamiri Tajik dance also shares this pantomime element.

Small bells, called *zang*, traditionally worn on the wrists and the ankles, are mentioned in numerous dance accounts and more recently documented in photographs. There is a mention from the 1940s of Iranian girls wearing ankle bells in dance,[103] a reminder of the Sasanian depictions of Anahita. Since the 1990s, Uzbek Bukharan dancers have stopped wearing ankle bells[104] but continue to wear wrist bells. Many Bukharan gestures and hand movements involve hitting the wrists together, strictly matching the dance rhythm. Hands can also quickly flutter or vibrate to create a tremulous sound with the bells. This can be done as the hands travel in various paths in front of the body with the hands in the characteristic "Aqilov" position[105] in which the thumb and index finger curve toward each other to create a circle. When the quivering movement occurs while

---

[102] Avdeeva, Introduction to Karimova, *Bukharskii Tanets*, p. 8. This is also confirmed by Nizam Nurdzhanov, Traditsionnyi Teatr Tadzhikov, Dushanbe, Aga Khan Humanities Project, 2002, volume I, p. 286.

[103] Ramazani, *The Rose and the Nightingale*, p. XIV.

[104] At one point, while studying dance in Uzbekistan, I was told that ankle bells were only worn by slaves.

[105] This hand position was described to me as "Aqilov style" by People's Artist of Uzbekistan, Viloyat Aqilova.

the arms are extended outward at the sides, fingers are tightly held together in the flattened position. While "running" on the knees on the floor, hands vibrate in this same flattened palm position with arms extended forward from the shoulders.

The hands can also travel rapidly in looping pathways with wrist circles. Wrist circles tend to rotate away from the body column in Bukharan dance.

A movement in imitation of brushing the hair can be performed by allowing one hand, palm down, to move above the head, as if stroking the hair, and continuing on a path down the back of the skull, then turning palm up, stroking under the chin. Both hands simultaneously perform this movement but beginning at different points to create this horizontal encircling motion, with hands traveling in opposite directions.

One hand can also gracefully rest above the forehead, palm facing outward, as if in imitation of a plume or aigrette on a hat or crown. Alternatively, the palm can turn inward for a gesture indicative of thought. These poses also occur in Kathak dance.

Both hands can be held under the chin, palms down, with some space between the fingertips of each hand, and wrists arched higher than fingertips, while the upper arms are held at the same level as shoulders. This movement is known as *lola* or "tulip," suggesting that the face of the dancer herself is the flower and her hands, the leaves.

A snake-like arm movement called *elon* (snake) brings all the fingers of each hand together to touch the thumb, creating a triangular shape similar to the head of a snake. This movement is performed with both hands leading the movement as the arms coil in toward the body, then move outwards away from the body. The arms can perform these motions synchronously or alternately.

While the head, arms, hands, and upper torso movements can be intricate and expressive, the traveling steps are limited. The most characteristic is a repetitive "flat-ball" step that does not alternate but is done with the same foot providing the "flat" accent. Both knees are slightly bent throughout this step, but the spine remains straight, and the head remains level, creating a smooth traveling step, without an up-and-down motion.

During a dramatic moment, the dancer may come up on the balls of her feet, lifting both heels off the floor. This can be done to accent a level change with the upper torso lifted and also with one or both arms lifted upward.

A step common to all Uzbek dance zones, *kaichi*—meaning "scissors"—can be done in place or as a traveling step. Both feet simultaneously and repeatedly alternate between touching the toes and both heels as a means of locomotion, smoothly traveling laterally. *Kaichi* can also be used to rotate in place with weight on one foot while the toe of the non-weighted foot alternately pushes toward the toe, then returning the heel to touch the instep of the anchored foot.

Movements on the Floor

The legacy of a dance form developed in the *ichkari*, with viewers on the floor, some elements of the dance were performed almost entirely while seated or kneeling on the floor in the center of the room or in a courtyard on carpets. In traditional performances of the *sozanda*, significant sections of a performance could be performed in a kneeling position, with delicate gestures moving in the front and upper part of the body's kinesphere. Here, minute movements of facial muscles could come into play, with directional glances of the eyes and isolations of the eyebrows framed by the hands. When kneeling, the dancer placed herself at the same level as her viewers who were seated on cushions on the floor, making her smallest movement easily seen. But these intimate dance moments were lost when women left the *ichkari* to appear on the proscenium stage. The advent of televised performance brought back some of these elements with close-ups, but for stage dance in large concert halls, they were less discernible.

The ascent to the floor can be done slowly and gracefully or more dramatically, with a "drop" following a quick spin, and even a small jump in place, landing with the dancer on her back and both knees tucked under her. From this position, the dancer can perform a "layback" by sweeping her arms outward, parallel to the floor, creating a circular path with her torso. She may also remain in the position with her shoulders and upper torso touching the floor, using her hands to create patterns in the space above her. (This position also occurs in the Azerbaijan *nalbeki* dance.)

As a teenager, Isaqar Aqilov became the first male to perform the sensational knee spins known as *charq do zoni*. Aqilov taught this technique to his eldest daughter and it became part of the more pyrotechnic versions of Bukharan stage dance for both male and female dancers.

Salomlar

Each dance zone has its own characteristic set of *salomlar* or bows. For Bukharan dance, there are several options. Both hands may simply cross over the chest as the dancer slowly bows from the waist. Or the dancer may extend the left arm out to the side while the right hand gestures over the end of the sleeve, as if to bring attention to its width and richness, while the right foot crosses behind with a slight bend of the knees; the same motion is repeated to show the right sleeve, as the left foot crosses behind.

5 KHOREZM DANCE

In Khorezm, everyone dances.

—LOCAL FOLK-SAYING

The land, the climate, the flora and fauna of a place, all shape human development. With both gifts and challenges, Nature dictates the means of survival and these necessities for survival all leave an imprint on dance. The Khorezm region, known historically as Chorasmia, extended along the Amu Darya River, the western part of present-day Uzbekistan, and to the area closest to the Persian Empire. Populations settled around the verdant oasis that is "surrounded by a girdle of terrifying deserts ... "[1] The steppes and desert were home to nomadic tribes. These different populations interacted in commerce as well as in conflict. Turkmen raiders preyed upon caravans coming from Persia, selling their captives in Khiva, one of Central Asia's slave-trading centers. One of the genres of *Lazgi* has been traced to Iranian hunters who trespassed in Khorezm.[2]

The Amu Darya River and network of tributaries provided a source of fresh water, a food source, and a means of transportation.[3] Not surprisingly, "the tradition of considering water as a source of life and a symbol of purity has survived

---

[1]Konstantin Konstanovich Pahlen, N. J. Couriss, and Richard A. Pierce. *Mission to Turkestan, Being the Memoirs of Count K.K. Pahlen, 1908–1909.* London: Oxford University Press, 1964, p. 163.

[2]This comes from a story that the Khorezm shah encountered skillful horsemen and archers while hunting. Upon his second encounter, he invited them to resettle on his territory. See Khorezm Lazgi Dance in Nine variations (2019) Khorazm Lazgi Raksining 9 Turing Tarikhi va Izhro Uslublari Yuenesko Yezilgan Varinti, www.facebook.com/100013572485293/videos/1305349800036302?idorv anity=562680813809835.

[3]Rahele, Koulabadi, Seyyed Mehdi Mousavi Kouhpar, Javad Neyestani, and Seyyed Rasool MousaviHaji. "An Overview of Goddess Anahita and Her Iconography in Ancient Iran." *Central Asiatic Journal*, 62, no. 2 (2019): 203–26. Accessed August 27, 2021. doi:10.13173/centasiaj.62.2.0203.

in Central Asia until the present day."[4] Reflecting this heritage, the Khorezm Zone includes the dances of settled populations as well as rituals of Turkmen peoples along with the more recently created Karakalpak dance, which was developed during Soviet times. And it is the Khorezm zone which gave birth to a unique dance known as *Lazgi*, claimed to have a 3,000-year-old lineage.

In the opinion of many scholars, Khorezm was the birthplace of Zoroastrianism, which emerged around 600–650 BCE and for more than a millennium served as the state religion in a number of cultural and historical regions of Central Asia. The three basic principles of Zoroastrianism—*Humara, Hukhta, Huvarshta* (Good Thoughts, Good Words, Good Deeds)—provided the ethical foundation for humanity which was part of a cosmic struggle between the forces of Light, led by Ahura Mazda, and those of Darkness, headed by Ahriman. This battle required active involvement from humans to overcome Evil and side with the forces of Good. A reminder of the Zoroastrian legacy can be seen in the stylized symbol of the winged deity Ahura Mazda,[5] evident today in unique turquoise-colored tiles embedded into the brick fortress walls that surround the ancient inner city of Khiva, the ancient capital.

In antiquity, the population of the region had links with ritual dances, sun worship, and goddess worship. Anahita, a goddess in the Zoroastrian pantheon, was the deity associated with water, fertility, and prosperity, with very specific abilities as one "who makes the seed of all males pure, who makes the womb of all females pure for bringing forth, who makes all females bring forth in safety, who puts milk into the breasts of all females in the right measure and the right quality."[6] She appears "as a maid, fair of body, most strong, tall-formed, high-girded, pure, nobly born of a glorious race … "[7] Her impressive adornments included, "square golden earrings" on pierced ears, and around her "beautiful neck" a "golden necklace." She bound upon her head a "golden crown, with a hundred stars, with eight rays … fillets streaming down." Completing this ensemble of sartorial splendor, Anahita wore "a mantle fully embroidered with gold."[8]

Ahura Mazda acclaimed her as one "who is worthy of sacrifice in the material world, worthy of prayer in the material world," as one "who hates the Daevas[9] and obeys the laws of Ahura."[10] Her qualities were manifold; she was "the life-increasing and holy, the herd-increasing and holy, the fold-increasing and holy,

---

[4]Adhamjon Ashirov, "Thoughts Related to the Cult of Water in Zoroastrianism." *International Journal of Multidisciplinary Research*, 6, no. 5 (May 2020): 492. DOI:10.36713/epra2013.
[5]The design in these tiles has been flipped from the horizontal depiction of Ahura Mazda to the vertical plane.
[6]Avesta, Chapter II, verse 2. http://www.avesta.org/ka/yt5sbe.htm.
[7]Avesta, Chapter XXX, verse 126.
[8]Avesta, Chapter XXX, verses 128 and 129.
[9]In the Avesta, the Daevas are demons causing chaos and disorder, maleficent beings.
[10]Avesta, Chapter II, verse 10.

the wealth-increasing and holy, the country-increasing and holy."[11] In return for her gifts of bounty, Anahita requested sacrifice from her supplicants:

> Who will praise me? Who will offer me a sacrifice, with libations cleanly prepared and well-strained, together with the Haoma and meat? To whom shall I cleave, who cleaves unto me, and thinks with me, and bestows gifts upon me, and is of good will unto me?[12]

In return for these offerings, Anahita could exercise control of the waters for both productive and destructive purposes. To help one warrior defeat an enemy, "a part of the waters she made stand still, a part of the waters she made flow forward, and she left him a dry passage to pass over the good Vitanghuha."[13]

An early account by the Greek historian Herodotus, written circa 425 BCE, describes the Massagetae people who lived on the present territory of Khorezm near the lower reaches of the Amu Darya, known by the Greeks as the Oxus. He wrote that the Massagetae would gather together and build a fire, then throw fruit from a special tree into the fire. The smell of the burning fruit (or perhaps it was the smoke) made "them as drunk with it as the Greeks are with wine, and more and more drunk as more fruit is thrown on the fire, till at last they rise up to dance and even sing."[14] Identification of this plant varies among scholars, but some, like Falk, recalling Aurel Stein, suggested that it was possibly *Ephedra sinica*, a plant found in ancient tombs.[15] Known among the Uzbeks as *isryk*, the plant is still used today in homes for ritual purification. Medically, it can help with bronchial infections. But perhaps the intoxication observed by Herodotus may not have come from the plant at all but from the act of singing and dancing. "Dance rhythms are contagious … They can seduce, magnetize and mesmerize the unsuspecting."[16]

Herodotus also mentions the deification of the Sun by inhabitants in his account of the battle between the Persian forces of King Cyrus the Great and the Massagetae tribe led by Queen Tomyris (570–520 BCE). At first, Cyrus tries to woo the widow, proposing marriage, but she understands his true motive is to add her lands to Persian territory. She rejects him and advises him to return home to his side of the river but, by trickery, he captures or kills part of the Massagetae army

---

[11] Avesta, Chapter I, verse 1.

[12] Avesta, Chapter I, verse 8, *Haoma* refers to the intoxicant used by populations such as the Massagata.

[13] Avesta, Chapter XIX, verse 78.

[14] Herodotus, *History Book One* 202 H & W. The plant may be *Ephedra sinica*, which is still used as a "smudge" in Uzbekistan to purify and drive away evil. It also has medicinal qualities.

[15] As Falk, recalling Aurel Stein's discovery of *Ephedra* plants interred at first-century CE Tarim Basin burial sites, notes: "an imperishable plant, representing or symbolizing the continuity of life, is most appropriate to burial rites". Harry Falk, "Soma I and II." *Bulletin of the School of Oriental and African Studies*, 52, no. 1 (1989): 77–90. doi:10.1017/S0041977X00023077. JSTOR 617914. S2CID 146512196.

[16] Steven Lonsdale, *Animals and the Origins of Dance*. New York: Thames and Hudson, 1982, p. 26.

and takes her son captive. Upon hearing this news, Queen Tomyris swears an oath of vengeance by the Sun god:

> Restore my son to me and get you from the land unharmed, triumphant over a third part of the host of the Massagetai. Refuse, and *I swear by the sun, the sovereign lord of the Massagetai*, bloodthirsty as you are, I will give you your fill of blood.[17] [Italics added]

Refusing to yield, the Queen defended her territory and fulfilled her oath with a grisly response, placing the severed head of Cyrus in a skin filled with blood. A powerful symbol for the Uzbek people, and still remembered today for her heroism, Tomyrys became the subject of the eponymous two-act ballet, with music by Uzbek composer Ulugbeg Musaev and choreography by People's Artist of Uzbekistan Ibragim Yusupov. Based on Yavdat Ilyasov's story *Spotted Death*, the work premiered in Tashkent in 1984 at the State Academic Bolshoi Theatre of Opera and Ballet named for Alisher Navoi.[18]

In addition to written accounts about trance dancing around fires and honoring the Sun as a deity, archeological discoveries offer clues about the early spiritual beliefs and dance traditions in Khorezm. The arid climate supplied readily available building material—sun-dried mud bricks—that could be used to construct the impressive fortresses known as *qala*, scattered throughout the region. These *qala* served as citadels—military and residential—but the site known as Topraq Qala reveals an ancient connection between dance and spiritual practices. In 1938, when the Soviet archeologist Sergei Tolstov, head of the Chorasmian Archeological–Ethnological Expedition, came across the ruins of Topraq Qala, the locals told him there was nothing of interest to be found there. However, within its crumbling walls, Tolstov and his excavation team found evidence of a sophisticated civilization, the site of a past capital which included a palace–temple complex and citadel, protected by an inner fortification wall. Inhabited from about the first century BCE until the site was abandoned around the third century CE, the palace complex contained several intricately decorated rooms. One of them became known as the "Hall of the Dancing Masks." Along the walls covered with polychrome paintings were molded reliefs of sixteen masked, life-sized couples, male and female, dancing together. The archeologist Yuri Rapoport speculated that the room of dancing masks found in the ruins of Topraq Qala

---

[17]Herodotus, I: 212: Herodotus, *The History*, George Rawlinson, trans. New York: Dutton & Co., 1862.
[18]A classical ballet in two acts, this production premiered on February 24, 2016, at the Alisher Navoi State Academic Bolshoi Theatre, Uzbekistan. Libretto by P. Uzakova based on Yavdat Ilyasov's story "Spotted Death" with choreography of People's Artist of Uzbekistan Ibrahim Yusupov.

could be the temple of Anahita.[19] These images of males and females dancing in pairs reflect a time before the advent of Islam that followed the Arab invasion of the seventh and eighth centuries, and the gender separation that followed.

In the center of the room, a raised platform with four columns, one at each corner, held up the roof. This has been identified as possibly an altar, but the central location as a raised platform also suggests a stage, or perhaps it served as both altar and stage if dance were part of sacred ritual.[20] The investment of effort, artistry, and resources involved in creating these dancing images indicate that dance played a central role in this culture. Significantly, this hall has been interpreted as a sanctuary for the Goddess Anahita, symbol of the matriarchate past of Khorezm who, with her power over life-giving waters, was the central key to human survival. The inhabitants of Chorasmia had long constructed canals to irrigate lands for agriculture, but, at times, these canals and dams were used as weapons against local populations, either by cutting off water supplies, or opening dams to release destructive floods.

The archetype of Anahita as a powerful goddess, covered in golden jewelry, surfaces in the women's dances of Khorezm. Archeological discoveries at Topraq Qala included pendants and amulets in the form of a bronze mirror.[21] "In Central Asia, the mirror was considered an attribute of the female deity of the earth and fertility (Anahita) and was associated with the cult of the sun, *kul'tom solntsa*."[22] This connection appears in a pantomime sequence in which the dancer pretends to hold and gaze into a mirror while applying makeup, darkening her eyebrows. (This also occurs in Bukharan, Persian, and Tajik dances, regions historically connected with the Sogdians and Zoroastrianism.) There were discoveries of other jewelry items associated with the cult of fertility, such as a large heart-shaped pendant.[23] The chest ornaments (*nagrudnovo ykrasheny*) known as *nosi-gardon* are still found today in Uzbek jewelry. And the intricate *takya-duzi* headdress,[24] covered with chains from which dangle beads connected to small leaves or pods, makes a delicate sound with every movement of the dancer's head. The special Khoream *zebigardon* worn today by female dancers features hundreds of tiny pendants that shiver with the vibrations of shoulders and upper torso, the quivering *titramish* movement characteristic of Khorezm dance, sounding like the tinkling of rivulet or a stream, reminiscent of Anahita's power over water.

---

[19]Yuri Rapoport, "Some results of the study of the palace on the ancient settlement," 1972, pp. 233–34, cited by Khulkar Khamroeva, *Gavkhar Matyokubova Izhod va Ilm Integratsiyasi*. Tashkent: Monografiya, 2022.

[20]Bukhara, with ancient Sogdian connections, once held summertime dance performances in courtyards on wide raised platforms made of burnt brick.Nazim Nurdzhanov, *Traditsionnyi teatr tadzhikov. Vols. I and II.* Published with the support of the Aga Khan Humanities Project in Dushanbe, Tajikistan, 2003. Nurdzhanov, vol. 1, p. 281.

[21]Delyara A. Fakhretdinnova, *Yuvelirnoye Iskusstvo Uzbekistana*. Tashkent: Gafur Gulyam, 1988, p. 30.

[22]Ibid.

[23]Ibid.

[24]Nafisa Sadikova and Yulduz Gaibullaeva. *Uzbek millii kiiimlari XIX–XX asrlar*. Tashkent; Sharq, 2014, p. 157.

The unique and sophisticated civilization that created Topraq Qala and revered the goddess Anahita has disappeared. Originally, it was considered that the area became depopulated for environmental reasons, when the Amu Darya River changed course, leaving irrigation canals without water.[25] Others surmise that Topraq Qala was abandoned only for political reasons, perhaps destruction by aggressive neighboring cultures. But these two theories of cultural demise— environmental change and foreign destruction—may not be mutually exclusive. Climate change, the alteration in the natural environment, may have weakened the infrastructure of Topraq Qala, making it less able to defend itself against enemies.[26]

Another insight into the region's past connections with fertility and the Divine Feminine comes from the twelfth-century epic poem, *Haft Paykar*, by Nizami Ganjavi (1140–1202). In this tale of King Bahram Gur and his marriage to seven princesses from the "seven climes,"[27] the poet identifies each princess with a specific geographical region, color, planet, day of the week, and moral virtue. Nizami selected Khorezm to represent the clime of Transoxiana, embodied by "the king of Khvarazm's[28] daughter Naz-Fari, graceful as a mountain-partridge in her gait." Her day of the week was Monday and her planet was the moon, which, in Nizami's time, was considered a planet. She was linked to the color green: "He judged her to the heavenly ones akin, so dressed her like the houris all in green."[29]

Better than yellow robes are green;
green well befits the cypress' form.
Green is the field of healthy corn;
in green the angels are adorned.
Green, above all, is the soul's choice;
green verdue makes the eyes rejoice.
The growing plants are green of hue;
green is the color of all that grows.[30]

---

[25]Heidi Oberhänsli, Nikolaus Boroffka, Philippe Sorrel, and Sergey Krivonogov. "Climate Variability During the Past 2,000 Years and Past Economic and Irrigation Activities in the Aral Sea Basin." *Irrigation and Drainage Systems*, 21, nos. 3–4 (Dec. 2007): 177–83.

[26]A present-day example exists in the recent warning that the President of the United States received from the Central Intelligence Agency that climate change posed the greatest national security threat to America "due to its effects on population movements, increased scarcity of land capable of growing food, and possible fighting over land." (And, I might add, water resources.) Could this also have been the case with Topraq Qala? Losey, Steve, Top General Pressed on Biden Remark About Climate Change's Threat toUS." https://www.military.com/daily-news/2021/06/10/top-general-pressed-biden-remark-about-climate-changes-threat-us.html.

[27]In medieval times, one of the seven climes was Khorezm, i.e., Khvarazm.

[28]That is, Khorezm.

[29]Nizami Ganjavi, trans. C.E. Wilson, *The Haft Piakar: Containing the Life and Adventures of King Bahrâm Gûr, and the Seven Stories Told Him by his Seven Queens*. London: Probsthain & Co., 1924, p. 171.

[30]Nizami Ganjavi, trans. Julie Scott Meisami, *The Haft Paykar, A Medieval Persian Romance*. Oxford: Oxford University Press, 1995, pp. 157–58.

This description contains echoes of the Zoroastrian goddess Anahita, the same deity connected with Topraq Qala, and like that goddess, the Princess of the Green Dome shares links with the moon, fertility, fecundity, and most importantly, with Khorezm. Because this princess represented the moral virtue of faith, green as the sacred color of Islam could resonate with Nizami's contemporaries. The poem also associates green with the verdant colors of nature and abundant growth, all attributes of the pre-Islamic goddess Anahita.

Only two decades after Nizami wrote his verses in praise of verdant Khorezm, another wave of invaders swept over the area. The Mongol conquest of Gurganc, then the capital of Khorezm, proved to be one of the most anthropogenic catastrophes in history. In 1220, the Mongols began their campaign by destroying a dam on the Amu Darya that controlled irrigation, flooding the area and turning it into a marsh. After Gurganc was conquered, young women, girls, and boys were given as slaves to the victorious troops. The remaining population was executed by command, with every one of the fifty thousand Mongol warriors ordered to each behead twenty-four persons. In addition to the devastating impact on the human population, the region's cultural legacy was also destroyed, with buildings and archives burned.

But dance is an embodied heritage and the resilient survivors preserved connections to the ancient sun cult in their dance movements. People's Artist of Uzbekistan Gavkhar Matyokubova, after spending many years of research to reconstruct Khorezm dance traditions, identified twenty-eight specific movements in the celebrated *Lazgi* dance that are associated with the sun.[31] The circling aspects of group dances still exist in other Turkic populations, like the Azeri *Yally* dance, the Uyghur *Sama* dance, and the Turkmen *Kushtdepa* ritual, all suggesting an ancient Turkic commonality. These rotational dances reflect a connection with natural phenomenon, imitating the movements of the solar system, in which "the nine planets perform a dance around the sun—a circle dance, the oldest known configuration."[32]

Through the efforts of Professor Gavkhar Matyokubova, *Lazgi* earned recognition in 2019 from UNESCO as an Intangible Cultural Heritage.[33] She recounted that her great-grandmother was a *khalfa*, called Ruzika Khalfa, who conducted ceremonies. In the center of the circle was a "fortune teller" who "stepped out of it" chanting "*ovaa, ovaa*" and "havo, havo."[34] This description

---

[31]Matyokubova, cited in Khulkar Khamroev, *Gavkhar Matyokubova Izhod va Ilm Integratsiyasi.* Tashkent: Monografiya, 2022, p. 21.

[32]Lonsdale, *Animals and the Origin of Dance*, p. 24.

[33]https://ich.unesco.org/en/RL/khorazm-dance-lazgi-01364.

[34]Gavkhar Matyokubova, Shukhrat Tokhtasimov, and Hulkar Khamroeva. *Khorazm "Lazgi"*. Raqsi: Tarikhi va Tavsifi. Tashkent: Zamon Poligraf, 2022, p. 29.

of circle dance combined with chanting bears resemblance to the Turkmen ritual *Kushtdepta* in which the entire community participates, male and female, and all ages.[35]

Professor Matyokubova emphasized the deep connections between movements and their meaning, from depicting heart beats to bringing down the life-giving energy of the sun to nourish the earth. Even minute facial expressions, from eyebrows to eyelashes, play a role in the dance. She herself began her dance journey as a child, first taking lessons at the *Dom Pionerov*.[36] As an adult, she began to investigate the roots of the dance, realizing the unusual nature of Khorezm dance with its unique rhythms, rhythms that even alone are sufficient for dance. For example, the dance *Narim Narim* has its own stately rhythm.

Linguistic Origins of "*Lazgi*"

Khorezm dances contain deep connections to the natural world, acknowledging the life-giving power of the sun. The very name of the famous Khorezm dance, *Lazgi*, emphasizes its unique trembling, quivering, and shivering aspects with the Indo-European roots "lezg," which means "to tremble." One proposal is that *Lazgi* is perhaps "definitely a corruption of the Persian ларзагӣ لرزگی *larz[a]gī* 'shaking; trembling.'"[37] It seems connected to *lekiz*, which in Kurdish means to play and dance. The Kurdish dance *Larzon* also contains active trembling shoulder movements.[38] While there may be linguistic connections in the Kavkaz dances *lezginka* or *lezgi*, they are two very different genres with different movement vocabulary and technique.[39] *Lazgi* dancers often mimic local animals, from the flight of birds and bird-like head movements to the postures and gestures of desert mammals. The attraction of imitating these creatures can be found throughout the dances of indigenous cultures.

> There is something uncanny about the compulsive regularity of animal movement that impresses man. The same fascination with sure, precise, athletic and rhythmic motion that impels the visual artist to capture the animal in action through works of art carries over into dance in choreographic imitations.

---

[35]"Kushtdepdi Rite of Singing and Dancing." *Unesco Intangible Cultural Heritage*. 2017. https://Ich.Unesco.Org/En/RL/Kushtdepdi-Rite-Of-Singing-And-Dancing-01259

[36]"House of Young Pioneers," government-supported cultural centers that offered free classes to children.

[37]Afsheen Sharifzadeh, *Origin of Khorezm Lazgi*, Borderlessblogger.com, December 5, 2021. https://borderlessblogger.com/2021/12/05/the-origin-of-khorezmian-lazgi/.

[38]Matyakubova et al., *Khorezm "Lazgi"*, pp. 19–20; etymology linked to "shivering" or "trembling" around a fire.

[39]In *Lezginka*, there is fast footwork while the upper body is held still.

Animals incorporate certain forces or qualities admired by humans, such as strength, speed, courage, or magical power over evil.[40]

The quickly fluttering hands[41] of Khorezm dance bring to mind a similar vibratory movement seen in Native American prayer dances, as well as the ecstatic *bandari* dance of the Persian Gulf, a reminder that in many indigenous cultures, worship of the Sacred is embedded in dance. Rather than being viewed as a frivolous or trivial activity, dance reinforces the position of humans as an integral part of the natural world, not something apart from it.

The *Lazgi* Series

Gavkhar Matyokubova has identified nine separate kinds of *lazgi*,[42] each with a special character or historical origin. First, the *Masqaraboz lazgi* comes from the syncretic Central Asian "clowning" tradition known as *masqaraboz*.[43] Social satirists who lampooned the rich and powerful, these folk entertainers performed humorous skits. They also danced, imitating not only animals, like jerboas, and people from various walks of life with easily identified professions or even at times imitating physically disabled persons. The *Masqaraboz lazgi* features pantomime to imitate some dances derived from hunting such as the Bear Dance and the *pishek kum* in imitation of the small but aggressive desert cat with beautiful fur.[44] A rhythmic sound created by men slapping the sounds of their open mouths, known as *pakapak*, is another humorous element.

The *Surnai lazgi* is performed to the piercing sounds of the Central Asian wind instrument known as *surnai* that was used in military music for battles. Revealing this bellicose connection, the militaristic *lazgi* was traditionally a stylized confrontation between two opposing sides.[45] Count K. K. Pahlen, who visited Khiva in 1908–1909 on an official mission from the Russian tsar, may have seen something like this when he was a special guest of the Khan. He was feted at a performance of their "national ballet" that included *bachas*. The program also included "war dances, with swords drawn in the glittering moonlight."[46]

Other kinds of *lazgi* are also linked to specific rhythmic and instrumental accompaniment. The *Kairoki lazgi* requires dexterity from the dancers to

---

[40]Lonsdale, *Animals and the Origins of Dance*, p. 11.
[41]Fluttering hands can also be seen in Native American prayer dances as well as the ecstatic Bandari dance of the Persian Gulf region.
[42]Matyakubova et al., *Khorazm "Lazgi" Raksi: Tarikhi va Tavsifi*, p. 9.
[43]To avoid this misapprehension, the term *masqaraboz* will be used throughout.
[44]Khamroeva, ibid., p.202.
[45]Ibid., pp. 202–03.
[46]Pahlen, *Mission to Turkestan*, p. 171.

accompany themselves with varied rhythms played on the *kairoki*[47] stone "castanets" while dancing. As suggested by the name, the *Dutor lazgi* is performed to music played on this stringed instrument.

The *Garmon lazgi* is performed to the *garmon*, a small Russian button accordion. According to ethnomusicologist Jean During, the *garmon* found its way into the music of the East through Russia, but only really caught on in Azerbaijan and Khorezm. The female entertainers, known as *khalfa*, performed at women's gatherings and celebrations in small "groups of two, three, or four, often including a dancer."[48] Theodore Levin noted that *khalfa* often came from lower social classes. "Many *khalfas* have been blind or crippled."[49] They added percussive elements by tapping on *piala* (tea bowls) with thimbles, wearing *zang*, or playing *kairok*—all items carried into the women's quarters.

The unusual *Changak lazgi*, meaning "twisted or crippled," includes an odd posture, limping movements of the legs, asymmetrical facial distortion, and arms and hands pulled in toward the body, similar to the symptoms of persons with muscular dystrophy. Two explanations exist for this disconcerting dance. One tells of Iranian hunters, skilled in horsemanship and archery, who encountered the Khorezm Shah in the forest. They escaped, but when they were met again, the ruler, impressed by their skills, rewarded them and settled them together with their families upon his lands. But this story does not explain the unusual posture and the twisting of the limbs in this genre of *lazgi*.

Another story mentions a specific individual who performed at the *saroy*— which means "palace"—where the *Saroy lazgi* was intended for the entertainment of the ruler, the khan or the *padshah*. This connects the tradition of dancing on a *lagan* (a platter or tray) to a women's *lazgi* competition that took place at the Khan's palace. A dancer named Anabibi Sobirova fell off a cart in which she was traveling with female musicians escorting a bride to the home of the groom.[50] During this accident, the dancer's leg and arm were seriously injured; even after recovery, both limbs were shortened, and she walked with a limp. But in a spirit of resilience, she participated in the palace competition, dancing on a platter or tray. Her movements were so confident and original that the khan thought they were purposeful, not the result of injury. The *Lagan lazgi* remains, challenging the creativity of the dancer to never repeat the same movement while performing in one place.

Whatever the origins may be, the *Changak lazgi* can be seen at folk gatherings and wedding festivities. (See filmography.) However, the disturbing elements seem like a parody. Do they stem from cruel mockery or, instead, do they celebrate the human determination to dance, in spite of physical challenges?

---

[47]Kairoki are the smooth river stones held in pairs in each hand.
[48]Levin, *The Hundred Thousand Fools of God*, p. 191.
[49]Ibid., p. 190.
[50]Another oral tradition says a jealous rival pushed or tripped her.

The *Khiva lazgi* portrays the beauty and grandeur of the city's architecture, the flight of birds, the flow of the Amu Darya.[51] The most recent genre, the *Khorezm lazgi*, comes from the innovation of the beloved Khorezm singer Komiljon Otaniyozov, who, in 1960, performed *lazgi* for the first time with poetic lyrics. Prior to that, the dance was done only to rhythm or instrumental music. This new approach was immediately embraced but the public and today most concerts feature *lazgi* dances to a song.

Body Posture

The upper torso is more relaxed than in other dance zones, sometimes swaying from side to side in a seemingly effortless manner. Both men and women will at times deeply bend forward and back from the waist. Forward, as if leaning to pick up something, or like a horseback rider trying to encourage their steed, or back, again as if on horseback. While only women wear wrist bells, both male and female dancers will at times snap fingers or play *kairoki*. Tiny isolations of the shoulders and head ornament the dance. The limp position of the hands, hanging down from the wrists, are similar to Turkish men's *kara deniz* (Black Sea) dances, with the vibration of the hands bringing to mind the spasms of a fish out of water, a reminder of the natural fisheries lost with the desiccation of the Aral Sea. Male dances can be especially playful and humorous, but for both men and women, the underlying sentiment conveys both mischief and joy.

The Magic and Science of *Lazgi*

Khorezmians insist that *lazgi* is danced by children as young as three or four, as well as grandmothers that are seventy to eighty years old. Even more elderly people, as old as one hundred, have been known to perform *lazgi*.[52] Upon hearing the tune, they begin shaking their hands, shoulders, and so on.[53] This trembling imitates the moment of the soul entering the body, filling it with the life force. And so contagious is the music that it is not uncommon for audience members to leave their seats and dance in the aisles, even during formal concert presentations of *lazgi*, creating a communal celebration of joy.

With its unique character, distinct from all other Uzbek dance, *lazgi* won official recognition from UNESCO as Intangible Cultural Heritage. The dance begins in the upper body in a pose with the arms raised above the head, a shoulder width

---

[51] As described in a documentary video about *lazgi*. (See filmography.)
[52] Khamroeva, Gavkhar Matyokubova, p. 21.
[53] Ibid.

apart, but "the legs are silent—*Oeklar zhim*." Slowly, movement begins, there is head movement, a glance, a flutter of the eyelashes, and "the raised arms begin to descend, fingers tremble." Energy and life begin to descend as if enlivened by the sun as "each body part comes alive. But the dancer must not repeat these movements."[54] For example, if the word for "hair" is mentioned, the dancer must perform a related gesture, but every time the word is repeated, a different movement related to "hair" must be used.

Link to Healing Aspect

Khorezm dance, especially *lazgi*, has connections with healing and brings blessings as well. Past humans may have ascribed benefits to supernatural intervention, but embedded in the folk-saying that "in Khorezm, everybody dances" there is "growing evidence that stimulating one's mind by dancing can ward off Alzheimer's disease and other dementia, much as physical exercise can keep the body fit. Dancing also increases cognitive acuity at all ages."[55] A study published in the *New England Journal of Medicine* analyzed various leisure activities in senior citizens and concluded that "dancing was the only physical activity associated with a lower risk of dementia."[56] The Center for Disease Control (CDC) has warned that senior individuals who live in social isolation have a fifty percent greater risk of dementia, something which communal dance could help to prevent.[57]

The characteristic "trembling" found in *lazgi* may protect against bone fragility in older adults.[58] One U.S. study found that rodents, when placed on a vibrating tray, developed stronger bones.[59] (In the case of rodents, the vibration came from an outside influence, but imagine how much more beneficial results could be if the individual initiated the vibratory movement.)

On September 5, 2021, a new ballet, *Lazgi*, premiered at the Alisher Navoi Theatre of Opera and Ballet, created by German choreographer Raymondo Rebeck working with Khorezm dance expert Gavkhar Matyokubova. One reviewer, describing a solo performance of *lazgi* within the ballet, noted that "the performer completes the dance with an almost ecstatic sense of pure joy

---

[54]Feruza Salikhova, "Uzbek Raqs San'ati Tarikhi Khaqid Airim Mulokhazalar." In *Materials of the First International Scientific–Practical Conference*. Tashkent: Bookmany Print, 2022, p. 233.
[55]https://socialdance.stanford.edu/syllabi/smarter.htm.
[56]*New England Journal of Medicine*, https://www.nejm.org/doi/full/10.1056/nejmoa022252.
[57]Centers for Disease Control, www.cdc.gov/aging/publications/features/lonely-older-adults.htm
[58]*New England Journal of Medicine*, ibid.
[59]Greg Gillepies, "Vibration Reduces Cellular Senescence in the Bones of Rats," May 5, 2021, www.lifespan.io/news/vibration-reduces-cellular-senescence-in-the-bones-of-rats/Baker; Tony, "Whole body vibration has same health benefits as walking," JagWire, March 16, 2017. https://jagwire.augusta.edu/whole-body-vibration-has-same-health-benefits-as-walking/.

and happiness, causing a storm of delight in the audience, as if after a protracted quarantine, they are being reborn to a new healthy happy life." The critic also surmised that "it is not surprising that this energetic and incendiary dance helped the ancient Khorezmians to survive in the conditions of cold harsh winters and endless internecine wars."[60]

Costuming and Jewelry

Women's costuming resembles traditional garments elsewhere in Central Asia with a shift-like dress, pants, and outer coat or jacket. Khorezm *chapans* are sometimes quilted as protection against the bitter cold of the region's winters. Unlike other areas, Khorezm *chapans* are often quilted with narrow vertical channels, or "wales." Strong colors are favored. Tamara Khanum, who spent two years in Khorezm studying the local dance culture, owned a costume of bright orange silk topped with a dark green velvet coat. Traditionally, Khorezm dancers wore belts, ornamented with several long tassels hanging from black twisted cord, adding a "delayed line" to the dancer's movements. For contemporary stage performances, dancers now sometimes favor long-sleeved dresses, fitted through the torso, then flaring out into a full skirt. In some, the former emphasis of the belt at the waistline has lowered to a "drop waist" closer to the hip level, even though hip isolations are absent in Khorezm dance, and indeed, for Uzbek dance in general.

Special jewelry adds auditory elements to the trembling movements of Khorezm dance. Hats embellished with tiny metal pods—not coins—create a tinkling sound whenever the head moves, especially during lateral head slides. They were made with silver, then sometimes gilded, a reminder of golden jewelry favored by the goddess Anahita. On the center of the crown of the hat is a large rectangular amulet, and in the past an elaborate jewelry piece hung down at the back of the hat, protecting the back of the skull, thought to be a remnant of the days when women fought in battles. On the left side of the hat—over the heart—small feathers grouped together to create a sort of aigrette.[61] The *qorabag'r* bird is favored, but owl[62] and duck feathers are also used, believed to bring luck.

Across the chest, female dancers wear a special pectoral that fastens on each side of the shoulders. The jewelry hangs down in three tiers,[63] each decorated with

---

[60]Guarik Bagdasarova, "Magiya tantsa: balet 'Lazgi' na stsene GABT im. A. Navoi." The article is about the ballet *Lazgi* on the stage of the State Academic Bolshoi Theater named for Alisher Navoi. www.kultura.uz/view_4_r_16923.html

[61]Normally, an aigrette uses heron feathers.

[62]The Eurasian eagle owl, an endangered species.

[63]One jeweler told me that ancient ornaments corresponded to the chakras of the human body, from belts on up to the crowns.

tiny pods. The center of each tier sometimes has a special stone, often carnelian, that can be carved with an inscription. This jewelry enhances the tiny trembling movements or "titratma" of Khorezm dance. Female dancers also wear wrist bells, or *zang*, during performances of *lazgi*, adding to the soundscape.

Unfortunately, these traditional ornaments have at times been replaced with gold-colored beaded fringe and plastic paillettes, which dramatically change the look and soundscape of the dance. The traditional ornaments, amulets, and feathers, imbued with ritual and symbolic meaning, have sometimes disappeared from stage performances in favor of the heavy beaded fringe, more familiar in Arabic *raqs sharqi* dance. Feathers from local birds, associated with good luck, have increasingly been replaced by tall ostrich plumes, which are not traditional because ostriches became extinct long ago in Central Asia.[64]

The magic of *lazgi* reaches across time and cultures, winning admirers from people who have never even seen a live performance. Recently, videos posted on YouTube have attracted global attention.[65] When in 2020 and 2021, the global quarantine lockdown during COVID-19 moved classes to the remote Zoom format, the 17th and 18th Central Asian Dance Camps offered virtual classes with Khorezm dance specialist Shanazar Boltaev.[66] The seemingly magical quality of "the melody and dance of Lazgi are so attractive that spectators start dancing voluntarily."[67] This buoyant, life-affirming energy may explain the resilience of a population that has endured so many destructive invasions through the centuries.

---

[64]Although ostriches did exist in Central Asia and their fossils have been found in Mongolia, they date from the late Eocene epoch and have long been extinct. https://americanornithology.org/ostrich-evolution-revealed-fossil-finds-shed-new-light-on-the-evolution-of-the-african-ratite/ See also Gerald Mayr and Nikita Zelenkov, "Extinct crane-like birds (Eogruidae and Ergilornithidae) from the Cenozoic of Central Asia are indeed ostrich precursors." *Ornithology*, 138, no. 4 (October 1, 2021): ukab048, https://doi.org/10.1093/ornithology/ukab048.

[65]Mr. Leonard Schneider, an 84-year-old resident of Augusta, Maine, happened to come across a YouTube video of the dance. Now, he is a huge fan of Khorezm culture—and of Khorezm singer and dancer Hulkar Abdullaeva. Schneider says that Lazgi is "like a rare, missing, but very essential vitamin to revive our souls and spirits." He feels happy he had lived long enough to discover this culture, even this late in his life. From Laurel Victoria Gray, "Dancing into the Future with Ancient Steps: Lessons on Healing and Restoration from Khorezm Traditions". Paper presented at International Cultural Forum "Central Asia at the Crossroads of World Civilizations," 2021.

[66]"Uzbek Dance Goes Virtual with the 17th Central Asian Dance Camp", on *Voices on Central Asia* website. https://voicesoncentralasia.org/uzbek-dance-goes-virtual-with-the-17th-central-asian-dance-camp/.

[67]https://ich.unesco.org/en/RL/khorazm-dance-lazgi-01364.

PART THREE

FROM THE *ICHKARI* TO THE CONCERT STAGE

6 MENTORS AND MARTYRS

Yusufjon-Kyzyk Shakarjanov—Carrier of Tradition

The *ustoz–shagird* tradition provided a system for rhythm and dance transmission connecting countless generations through information passed experientially and orally from master to student. Turkic Central Asians, and other peoples of the East, with their love of poetry recitation and oral epics, have well-developed skills of memorization.[1] However, this lineage also imparts a certain fragility to tracing the history of dance because the chain of knowledge can be broken when a master passes, leaving behind stories and legends that are difficult to verify. One documented carrier of oral traditions was Yusuf-Kyzyk Shakarjanov. His remarkable life spanned ninety years of immense change; he performed at the court of the khan of Kokand and, in 1909, for Russian Emperor Nicholas II, then later for Lenin himself and, eventually for Khrushchev. In his lifetime as an artist, he embodied all the genres of Uzbek performing arts, as a dancer, percussionist, musician, puppeteer, circus performer, comedian, actor, humorist, and *ustoz*.

Yusufjon-Kyzyk was born in 1869 in Margilan, the cultural center in the Ferghana Valley that was the birthplace of many of the early pioneers who shaped Uzbekistan's stage traditions in the twentieth century. His father, a maker of *tandoor* ovens, had so delighted his community with his quick wit that they called

---

[1] G. I. Gurdieff in *Meetings with Remarkable Men*, London: Arkana, 1985, p. 36. Gurdieff, not always the most reliable of sources, claimed that his father and his friends who were traditional bards often recited stories that turned out to come from the epic of Gilgamesh, even though the written version of this ancient poem had only been rediscovered in 1853—"this legend had been handed down by the *ashoks* from generation to generation for thousands of years."

him "sweet-tongued," *shakar*.[2] This ability to play with language emerged in his son as well and would eventually earn Yusup the honorific of "kyzyk" given to outstanding performers of humorous folk traditions. Also a talented musician, Yusuf-Kyzyk attributed his own musical skills to his grandfather Rizo, who was known as a *hofiz*, a folk poet and singer, asserting that "I am a hereditary artist" (*ya potomstvennyy artist*).[3]

Yusuf's father enrolled him in a *madrassa* so he could receive an education, but the lively boy was not keen on the dry, rote learning taught there that focused primarily on Qu'ranic studies. Later, he confided to Peoples' Artist of Uzbekistan Ganjian Tashmatov that, instead attending classes, it was "better to spin around in the *chaikhona*" (*luchshe v chaykhane pokrutit'sya*) where he could eat his fill and listen to stories.[4] The boy knew the difference between these two places from experience because, when his father died, Yusuf-Kyzyk left the *madrassa* around age eight and went to work in a *chaikhona* to support the family, delivering food, washing dishes, running errands, and dancing. According to Avdeeva, he had already begun dancing at age six.[5] Yusuf-Kyzyk soon became known for his ability to entertain guests, amusing them by mimicking animal sounds, doing impressions of famous people, telling jokes, singing and dancing—talents which drew the attention of the local population in Margilan who heard of his amusing ways and came to this chaikhona just to see his performances.[6]

Insight into Yusuf-Kyzyk's early career can be found in nineteenth-century travelers' descriptions of folk entertainment in Russian Turkestan, which merged vocal and instrumental music with clowning, puppetry, dance, and acrobatics. One vintage photograph shows a boy performing the "bridge," an acrobatic posture in which a dancer leans back to touch the ground with his hands, forming an arch with his body. Count Pahlen, when traveling in what was then Russian Turkestan in 1908–1909, recalled that in addition to the *bacha* performance in Khiva, "we were treated to other types of entertainment, also accompanied by the orchestra, which were really more like circus turns than anything else. I remember a small boy who was tossed like a ball high in the air by his partners and who never failed to come down on his feet, bowing gracefully to his audiences."[7]

---

[2]Mukhtar Ganiev, "*Shut Margilanskiy*" (Jester of Margilan), *Pis'ma o Tashkente*. December 31, 2020. Online article, no page numbers. https://mytashkent.uz/2020/12/31/shut-margilanskij/
[3]Ibid.
[4]Yusufjon-Kyzyk Shakarjanov cited by Ganijon Tashmatov in Mukhtar Ganiev's article, "*Shut Margilanskiy*."
[5]Avdeeva, *Tantseval'noye iskusstvo Uzbekistana*, p.27.
[6]Ganiev, "*Shut Margilanskiy*."
[7]Pahlen, trans. N. J. Couriss, *Mission to Turkestan, Being the Memoirs of Count K.K. Pahlen*. London: Oxford University Press, 1964, pp. 170–71.

Yusufjon remembered that from as early as age five, he realized he had the ability to make people laugh and this skill made him happy.[8] He related in conversation with the famous art historian and researcher of traditional Uzbek folk theater Mikhail Verkhatsky that from ages seven to fifteen, his first teacher was Usta Saadi Mahdi, who eventually took him to Kokand and included him in his troupe of court entertainers. Young Yusuf also studied with Usta Khudaiberdy. Both masters taught him numerous *usuls*—the foundational rhythms of Uzbek dance.[9] By age eleven, the boy was already known as an exceptional dancer.

At age twelve, Yusufjon left his work in the chaikhona to join a traveling circus group and he began the traveling life of a professional Central Asian folk artist. He was skilled in *askiya* contests of improvisational wit, often involving clever and elaborate play on words. Yusuf-Kyzyk worked with the troupe until about age twenty, performing in three unique and somewhat difficult to describe genres of Uzbek entertainment—*kizikchi* (comedic clowning), *masqaraboz* (masked comic actors), and *qoghirchoqbozlik* (puppetry). His *ustoz* Saadi Mahsim, who had for thirty-six years performed under three different khans, became Yusufjon-Kyzyk's main mentor in life.[10] The free-spirited improvisational nature in *masqaraboz* performances belied the training that shaped their art. Training was strict. To learn the distinctive *shokh* turn, his teacher blindfolded him and forced him to repeat the movement fifty times. If he became tired or fell, he was beaten.[11] Reputedly, Usta Saadi trained his performers for two years on mastering expressions of the face and eyes. This attention to facial expression also emerged in women's dances, often performed to deeply emotional songs in which the dancer's countenance must match the thematic content.

The opening of the railroad in Russian Turkestan, with the Trans-Caspian railway extended to Samarkand in 1888, facilitated transportation for Russian and European circus and theater troupes to tour colonial Turkestan to entertain the Russian population. The railroad also made travel easier for local entertainers to visit other regions and countries. At the end of the nineteenth century, Yusuf-Kyzyk toured Iran, Turkey, and Afghanistan.[12] For a time, Yusuf-Kyzyk worked in Bukhara at the theater of Said Kissach but, by 1904, he had relocated to Tashkent, performing as a clown in Turkestan's first national circus.

Yusuf-Kyzyk performed in the major celebrations and events of the new Soviet state. In 1920, he worked as a member of Hamza's AgitProp train "Red East" that served the Trans-Caspian front and participated in a national celebration marking

---

[8]Yusufjon-Kyzyk Shakarjanov quoted by Avdeeva in *Tantseval'noye Iskusstvo Uzbekistana*, p. 27.
[9]Ganiev, "*Shut Margilanskiy.*"
[10]Ibid.
[11]Avdeeva, *Galia Izmailova.* Tashkent: Gafur Gulyam, 1975, p. 65.
[12]Avdeeva, *Tantseval'noe iskusstvo Uzbekistana*, p. 28.

the overthrow of the Emir of Bukhara. He was part of the historic 1923 ethnographic concert of the All-Union Agricultural Exhibition in Moscow, with Uzbek artists including Tamara Khanum and Maria Kuznetsova, making a sensational entry in camel-drawn carts, filled with musicians playing drums and karnai trumpets.[13] In 1926, Yusufjon-Kyzyk joined the Ethnographic Ensemble of Mukhitdin Kari-Yakubov. He traveled again to Moscow in 1930 for the All Union Olympiad of Folk Art and, in 1937, for the *Dekada* of Art and Literature in Moscow.[14]

A photograph from 1927 shows Yusuf-Kyzyk playing the *nagora* kettle drums in the ensemble of Kari-Yakubov, which included fifteen other men and a solitary female, the dancer and singer Tamara Khanum. In addition to playing *doira* and *nagora*, he also learned to play *dutar*, *chang*, and *nai*, "but most of all" he loved playing *doira* and in his remarkable memory stored "about a hundred rhythms of Uzbek dance."[15]

Yusufjon possessed both physical and mental agility, whether turning in dance or turning a phrase. Indeed, it was Yusufjon's quick thinking that saved the life of Tamara Khanum when, during one of the performances of the AgitProp troupe, *basmachis* appeared in the audience, seeking to kidnap or kill the young dancer. Yusuf-Kyzyk grabbed a *paranjah* and threw it over Tamara, allowing her to disappear into the crowd of veiled women.[16]

Tall and good-looking, Yusuf was sometimes called "painted," or "buyak," because he dyed his hair and brows with *usma* (henna), powdered his face, and used *surma* (antimony or kohl) on his eyelashes and to rim his eyes.[17] Although not commonly done by Uzbek men in the Soviet era, the use of kohl was a traditional practice of some Muslim men and attributed to the Prophet Muhammad according to various *Hadith*, to both brighten the eye and protect it.[18] Yusufjon emphasized the need for an artist to cultivate a distinguished appearance.[19]

The 1959 Uzbek film *Qo'shiqlar Uchadi* (Songs Fly) includes a cameo appearance by Yusuf-Kyzyk, along with other celebrated Uzbek artists traveling by train. Yusuf-Kyzyk walks through the corridor, looking into different compartments to view rehearsals and joke with the performers. Close-ups of his face and his intense gaze, as well as his interactions with Tamara Khanum and others, give a short but vivid impression of the artist who was about ninety years old when this was filmed.

---

[13]Ganiev, "*Shut Margilanskiy.*"
[14]Avdeeva, *Tantseval'noe iskusstvo Uzbekistana*, p. 30.
[15]Ibid.
[16]Ganiev, "*Shut Margilanskiy.*"
[17]December 3, 2022. In a conversation with Uzbek actor Yuldash Juraboev about makeup traditions, he remembered that his grandmother created small, permanent marks on her face after the death of each of her three children in infancy.
[18]For a discussion of various *hadith* regarding the permissibility of using kohl, see https://islamqa.info/en/answers/44696/pure-kohl-is-beneficial-to-the-eyes-and-is-not-harmful.
[19]Ganiev, "*Shut Margilanskiy.*"

Yusufjon-Kyzyk Shakarjanov's remarkable career spanned three distinct epochs of rulers and took him before major political leaders in the transformational years of the late nineteenth century, the Revolutionary period, and into the post-Stalin Soviet Union under Khrushchev. Khans, tsars, and commissars all yielded to his bright, entertaining spirit. He passed his knowledge and training on to the artists who shaped Uzbekistan stage arts, not only Tamara Khanum, but also Usta Olim Kamilov, who studied dance skills with Shakarjanov.

Tamara Khanum

Born in 1906, in a small *kishlak* known as Gorchakova Station near the town of Margilan in what was then Russian Turkestan, Tamara Artemyovna Petrosian was the second of five daughters born to an Armenian couple banished from Baku for their Revolutionary activities the previous year. Tamara thoroughly absorbed the language, culture, and traditions of her Uzbek neighbors. As *Izvestia* later wrote of her: "Armenian by origin, she is inseparable from the Uzbek national art. She comprehended its depths, revealed the beauty of the song and dance creativity of the peoples of Uzbekistan and other republics of Central Asia."[20]

As a child, she saw performances by traveling players, presenting traditional Central Asian folk entertainment like magic tricks, juggling, tightrope-walking, and more. Together with her sisters, they put on their own shows in the desert behind their home, with her sister Elizaveta playing the role of the *askiya* humorist.[21] Early on, their mother Anna would predict that Tamara would someday "dance in Paris," a seeming impossibility that caused everyone to laugh[22] but which would become a reality.

Tamara's radiant personality, and her gift for music and dance, made her known among their neighbors. As early as age 12, she performed at weddings, but in the women's quarters. Even so, news of her "inappropriate behavior" spread in the local Uzbek community and her father received warnings to control his child. Like many legendary figures, several stories exist about her early life, but according to Langston Hughes, in 1918 the girls were sent away to Tashkent, and reactionary *Basmachi* forces attacked their home, robbing and murdering their

---

[20]*Tamara Khanum, Muse of the East*, interview by Tatyana Simbertseva on *Koryo-Saram*. https://koryo-saram.site/muza-vostoka-tamara-hanum-i-ee-korejskie-pesni/
[21]Avdeeva, *Tantseval'noye iskusstvo Uzbekistana*, p. 131.
[22]Often quoted comment, see Zilola Safarova, "Life Dedicated to Art," *European Journal of Business*, 2, no. 5 (2022), p. 32.Z. S. Safarova. "Art by Tamara Khanum and Roza Karimova." *Middle European Scientific Bulletin*, 1 2020): 34–39. 10.47494/mesb.2020.1.137.

father.[23] The following year, Tamara stepped onto the public stage for the first time and for many years, she herself was the target of murder attempts.

As Tamara herself recalled, her love for art began early, from childhood. She wanted only to dance.

"I was 13 years old when I started performing," recalls Tamara Khanum. It was in Margilan, my native village in the Ferghana Valley. Since then, the flame of love for art has been burning in my soul. It's even impossible to convey. From childhood, I wanted only one thing—only to dance, only to be where karnai and surnai play, where puppeteers and tightrope walkers give performances.[24]

Later, as an adult, when she had learned the songs and dances of dozens of nationalities beyond those found within the USSR, the Polish literary critic T. Komar would tell her, "you are the daughter of all the nations whose songs you sing."[25] In this spirit of artistic multi-culturalism, Tamara Khanum continued and expanded the previous practice of the *bachas* who included the dances of different regions and ethnicities in their performance repertoires.

Determined to promote the goals of the Revolution, in particular women's emancipation, Tamara Khanum performed as part of the "AgitProp"[26] drama theater brigade of the Turkestan front, directed by Hamza Hakimzade Niyazi (1889–1929)—the writer, composer, and political activist who championed the cause of female emancipation in his plays and songs. The performers traveled to villages, spreading information about the new Soviet state and its goals with Tamara and the other girls campaigning for women to take off the veil. The conditions of the work challenged the artists physically as they often went without adequate food or a place to sleep. They carried their own costumes and instruments, often walking from village to village. Tamara Khanum recalled those years. "I danced anywhere—on rooftops, in the streets, in the villages. I remember walking with a baby at my breast, another child at my side, holding my hand, and, on my back, a bundle filled with my costumes. Like this I walked to the villages and danced, while in the audience sat women still wearing the paranjah."[27] But the performers remained dedicated to their cause despite these difficulties. As Mukhidtin Kari-Yakubov[28] often observed, an artist must always

---

[23]Langston Hughes, "Tamara Khanum, Soviet Asia's Greatest Dancer." In *Theatre Arts Monthly*, 1934, p. 834.

[24]Tamara Khanum, quoted in Avdeeva, *Tantseval'noye iskusstvo Uzbekistana.*

[25]Komar quoted in Avdeeva, *Tantseval'noye iskusstvo Uzbekistana*, p. 82.

[26]"AgitProp"—from the Russian words for "agitation" and "propaganda"—refers to political propaganda campaigns that spread Communist concepts through performances and the arts.

[27]Tamara Khanum cited by Laurel Victoria Gray in "Tamara Khanum, Uzbekistan's Heroine of Dance." *Arabesque*, X, no. V, January–February 1985, pp. 14–15.

[28]Kari-Yakubov will be more fully introduced in Chapter 7.

remain in good spirits, "even if hungry, in ragged clothing, the artist knows how to work miracles."[29]

The local populace often assumed that members of the AgitProp troupe were *masqaraboz*, the traveling players of Central Asia who performed masked or in "white face," clowning and presenting humorous skits on everyday life, often mocking the wealthy and powerful. When the brigade's *arba* cart became stuck in a river, they found that the locals were not keen to assist the artists; the villagers had troubles of their own. But when the AgitProp team presented a concert in a *kishlak* that brought up topics like the new Soviet programs of land and water reform, issues crucial to rural populations, the villagers often stayed after the performance to ask questions, even inquiring about electricity and Lenin.

The Uzbek film series about Hamza Hakimzade Niyazi includes one episode, *Paranji Tashlangan Kun*, dramatizing the *Hujum* ("attack") unveiling campaign of March 8, 1927. One by one, veiled women, encouraged by Hamza, remove their *paranjahs* and throw them into a fire, reciting Hamza's verses. They begin to sing and dance, all the while threatened by the *mullahs* and men of the village. It reflects a similar circumstance in Tamara Khanum's own life, when she sang the revolutionary words of Hamza with lyrics encouraging women to cast aside the *paranjah*.

> Make haste, dear sisters, and rejoice,
> Take part in glee that all the women voice.
> Come, fling the hideous veil into the flames
> To make this world a warmer, brighter place,
> To celebrate the State that set us free at last.
> So let us join our hands and freely sing and dance.[30]

Hamza saw in the young and talented Tamara Khanum not only a good artist, but a living example of emancipation, a tremendous weapon in the propaganda campaign. It was perilous work because the AgitProp group faced genuine danger from the *Basmachi* who hunted them, threatened by their revolutionary ideas. Tamara Khanum's historic appearance onstage without a *paranjah* and *chuchvah* was not a singular event. She repeatedly risked her life whenever she performed in public. By her bold act, Tamara Khanum inspired other women to take the same step, but change came slowly. Research on accounts of the *Hujum* campaign suggest that the dramatic unveilings were short-lived, with many women soon veiling again, pressured by their traditional families and communities.[31] Eventually,

---

[29]Manuscript "Uzbek Chaliapin" shared by Elena Kari-Yakubov, pages unnumbered.
[30]The English-language translator of the Hamza poem is unknown.
[31]For a detailed analysis of the complex issues surrounding the *Hujum* campaign, see Northrop, *Veiled Empire: Gender and Power in Stalinist Central Asia*. Ithaca, NY: Cornell University Press, 2004.

the practice of wearing the *paranjah* was discontinued, although some women in remote areas continued to wear it for many years.

The American socialist Anna Louise Strong recorded incidents of retribution against those who removed the *paranjah*. One young female activist, a member of a student youth organization, went to a village to share the message of women's emancipation. The following day, she was "returned" to her team members "in a peasant cart, cut into small pieces. These words accompanied the body: 'This is your women's freedom!'"[32] Another incident involved the young wife of the new secretary of the village soviet of Yan-Kabak, who dared to unveil. "A group of seventeen men attacked her in the eighth month of pregnancy, violated her in turn, killed her and threw her body in the river."[33]

One woman who survived mutilation by the *Basmachi* was Mayna Khasanova (1903–1943), born in Bukhara, the first Uzbek woman to join and fight with the Red Army during the Civil War. In 1922, she was captured by the *Basmachi* while conducting an intelligence operation. They amputated her hand, cut out her tongue, tied her to a tree, stabbed her while galloping on horses, then buried her up to neck, leaving her to die.[34] The Red Army found her and, after her recovery, sent her to study in Moscow at KUTV[35] where Maryam Yakubova (1909–1987), one of Uzbekistan's first actresses, was also enrolled. Yakubova recalled that the girls, seeing Mayna's disfigurement, "could not look at her without tears." Khasanova's life became the subject of the 1980 film *Devushka iz legendy* (Girl from the Legend).

Artists were also targeted by their own family members. Tursunoi Saidazimova (1911–1928), an actress and singer known as "the Uzbek nightingale," was killed in Bukhara by her own husband. She had studied theater at the Uzbek Drama Studio in Moscow from 1925 to 1927, then joined the Uzbek drama theater directed by Hamza. Upon her death, Hamza wrote a poem in her memory, *Tursunoi Marsiyasi*, memorializing her martyrdom for art.

For the performing artists of the AgitProp brigade, murder took one of their members when, on July 1, 1929, the sixteen-year-old Nurkhon Yuldashkhojaeva—sister of Usta Olim's wife—was murdered by her own brother, who repeatedly stabbed her. Nurkhon's story has often been trivialized and even incorrectly reported that she joined a "Russian ballet troupe"[36]—it was actually Hamza's

---

[32]Louise Anna Strong, *Red Star in Samarkand*. New York: Coward-McCann, Inc., 1929, p. 256.
[33]Ibid.
[34]This account comes from Mariam Yakubova's memoir, *Kak ya Stala Aktrisoy*, 1984, and appears in Gulmira Rakhimova, *Tuhfakhon, The Greatest Sozanda*, pp. 258–79.
[35]KUTV is the acronym for the Communist University of Workers of the East—Kommunisticheskiy universitet trudyashchikhsya Vostoka. It was founded in Moscow in 1921 and drew students from the USSR as well as nations of Asia and Africa.
[36]In my article on Uzbek dance for the Oxford University Press *International Encyclopedia of Dance*, I wrote that Tamara Khanum joined a ballet troupe. This was based on a translation in Russian before I learned that the term "ballet" was often used to characterize any stage dance. The nature of the dance group is still unclear.

Uzbek AgitProp brigade—and that she went on stage without a face veil or a head scarf, and not the totally enveloping *paranjah* and *chuchva*. Nurkhon had been purposely lured to return home for a visit, not knowing that her own father, encouraged by the local *ming-boshi*[37] and Mullah Kamal G'iasov, had forced his son to swear on the *Qur'an* to murder Nurkhon. She returned home, and wore "in the last hour of her life, a pleated skirt, a white batiste blouse, pink stockings and black shoes with high heels"[38]—Western clothes she had purchased when the company performed in Samarkand. She died in these clothes.

The memory of Nurkhon and her painful death haunted Tamara Khanum; they had performed together on stage. She kept a photograph of the girl in her home museum.[39] Thousands of people attended Nurkhon's memorial service and women tore off their *paranjahs* in front of her coffin.[40] In spite of this tragic loss, the artists remained determined to continue their work and Kari-Yakubov stood by the girl's coffin and affirmed that "regardless of the death of our Nurkhon, I believe that hundreds of Uzbek women will come to art."[41] The story of the first martyr of Uzbek dance became the subject of the musical drama, *Nurkhon*, by Kamil Yashin, a native of Andijan, another of the brilliant talents to come out of the Ferghana Valley. He later became a member of Hamza's Agitprop brigade.

As for Hamza himself, that valiant promoter of women's rights was martyred in 1929, stoned to death by angry men in Shohimardon in an incident involving the dismantling of a saint's shrine.[42]

Mukarram Turgunbaeva

Mukarram Turgunbaeva was one of the very first girls—and they were indeed girls—to follow the example of Tamara Khanum. Like other Uzbek girls, she danced in her home but had no recollection of anyone teaching her to dance— "I danced like all those around me danced." Her friends and her grandmother's friends recognized her talent, telling her that "the dance lived in my soul." Her grandmother cultivated her propensity for dance (Figure 6.1), playing the *doira* while Mukarram improvised, creating "entire dance scenarios based on fairy tales and songs."[43] She made her decision to become an artist after seeing a performance

---

[37]A "*ming-boshi*"—a title with military origins, literally meaning head of a thousand, refers to an office holder.
[38]Mukarram Turgunbaeva, cited in Avdeeva, *Tanets Mukarram Turganbaevoi*. Tashkent: Gafur Gulyam, 1989, p. 58.
[39]Gray, "Tamara Khanum, Uzbekistan's Heroine of Dance."
[40]This assertion is repeated online but without source.
[41]"Uzbek Chaliapin" manuscript.
[42]Adeeb Khalid, *Making Uzbekistan: Nation, Empire, and Revolution in the Early USSR*. 1st ed. Ithaca, NY: Cornell University Press, 2016, p. 352.
[43]Mukarram Turgunbaeva quoted in Avdeeva, *Tanets Mukarram Turganbaevoi*, p. 352.

by Tamara Khanum and Mukhitdin Kari-Yakubov. Walking home through the darkened streets after the concert, Mukarram resolved to join the theater, even though she would face opposition from her uncle, head of the family after her parents died. It took her two years to be able to follow through with her resolution.

In a profound assessment born of personal experience, Mukarram noted that while much had been written about the *Hujum* unveiling campaign and the struggle for female emancipation, the historians, journalists, and writers all "talk about social, religious oppression, they talk about the humiliating laws of Sharia, *adat* [the local customary practices of Muslim communities] ... rarely do they dwell on the fact that all these laws: social, economic, and moral—have formed the character of a woman—the historical national character."[44] Social reforms could take the woman out of the *ichkari*, but they could not take the *ichkari* out of the woman. "All the concepts of what can and should be done, how to act, even how to think and feel, were brought up in us, women, from century to century, from generation to generation. And therefore, fighting for the liberation of a woman, it was necessary to fight with the woman herself."[45]

This struggle was not only difficult, but multi-ethnic. Mukarram noted that their first examples, their ideals—"Tamara Khanum, Gavkhar Rakhimova,

FIGURE 6.1 Tamara Khanum (right) and Mukarram Turgunbaeva (left) performing the Ferghana dance gesture imitating the crushing of leaves to make *"usma"* to darken eyebrows.
Photo source: Archive of Tamara Khanum Museum.

---

[44]Mukarram quoted by Avdeeva, p. 52.
[45]Ibid.

Maria Kuznetsova,[46] Maksuma Karieva[47]—were not of Uzbek origin—they were Armenians, Russians, and Tatars." The fact that these first female stage performers were not Uzbek reflected a practice in Muslim societies where the niche of performing artists was often filled by non-Muslims such as Armenians, Russians, Bukharan Jews, and *Luli*.

All this made more challenging the effort to persuade Uzbek women and girls to join the performance ensemble. The wife of Usta Olim Kamilov told Mukarram how hard she had worked in order to persuade her sister Nurkhon, as well as the talented singer Tuhfakhon, to join the ensemble. Although these two did eventually join the performance group, they worked in the theater only for a very short time before they were murdered.

And they were not the only victims. Even women who did not perform on stage, but had only removed the *chuchva*, or attended educational programs, were killed. One disturbing account was recalled by Gavkhar Rakhimova, who attended a boarding school as a student and young member of one of the early performance groups that traveled together with a brass band to the town of Aravan in the Ferghana Valley. She sang and danced. Their group was accompanied by Taji-zade, the secretary of the district Komsomol (Young Communist) committee who recited political verses and invited the audience to attend an educational rally held after the concert. The rally was disrupted by *Basmachi* who "flew in"—probably on horseback. At dawn the following morning, Gavkhar, together with several students of the boarding school, made their way to the train station to return home.

> Passing through the covered market at the station, we heard a groan in the meat row. It was dark and we could barely see the girl the *basmachi* had hung on the meat carcass hook. Her body had been tortured. We urgently informed Red Army soldiers from the armored train that was standing at the station. The soldiers transferred the girl to the Medical Center, but she died without gaining consciousness. She was killed for attending an educational program.[48]

In the local communities, news of every beating of a woman, every murder, "flew from gate to gate." Mukarram recalled understanding that, in those times, the decision "to come to the theater meant to condemn yourself to deprivation, to break with your family, to break with many loved ones."[49] When she ran away from home to join the theater, she stayed with other young girls who, like her,

---

[46]A Russian opera singer and dancer who performed with the Ballets Russes.

[47]Actress who performed the Schiller drama *Love and Intrigue* in 1921, staged for the first time in the Uzbek language with many women in the audience still attired in *paranjah* and *chuchva*.

[48]This happened at the Gorchakova Station, the railway station of the city of Ferghana. Testimony of Gavkhar Rakhimova, cited by Avdeeva, *Tanets Mukarram Turganbaevoi*, p. 52.

[49]Mukarram Turgunbaeva, cited in Avdeeva, *Tanets Mukarram Turganbaevoi*, p. 53.

had never lived independently. They spent their stipend within the first few days, then survived on bread and sour milk.[50] Mukarram recalled that she could endure the privations, but what most troubled her was a fear that would not leave her, the dread that at any moment her uncle would appear, or would send someone to kill her, just as Nurkhon had been murdered only six months earlier.[51] And, in the kishlaks—the villages—the performers also feared the revenge of the *basmachi* "who threatened to cut both the artists and the audience."[52] Usta Olim Kamilov and his wife, sister of the murdered Nurkhon, stepped in to adopt Mukarram. "I began to live with them and gradually calmed down but for the rest of my life, there was a memory of the endless tension of these years."[53] Only in performances did she become truly happy and joyous. She recalled that "even my shoulders straightened,"[54] perhaps a reflection of how deeply the physical toll of constant fear and anxiety manifested in her body. But Mukarram always remembered that the decision to come to the theater exacted a price that meant enduring privation, as well as "cutting ties with family and many loved ones."[55]

Usta Olim, for whom Nurkhon's death was also a family tragedy, continued to teach, training a new generation of dancers like Galia Izmailova and Gulnara Mavaeva, as well as his own daughter, Halima Kamilova. But the murder of Nurkhon caused other young recruits to the ensemble to quit and, for a time, Tamara Khanum was the first and only female in the ethnographic ensemble that her husband Mukhitdin Kari-Yakubov founded in 1926 together with Usta Olim and Yusufjon-Kyzyk Shakarjanov.

---

[50] Ibid.
[51] Ibid.
[52] Ibid.
[53] Ibid.
[54] Ibid.
[55] Ibid.

7 CROSS-POLLINATION: MOSCOW AND PARIS

After the Bolshevik Revolution, performing artists from Uzbekistan[1]—sent by the new government—began to travel to Moscow, eager to explore exciting new possibilities with leaders in avant-garde performing arts. This atmosphere of openness was very different from the ideological rigidity that characterized Moscow in later decades. Experimentation was in the air, with artists seeking new ways to express a new society. Many of the creative forces of Russia's cultural "Silver Age" (c.1890–1917) were still alive and in the country, working and creating, part of the innovative, revolutionary spirit that characterized dance in the West as well. Described "as a turning point for Russian fine arts, performing arts, and scientific research,"[2] Russia's Silver Age included fresh creativity in dance. Isadora Duncan, considered "the Mother of Russian Modern Dance," made her debut at the Hall of Nobles in St. Petersburg in 1904. The following year she went on to tour Moscow and Kyiv. "Many of Russia's poets, artists, scientists, philosophers, and musicians understood Duncan as a fellow innovator and fully supported her."[3] Maurice Magnus, manager for her 1907–1908 Russian tour, maintained that the advent of Isadora in Russia "was the opening epoch of the new school of the dance for all the world. It was through it and the consequent Russian Ballet … that the Renaissance of the Dance took permanent root."[4]

---

[1]Known as Turkestan until 1924, when officially designated as the Soviet Republic of Uzbekistan.
[2]Overview of a joint lecture by Elena Yushkova and Lori Belilove, *Isadora Duncan: A Revolutionary Dancer in Revolutionary Russia*. Lecture presented on January 29, 2008, at the Wilson Center. Yushkova is a Senior Lecturer, Vologda Branch of the Moscow Academy for Humanities, and Fulbright-Kennan Institute Research Scholar, Kennan Institute. Lori Belilove is the Artistic Director of the Isadora Duncan Dance Foundation. www.wilsoncenter.org/event/isadora-duncan-revolutionary-dancer-revolutionary-russia
[3]Ibid.
[4]Maurice Magnus, quoted by Louise E. Wright, "Touring Russia with Isadora: Maurice Magnus' Account." *Dance Chronicle*, 23, no. 3 (2000): p. 259.

Some of these ground-breaking Russian artists who remained in the country after the Bolshevik Revolution had produced the 1920 mass spectacle recreating the 1917 storming of the Winter Palace, with eight thousand re-enactors, including students from the Imperial Theatre School where the young George Balanchine studied ballet.[5] These productions set the stage for future mass celebrations that eventually grew into the ossified Soviet celebrations of May Day and the October Revolution. The event producers learned how to coordinate large groups in the open air, often located quite far from each other, at times requiring a motorcyclist to ride between the different teams with cues to each director who was embedded within a particular group.

Other innovations included unexpected soundscapes and performance sites. Factory sounds became the inspiration for the 1922 rooftop "hooter" symphony by Arseniy Avraamov, which incorporated factory sirens and industrial horns to celebrate the seventh anniversary of the Revolution.[6] A new genre of amateur theater called *proletkult* (from "proletarian culture") sprang from factory workers who created purpose-driven productions with political content, seeking to build a new culture. The famed film-maker Sergei Eisenstein began his theater career working for *proletkult*, producing the 1924 play "Gas Masks," written by Sergei Tretyakov, that was staged at a Moscow gasworks. Even the Ballets Russes in Paris explored machine-inspired movement in the 1927 ballet *Le Pas d' Acier* (*The Steel Step*), with choreography by Leonid Massine and a score by Prokofiev.

Russian Orientalism

Although the Ballets Russes never performed in Russia, it was developed by many artists of the Silver Age who represented the ebullient *fin de siècle* blossoming in dance, music, design, literature, and art. Russian Orientalism developed more fully in the nineteenth century as the empire continued to expand its borders to the East, including the conquest of Turkestan, the territory of present-day Uzbekistan. Orientalist music, theatrical sets, and costume design all contained the *element vostochnyi*, the "Eastern element," that most fully emerged in the literature and art of nineteenth-century Russia. But while Western European Orientalism was intertwined with imperialist incursions into distant foreign countries, Russian Orientalism reflected their centuries of direct interactions with Eastern peoples with whom they shared contiguous borders. From early interactions with

---

[5]Jennifer Homans, *Mr. B: George Balanchine's 20th Century*. New York: Random House, 2022, pp. 78–79.
[6]Alex Sakalis, "Arseny Avraamov: The forgotten Soviet genius of modern music," November 6, 2022. www.bbc.com/culture/article/20221103-arseny-avraamov-the-man-who-conducted-a-city. A recording of the reconstructed *Hooter Symphony* can be heard on YouTube at https://youtu.be/Kq_7w9RHvpQ.

Scythians to conflicts between Kievan Rus and the Cumans and Polovestians, to the struggle under the "Mongol Yoke," and subsequent conflicts with Ottoman and Persian empires, the Russian vision of the East was complicated and extensive. Several prominent Russian families could trace their lineage and surnames to these Eastern ancestors. The oft-cited proverb "scratch a Russian and find a Tatar"[7] could be interpreted to describe not only temperament, but also a genetic reality.

The *element vostochnyi* in music and art dazzled Europe when the Ballets Russes served up a heady mixture of Orientalism with its ballets *Cleopatra* (1909), *Polovtsian Dances* from the opera *Prince Igor* (1909), *Les Orientales* (1910), *Scheherazade* (1910), *Le Dieu Bleu* (1912), and the lesser-known *Thamar* (1912). Their stories centered around themes of sensuality, seduction, and death. Colorful set designs, exotic costumes, and "Oriental" tonality in musical scores all presented a Russian vision of the East that captivated Paris and the world, impacting trends in fashion, interior decor, and even perfume.

Under Stalin, this vein became officially promoted in Russian classical music when "folklore, realism, and Russian imperialist expansion fused in the last central characteristic that came to define the 'Russian classics,' orientalism. Its defining characteristic is the musical presentation of a passive, eroticized East through a series of easily legible codes."[8] These "Eastern elements" were embraced by "Stalinist cultural policymakers, and orientalism remained an important component of Russian-based and Russian-trained composers' relations with their counterparts in the national republics, especially in the Caucasus and Central Asia, where composers willingly took up orientalist codes to propagate musically orientalist national traditions in the 1930s."[9]

Russian artists had been imagining the East for decades, but in the 1920s, the East came to Moscow in person. Young artists of Uzbekistan[10] arrived to study with legendary figures such as Vsevolod Meyerhold, who had trained at the Moscow Arts Theatre founded in 1898 by Vladimir Nemirovich-Danchenko and Konstantin Stanislavsky. Theater director Nemirovich-Danchenko, born in Georgia, was known for his productions that emphasized naturalism; he traced his lineage to Russian nobility as well as mixed Armenian–Ukrainian descent. Meyerhold, with a reputation for frequently controversial theatrical innovations, had worked with Diaghilev, Prokofiev, Fokine, and many others linked with the Ballets Russes,

---

[7]This aphorism, often attributed to Napoleon, *Grattez le Russe, et vous verrez un Tartare*, has a multilayered history that even Dostoyevsky discussed.

[8]Kiril Tomoff, "Uzbek Music's Separate Path: Interpreting 'Anticosmopolitanism' in Stalinist Central Asia, 1949–52." *The Russian Review (Stanford)*, 63, no. 2 (2004): 217.

[9]Ibid.

[10]In 1922, Uzbek singer Mukhitdin Kari-Yakubov studied at the KUTV (Communist University of Workers of the East). His interest in theater intensified after visiting the acting classes of Meyerhold. See M. A. Khamidova, *Akterskoye iskusstvo uzbekskogo muzykal'nogo teatra.* Tashkent: Fan Publishing, 1987, p. 29.

but while several of Russia's theater artists left the country after the Revolution, Meyerhold stayed, joining the Bolshevik Party with the goal of introducing radical elements into theater. He became increasingly drawn toward dance as a means of pure emotional expression and was originally intrigued by the dance of Isadora Duncan in 1905, but "by the 1920s, his view that movement should reflect total control of the actor's body led him into a different opinion: 'The loose condition of a physically uncontrolled person (Duncanism) is inadmissible.'"[11] His inclusion of Duncanesque dance numbers in *Hostages of Life* was criticized as "long sessions in the taste of barefoot bumpkins".[12]

Originally trained as a musician, Meyerhold's system of "biomechanics" emphasized rhythm. Prior to the Revolution, he had worked for ten years as

FIGURE 7.1 Tamara Khanum and Mukhitdin Kari-Yakubov performing a "*lapar*" duet at the Moscow Theatre Studio, 1924.
Photo source: Archive of Tamara Khanum Museum.

---

[11]Anna Kisselgoff citing Meyerhold in "Dance View; Meyerhold, Dance and Avant-Garde Theater in 1920s Russia." *New York Times*, December 6, 1981.
[12]Konstantin Rudnitsky, *Meyerhold, The Director*. Ann Arbor: Ardis, 1981, p. 180.

an opera director at the Imperial Theatre. He believed in the need for harmony between movement, music, and intentions, the very elements which characterized Central Asian dance and music. When the carriers of Uzbek culture like Tamara Khanum and Mukhitdin Kari-Yakubov arrived at his studio in the early 1920s, they brought with them a long Eastern tradition of connection between music, poetry, rhythm, and movement. Meyerhold's interaction with his Central Asian students deserves more inquiry. Unfortunately, information about his life was suppressed after Meyerhold, a victim of Stalin's purges, was arrested in 1939 and tortured, then executed by firing squad in 1940. His wife, the beautiful actress Zinaida, was hideously murdered in their apartment after her husband's arrest. Although some files have more recently been released and "there is a considerable amount of scholarship on Meyerhold today, his legacy had been difficult to evaluate and restore, since for years he was persona non grata within the Soviet Union, and important archives were closed to scholars."[13] But with his musicality and dedication to the full integration of movement and meaning, his recognition of this innate quality in the essence of Uzbek music and dance culture may explain his support for his Central Asian pupils.

Two portraits of Meyerhold suggest an intriguing connection with the East. In Boris Grigoriev's 1916 "double portrait," the actor and theater director appears in the foreground in European attire, but behind him, in shades of red, there lurks a costumed Turkic warrior in wide-legged nomad trousers, ready to loosen an arrow—an image straight from *Polovtsian Dances*. A later, 1938 color-drenched portrait by Pyotr Konchalovsky depicts Meyerhold lounging against a background of a huge Uzbek embroidered wall hanging known as a *suzani*—perhaps a gift from one of his Uzbek protégées.

The talented baritone Mukhitdin Kari-Yakubov (1896–1957) was one of those Uzbek students. He had first gone to Moscow in 1922 to study but was not immediately accepted into the course because of his weakness in the Russian language. Meyerhold's wife—formerly married to the poet Yesenin, who later married Isadora Duncan—took the Uzbek artist under her wing, introducing him to the Moscow theater scene. When Kari-Yakubov returned home to Turkestan during summer break, he saw a brave young girl named Tamara defy tradition and perform in a public concert; he went backstage to speak to her. The concert organizers arranged for the two to appear together on stage the following day, performing a *lapar*—a witty Uzbek folk duet combining song and dance,[14] and

---

[13]Dolja Dragasevic, "Meyerhold, Director of Opera: Cultural Change and Artistic Genres" (PhD Dissertation, Goldsmiths College, UK), p. 3. https://core.ac.uk/reader/42383650.

[14]Shakhrinsa Komiljon kiz Mirzayeva, "Lapar is the Treasury of Uzbek Folklore." *Journal of Advanced Research and Stability*, 2022. https://sciencebox.uz/index.php/jars/article/view/3491/3174.

a genre she would later more fully develop in her career (Figure 7.1). They soon married and, in 1924, the couple traveled to Moscow, to study at GITIS.[15]

Legacy of Isadora Duncan

Tamara attended classes in Moscow at the dance studio of Vera Maya, who taught the then fashionable style introduced by Isadora Duncan known as "modern" and "*plastique*."[16] Born Vera Vladimirovna Bogolyubova (1891–1974), she began calling herself Vera Maya after 1917. She opened a dance studio in 1923, one of the first to promote the so-called "Duncan style" that had popped up everywhere in Russia, sometimes presented by dancers who had no solid connection with Duncan. Vera, along with other Duncan followers Nikolai Poznyakov and Lev Lukin, all "underwent conservatory training, prepared for a career as performing musicians and only then created their own dance studios. Having received no special choreographic training, they came from music in their dances, and classes in their studios turned into musical improvisation."[17] Vera Maya created her own set of innovative preparatory movements that were not based on ballet and not done at a barre. By coincidence, or perhaps inspired by the dance of Tamara Khanum, "Vera Maya paid special attention to the development of flexibility of the arms, neck, shoulders and body. While studying anatomy, she discovered a number of 'forgotten' muscles, not usually used in dance … that are usually underdeveloped and came up with special exercises to train them."[18] (One can only wonder how she reacted to the lateral head slides and seemingly "boneless" arm undulations of Uzbek dance.) She introduced acrobatics into her movements and investigated biomechanics, as did Meyerhold. Vera Maya experimented with the "mechanical" dance style in which performers imitate machinery, turning like cogs and moving to hammering sounds. She herself was an accomplished pianist, and in 1924 introduced folk music into her presentations, creating a work called "My Village." Intriguingly, this coincided with the time that Tamara Khanum studied with her in Moscow, perhaps sparking an interest in the folk music and dance traditions of the East. Maya later embraced "exoticism" and invited visiting student Si-Lan

---

[15]GITIS is the current acronym for Russian Institute of Theatre Arts (GITIS) (Российский институт театрального искусства—ГИТИС) located in Moscow. It has worn various names since its founding in1878.

[16]*Plastique* or plasticity, a fluid lyrical use of the body. For Russian reaction of Isadora Duncan, see Elena Yushkova, "Isadora Duncan's Dance in Russia: First Impressions and Discussions. 1904–1909." *Journal of Russian American Studies*, 2, no. 1 (May 2018).

[17]Irina Sirotkina, Айседора Дункан: Сто десять лет свободного танца by Ирина Сироткина журнал ТЕАТР №20, 2015 год (One Hundred and Ten Years of Free Dance), https://oteatre.info/ajsedora-dunkan-sto-desyat-let-svobodnogo-tantsa/.

[18]Ibid.

Chen—daughter of a Chinese diplomat and Afro-Caribbean mother—who was studying in Moscow to tour with her group traveling to the Soviet Far East, and there "discovered" Korean dancer Anna Kim.[19] Chen later described Moscow as a "wonderfully stimulating place" characterized by "all kinds of experimental thinkers ... and artistic activity was intensely encouraged."[20]

Attentive and enthusiastic, Tamara appreciated the flexibility of the Vera Maya style which, like Duncan's approach, employed a "natural foot" and classical lines inspired by ancient Greek art. However, the young Tamara discovered that the classes did not offer possibilities for emotional expressiveness, a quality central to Uzbek dance.[21] Yet, she may have learned something of Vera Maya's mechanical *massovyi* dances, which involved large groups of performers imitating machine-like movements of industrialization, much like the earlier *proletkult* productions; she later tried out this approach when developing a group choreography for *Pilla* ("silkworm"), a dance she had originally created as a solo with Usta Olim Kamilov. It proved unsuccessful for Uzbek audiences, and she omitted it from future performances.[22] Several years later, when Si-Lin Chen studied with Vera Maya, the teacher was no longer actively moving during class sessions, and conducted her classes from a chair.[23]

At the Moscow concert of the Communist University of the Toilers of the East (KUTV), Tamara Khanum performed the acrobatic etudes of Vera Maya in the style of so-called "Eastern miniatures," but it was her performances of actual Uzbek folk dances like *Dilhiroj* and *Kari Navo* that won applause. The acclaimed writer, playwright, and political activist Maxim Gorky, who attended the concert, advised people to see Tamara perform. Anatoly Lunacharsky, the first People's Commissar for Education (1917–1929), gave a final speech at the Eastern Evening, in which he called Tamara Khanum "the first swallow of the East."[24]

Lunacharsky was one of the first to notice young Tamara's considerable personal charisma. As she would later explain, "as soon as I take a step out of the wings to meet the audience, I physically feel thousands of invisible threads that quickly arise between me and the audience. The more of these threads, the better my voice sounds, as if I am possessed by thousands of demons, who create my dance."[25] This connection would enable her to connect with people of countless nationalities throughout her career.

---

[19]Ibid.

[20]Elizabeth E. Sine, "The Radical Vision of Si-lan Chen: The Politics of Dance in an Age of Global Crisis." *Small Axe*, 20, no. 2 (2016): 28–43. muse.jhu.edu/article/622467.

[21]Avdeeva, *Tantseval'noe Iskusstvo Uzbekistana*, p. 49.

[22]Ibid.

[23]Leyda, *Footnote to History*, p. 107.

[24]Avdeeva, *Tantseval'noe Iskusstvo Uzbekistana*, p. 49.

[25]Z. S. Safarova, "Art by Tamara Khanum and Roza Karimova." *Middle European Scientific Bulletin*, 7 (Dec. 2020), p. 36. https://doi.org/10.47494/mesb.2020.1.137.

She also caught the attention of Russian theater director Vladimir Nemirovich-Danchenko, who was then staging a production of the Rimsky-Korsakoff opera, *Le Coq D'or* based on Alexander Pushkin's poem, *The Tale of the Golden Cockerel*, in the original Russian *Zolotoy Pyetushok*. He invited her to attend rehearsals and coach the performers on Eastern mannerisms and gait.[26] Not surprisingly, he cast Tamara to portray in dance the role of the Queen of Shemakha, perhaps during the exquisite aria "Hymn to the Sun" created for lyric coloratura soprano. This role matched her Armenian ethnicity, as the "real life" city of Shemakha[27] in Azerbaijan had, at one time, an Armenian population. (The Armenian dancer Armen Ohanian (1887—1976), author of *The Dancer of Shamahka*,[28] wrote of her early life in the town and a devastating 1902 earthquake,[29] which led to Ohanian's family moving to Baku.)

From these innovative directors, the young Central Asian artists learned new ways to broaden their craft to fit the concert stage. Just as the art of Eastern miniature painting had reached a zenith with Kamoliddin Bekhzod (1450–1535), often requiring a brush with a single hair for the most minute details, so too had women's dance developed a delicacy within the circumscribed framework of the *ichkari*. But given a larger canvas, the same aesthetics of miniature paintings could enlarge in scope, as beautifully demonstrated by Uzbek artist Chingiz Akhmarov (1912–1995), who trained at the Surikov Institute in Moscow, creating the memorable frescoes in the foyer of Tashkent's Alisher Navoi Theatre of Opera and Ballet. Embracing the same creative potential, Uzbek dance pioneers would also expand their traditions when they stepped onto the proscenium stage.

Performance in Paris 1925

Both Kari-Yakubov and his young bride passed the auditions in Moscow[30] to be included in the team of artists sent to represent the fledgling USSR at the 1925 World Exhibition of Decorative Arts (*L'Exposition Internationale des Arts*

---

[26]Avdeeva, *Tantseval'noe Iskusstvo Uzbekistana*, p. 49.

[27]Known today as Shemaxi.

[28]Armen Ohanian, *The Dancer of Shemakha*. London: J. Cape, 1922; and Vartan Matiossian and Artsvi Bakshinyan, *A Woman of the World: Armen Ohanian, The Dancer of Shamakha*. Fresno: California State University, 2022.

[29]Shemaxi was earthquake-prone and was devastated many times. The February 13, 1902 earthquake may have been the one Ohanian wrote about, but she said it happened when people were attending Easter services. Armenian Orthodox Easter occurred on April 7,1902.

[30]Laura L. Adams in her work *The Spectacular State* incorrectly asserted that Tamara Khanum only began to tour internationally in the 1930s, and then "under the management" of her husband. But her inaugural tour abroad, as well as subsequent trips, was under the auspices of the Soviet state. Tamara's 1935 performance in London was after the two had divorced and married other people. She appeared with Usta Olim and two other musicians, not with Kari-Yakubov's ensemble.

Decoratifs et Industriels Modernes), "deemed to be where Modernism and Art Deco were born and transported around the world."[31] The Soviet presence at the 1925 Paris Exposition upstaged the French, creating a sensation with the modern design of the national pavilion, the avant-garde quality of the theater presentations, and the unique ethnographic programs featuring Uzbek, Kirghiz, Tatar, Bashkir, Russian, and Ukrainian folklore. "Of all the exhibits on display in Paris, by common consent the Soviet theater arts were considered the most radical and thus were the most consistently discussed, lauded, and attacked."[32] Alexander Rodchenko, Russian modernist artist and designer who was one of the founders of constructivism, declared that "almost all the newspapers are writing about the Russian exhibition, this much hasn't been written about any of the others, and this—is a definite kind of success."[33]

The performers who represented the new republic of Uzbekistan were praised by Julien Autran, who wrote that "the concert ended with a lovely duet, sung and danced by Tamara Khanum and Kari-Yakubov, who delighted and at the insistence of the hall, 'bis' [encore]."[34] Tamara in particular captivated the Parisian public with her lyrical movements of hands and arms. Her performance of the characteristic Uzbek lateral head slide, known as *kigiir buyin* ("bird neck"), reportedly mystified Isadora Duncan, who happened to be in the audience.[35] She came backstage afterward and asked to touch Tamara's neck and arms, thinking the secret in the flexibility could be found in some skeletal oddity.

Paris had other memories for the young couple who had come a long way from their birthplace in the Ferghana Valley. Once while strolling through Parisian streets, Kari-Yakubov paused, alerting Tamara to the Muslim call to prayer. They followed the sound to a mosque and Tamara waited outside while her husband entered. As signified by the honorific prefix of "kari," Mukhitddin was known as a reciter of the Qur'an. Soon his young bride outside the building could hear her husband's voice as he intoned the sacred verses within the mosque. Reportedly, he later began to sing some folk songs and, as a result, received invitations to the homes of local residents.[36]

This Parisian trip also provided Kari-Yakubov with the opportunity to fulfill his long-held wish to hear the voice of the celebrated Russian opera star, Fyodor Chaliapin, who happened to be performing in Paris at the time. The

---

[31] https://artdecosociety.uk/2019/06/01/l-exposition-internationale-des-arts-decoratifs-et-industriels-modernes-1925-paris/.
[32] Irena R. Makaryk, April in Paris: Theatricality, Modernism, and Politics at the 1925 Art Deco Expo. Toronto: University of Toronto Press, 2018, p.4. www.Jstor.Org/Stable/10.3138/J.Ctv2fjwwjz.
[33] Aleksandr Rodchenko , ibid., pp.106-07.
[34] The review was published on July 14, 1925, Bastille Day.
[35] Other versions have this meeting taking place in Germany.
[36] "Uzbek Chaliapin" by Mastur Iskhakov, manuscript shared by Elena Kari-Yakubova. Iskhakov used fragments from the documentary monograph of L. Avdeeva, "Mukhitdin Kari-Yakubov."

couple purchased tickets but were turned away from the entrance to the opera house because Kari-Yakubov was wearing an Uzbek *chapan* robe, which was not considered appropriate Parisian opera attire. The obstacle was eliminated when he purchased the *de rigueur* white tie and tails, but Kari-Yakubov found a way to assert his national identity by draping his Uzbek *chapan* over his shoulders.[37]

At the end of the final performance of the couple in Paris, Tamara Khanum became feverish and fell unconscious after the concert. She had contracted "gangrene of the lungs," i.e., tuberculosis. At age 19, Tamara found herself in a foreign country, seriously ill, unable to speak the local language. However, it happened that there was in Paris at that time a Russian woman who specialized in treating tuberculosis, Rosalie Plekhanova (1856—1949). She was the wife of the Russian revolutionary Georgi Plekhanov, who had died in 1918 after suffering for many years from tuberculosis. Madame Plekhanova had trained as a doctor in Russia but had not been allowed to graduate because she was female. She completed her medical training in Switzerland and had once run her own sanitorium.[38] Madame Plekhanova oversaw Tamara's treatment, sending her to a hospital in Germany. Tamara's recuperation took six months and when she returned to the new Soviet Republic of Uzbekistan, she would need all her strength to fight the battle for women's emancipation. While she had been feted for her dance in Paris, she faced bullets at home for performing those same dances.

---

[37]Ibid.

[38]For more about Rosalia Plekhanova's medical background, see M. T. Iovchuk and Irina Nikolaevna Kurbatova, *Plekhanov*, 1977. Special thanks to Don Van Atta for sharing this book with me.

8 FROM REVOLUTION TO EVOLUTION

A New Path to Dance Education

Public education, a primary goal of the new Soviet government, included arts education. Free dance lessons for children was part of this. Russian ballet training was readily available and had developed generations of technically skilled artists. But in Central Asia, arts training was traditionally achieved through the *ustoz-shagird* system (master–disciple) which was, and still is, common to many Eastern cultures, not only for the arts, but for various crafts and trades. In the female dance genres such as the *sozanda*, this was the system by which not only dance but the many layers of performance were transmitted—poetry, blessings, songs, rhythm patterns, skits, rituals, and costuming. Performed in the confined space of the *ichkari*, women's dance explored movement within the almost stationary body, developing a vocabulary of gestures, known as "*harikat*," and facial expressions reflecting inner emotions. The appreciation of this internal quality was expressed in the Uzbek saying *yaxshi raqqosa bitta joyda o'nayshi mumkin*—"a good dancer can perform in one place."

The American journalist Anna Louise Strong described a dance in the *ichkari* when she traveled in Soviet Central Asia during the turbulent 1920s. As a female, she was permitted access to the women's quarter of an Uzbek home where she saw a little girl dancing in the inner courtyard, accompanied by her mother and grandmother playing *doiras*.

The child's feet tapped at the stones, without leaving their place, there was no room to move in any direction. Nor was such movement needed for the dance, which consisted of the slow swaying of the body and movements of the arms. Mingled with the awkward grace of a child of six was already a naive feminine seductiveness: the baby seemed pleasantly and self-consciously aware that her motions were charming to us.[1]

When American diplomat and writer Eugene Schuyler called the Uzbeks "dance mad natives"[2] after witnessing numerous performances of the *bachas*, his disparaging assessment did acknowledge the central role of dance as expression in Central Asian life. Had he been permitted access to the *ichkari*, he would have found a similar love of dance among the women and girls. As explained by an Uzbek woman who grew up in a Khorezm region village, "our eastern dances use movements of the arms and the head and facial expressions to tell the story of our lives and our culture: about picking cotton, weaving carpets, about our gardens and our vines ... These dances express the states of the soul—both joy and sadness."[3] Or, as one Uzbek diplomat disclosed, there is a saying that if "people live to dance, Uzbeks dance to live."[4]

Significantly, three persons of color born in the West, and all artists themselves, witnessed Uzbek dance in the 1930s USSR - Langston Hughes, Si-Lan Chen, and Paul Robeson. Each one met Tamara Khanum and recognized the powerful heritage of her art. Langston Hughes, "the first American writer translated into any Central Asian language,"[5] witnessed Tamara Khanum on stage, visited her in her Tashkent home, and heard stories of the dancing boys from older Uzbek male musicians. Si-Lan Chen found Uzbek dance captivating and studied with Tamara's teacher and collaborator Usta Olim, adding Central Asian dance to her own performance repertoire of ethnically specific choreographies. Celebrated concert artist and actor Paul Robeson (1898–1976), son of a runaway slave, was keenly aware of the importance of cultural roots. Like Tamara Khanum, he understood the power of art for direct communication, often performing foreign folk songs in over twenty languages including Russian, Basque, and Yiddish.[6] Lloyd L. Brown, friend and biographer of Robeson, described him in a way that is equally applicable to Tamara Khanum, as an artist who "sings the songs of the peoples of the world in the languages of those peoples and touches their hearts ..." Robeson attended the 1937 concert at Moscow's Bolshoi Theater featuring the "Uzbek National Theater, headed by the highly gifted Tamara Khanum. The orchestra was a large one, with instruments both ancient and modern."[7]

[1]Anna Louise Strong, *Red Star in Samarkand*, New York: Coward-McCann, Inc., 1929, pp. 238–39.
[2]Schuyler, *Turkistan*, p. 62.
[3]Bibish, *The Dancer from Khiva*. New York: Grove/Atlantic, Inc., 2008, p. 84.
[4]Personal communication with an Uzbek diplomat in Washington, DC, 2022.
[5]David Chioni Moore, "Colored Dispatches from the Uzbek Border: Langston Hughes' Relevance, 1933–2002." *Callaloo*, 25, no. 4 (2002): 1115–35 (this quote from p. 1118). www.jstor.org/stable/3300273.
[6]Paul Robeson: "Here I Stand" (1999), includes footage of his performances in these languages. https://youtu.be/BUki-v-NvoE?si=6ybOsHtl8Kq86_UV.
[7]"To You Beloved Comrade." Originally published in *New World Review*, April, 1953. Public Domain: Marxists Internet Archive (2008). www.marxists.org/reference/archive/stalin/biographies/1953/04/x01.htm.

The wonderful performance began, unfolding new delights at every turn—ensemble and individual, vocal and orchestral, classic and folk dancing of amazing originality. Could it be possible that a few years before in 1900–1915—these people had been semi-serfs—their cultural expression forbidden, their rich heritage almost lost under the Tsarist oppression's heel?[8]

London International Folk Dance Festival

While Hughes, Chen, and Robeson all met Tamara Khanum in the 1930s during their travels in the USSR, she brought her dance to the West at London's International (European) Folk Dance Festival, held July 15-20, 1935. Organized by the English Folk Dance and Song Society (EFDSS) and the British National Committee on Folk Arts of the League of Nations, "its object was to promote understanding and friendship between nations through the common interest of Folk Dance"[9] – a goal long pursued by Tamara Khanum. However, the event organizers deemed necessary to limit the Festival to European countries,[10] because it involved hosting over five hundred dancers representing seventeen countries along with hundreds of traditional British dancers. When the USSR agreed to participate, Frank Howes of the EFDSS noted that the "presence of the Russian folk dancers at our festival is a very acceptable indication of a desire for more cordial and intimate relations."[11] However, the 38-person Soviet delegation went beyond the ambit of the festival when it included non-European artists along with their Russian, Ukrainian, and Georgian teams. A June 20,1935 article in the Daily Telegraph entitled "Asiatic Dancers" - and attributed to "our own" Moscow correspondent - stated that the "Soviet authorities have decided to send three professional ballet dancers from the State theaters in Tashkent to exhibit Usbek [sic], Tajik, and other Central Asian native dances…."[12] In addition to Tamara Khanum, who was identified by name, the newspaper mentioned that "a professional dancer from the Tashkent Jewish theatre will also display the local dances of his race in Turkestan."[13] The latter was undoubtedly the 21-year-old Isaqar Aqilov, known for his spectacular *charkh do zoni*, knee spins. The third "ballet dancer" may have been his new bride, Margarita,

---

[8]Ibid.

[9]Frank Howes. "The International (European) Folk Dance Festival." *Journal of the English Folk Dance and Song Society* 2 (1935): p. 3. http://www.jstor.org/stable/4521057.

[10]Ibid.

[11]Ibid., p. 8.

[12]Cited by Rosa Vercoe, "How they met Tamara Khanum in London and the secret of Usto Olim Komilov's turban." Voices on Central Asia online, October 22, 2019. I am indebted to Rosa Vercoe for her detailed account of the Uzbek delegation, illustrated with historic photographs. Note that the newspaper account mentions "ballet dancers," a frequent and continuing conflation of terms by Uzbeks to distinguish professional Uzbek dancers as artists.

[13]Daily Telegraph, cited by Vercoe, ibid.

from Tajikistan. Aqilov was prevented by the NKVD from leaving the USSR when it was discovered he had family in England.[14] The only dancer from Uzbekistan who arrived in London was Tamara Khanum, accompanied by her mentor and collaborator, Usta Olim Kamilov, and the accomplished musicians Tokhtasyn Jalilov and Abdukodir Ismoilov. The well-coordinated schedule of more than one thousand participants combined formal concerts at the Royal Albert Hall attended by King George V and Queen Mary, and several public performances in various parks blessed by good weather –"never has the English climate behaved better to foreign visitors."[15] When the festival participants traveled by steamer to Greenwich for a special performance, the shared dance enthusiasm led to "the fraternization among the teams, the tongueless exchange of courtesies through feet, as people without a common language began to teach each other their dances."[16]

The Central Asian performers both captivated and puzzled audiences. During the festival Tamara Khanum, who performed Katta O'yin, Pilla, Kari Navo, and Gul O'yin, was described by dance critic Arthur Batchelor as "a lady of a pronounced Mongol type" who as "the smiling but inscrutable enigma "gave an interesting solo dance "which reminded one of a Nautch."[17] He characterized Usta Olim Kamilov as a "marvelous musician" and an "aged Asiatic" who "really thrilled to the marrow every musician and dancer in the hall"[18] including the king and queen who gave a special award to the doirist.[19]

Tamara Khanum's dances, as well as the ecstatic pagan ritual of the Romanian Călușari, left some English folk dance purists nonplussed. Douglas Kennedy, head of the EFDSS, in his closing remarks to members, diplomatically suggested that "we should not be so afraid of the unusual or the unknown," reminding them that "joy is a human appreciation of an internal resurrection – a renewal of energy, spiritual and physical."[20]

> The woman dancer from Uzbek [sic] illustrates her own form of 'joy.' Some of us may dislike it as a form, but I think that is due to our lack of comprehension and to our own immediate environment and upbringing…We must try to view dancing not only in terms of physical activity, but to include an artistic

---

[14]For the rest of his life, Isaqar Aqilov was never allowed to travel out of the USSR. The story of Aqilov's removal from the London delegation was relayed to me by Rafael Nektalov, Coordinator of the Congress of Bukharian Jews of the USA and Canada and Editor-in-Chief of The Bukharian Times.
[15]Frank Howes, "The International (European) Folk Dance Festival." Journal of the English Folk Dance and Song Society 2 (1935): p. 2. http://www.jstor.org/stable/4521057.
[16]Ibid., p. 12.
[17]Arthur Batchelor, "A concert of Europe." In: E. F. D. S. S. News. The Magazine of the English Folk Dance and Song Society, Number 42, Volume IV, Part 8, p. 251–252. Cited by Vercoe, ibid.
[18]Batchelor, ibid., p. 250, cited by Vercoe, ibid.
[19]For details on their tribute to Kamilov, see Vercoe, ibid.
[20]Douglas Kennedy, "The Conclusion of the Conference," Journal of the English Folk Da 2nce and Song Society 2 (1935): p. 108. http://www.jstor.org/stable/4521072.

perception based on sympathetic feeling and a real understanding of the effect of rhythm on the human being from inside. Then we shall know what it is like to be a Călușari or an Uzbek dancer.[21]

People's Artist of Uzbekistan Galia Izmailova explained that most Uzbek dances "are imbued with deep feeling. A dancer must express these sentiments with her entire being so the emotion is actually experienced emotionally." Izmailova emphasized that "traditionally women's dances were strictly solos. Now we have *massovyi* choreographies with over a hundred dancers participating. These pieces are presented at large public gatherings such as events held at our sports stadium"[22] (Figure 8.1). But when the dance expanded into the public performance sphere, the opportunity for greater movement revealed the need for uniform, formalized training that became central to the development of professional dance in Uzbekistan. Bernara Karieva—also People's Artist of Uzbekistan—noted that "the old dances were often quite stationary" but "modern choreographies use greater space and performers utilize broader, more expansive movements."[23] People's Artist of Uzbekistan Gavkhar Matyokubova understood that performances in

FIGURE 8.1 Tamara Khanum, wearing her Bukharan velvet coat with *zardozi* embroidery, performing with other artists for workers during the construction of the Great Ferghana Canal in 1939.
Photo source: Author's personal archive. Photographer unknown.

---

[21]Ibid.

[22]Personal communication with Galia Izmailova, cited in Gray, "Uzbek Women's Dances, Past and Present." *Viltis*, 43, no. 6 (March–April 1985): 8–9.

[23]Personal communication with Bernara Karieva, cited in Gray, ibid.

stadiums, "if the width of the stage is 80 meters, the dancer is required to move quickly to perform the dance. If you walked half a meter in half a second, now you need to walk ten meters. In a sense, the grace of the dance is lost, and dexterity takes its place."[24]

Tamara Khanum had experienced informal dance transmittal in her childhood, listening, watching, and copying the songs and dance she had seen in the *ichkari* of her neighbors, as well as the repertoire of the female dancers known as *yallachi*. Through Usta Olim Kamilov and Yusuf-Kyzyk Shakarjanov, she entered the *ustoz-shagird* system, learning from them the *usuls* and movements used by professional Uzbek boy dancers. The first dance co-created with Usta Olim was *Pilla*, depicting the gestures and tasks of sericulture, was set to *doira* accompaniment only. Understanding the centrality of rhythm in Uzbek dance, Usta Olim taught Tamara the elements of *Katta O'yin*, the famous dance of the *bachas*. From this they developed the seminal rhythm and dance etude, *Doira Dars*, basic to all Uzbek dance training, and still used today in classes throughout Uzbekistan.

The traumatic experiences endured by these young dance pioneers provided the impetus for future choreographies. As Mukarram recalled of the Basmachi attacks, "we all survived the raids of these desperate, atrociously cruel thugs." Several of the first dance productions centered on the early struggle for female emancipation. One work entitled *Ballerina* (later called "*Gulnara*" after the heroine) followed the story of a young worker who, on the advice of her teacher, leaves the collective farm to study dance in Tashkent in spite of opposition from her father. Another piece, set by Isaqar Aqilov, portrayed a deceptive practice of the Emir of Bukhara who sent his troups, disguised as *Luli*, to visit the home of Jews and report beautiful young girls in the family.

When Tamara Khanum trained in Moscow at the theater school in 1924, she was 18 years old, too late to begin a career in ballet, if that had ever been a goal. She understood her own limitations and, while traveling back on the train from the 1937 *Dekada* in Moscow, admitted to Mukarram that "I am a 'lapar' artist, but you are a performer of ballet and national dance," and encouraged her to keep working to become a better ballerina.[25] Still, Tamara Khanum understood that a systematic, formalized approach to dance training was required for the evolution of stage dance in Uzbekistan. The example readily at hand was the well-developed system of Russian ballet, offering young students their first experience in a dance class with clear structure. Ballet terms entered the Uzbek dance lexicon, at times confusing outsiders when certain words with very specific meaning in the West took on a broader meaning in Uzbekistan. For example, "ballet" was sometimes applied to any stage dance and "ballerina" could indicate any professional dancer. The term "ballet

---

[24]Gavkhar Matyokubova, quoted by Khulkar Khamroeva, *Gavkhar Matyokubova Izhod va Ilm Integratsiyasi*. Tashkent: Monografiya, 2022, pp. 194–95 (translator unknown).
[25]Mukarram Turganbaeva cited in Rakhimov, *Mukarramkhonim "Tanovar"i*, p. 32.

master"—conventionally defined as the person responsible for training, rehearsing, and sometimes choreographing works for a ballet company—came to be used in Uzbekistan as a general term for a choreographer, although not specifically a maker of ballets. Thus, a Soviet ballet encyclopedia, published in Moscow, listed Usta Olim Kamilov, as a "ballet master," acknowledging his role as a creator of Uzbek dances even though he had no training in ballet.[26] As noted by Uzbek dancer and scholar Gul'sum Khamraeva, the term "ballet" is used abroad to distinguish Bakhor as a professional ensemble and not an ethnographic group.[27] As recently as 2022, the members of the Bakhor Ensemble were identified as ballet dancers in promotional materials. This linguistic confusion may partially explain the claim by post-Soviet Western scholars that Uzbek stage dance was based on ballet.

Young dancers in Uzbekistan did benefit from systematic ballet training, learning body alignment and spatial awareness as well as the physicality of presentation on a proscenium stage. Dancing within the four walls of the *ichkari* now evolved to dancing within three walls[28] because their performances would take place in a space that was open only to the one side where the audience was seated. Central Asian women's dance, with its improvisational nature, emerged from centuries of a "site-specific" performance tradition to explore the possibilities of the European concert stage while at about the same time modern dance in the West began to shift away from structured choreography in the proscenium setting to explore improvisational movement in other venues. Ballet, especially *maso* choreographies, required a different spatial awareness as dancers entered into the geometry of stage patterns. Here, the sophisticated, intricate heritage of Central Asian architecture and design appeared in the staging of Mukarram Turgunbaeva, whose diagrams of stage "figures" sometimes looked like the designs of the *suzani* tapestry, with spinning suns and flowers.

But not all in the dance community were keen on adopting methods from ballet, which was, after all, a *European* classical dance form. "Some Uzbek dancers were afraid that it would ... kill Uzbek dance" and that the "frozen" hand positions and "hard back" of the ballet canon would be harmful to the inherently lyrical Central Asian styling, and not allow the dancer to "open and close the rose bud,"[29] a phrase often used to describe the flowing movements of Ferghana dance, but Yusuf-Kyzyk Shakarjanov and Usta Olim disagreed. They were both well-versed in the "plasticity" of Ferghana dance and had taught it to Tamara Khanum, Mukarram Turgunbaeva, Rozia Karimova, and Galia Izmailova. With that technique firmly

---

[26] *Balet: Entsiklopediya*, Iu. N. Grigorovich, ed., Moscow, 1981; entry for Usta Olim Kamilov, p. 235.

[27] Gul'sum Rakhmedova Khamraeva, *Obshchie zakony stsenicheskoy choreographii natsionalnaya obraz tantsa* (PhD diss.). Tashkent: Institute of Art Studies, 1986, p. 3.

[28] Development of the impact of this change in performance venue emerged in conversation with Dana Tai Soon Burgess.

[29] Avdeeva, *Galia Izmailova*. Tashkent: izdatel'stvo literatury i iskusstva im. Gafura Gulyama, 1975, p. 66.

ingrained, they believed that dancers could also learn from European classical dance while keeping it distinct from their native style.

The fundamental difference between ballet and Central Asian was as Avdeeva emphasized: "'European dance' is first of all a dance of the legs, the hands only accompany the dance." Uzbek classical dance "like all classical dances of the East, is the dance of the whole body," and the movement of the hands grow from movements of the body, the movement of the case "grow from rhythmically complex dance moves."[30]

Founding a Dance School

In 1933, Tamara Khanum, together with Usta Olim Kamilov, founded Uzbekistan's first official dance school. Dedicated dance professionals like Vera Gubskaya (1906–1953), who was a graduate of Moscow Ballet School and who had danced leading ballet roles such as Odette-Odile in *Swan Lake*, *Kitri* in *Don Quixote*, and *Zarema* in *Fountain of Bakhchisarai*, joined the faculty of the Ballet School of Tamara Khanum. She taught there from 1935 until the school was closed in 1941 because of the war. (She returned to teaching after the war years.) Gubskaya also organized and taught ballet classes at the *Dom Pionerov*, where the State provided free classes for children in many subjects. She collaborated with Tamara Khanum and Usta Olim in choreographing elements for the hybrid folk and ballet production of *Gulyandom*.

Another early faculty member was Yevgeniya Obukhova (1874–1948), a graduate of the St. Petersburg Theater School. She worked at the Mariinsky Theater from 1992 to 1910, dancing roles in *La Bayadere*. She taught at Tamara Khanum's school in 1935–1941 and the ballet studio at the Navoi Theatre of Opera and Ballet from 1944 to 1948. Many of her students emerged as Uzbekistan's leading artists of that first generation of "trained" dancers—Galia Izmailova, Mukarram Turgunbaeva, Halima Kamilova, Gulnara Mavaeva, Rajab Tanguriev, and Klara Yusupova. Several of them became "crossover" artists who mastered ballet as well as Uzbek dance.

In this new generation of professional dancers, Galia Izmailova was a pivotal figure who was able to blend Uzbek and other Eastern styles without the stiff shoulder girdle that characterizes traditional ballet technique. A petite woman, she also performed traditional Central Asian spins up on the balls of her feet, lengthening the look of her legs, creating more height. Galia Izmailova made Uzbek dance history by performing the role of the legendary *Simurgh* bird *en pointe* in the 1943 production of the "hybrid" ballet *Ak Bilyak*.[31] The choreography had been created by Fyodor Lopukhov (1886–1973) who, together

---

[30]Ibid., p. 65.
[31]Ibid., p. 89.

with Mukarram Turgunbaeva who set the Uzbek dances, carefully blended ballet with Uzbek dance, moving toward the creation of a new genre—Uzbek ballet—distinct from Uzbek stage dance with its roots in traditional dance.

Learning from Ballet Pedagogy

Ballet provided a system of basic positions and terminology which has proven effective in creating awareness of posture and body placement. The upper body ballet *port de bras* harmoniously suits the lyrical fluidity of the arms, hands, and upper torso in Central Asian women's dance. But other elements, such as extension of the legs, required for movements like *arabesques*, are not used in traditional Uzbek dance. Ballet posture training had the benefit of creating a standardized "look" for a corps of dancers, but at times fought against native Uzbek styling, such as Ferghana dance, with its slight forward inclination of the upper torso. The tight balletic position of the shoulder girdle and neck froze the very muscles that needed to remain relaxed and flexible for head and shoulder isolations and trembling vibrations characteristic of Central Asian dance.[32] Also antithetical to Uzbek dance was the "turn out" of the legs, knees, and feet. The modesty of Central Asian culture requires that women keep their feet relatively close together. Deep pliés are absent from women's dance, although they appear in Khorezm men's dances that imitate animals and elements of horseback riding. And, as Avdeeva wrote about Uzbek women's dance, "there is no leap in Uzbek dance."[33] Other hallmark gestures such as elaborate wrist circles, along with undulations of hands and arms[34] and head slides, are entirely absent from classical ballet, although in the wrist flourishes, there is a bit of kinship with baroque traditions.

As dance training evolved and changed, so did the name of the dance school, eventually becoming the Choreographic Institute. Students trained in both Uzbek dance and ballet but specialized in one of the forms for their professional careers. Even the professional Uzbek folk ensembles today still begin rehearsals with a ballet barre, before moving on to center floor drills of Central Asian spins accompanied by *doira* rhythms and music played by folk musicians. Prospective students are evaluated according to body type, musicality, coordination, and other qualities.

---

[32] People's Artist of Uzbekistan Kizlarkhon Dusmukhamedova commented when viewing a ballet-trained American dancer attempting to perform Uzbek dance that her style was "too stiff, too European, too tight through the shoulders." Personal conversation with author during dance rehearsal in Washington, DC.

[33] Avdeeva, in her introduction to E. A. Petrosova, *Karakalpakskii Tanets*, Tashkent: Literature and Art Press named for Gafur Gulyam, 1976, p. 233.

[34] The notable exception is, of course, *The Dying Swan*, which considering the popularity of "exotic" themes and technique at the time it was created may owe its distinctive arm undulations to Eastern dance forms.

Contribution of Rozia Karimova

From the first generation of Uzbek dancers, People's Artist Rozia Karimova (1916–2011) trained with both Tamara Khanum and Usta Olim. Born in Kazan, she was an ethnic Tatar and, like many young dancers of the era, an orphan whose situation allowed them to study dance without interference from family. She participated in the first dance ensembles, and was among the Uzbek dance artists who during the Second World War performed at the front as well as for those in hospitals in Uzbekistan. Rozia Karimova was one of the group of artists from Uzbekistan chosen to perform in a concert at the historic 1943 Tehran Conference of WWII Allies Stalin, Churchill, and Roosevelt.

The *ustoz–shagird* tradition of dance transmission required a close, in-person relationship between master and student, which did not allow for the broad dissemination of training. As a result, "Uzbek dance existed only in the memory of its performers and spectators."[35] Rozia Karimova sought to remedy this and was the first to create "full-fledged textbooks. For the first time in history, she recorded Uzbek dance as a choreographic work," describing, designating, and creating "a unique system of movements, positions, gestures."[36] As the author of a remarkable series of books, Rozia Karimova presented works devoted to each dance "school" as well as other volumes, some focusing on the choreographies in the repertoire of the Bakhor Ensemble. The books provided an introduction to the basic postures of the different styles of Uzbek dance and detailed instruction on the group and solo dances, creations of Uzbekistan's most famous choreographers. Published by the Institute of Art Research named for Hamza Hakim-zade Niyazi, the books were issued under the supervision of the Ministry of Culture with the goal of "creating a manual for Uzbek dance intended for teachers of folk dance and ballet ensembles, leaders of amateur art groups" covering "the basics of Ferghana dance—basic positions, movements, rhythms" and dances created from these elements.[37]

The generosity of this act of sharing Uzbekistan's repertoire of the most famous stage dances deserves consideration. These are not simple step progressions of folk dance done in a line or circle, but they involve a level of dance competence beyond that of a simple amateur. Some choreographies require a proficiency in fast spins and deep backbends, but with training, any dance group could recreate and perform these pieces.

In the Soviet era, many amateur dance ensembles existed throughout Uzbekistan; some were originally connected with trade unions, like the Parvoz Folk Song and Dance Ensemble, which was financially supported by the Tashkent

---

[35]Z. S. Safarova, "Art by Tamara Khanum and Rozia Karimova." *Middle European Scientific Bulletin*, 7 (Dec. 2020): 38. https://doi.org/10.47494/mesb.2020.1.137.
[36]Ibid., pp. 38–39.
[37]Introduction from the Institute of Art Studies to R. Karimova, *Ferganskii Tanets*. Tashkent: Literatura i Isskustvo, 1973, p. 3.

Aircraft Corporation. They rehearsed three times a week, in three-hour sessions, creating a "diversified program lasting an hour and a half made up of Uzbek songs and dances which alternate with the songs and dances of other peoples of the Soviet Union and foreign countries."[38]

Enriched by her own experience as an accomplished dancer, Karimova describes the basic positions of the feet, arms, and hands, then provides details about some of the characteristic movements. The books include instructions for specific, well-known choreographies with measure-by-measure explanations of the movements, augmented by stage diagrams. Costume descriptions, as well as the musical notation for each dance, make it possible to recreate these choreographies.

Rozia Karimova thoughtfully adapted from ballet the pedagogical device of defining basic positions of the feet, arms, hands, and head, analyzing the distinct qualities of the three dance "schools"—Ferghana, Bukhara, and Khorezm. Developed in the spatially limited environment of the *ichkari*, footwork in Uzbek dance remains simple and grounded, so Karimova applied the same basic positions of the feet to all three genres. Lacking complex footwork, Uzbek dance focuses primarily on intricate movements of the upper torso, the arms, head, and the face.

In Karimova's system of positions or poses, the arms travel along the same pathway. In first, both arms are extended out to the sides; second, both arms are held above the head; third, one arm lowered to extend out from the side; fourth, the extended arm is brought across in front of the body; fifth, the remaining raised hand is lowered and extended out to the side; sixth, both hands are extended forward in front of the body at chest level; seventh, both hands are brought to rest at the waist. The regional distinctions of the dance zones most clearly emerge in the different positions of the hands as the arms move through these poses. For Ferghana dance, the fingertips point skyward, with the palm facing out. (Intriguingly, in two separate early photographs of Tamara Khanum and Mukarram Turgunbaeva, they both have their fingers touching in second position, where the arms are held above the head, but now it is done with a slight space between the hands.) In Bukharan dance, palms also face outward, and at times upward, but they are flat with fingers and thumb held tightly together. Khorezm dance shows a somewhat surprising hand position that is also characteristic in the Turkish *Kara Deniz* (Black Sea) men's dances, with fingers relaxed and hanging down from the wrist, from which they tremble. Rozia Karimova also noted differences in the characteristic head movements for each regional style as well as variations in the distinct *salom*—or bow—used in each style.

Through Karimova's efforts, the *Doire Dars* was transcribed and published in 1987 with the goal of training dancers to understand the basic dance *usuls* and the movement they normally accompanied. In this, the lineage of past dancers and doirists like Usta Olim Kamilov, Yusufjon-Kyzyk Shakarjanov, and the generations

---

[38]Allan Davidov, "World of Song and Dance." *Soviet Uzbekistan*, no. 9 (287) (1986): 20.

who preceded them should be recognized. Some of the movements had no names, only links to certain musical rhythms, but those names were sometimes obscure and did not always correspond to the meaning of the dance movements. Karimova gave the names to the majority of movements according to their semantic meaning, creating an Uzbek dance vocabulary.[39] She affirmed that the ubiquitous *shoh* rotation in place is only done turning to the left, and this is also the case in Tajik dance.

Dance Training

After Independence, the dance school changed again. The 1997 decree by the President of the Republic of Uzbekistan, I. A. Karimov, gave a new status to the "Tashkent State Higher School of National Dance and Choreography" as a specialized educational institution with the goal of "developing national dance and the art of choreography." It served as the primary training institute for future professional dancers and dance educators, not only for Uzbekistan, but for other parts of Central Asia as well. Daily classes included several hours of dance training along with an academic curriculum taught in regular schools. Because many children came from outside of Tashkent, and even other republics, some lived in the school's dormitory.

Children were accepted into the school according to body type, musicality, and flexibility. The preferred body type for female dancers began to shift away from the rounder, more "womanly" figure of early dance pioneers toward an aesthetic ideal of the slender, long-limbed ballerina, even for those specializing in folk dance.

State Examinations at the Choreographic Institute

Final examinations determine the professional future of the young dancers. Dance experts, often directors of various ensembles, are the judges evaluating the students' abilities. Together the dancers in the graduating class present barre exercises, then move to center floor. As a group, they perform *massovyi* choreographies; individuals also present a solo dance. Students are graded on a scale of one to five, with five being the highest grade. When their marks are announced, the students are then offered positions according to their achievements. Those who earn "five" receive invitations from the Tashkent top ensembles, the most prestigious for the girls being the Bakhor Ensemble. Others might be invited to join companies outside of the capital of Tashkent. Their employment would last at least twenty

---

[39]Rozia Karimova, *Urok uzbeksyaya tantsa*. Tashkent: O'qituvchi Publishing, 1987, p. 3.

years, with most retiring from the stage by age forty. Some leave the profession even earlier upon marriage because the dancer's new husband and his family might not consent to her continuing in dance. But other dancers could take a leave of absence during pregnancy and return after giving birth.

In 2020, the dancescape of Uzbekistan changed dramatically with a new name and a new building. On the initiative of Uzbekistan's President Shavkat Mirziyoyev, the dance school that was founded in 1933 now had an elevated status as the "Uzbekistan State Academy of Choreography,"[40] and the "long-awaited complex of buildings of the State Academy of Choreography of Uzbekistan appeared as a triumph."[41] The school's longtime rector, Shukhrat Makhmutovich Tokhtasimov, remains at the helm. Leading choreographers and specialists like People's Artist of Uzbekistan Kadir Muminov have joined the faculty, bringing with them years of performance experience and specialized training. With beautiful new facilities, the Academy planned scientific conferences on different aspects of dance, inviting specialists from around the world to participate. When the COVID-19 quarantine eliminated the possibility of in-person gatherings, the conferences were held in a virtual format but with local experts participating in person. Faculty members increasingly began to publish short essays on various aspects of Uzbek dance in online journals. More than ever, the door opened for active communication between dance scholars. A growing global interest in Uzbek dance, the revivification of the Bakhor Ensemble, and new choreographic collaborations on the part of Navoi Theatre[42] all suggest an exciting new chapter in the history of Uzbek women's dance as the future of art looks increasingly toward Asia.

[40]Online newspaper article "Uzbekistan State Choreography Academy established," 05/02/2020, Uzdaily.com www.uzdaily.uz/en/post/54581?fbclid=IwAR1d2LFE5uIX0Q2BppyBnq-dKLBbj7iK4d-1us9yLebgIrg2pQBNe_BggN0.
[41]Statement by the Academy's Rector, Shukhrat Makhmutovich Tokhtasimov, in a post on the Facebook page for the O'zbekiston davlat xoreografiya akademiyasi.
[42]Officially, the Navoi Theater is GABT, the State Academic Bolshoi Theater of Opera and Ballet named for Alisher Navoi.

PART FOUR

TERROR AND WAR

9 UPROOTED: KOREANS AND CRIMEAN TATARS

The dance legacy of the Silk Road comes from countless generations of humans who carried their embodied dance heritage into Central Asia, mingling with settled groups. Sometimes these cultural exchanges grew out of commerce, but other encounters resulted from violent conquest, when entire populations were captured and enslaved, uprooted from their homeland and carried off to new regions. Natural catastrophes, famine, and political upheaval also pushed people to voluntarily migrate in hope of a better life. The details of these arrivals in past centuries may be lost, but during the Soviet era, several ethnic groups were subjected to mandatory migration when they were deported from their homes by order of Stalin. Koreans and Crimean Tatars were two such groups who were sent to Uzbekistan and, in both cases, the Soviet government used suspicions of espionage and disloyalty to justify the extreme cruelty of the relocations, which led to a high death toll in both communities. After surviving the initial years of privation, both groups created music and dance ensembles, preserving their folk traditions. The consequences of these deportations continue to ripple down through many generations, enriching Uzbekistan's dance culture.

Origins of the *Koryo-Saram*

Koreans known as *Koryo-Saram*—literally, "Korean people"—first arrived on Russian soil after 1861, when Tsar Alexander II encouraged the development of sparsely populated regions in the Far East that had been recently acquired by treaties with China in 1858 and 1860. "On 27 April 1861, the Russian tsarist government enacted a law to encourage and expedite the migration of the Russian peasants into the Amur and the Maritime Provinces (the Primorskaya Oblast). According to the law, not only Russians but foreign immigrants were also granted various benefits from the government as new settlers."[1] During the late nineteenth century, peasants from the northern area of Korea seeking to avoid conditions of "famine, punitive taxation, and tyranny of government officers and landowners" under the Joseon Dynasty began to move north into this neighboring region of Russia to farm the land there.[2]

By the 1880s, about 761 families had migrated into the area. There they created a Korean theater, keeping their traditions alive in the new land. The political disruption and national trauma created by the vicious and brutal 1895 assassination by Japanese *Ronin* of Korea's Queen Min[3] marked increased Japanese influence. This worsened when Japanese colonial rule of Korea began in 1910, motivating some Koreans to seek better conditions in Russia. Although the Japanese occupation of Korea brought more settlers into Russia, it also made those immigrants susceptible to Russian accusations of collaboration with the Japanese government, because many of the *Koryo-Saram* still had vulnerable families under Japanese jurisdiction. In 1937, with the goal of "frontier zone cleansing," Stalin announced the "deportation of all Korean population from the border regions of the far east,"[4] relocating them to the southern area of Kazakhstan, as well as Uzbekistan and land near the Aral Sea to work in agrarian or fishery kolkhozes.[5] The decree was delayed only long enough for people to harvest their crops, then Soviet troops came to homes without warning, sometimes allowing as little as 30 minutes for families to collect belongings, documents, and food before boarding cattle cars for the four thousand mile train journey west which lasted between thirty and forty days.[6] Of the 172,000 deportees, about five hundred died on the "Ghost Trains," so-called because Koreans feared that the unburied bodies of their loved ones, callously dumped along the railway, would turn into ghosts.[7] Other estimates state that "several thousand people died due to diseases, starvation, and train incidents."[8] More deaths followed when the *Koryo-Saram* arrived in Central Asia, encountering bleak living conditions, even digging holes in the earth for basic shelter. Exposed to severe climate, disease, and starvation, an estimate of between

---

[1]Woosung Lee, "The Korean's Migration to the Russian Far East and their Deportation to Central Asia: from the 1860s to 1937" (MA Dissertation), University of Oregon, 2012, p. 9.
[2]Ibid., p. 12.
[3]Planned by the Japanese with Korean collaborators; 48 *Ronin* were later tried for the murder but let off by the Japanese government.
[4]Decree No. 1428-326ss, signed by Stalin and Molotov on August 21, 1937. Cited by Woosung Lee, *Korean Migration*, p. 68.
[5]Lee, *Korean Migration*, p. 80.
[6]Victoria Kim, "Lost and Found in Uzbekistan." 2015. https://centralasiaprogram.org/initiatives/cultures-and-societies-initiative/lost-and-found-in-uzbekistan-the-korean-story.
[7]Y. David Chung and Matt Dibble. *Koryo Saram—The Unreliable People*. Documentary film (2007). http://www.koryosaram.net/about_film.html.
[8]Lee, *Korean Migration*, p. 75.

ten and twenty-five percent[9] of the deportees died as a result. The communal trauma of the forced deportation of the Koryo Saram proved devastating to their economic, social, and cultural development.

While the majority of *Koryo-Saram* were settled in southern Kazakhstan, others were sent to Tashkent, Samarkand, Namangan, and Ferghana. Some were relocated to Nukus, participating in the fishing industry that existed at that time around the Aral Sea. Finally, in 1947, they were allowed to have passports, but only for use within the area of Soviet Central Asia. Despite these difficult conditions, dance was so deeply embedded in their culture that "during all those years, Koreans living outside of their ethnic motherland performed their folk dances at family or traditional holiday celebrations."[10] Even as early as the Zhou dynasty (1046–256 BCE) the region that became Korea was described by the Chinese as "a land of dance and music that is forever filled with vigor and vitality."[11] The *Koryo-Saram* who immigrated from the Joseon Kingdom to the Russian Far East came primarily "from the Northern Provinces of the Korean Peninsula: Hamgyŏng-do and Pyŏngan-do. Therefore, they were familiar with the regional peculiarities of Korean folk dances."[12] When the 1945 division of the peninsula divided their homeland into North and South Korea, the Soviet Union aligned with the communist North. The Cold War narrowed opportunities for cultural exchange, so only the dances of North Korea were known in the USSR, influencing the folk dances of Soviet Koreans.[13] The *Koryo-Saram* were further alienated from their roots when they were forbidden by the Soviet government to teach the Korean language. As a result, successive generations lost their mother tongue, but the Soviet regime allowed folk music and dance and Korean cultural centers opened in Bukhara, Samarkand, and Nukus.

By 1955, a Korean Music and Drama Theater was established within Tashkent's Theatrical Institute, which trained young people for careers in the performing arts.[14] In Uzbekistan and Kazakhstan alike, professional, semi-professional, and amateur dance groups developed, finding a place within national celebrations. One North Korean dancer, Hwang Jeong Ok, graduated from Tashkent's Choreographic Institute and became a member of Uzbekistan's celebrated Bakhor Dance Ensemble. With her expertise she "laid the foundation of the Soviet Korean

---

[9]Typhus and malaria took an estimated 165,00–282,00 lives.
[10]German Kim, "Dances of Divided Korea on Central Asian Soil." *S/N Korean Humanities*, 7, no. 1 (2021): 74.
[11]Zhou Dynasty text *Chou-Ye-Chu'un Kwan Ju*, cited in Heyman, *The Traditional Music and Dance of Korea*. Seoul: Song Lim Printing Co., Ltd., p. 9.
[12]German Kim, *Dances of Divided Korea*, p. 80.
[13]Ibid.
[14]Ibid., p. 81.

ensemble *Chen-Chun*."[15] Later, in 1989, Artistic Director Yelizaveta Kim founded Ensemble *Sin-Sen* under the auspices of Uzbekistan's Union of Theatrical Workers.

Korean and Uzbek Dance Commonalities

Distinct, ancient, and intricate, traditional Korean dance shares some commonalities with Uzbek dance. The "rising and falling" characteristic of Korean dance reflects a "groundedness," and the creation of level changes by bending the knee occurs in several Uzbek styles that emphasize bent knees in some basic steps. Both dance traditions share shoulder isolations and are highly gendered, with women having their own special dances. Rhythms can be quite complex and often shift during a piece, increasing in speed and intensity to a point of ecstasy, similar to the pattern noticed in the dances of *bachas*. In certain pieces such as *chonggoch'um*, the dancer plays an hourglass-shaped drum attached to her body; in *popkoch'um*, the traditional Buddhist dance, women dance while using mallets to play complex rhythms on three, five, seven, or even nine separate drums hung from standing frames.

Regal and elegant, Korean court dances employ the use of extended sleeves called *saekdong* to create graceful, delayed lines. This also occurs among Tajiks in historically Sogdian areas like Samarkand, suggesting a shared link to Han and Tang Dynasty sleeve dance traditions, although the sleeves in the Sogdian/Tajik dances are not as long as those in Korean dances. Both kinds of sleeve dances have a wrist flick that propels movement of the sleeves. But while Korean court dances have been preserved and are still performed, the Soviet political ideology that brought an end to the khans and emirs in Turkestan may have also ended the Uzbek court dance tradition. Only some solo dances seem to have survived.

Koreans and Uzbeks share a shamanic tradition, but during the Soviet era, shamanism in Uzbekistan came under attack from the central government, which viewed it as a vestige of backwardness and superstition, so shamanism was practiced surreptitiously. In Korea, shamanism is a living tradition; people attend public and private ceremonies, known as *kut*, consulting shamans for auspicious undertakings and when faced with difficulties. Most Korean shamans are female and, in dance, turn to the left, just as in Central Asian traditions with links to the Sogdian Whirl. In an interpretive stage version of the *salp'uri*, a dance to expel demons, the left–right distinction continues with the fan held in the right hand and the shaman's bells held in the left.

The farmer dance *nongak*, traditionally performed by males—although now some women can be seen among the drummers—contains spinning elements like

---

[15]Kim, *Dances of Divided Korean*, p. 81, on the contributions of Hwang Jeong Ok.

traveling in a counterclockwise path around the performance space and turning to the left when performing leaping sagittal spins. This dance also contains circular movements of the head, reminiscent of hair tossing in the Afghan *Attan* dance, but Korean dancers wear special hats called *sangmo* with a long, thin ribbon attached to a flexible rod that creates patterns in the air.

Korean dance traveled beyond their uprooted community to find inclusion into the repertoire of prestigious dance artists and companies in Uzbekistan. Tamara Khanum sought out the *Koryo-Saram* soon after their arrival in Uzbekistan, eventually visiting all their collective farms, watching and listening to "beautiful Korean songs and dances." With her deeply held belief that music and dance reveal the "soul of a people," she had continually expanded her repertoire of songs and dances of various nationalities. With the help of singer Olga Kogay, she learned, performed, and recorded the Korean song *Doraji taryeong*,[16] and included a Korean dance as part of her growing repertoire of international songs and dances. (Tamara's Korean dance costume is part of her personal museum collection.[17]) In 1956, she met North Korean dancer and choreographer Zhao Dexian[18] (1913–2002), who was visiting the USSR. Tamara Khanum's inclusion of Korean songs and dances in her concert repertoire was deeply appreciated by the *Koryo-Saram,* because she shared their cultural heritage with world audiences.[19] Galia Izmailova included a Korean dance in her repertoire,[20] as did Uzbekistan's Bakhor Ensemble, adding a Korean drum dance to their concert program. Kizlarkhon Dusmukhamedova frequently performed a Korean dance choreographed by Diana Kwon San.

North Korean dancer Hwang Jeong Ok was studying in Moscow when the 20th Party Congress denounced Stalin's "cult of personality." As a result of this political development, "Pyongyang urgently forced all North Korean students to return home" but, defiantly, Hwang Jeong Ok refused to follow the order and ended up in Uzbekistan, where she graduated from the Tashkent Choreographic School and eventually performed with the famous Bakhor Ensemble for many years.[21] Hwang Jeong Ok "laid the foundation for the Korean dance repertoire of the famous

---

[16]Doraji, Korean for "the bellflower."

[17]Interview by Tatyana Simbirsteva, «Муза Востока» Тамара Ханум и ее корейские песни, *Koryo-Saram*, Dec 11, 2014. https://koryo-saram.site/muza-vostoka-tamara-hanum-i-ee-korejskie-pesni/.

[18]Photo citation "Zhao Dexian Portrait". https://quod.lib.umich.edu/d/dance1ic/x-zd00015/zd00015. University of Michigan Library Digital Collections. Accessed August 30, 2022. Zhao, like many dance artists, crossed cultures and national boundaries during his dance career. Born in Pyongyang (now North Korea), he moved in 1938 to join a Russian ballet ensemble in Harbin, a city which had been "Russianized" by builders and employees of the Chinese Eastern Railway in the late nineteenth century, then moving again in 1948 to Yanji where he founded the Yanbian Song and Dance Ensemble.

[19]Tamara Khanum quoted by Simbirsteva, «Муза Востока» Тамара Ханум и ее корейские песни.

[20]Avdeeva, on Galia Izmailova in *Tantseval'noe Iskusstvo Uzbekistana.* Tashkent: Gosudarstvennoe Izdatel'stvo Khudozhestvennoi Literatury, 1963. "Galia Izmailova is the first Uzbek ballerina" and "a milestone in the history of the art of a people."

[21]Kim, *Dances of Divided Korea*, p. 81.

Soviet Korean ensemble *Chen-Chun*" as well as creating many pieces that became popular with amateur ensembles.[22]

When Uzbekistan achieved independence in 1991, the nation sought closer political and economic ties with South Korea, which was the first Asian Pacific country to recognize Uzbekistan as an independent nation. By January 1992, diplomatic ties with South Korea were established, clearing the way for expanded cultural contact and dance research. The focus of Korean Studies "shifted from North to South Korea,"[23] and Russian scholars began to study Korean dances, noting a "lack of fundamental research of the traditional choreography of Korea and no complex studies of the topic."[24]

South Korean popular and folk culture began to dominate the *Koryo-Saram* community, with Korean-language study getting a boost from interest in the K-Pop genre. Even during COVID-19, the popularity of K-Pop continued; on July 15, 2021, the Embassy of the Republic of Korea in the Republic of Uzbekistan hosted an online event "K-Pop World Festival 2021".[25]

In July 2017, to mark the eightieth anniversary of the arrival of the deported *Koryo-Saram* in Uzbekistan, the Seoul Park opened in Tashkent, with buildings in the Korean architectural style. The Mayor of Seoul attended the opening ceremonies, which featured performances of Korean music and dance, and the park became the site of Korean community celebrations. It is also the site of a monument to King Sejong who created the Korean Hangul alphabet in 1443, spreading literacy among his people.[26]

Today, there are currently about 180,000 ethnic Koreans in Uzbekistan. In an impressive symbol of Uzbek–Korean relations, the House of Korean Culture opened on April 22, 2019. Built in Tashkent on land donated by Uzbekistan, with construction done by a Korean firm, the center's design included "modern architectural solutions … harmoniously combined with elements of traditional Korean culture." The facility houses a 478-seat cinema and concert hall, library, art gallery, and restaurant. President of the Republic of Uzbekistan, Shavkat Mirziyoyev, and the President of the Republic of Korea, Moon Jae-in, together with their spouses, attended the opening ceremony. President Moon recognized

---

[22]Ibid., p. 82.

[23]Ibid., p. 74.

[24]I. N. Tolstykh, *"Traditsionnye narodnye tantsy Korei:etnograficheskii aspekt"* [Traditional Korean folk dances: its ethnographic aspect]. Vestnik DVO RAN 2: 96–100, 2010, cited by Kim, *Dances of Divided Korea*, p. 76.

[25]Prazdnik druzhby yi soglasia mezhdu molodyozhyu dvukh stran. July 28, 2021. https://koryo-saram. site/?s=K-pop.

[26]"Kim Chang-Keon: 'I am glad to contribute to the development of cultural relations between the Republic of Korea and Uzbekistan." https://uza.uz/posts/440873 UZA Uzbekistan National News Agency. This is planned for 2023. https://uza.uz/en/posts/kim-chang-keon-i-am-glad-to-contribute-to-the-development-of-cultural-relations-between-the-republic-of-korea-and-uzbekistan_440873?q=%2Fposts%2F.

the facility as "a center of friendship and harmony" expressing hope that it would become "a common home for the Korean diaspora in Uzbekistan, Koreans and all Uzbekistan people working here."[27] A concert of traditional Korean music included the *popkoch'um* drum dance and the finale featured dancers in Korean and Uzbek costumes performing together on stage. In 2021, a special program featuring Korean traditional *hanbok* dresses sewn from Uzbek *khan atlas* fabric emphasized cross-cultural exchange between populations.

The documentary film *Koryo Saram—The Unreliable People* (2007) "is a fascinating testament to the power of cultural heritage," revealing how "Koreans integrated with Soviet society while maintaining their traditional identity alongside other deported people."[28] It raises a question: "In a world where culture is no longer tied to territory, what are the ways people of countries with age-old traditions use to forge an identity from the dominant society?"[29] Clearly, dance is an answer.

Mandatory Migration of Crimean Tatars

Like the *Koryo-Saram*, the Crimean Tatars experienced a similar uprooting of their entire population, forcibly removed from their homeland in the Crimea. They were conquered by the Russian Empire in 1783 and absorbed into the Soviet Union in 1921 as the Crimean Autonomous Soviet Socialist Republic. For the dance world, Crimean Tatars are probably best known in connection with the ballet *The Fountain of Bakhchisarai* (*Bakhchisaraïskiï fontan*). Inspired by the poem by Alexander Pushkin, the ballet derives from a fictionalized account of a Polish noblewoman who was kidnapped by the Crimean Tatar ruler, Khan Girey. In this Soviet Orientalist ballet, the dangerous, violent Khan threatens the kidnapped Christian woman; his overtures to her arouse the jealousy of the chief wife, Zarema, who stabs and kills her rival. First choreographed by Rostislav Zakharov (1907–1984), the ballet premiered in Leningrad at the Kirov Theatre[30] on September 28, 1934,[31] and applied Stanislavsky's theatrical methods to the creation of realistic dramatic characterizations. Even though the composer, Boris Afasyev (1884–1949), was a native of Astrakhan—once the capital of the Astrakhan khanate—his musical score, while often quite tender, has little of the "Eastern" coloring of the earlier Russian Orientalist composers such as Borodin and Rimsky-Korsakov. The

---

[27]Hanna Lee, "House of Korean Culture & Art, Symbol of Korean–Uzbek Future," *Korea*. https://www.korea.net/NewsFocus/policies/view?articleId=136474.
[28]Website of film *Koryo Saram—The Unreliable People* (2007). www.koryosaram.net/about_film.html
[29]Ibid.
[30]The Kirov is now known as the Mariinsky Theater.
[31]Entry on *Bakhchisaraïskiï fontan*, in *Balet: Entsiklopediya*, edited by Iu. N. Grigorovich, Moscow; 1981, p. 60.

costuming for the female dancers of the harem has more in common with the Ballets Russes production of *Scheherazade* than any actual elements of Crimean Tatar women's clothing, although the garments of Khan Girey and his warriors have a more traditional flavor. Zakharov's choreography also references elements from *Polovtsian Dances* along with a few balletic "Eastern" poses by women of the Khan's harem that are something of a Soviet shorthand for "oriental dance."[32] In 1936, the celebrated ballet was included in the 4th USSR theater festival. However, in May 1944—a decade after the ballet's premiere—Stalin ordered the deportation of the entire Crimean Tatar population from their homeland. With little advance warning, Crimean Tatars from every village and town were forcibly loaded into cattle cars with no food and only a little water. Only tiny windows barred with barbed wire let in fresh air.[33] The deportees were shipped to Central Asia and the Ural Mountains, resulting in an estimated loss of over thirteen thousand lives during the evacuation, but Crimean Tatar census committees have concluded that forty-six percent of their population perished as a result of the deportation and settlement process.[34]

The 2013 film *Haytarma* (Return) tells of this deportation, opening with a scene of a couple dancing the eponymous dance. Later in the film, a village celebration depicts everyone dancing—even those missing limbs from war injuries—all with an exhilarating pride and a sense of community, clues to their resilient survival.[35]

Many of the deported Crimean Tatars ended up in Uzbekistan, but it was not until 1957 that survivors were granted governmental permission to organize their own folk-dance company, which became known as *Khaytarma*,[36] in order to preserve and present Crimean Tatar folk dances, music, songs, plays, sketches, and concerts.[37] First directed by the well-known composer Ilyas Bakhshish, the ensemble gave Crimean Tatars hope and reminded them of their lost homeland. It "played a great role in saving and developing Crimean Tatar culture in exile."[38] Bakhshish helped with the development of Uzbekistan's Navoi Theater of Opera and Ballet, as well as the organization of folk dance, song, and music groups.[39]

One child, Dilyara Kerimova, was part of the mass deportation when she was six years old. She was born in Alushta, now a resort town on the coast of the Crimean Peninsula. In 1948, four years after her arrival, she was taken from the orphanage

---

[32]The ballet has been restaged by other choreographers throughout the USSR.

[33]Documentary film interview with deportee. "Deportation Of The Crimean Tatars In 1944. How It Happened," https://youtu.be/nlyeec3dZVc?si=jYjn16XRiCZ-M-VT.

[34]Oksana Grytsenko, "'Haytarma', the first Crimean Tatar movie, is a must-see for history enthusiasts." *Kyivpost.* July 8, 2013, www.kyivpost.com/post/9269

[35]Ibid.

[36]Also spelled *Qaytarma* and *Haytarma*.

[37]Risa Gulum, "Rituals, Artistic, Cultural and Social Activities," in *The Tatars of Crimea: Return to the Homeland*, edited by Edward Allworth, p. 87.

[38]Video celebrating the ensemble's 60th anniversary, "Khaytarma Ensemble Marks its 60th Anniversary," https://www.youtube.com/watch?v=MScs8fb9G90.

[39]Gulum, "Rituals, Artistic, Cultural and Social Activities," p. 92.

where she had been placed and sent to study at Tashkent's Choreographic Institute. After graduating from school, Dilyara worked at the Navoi Theater of Opera and Ballet, where she was seen by Mukarram Turgunbaeva, who invited her to join the Bakhor Ensemble. Dilyara became a soloist in the company, but when Bakhor traveled to Austria for the 1959 World Festival of Youth and Students, the Soviet government did not grant her permission to leave the USSR, her Crimean Tatar ethnicity still marking her as suspect. However, as the director of Bakhor, Mukarram herself supported Dilyara, protecting her dancers so their rights were not infringed as a result of nationalism ("*ne ushchemlyali iz-za natsional'nosti*"). Mukarram also made it possible for Dilyara to create a *massovyi* Crimean Tatar choreography for Bakhor and her talent subsequently earned her the title of People's Artist of Uzbekistan. In 1989, Dilyara managed to return to Crimea, where she taught dance.[40]

Characteristics of Crimean Tatar Dance

Like Uzbeks, Crimean Tatars are a Turkic people, but their dances are quite distinct from each other. Crimean Tatar women's dances share a greater resemblance to other traditions of the Caucasus—such as Azeri, Armenian, and Georgian dance—and are characterized by a proud, erect carriage and lifted head, a posture encouraged from childhood.[41] With precise and fluid movements of the arms and hands, the upper torso remains somewhat stationary, ornamented with crisp and controlled shoulder accents. At times, men and women dance together in pairs, facing each other but not touching, with the male dancer often circling the woman.[42] Slower, elegant dances like *Emir Jalal* feature stately poses accented only with small, sharp shoulder movements. Level changes are achieved by keeping both knees close together, then simultaneously bending then straightening them according to a musical accent. The virtuoso solo *Tim Tim* emphasizes nuanced control of fingers, in imitation of plucking the strings of a violin. It began as a male dance, depicting the intense emotion of a violinist for a young woman; with trembling hands, he plucks the strings of his instrument.[43] *Tim Tim* is now often danced by a female soloist, made famous by Remziye Bakkal.[44] Another interesting

---

[40]Arzy Abdullah, "*Dilyara Kerimova byla solistkoy legendarnogo ansamblya 'Bakhor'*" (Dilyara Kerimova was a soloist of the legendary ensemble Bakhor) https://www.crimeantatars.club/culture/art/dilyara-kerimova-byla-solistkoj-legendarnogo-ansamblya-bahor.

[41]"Pride of the Nation: Crimean Tatar Folk Dance," *Golos Krimy—Kul'tura*, July 14, 2020. https://culture.voicecrimea.com.ua/en/pride-of-the-nation-crimean-tatar-folk-dance/.

[42]Couple dances are rare in the Islamic world, but do occur in the region of the Caucasus.

[43]Gulum, "Rituals, Artistic, Cultural and Social Activities," p. 93. The *Tim Tim* choreography was created by Huseyn Bakkal for comedian Bilal Parik, as a scene in the production *Altin Beshik* (The Golden Cradle).

[44]Ibid., p. 94.

characteristic of Crimean Tatar dance occasionally involves rapidly traveling backwards in a circle. Set to a 7/8 rhythm, the lively *Khaytarma* dance includes both men and women and involves fast, smooth traveling steps, arms often opened like wings, and quick footwork by the men.

Crimean Tatar dance music reflects its original homeland with the use of accordion and brass instruments like trumpet and wind clarinet. When it moves into the 7/8 rhythms, the dance music sounds very Balkan, reflecting the traditions of the Roma musicians who were employed to play at weddings and celebrations by Muslim Tatars who had sometimes had a sense of moral ambiguity surrounding the propriety of music.[45]

Traditionally there was no Crimean Tatar stage dance; it naturally unfolded in social settings. When people gathered at celebrations, such as weddings, they simply improvised to music. Guests would sometimes tuck money under the hat of the best dancers who would later pass it on to the musicians.[46] Drawing from these folk elements, "almost all the national dances of Crimea were created by Huseyin Bakkal" who staged the dances and trained the best dancers.[47]

Bakkal's daughter, Remziye, contributed to the development of Central Asian stage dance in neighboring Tajikistan where she became a noted actress and choreographer. One of her pieces was featured in the opening ceremony of the 1980 Moscow Olympics.[48]

Remziye Bakkal served as an authority on Uzbekistan's Crimean Tatar dance ensemble *Khaytarma*, contributing elements to their choreography, bringing in an additional six female dancers, and traveling to Tashkent to stage several pieces for the ensemble.[49] Several of her students achieved prominence in the dance arts. Zulfira Asanova won many dance competitions as a child, going on to dance the role of Zarema in a production of *Fountain of Bakhchisarai* staged in Dushanbe, Tajikistan. Other pupils included Zebo Amin-zade, founder of the celebrated Zebo Ensemble, which performs the diverse dances of Tajikistan, preserving the ancient and distinct regional traditions that developed in remote, isolated areas.[50] Most recently, this company performed at the Lazgi International Dance Festival in Khiva, Uzbekistan.

---

[45]Observation by Razia Sultanova; see her discussion of music and Islam in *Turkic Soundscapes: From Shamanic Voices to Hip-Hop*. New York: Routledge, 2018.
[46]"Pride of the Nation: Crimean Tatar Folk Dance", *Golos Krimy—Kul'tura* July 14, 2020. *https://culture. voicecrimea.com.ua/en/pride-of-the-nation-crimean-tatar-folk-dance/*.
[47]Gulum, "Rituals, Artistic, Cultural and Social Activities," p. 93.
[48]Historic footage from the Moscow Olympics, *Танцы народов СССР—часть 1*, begins at 5:56 into the video. https://youtu.be/uDdPhntSGNQ?t=356.
[49]Gulum, "Rituals, Artistic, Cultural and Social Activities," p. 94.
[50]*Lazgi International Dance Festival* was held in Khiva, Uzbekistan, April 25–30, 2022 and included a conference on dance research.

Another student of Remziye Bakkal is the dazzling soloist, Malika Kalontarova. Of Bukharan Jewish origin, with both parents born in Samarkand, she grew up in Tajikistan, the youngest of seven children. Her dynamic performance style made her famous throughout the Soviet Union and in 1984, she was awarded the title of People's Artist of the USSR. Malika received international attention when she toured as a soloist with the Moiseyev Dance Company. Igor Moiseyev himself called her "an Eastern miracle" who "made a revolution in Oriental popular dancing."[51] Malika includes Uzbek dances in her repertoire and today lives in Queens, NY, passing her training down to young students and her daughter, Samara Sitara.

These examples of overlapping dance teachers, training, and traditions exemplify the centuries-old cultural interweaving of Silk Road dance arts. One method of preserving cultural distinctions is through clothing. Crimean Tatar women's stage dance costumes follow the lines of traditional folk clothing with long-sleeved dresses, or coats, tightly fitted through the upper torso and arms, then belted and flaring out from the waist. Intricate filigree work characteristic of Crimean Tatar jewelry ornaments includes belts worn at the waist. On the bodice, women wear *monitso*, a three-tiered gold-tone coin necklace. A fez-like hat, called a *tepelik*, completes the costume, ornamented with a round decorative piece on the center top—visible in the opening dance sequence of the film *Haytarma*—with a long veil hanging from the back of the headdress. Women's hair also signifies identity. Crimean Tatar women wear two long braids that fall over each shoulder and reach down to their waists.

While based in Uzbekistan, *Khaytarma* presented professional concerts featuring women's group and solo dances, men's dance, and mixed gender *massovyi* dances, all interspersed with vocalists and musical numbers. Their live performances were well attended by members of the Crimean Tatar community, for whom the ensemble served as an important symbol of identity.[52] Some scenes depicted familiar folk traditions, such as a suite depicting the preparation of a bride and the subsequent wedding celebration. After Uzbek independence, the Crimean Tatars received permission to return to their homeland but, for the generations who had grown up in Uzbekistan, this return proved bittersweet, because Uzbekistan was the only home they had ever known. Still, the members of Ensemble *Khaytarma* boarded trains in Tashkent in 1992 to travel back to the Crimea. There they found that their family homes had been destroyed or were now occupied by Russians. The returnees had to build new shelters, surviving in the challenging years following the dissolution of the USSR, when infrastructure broke down. *Khaytarma* survived and as recently as December 2021 was still

---

[51]Igor Moiseyev on Malika Kalontarova, quoted in "Bukharan Jewish dancer Malika Kalontarova is born," *Jewish Women's Archive*, September 2, 1950. https://jwa.org/thisweek/se,/02/1950/bukharan-jewish-dancer-malika-kalontarova-born.

[52]Allworth, *Tatars of Crimea*, p. 20.

performing in the Crimea. Although Ukraine had become independent from the USSR in 1991, Putin's annexation of the Crimea in 2014 dashed Tatar dreams of recognition of rights to their language, culture, religion, and independence. Russia's military invasion of Ukraine that began in February 2022 makes existence even more uncertain. Recent reports of harassment and violence toward Crimean Tatars by the Russian population suggest a grim outlook.

Not all of Uzbekistan's Crimean Tatar population returned to their original homeland, and some who had migrated to the Crimea later returned to Uzbekistan to live among their fellow Muslims. The Crimean Tatar diaspora community in Tashkent participates in festive gatherings, such as celebrations of Uzbekistan's Independence Day, wearing their distinctive costumes and proudly sharing their dances, another sparkling facet of the nation's varied dancescape.

10 THE WAR FRONT AND THE HOME FRONT

Vse—dlya fronta, vse—dlya Pobedy

(EVERYTHING FOR THE FRONT, EVERYTHING FOR VICTORY)

The opposite of war may not be peace, but Art; war actively destroys, while art actively creates. In Uzbekistan, wartime "gave a new impetus to the development of art, and in particular the art of dance" in response to the attack on the homeland.[1] Dancers willingly performed in difficult and dangerous conditions, creating programs designed to instill patriotic zeal at the Front, and to encourage those at home, living in the tumult and deprivation caused by war. As one Uzbek scholar observed, even during the harsh war years, art made "a strong emotional and ideological impact on the audience" fulfilling the "dire need of bright and joyful impressions."[2]

News of the outbreak of war came to people throughout the Soviet Union on June 22, 1941, when they heard the voice of Radio Moscow announcer Yuri Levitan deliver the shocking news: "Citizens of the Soviet Union, today at 4 a.m., without a Declaration of War, German armed forces attacked the borders of the Soviet Union. The Great Patriotic War of the Soviet people against the German Fascists has begun."[3] Upon hearing these words, Mukarram Turgunbaeva[4] and her colleagues rushed to the Sverdlov Theater where they worked.[5] Tamara Khanum

---

[1] Z. S. Safarova, "Art by Tamara Khanum and Roza Karimova." *Middle European Scientific Bulletin*, 7 (Dec. 2020): 38. https://doi.org/10.47494/mesb.2020.1.137.
[2] Ibid.
[3] The original Radio Moscow announcement is available on YouTube: https://youtu.be/hVJCbJD-xJA
[4] Mukarram Turgunbaeva quoted in Avdeeva, *Tanets Mukarram Turganbaevoi*, p. 60.
[5] In 1939, the Uzbek Ethnographic Ensemble established in 1929 by Kari-Yakubov was renamed the Uzbek State Opera and Ballet, combining both Central Asian and European genres and housed in the Sverdlov theater.

sent a telegram to Moscow asking for permission to perform at the Front. The reply came with thanks, but also a caveat that "while it is necessary to conduct a tour of Central Asia—the Front needs money."[6] Artists unified in spirit with the slogan, with "Tamara Khanum, Mukhitdin Kari-Yakubov, Halima Nasyrova, Gavkhar Rakhimova, Liza Khanum Petrosova, Mukarram Turgunbaeva, Isaqar Aqilov, Rozia Karimova and many other artists" responding to the call of "Everything for the Front! Everything for Victory! *(Vse dlya fronta! Vse dlya Pobedy!)*"[7]

Tamara Khanum transferred the monetary award from her USSR State Prize to the Defense Fund. She also gave benefit performances, raising enough money to finance a tank—and a plane—to send against the Nazi invaders. Officially awarded the rank of captain in the Soviet Army, Tamara Khanum recalled that, "I wore a uniform and carried a pistol. But I never shot anyone! I did my shooting with my songs and dances."[8] Gavkhar Rakhimova, a talented younger sister of Tamara Khanum, also created a team of artists who presented over 1,200 performances for Red Army soldiers at the Front.[9] Those first months—the summer, autumn, and winter following the outbreak of the war—found dance artists as part of performance brigades that traveled throughout Kyrgyzstan and Uzbekistan, where they gave concerts to the rear and the wounded … "[10]

"Art and literature workers faced a responsible and grateful task: preparation of the latest military–patriotic repertoire, organization of concert brigades, the deployment of patronage work in military units, hospitals, on people's construction sites, collective and state farms."[11] Dancers presented concerts for those military units preparing to go to the front, traveling in trains, cars, and wagons to various cities and towns, aware that these soldiers were heading to battle and perhaps death. As Halima Nasyrova recalled, "each soldier wanted to hear his favorite song," so the artists "sang everything that was asked of us, danced, played everything that the fighters wanted. Their grateful faces and friendly applause were a reward for us."[12]

Tashkent became an evacuation center for theaters, film studios, and conservatories from Ukraine, Russia, Belarus, Latvia, Lithuania, and Estonia. There simply were not enough buildings to house them all, so the Tashkent ballet school

---

[6]Elena Kari-Yakubova, "Tanets Cherez Prizmu Voinu." Iskusstvo i Khoreograficheskoi Obrazovaniye v Godu Velikoi Otechestvennoi Voiny. Moscow: Moscow State Academy of Choreography (МГАХ), special issue IV, no. 2 (50), (2020): 62–7.

[7]Ibid., p. 62.

[8]Tamara Khanum, cited by Laurel Victoria Gray, "Tamara Khanum: Uzbekistan's Heroine of Dance." *Arabesque Magazine*, X, no. V (January–February, 1985): 15. Information based on author's personal interview with Tamara Khanum.

[9]Kari-Yakubova, *Tanets cherez prizmu voyny*, p. 62.

[10]Ibid., p. 63.

[11]Zilola Safarova, *"Deyatel'nost' Intelligentsii Uzbekistana V Gody Vtoroy Mirovoy Voyny."* Mirovaya nauka, vol. 5, no. 2, 2016, p. 9.

[12]Halima Nasyrova, cited by Elena Kari-Yakubova, *Tanets cherez prizmu voyny*. Special Issue IV, no. 2 (50), 2020, p. 65, in *Academia: Tanets, Muzyka, Teatr, Obrazovaniye*. Moscow State Academy of Arts, p. 64.

became the war-time home of the Leningrad Conservatory.[13] Dance training was suspended and younger students attended academic classes at a boarding school elsewhere,[14] but even these young people participated in the war effort. Although she was only ten years old at the time, Gulnara Mavaeva later recalled that after classes, she ran to the hospital with other students, helping to wash and dry the bloody bandages. Then they went into the different wards "and danced in front of the wounded soldiers, trampling to the beat of the rhythm of the dance." Her classmates—Raya Khojisaidova, Kunduz Mirkarimova, and Rajab Tanguriev—presented Uzbek dances while Gulnara performed a dance of the Caucasus. "The wounded smiled and applauded—some with a stick, some with a spoon, some stomping their feet."[15] Three of those four children—Gulnara, Kunduz, and Rajab—all became Peoples' Artists of Uzbekistan in their adult dance careers. Other dance artists, including Rozia Karimova—who also achieved the status of People's Artist—performed concerts for the injured in hospitals in Tashkent, Urgench, and Bukhara.

Those who had been part of the AgitProp Brigades in the early years following the Revolution, with experience in performing under difficult conditions, recalled past programs that had proven effective in rallying spirits, like the Budyonny March (Марш Будённого), which celebrated Marshall Semyon Budyonny, commander of the Red Cavalry during the Russian Civil War. Mukarram recalled that while driving to perform for the troupes in Krasnovodsk and Baku, the artists planned the dance program on the road. A scenario emerged with assistance from Yevgeny Baranovsky (1907–1981), a dancer and choreographer at Tashkent's opera and ballet theater from 1929, who had originally trained as an acrobat and had performed in the circus. Baranovsky had learned Uzbek dance from Usta Olim and Mukarram Turgunbaeva and had studied ballet with Yevgeniya Obukhova (1874–1948), who was a graduate of the St. Petersburg Theatre School. (She later taught at the Tamara Khanum Ballet School 1935–1941, and the ballet school of the Navoi Theatre, 1944–1948.) Turgunbaeva and Baranovsky collaborated to create a new piece depicting a wounded hero who first crawled, then rushed, into battle. Mukarram felt that the choreography met with success not only because of the theme, but also the powerful rhythms of the Uzbek *doira* that "created the necessary and truly combative mood."[16]

For these performances at the Front, the main musical offering was the song "Forward," written by the composer Pulatjon Rakhimov,[17] a setting of

---

[13]Avdeeva, *Tantseval'noe Iskusstvo Uzbekistana*, pp. 146–47. Avdeeva wrote that the ballet was moved to the theater—probably the Sverdlov—but other accounts differ.

[14]Kari-Yakubova, *Tanets cherez prizmu voyny*, p. 66.

[15]Ibid., p. 64.

[16]L. Avdeeva, Tanets Mukarram Turganbaevoi. Tashkent: Gafur Gulyam, 1989, p.60.

[17]Pulat Rakhimov was the second husband of Tamara Khanum, after she and Kari-Yakubov had divorced.

verses by Rozia Karimova's husband, Nasrullo Ohundi.[18] The sheer presence of artists themselves, with their "national clothes, their songs and dances, caused inspiration."[19]

"Tanovar" Comes to the Stage

A choreography that became one of the classics of Uzbek stage dance, *Tanovar*, emerged quite unexpectedly during the war years. Originating in the Ferghana Valley, this was a "centuries-old" genre of a "lyrical song ... accompanied by dancing" and originally performed for an all-female audience.[20] Men sang a version that came from the verses of Muhammad Aminkhoja Mukimi (1850–1903) while women chose[21] lyrics that expressed personal desires, the "refined nature of their thoughts and aspirations." *Tanovar* "was performed by women of all age groups and each found in the song and dance a specific form of expression."

Drawing from this traditional genre, Mukarram Turgunbaeva had been working to create a choreographed solo version of *Tanovar* since the 1930s after seeing the celebrated Russian ballerina Yekaterina Geltser (1876–1962) perform Mikhail Fokine's 1905 choreography, *The Dying Swan*.[22] This dramatic, psychological piece inspired Mukarram to create a similar dance poem to depict "the experiences of Uzbek women and girls over a long difficult historical period." She drew from pre-Revolutionary Ferghana dance traditions where *Tanovar* existed in over a dozen variations, expressing women's longings.[23] The two pieces, *The Dying Swan* and *Tanovar*, staged almost forty years apart and based on completely different movements, costumes, and music, outwardly bear no resemblance, but both share a deeply emotional content, a sense of loss and longing. At first, artists avoided presenting such melancholy dances in their war-time programs, thinking they were "not needed" by audiences and "even harmful" when people needed encouragement to keep up their fighting spirits. But in 1942,[24] Mukarram decided to bring the dance to stage after noticing the "anxious eyes of women waiting for news from their husbands from the front ... " as well as seeing "so much longing for their loved ones in the eyes of the bravest fighters."[25] She began to perform *Tanovar*, "dedicating it to the wives of the soldiers" and assuring the warriors,

---

[18]Kari-Yakubova, *Tanets cherez prizmu voyny*, p. 67.
[19]Ibid.
[20]Rozia Karimova, "Tanovar—an Uzbek dance," *Soviet Uzbekistan*, 291, no. 1198 (1987): 18–19.
[21]Ibid., p. 18.
[22]Mukarram Turgunbaeva, quoted in Avdeeva, *Tanets Mukarram Turganbaevoi*, p. 55.
[23]Research by television director Hamid Khakhramonov.
[24]Karimova states that the dance by Mukarram Turgunbaeva premiered in 1943, "Tanovar—an Uzbek dance," p. 19.
[25]Mukarram Turgunbaeva, quoted in Avdeeva, *Tanets Mukarram Turganbaevoi*, p. 55.

through dance, that those back home "are faithful to them, that they are waiting for them, that they remember them every hour, every moment."[26]

Uzbek Dance in Iran

The railroad served as a crucial lifeline during the war, not only for moving the wounded and evacuees, but also for moving supplies. The 1941 invasion of the USSR, known as Operation Barbarossa, raised alarms in London and Moscow about the German population living in Iran,[27] pressuring the Shah to expel all Germans from his country. Britain and the USSR also grew concerned about the security of the rail line that brought Allied supplies into the Soviet Union. On August 25, 1941, the Anglo-Soviet invasion of Iran began with the goal of securing the oil fields and protecting the Trans-Iranian railway for transport. As one Iranian dancer remembered, "the war raging in Europe came to Iran's very doorstep. With unimaginable consequences, Great Britain and the United States started using Iran as a transit route to supply war ammunition to the Soviet Union in its fight against Nazi Germany."[28] The following year, in 1942, Uzbek dance artists were sent on a performance tour of Iran, an undertaking that "during the terrible, anxious war months, was a genuine cultural mission."[29] They performed "in concert halls, and in cinemas, and on village squares, and … in private courtyards where only women gathered," traveling in cars and on horseback, living and sleeping wherever they were caught at night.[30] Mukarram Turgunbaeva recalled that her dances and those of her colleagues, "especially Tamara Khanum, were perceived as a revelation, because we were Muslim and so unlike the Iranian women wrapped up in a veil."[31]

Whatever the motivation behind this "cultural mission" to Iran, the three leaders of the anti-Hitler coalition at the 1943 Tehran conference expressed a "desire for the maintenance of the independence, sovereignty, and territorial integrity of Iran."[32] At that same historic conference, dancer Rozia Karimova joined other leading Uzbek artists at a special concert for Roosevelt, Churchill, and Stalin.[33]

---

[26]Ibid.

[27]F. Eshraghi. "Anglo-Soviet Occupation of Iran in August 1941." *Middle Eastern Studies*, 20, no. 1 (1984): 27–52. www.jstor.org/stable/4282976. p. 47

[28]Nesta Ramazani, *The Dance of the Rose and the Nightingale*. Syracuse, NY: Syracuse University Press, 2002, p. xiv.

[29]Mukarram Turganbaevoi remembrances, cited in Liubov Avdeeva, Mukarram Turganbaevoi. Tashkent: Gafur Gulyam, 1989, p. 61.

[30]Ibid.

[31]Ibid.

[32]Milestone: 1937–1945 Office of the Historian. THE TEHRAN CONFERENCE 1943, https://history.state.gov/milestones/1937-1945/tehran-conf.

[33]Safarova, "Art by Tamara Khanum and Roza Karimova," p. 38.

Tashkent

Uzbekistan was behind the lines, so many of the wounded soldiers were sent there along with civilian evacuees, arriving in Tashkent—City of Bread[34]—by train. The unusually wide gauge of Soviet railroad tracks provided some protection against further invasion because German trains were too narrow to use them without adapting the tracks and they had not captured enough Soviet rolling stock to use them for their purposes. Nazi advances were slowed as additional rail was laid inside existing Russian tracks. The war-time tumult and confusion of the Tashkent train station was depicted in the 1962 Uzbek film "You are Not an Orphan" (*Ты—не сирота*), which depicted the famous story of an Uzbek couple—blacksmith Shaakhmed Shamakhmudov and his wife Bahri Akramova—who provided a home for fifteen displaced children of different ages and nationalities. Many other Uzbeks also took in very young refugee children, helping to ameliorate some of the impact of war.

"The war years saw a substantial rupture in Soviet cultural life in countless ways, but one of the most significant was created by the evacuation of arts institutions from the pre war Russian culture capitals, Moscow and Leningrad."[35] The personnel from these institutions, leading artists, "were compelled to depart not only by a devastating war but by a government, their own government, which sought to protect the lives of its citizenry, to keep valuable 'human resources' from falling into enemy hands, and to assure the security of the state by clearing frontline regions."[36]

The rescue of the artistic intelligentsia and the preservation of the country's cultural heritage became a top priority for the Soviet government … In extreme circumstances, under bombardment from the air, the packed train carriages departed eastwards—to Asia and the Trans-Urals—carrying from Moscow, Leningrad, Kiev and Kharkiv art institutions, theatre companies, film studios and museum collections. Living as evacuees in Samarkand, Tashkent, Almaty, Tbilisi, Nalchik, Kuibyshev (now Samara) and Ufa, artists, composers and directors fully committed themselves to their creative endeavours, transforming these cities into dynamic and busy working spaces. These difficult, horrendous and at the same time productive years … bring into relief the incredible efforts

---

[34]Tashkent was known as "City of Bread" after the 1923 story by Aleksandr Sergeevich Neverov (real surname Skobelev, 1886–1923) about a starving boy who, facing great difficulties, traveled to Tashkent to get food for his family during a famine.

[35]Kiril Tomoff, "Uzbek Music's Separate Path: Interpreting 'Anticosmopolitanism' in Stalinist Central Asia, 1949–52." *The Russian Review*, 63, no. 2 (2004): 219. www.jstor.org/stable/3664082.

[36]Rebecca Manley, "Escape to Tashkent: Fleeing Operation Barbarossa." *War History Network*, Summer 2011. https://warfarehistorynetwork.com/escape-to-tashkent-fleeing-operation-barbarossa/.

that went into preserving the country's cultural legacy, and to show that the bloodiest and most destructive war in history was also a period of intense cultural activity.[37]

Young students from military music schools, as well as professional musicians, were relocated to Tashkent, which "became one of the largest concentration centers for evacuated musicians."[38] In fact, the Leningrad Conservatory spent its war years in Tashkent, conducting classes and giving concerts. The past cultural cross-pollination of the 1920s in Moscow now shifted geography during the war years, allowing a Soviet European population to absorb the culture of Central Asia. As one representative from the Uzbek Composers' Union observed, "the evacuation introduced Uzbek folklore to a large group of talented professionals who could assimilate it in their own work."[39] This facilitated "creative collaboration of Uzbek and Russian-based composers and introduced Uzbek composers to a host of popular music genres that were either previously unknown or poorly developed in the republic."[40] Artists also absorbed the eastern influences of this new environment, as had Alexander Nikolayev in the 1920s, who adopted Islam and an Uzbek name—Usta Mumin. His absorption of Central Asian culture and aesthetics emerged in his early paintings of *bachas*. Later, he designed the sets and costumes for the opera *Ulugbek*.[41]

Premiere of New Uzbek Ballet

Distinct from Uzbek women's stage dance, Uzbek ballet derives from the Soviet system developed by Agrippina Vaganova (1879–1951). However, there have been several "cross-over" artists such as Galia Izmailova, who mastered both genres. In addition to presenting the classics of European ballet, Uzbek ballet developed its own masterpieces, with productions designed by their own artists, based on Eastern themes, and "quoting" characteristic Uzbek gestures of hands and arms. During all the war years, only one new "hybrid" ballet, *Ak Bilyak* was staged. Based on an Uzbek folk story, it combined both Uzbek traditional dances, choreographed by Mukarram Turgunbaeva, and ballet sequences, set by the innovative Fyodor Lopukhov, who was appointed the artistic director at the Kirov in 1922 but was

---

[37]Ksenia Karpova, "Art in Evacuation." *The Tretyakov Gallery Magazine*, #2, 2015 (47). www.tretyakovgallerymagazine.com/articles/2-2015-47/art-evacuation.
[38]Tomoff, "Uzbek Music's Separate Path," p. 219.
[39]Ibid.
[40]Ibid., p. 220.
[41]R. V. Eremian, *Usta Mumin: A. Nikolaev*. Tashkent: Gafur Gulyam Press, 1981, p. 25.

later relocated to Tashkent.[42] Lopukhov had trained at the St. Petersburg Theatre School, as did his younger sister Lydia. As a child she had performed for the Tsar. Lydia toured as a "child star" with Diaghilev's Ballets Russes in 1910. (Later, in 1925, she married John Maynard Keynes.) *Ak Bilyak* provided work for young people who had danced in operas and ballets but, because of the war, no longer had work. When Tamara Khanum's ballet school closed in 1941 because of the war, the training of future professionals came to a halt, creating another obstacle to dance development. In response, pedagogue and choreographer Pavel Yorkin (1891–1952) created a dance studio in 1943, gathering girls and youths who had not yet graduated from the ballet school, helping these young people continue their training. Only in 1947 was a formal choreographic school organized. Before then, the Palace of Young Pioneers in Tashkent had a professional-level ballet school taught by Vera Gubskaya (1906–1953)[43] and Rimma Sanin.

In an ironic twist, in 1945—a year after the forcibly relocated Crimean Tatars arrived in Uzbekistan—the Orientalist ballet "Fountain of Bakhchisarai," with its setting in the Crimea, was staged in Tashkent. Pavel Yorkin, who choreographed this new production, cast Baranovsky as the Crimean Tatar, Khan Girey. Mukarram Turgunbaeva danced the role of his favorite wife, Zarema, who out of jealousy murders the captive Polish noble woman with whom Khan Girey had fallen in love. Mukarram had been learning to dance *en pointe*, but after she fell once in class and hurt her leg, Yorkin told her to dance the role as rehearsed, but in *relevé*, wearing ballet slippers instead of toe shoes.[44] While she felt she lacked the needed technique, Mukarram called on her acting skills, imbuing her character with the emotions of "passion, heartache, the desire to be free … " to carry off the role.[45] Mukarram felt that "Zarema herself helped me, I merged so much with my heroine that I suffered completely and seriously" and "could not recover for a long time" after rehearsals. As Mukarram recalled, she loved the character of Khan Girey, "so much … that I forgot myself. I forgot shame, fear, I was ready for both heroism and cruelty."[46] Zarema's sense of helplessness may have triggered memories of Mukarram's own childhood spent in the *ichkari*, unable to choose her own fate.

---

[42]One of his collaborators, a librettist, was sent to a Russian *gulag* earlier, so Lopukhov may have been sent to Tashkent to get him out of the way.
[43]Vera Nikolayevna Gubskaya (1906–1953) graduated from the Moscow Ballet School in 1923. She taught at Tashkent's Palace of Pioneers 1934–1945, and at the Ballet School of the Republic of Uzbekistan 1935–1941. Gubskaya became People's Artist of Uzbekistan in 1944.
[44]Mukarram Turgunbaeva, cited by Avdeeva, *Tanets Mukarram Turganbaevoi*. Tashkent: Gafur Gulyam, 1989, p. 60.
[45]Ibid.
[46]Ibid.

Japanese Prisoners of War

Evacuees, orphans, and the wounded were not the only groups sent to Uzbekistan. Japanese prisoners of war, captured after the Soviets invaded Manchuria in 1945, were shipped to detention centers throughout the USSR. Some of those sent to Tashkent contributed to the development of Uzbekistan's performing arts in a manner reminiscent of the practices of Tamerlane, who selected skilled craftsmen from his war captives to work in Samarkand. In similar fashion, some of the Japanese prisoners sent to Tashkent worked as forced labor on the construction of the new Theater of Opera and Ballet. The architect Alexey Shchusev (1873–1949), whose long career had begun under the Romanovs, designed the building in the "Soviet Orientalist" style for which he won one of his four Stalin Prizes. Shchusev had studied at the Imperial Academy of Arts, first designing Russian churches and railway stations. After the Revolution, he found patronage under the Bolsheviks, winning the design for the Lenin Mausoleum on Red Square. In Tashkent, work on the theater began in 1942. The approximately 400 Japanese prisoners assigned to the construction arrived in 1945, working on the interior of the 1,400-seat theater and contributing details, such as the "casting" technique used for the ornamentation on the walls of the Bukhara, Khiva, and Kokand halls, according to Jalal Sultanov, director of Tashkent's Museum of Memory of Japanese Internees. These men also planted trees around the theater that are still standing.[47] More significantly, the workers may have contributed to the safety design. The devastating Tashkent earthquake of April 26, 1966, destroyed eighty percent of the city and left almost 300,000 homeless and some experienced heart attacks from "seismophobia."[48] Over a thousand aftershocks continued until December 31, 1969, deeply traumatizing many citizens who initially thought Tashkent had been bombed.[49] In the surrounding neighborhood, only the Navoi Theater escaped unscathed, often credited to the architectural skills of Japanese workers. As the late Japanese Prime Minister Shinzo Abe stated in a 2015 speech, even though the detainees were forced laborers, they "wanted to construct something great, and so they gave their all to their work, came up with novel ideas, and worked diligently to create great things."[50] Today, a plaque on the exterior of the building, with text in Uzbek, Japanese, and English, acknowledges their contribution: "In 1945–1946,

---

[47]Teatr imeni Alishera Navoi—kul'turnoye serdtse Tashkenta. *Sputnik Uzbekistan*, October 8, 2015. https://uz.sputniknews.ru/20151008/676086.html.

[48]"1966 Tashkent earthquake" on Vnimaniye! Zemletryaseniye! (Attention! Earthquake), personal site of the seismologist V. I. Ulomov. http://seismos-u.ifz.ru/personal/1966-1975.htm.

[49]«То ли бомбят, то ли что-то другое»: как Ташкент пережил землетрясение, *gazeta.ru*, April 26, 2021. https://www.gazeta.ru/science/2021/04/25_a_13572272.shtml.

[50]"Prime Minister Abe Visits Uzbekistan," Japanese Prime Minister Shinzo Abe 2015 visit to Tashkent, online article www.mofa.go.jp/erp/ca_c/uz/page3e_000402.html.

FIGURE 10.1 Photo session in 1985 for the Bakhor Ensemble, held in one of the galleries at the Uzbekistan State Academic Bolshoi Theater named for Alisher Navoi, which was built during the war years. Costumes and jewelry are based on historical styles. Photo credit: Laurel Victoria Gray

the hundreds of Japanese citizens deported from the Far East took an active part in the construction of the theater named after Alisher Navoi."[51]

The impact of the Second World War, with its sacrifices and disruptions, provides insight into the consequences of past centuries of war that swept over the territory of what is now present-day Uzbekistan. Performances during the war years took dance artists to new regions at the same time that refugees and relocated peoples came into the territory of Uzbekistan. However, the resilient spirit of artists provided a positive focus, their creativity giving them a sense of accomplishment amidst destruction. Uzbek dance researcher Elena Kari-Yakubova, in her article "*Tanets cherez prizmu voyny*" (Dance through the Prism of War), compared the influential power of art to high diplomacy, but "on an emotional level." She observed that the "task of dance art is not only to preserve the memory of those who gave us peace at a high price. Creating highly artistic works, artists, choreographers, composers, are called upon to awaken with their creativity the best qualities inherent in each person" (Figure 10.1).[52]

---

[51]Officially named the Uzbekistan State Academic Bolshoi Theater of Opera and Ballet named for Alisher Navoi.

[52]Kari-Yakubova, *Tanets cherez prizmu voyny*, p. 67.

PART FIVE

THE ARRIVAL OF SPRING

11 THE BLOSSOMING OF THE BAKHOR ENSEMBLE

The "Thaw" Prepares the Ground

In dance, timing is everything. Several factors—political, cultural, and regional—aligned to facilitate the birth of the Bakhor Ensemble, which became Uzbekistan's world-famous company. In 1956, the Communist Party of the Soviet Union held the first party Congress to occur after Stalin's death in 1953. Khrushchev's "Secret Speech" at the Congress on February 25, 1956[1] denounced Stalin and his reign of terror, heralding a new trend toward cultural liberalization known as the "Thaw." This policy shift dramatically manifested in the 6th World Festival of Youth and Students, held in Moscow from July 28 to August 5, 1957, with 34,000 participants from 130 countries. With the theme of *Mir—Miru* ("Peace to the World,") symbolized by a dove, it reflected concerns of the world after the Second World War, shaken by the reality of nuclear warfare. One featured speaker, a young Japanese girl from Nagasaki, spoke about the horrors of the atomic bomb.[2] With a yearning for peaceful coexistence, this global gathering of young people gave them the opportunity to meet each other, showcase their national culture, and forge friendships that could lead to improved world understanding. The festival program included art, culture, films, and sports, with the now famous song "Moscow Nights" debuting at the event. Young people from the USSR who participated "were firmly convinced of the fruitfulness of international solidarity. By means of art, the power of the emotional impact made its way to the hearts

[1]For the background to the speech and American response to it, see the post on the website of the National Archives, https://text-message.blogs.archives.gov/2020/12/03/khrushchevs-secret-speech-1956/.

[2]A Pathé film depicting the festival participants shows them creating giant formation on the stadium field depicting the silhouette of a bomb, then crossing it out, and turning into "МИР," the Russian word for "peace." https://youtu.be/j8-3TtgFcKs.

of young people, opened the way to the mutual contacts infected with a thirst for understanding and friendship."[3] The festive atmosphere was heightened by "the sheer presence of foreigners from outside the Soviet bloc mixing freely[4] with crowds of Soviet citizens ... "[5]

For dance, the political shift heralded by the Thaw opened new possibilities, stimulating "the development of a vibrant post-Stalinist Soviet popular culture. ... Whereas late Stalinist artistic life had been carefully scripted to adhere to rigid ideological formulas, the Thaw years celebrated improvisation and openness."[6] Along with this creative freedom came "new opportunities for international travel and transnational cultural exchange, since Soviet authorities came to rely on artists, musicians, and dancers for popular diplomacy in the Cold War."[7]

The ethnic diversity of the USSR was highlighted throughout the festival performances and color-illustrated booklets of regional folk costumes were some of the many special items created for the event.[8] Glimpses of Uzbek dancers appear in historic film footage from the festival, with girls in Bukharan costumes and in Ferghana khan atlas dresses, along with Uzbek men wearing the black and white *dupi*. In this intoxicating atmosphere, the recognition of their prize-winning performance in Moscow revealed the powerful appeal of dance in creating an international presence. A promotional booklet about the Bakhor Ensemble states that the group was "organized in preparation for the VI World Youth Festival in 1957,"[9] although a poster from that event describes the performers as "Tashkent Youth." However, a newsreel promoting the festival identifies the Bakhor Ensemble rehearsing for the event with Mukarram Turgunbaeva featured in the choreography.

Uzbekistan's festival participants also had the opportunity to see dance groups from other cultures. One group that Mukarram Turgunbaeva had long admired was the all-female Russian State Academic Choreographic Ensemble *Beriozka*, founded in 1948. The company's founder, Nadezhda Nadezhdina, drew inspiration from a genre of Russian women's circle dances, known as the *khorovod*,[10] as well

---

[3]"6th World Festival of Youth in USSR," 1957. https://soviet-art.ru/6th-world-festival-of-youth-in-ussr/
[4]Babies of mixed non-Russian ethnicity born nine months after the event were known as "Festival Children."
[5]James von Geldern, "International Youth Festival." *Seventeen Moments in Soviet History*, https://soviethistory.msu.edu/1956-2/international-youth-festival/.
[6]Erik R. Scott, "Dances of Difference," In *Familiar Strangers: The Georgian Diaspora and the Evolution of Soviet Empire*. New York: 2016, pp. 123–54. Online edition, Oxford Academic. https://doi.org/10.1093/acprof:oso/9780199396375.003.0005.
[7]Ibid.
[8]One example is the color illustrated booklet, *Folk Costumes of the USSR*, 1957, which had the Festival logo on the cover.
[9]*Gosudarstvennyi Ansambl' Tantsa UzSSR Bakhor*, informational booklet with photographs.
[10]For more on the ancient connections of the *khorovod*, see Elizabeth Wayland Barber, *The Dancing Goddesses, Folklore, Archeology, and the Origins of European Dance*. New York: W.W. Norton & Company, 2013.

as from traditional folklore and costuming, interpreting it in a fresh way for the stage. Mukarram saw in *Beriozka* the possibility of creating a similar dance company based on Uzbekistan's wealth of dance forms with abundant material for an ensemble.

At the time of the festival, an Uzbek countryman born near Tashkent, Nuritdin Mukhitdinov (1917–2008), had recently been named a Candidate Member of the 20th Presidium of the Central Committee of the Communist Party. Mukarram visited him in his Moscow home, taking with her several young dancers—Rano Nizamova, Dilbar Abdulaeva, and Gulnara Mavaeva. Mukarram proposed the creation of a dance ensemble in Uzbekistan along the lines of *Beriozka*. It was a bold vision because, up to that point, there were several small dance "brigades" at Tashkent's Philharmonic, but nothing on the scale of *Beriozka*. For major events in Moscow, such as past *dekadas* and the recent festival, dancers were gathered from different Uzbek groups to create a large ensemble, but while they were always well received, they existed only as temporary endeavors and not an official company with a sustainable repertoire. The future of Uzbek dance needed something permanent, something that could share Uzbek culture beyond national borders. Mukhitdinov accepted Mukarram's request, and the Bakhor Ensemble was officially formed in 1957.[11]

Bakhor means "spring" in Uzbek, a fitting name for the ensemble "dedicated to glorifying the mighty forces of nature awakened from her long winter sleep."[12] The company's stated significance embraced a dedication to "the spring of life, to the happiness of youth and love, to the boundless joy of free labor."[13] In pre-Revolutionary Central Asia, with its past history of slavery, as well as slave-like conditions of women and agricultural workers, the concept of "free labor" held a significance in harmony with socialist goals and values.

Mukarram frequently called the Bakhor dancers *mening asal baxor kizlarim*, "my honey Spring girls."[14] She herself deeply identified with the symbolic meaning of spring, hope, and growth. When she ran away from her uncle's home to become an actress as a teenager, she changed the date of her birth from September 16 to a spring date, May 31, to mark the first day of her personal freedom and her birth as a true artist.[15] Mukarram devoted the remainder of her life to *Bakhor*, creating

---

[11]According to a conversation with Gulnora Musaeva, Director of Bakhor Ensemble, September 15, 2022.

[12]Text from the above-mentioned *Bakhor* souvenir album presented to me in 1979, after Bakhor's performance at Seattle University.

[13]Ibid.

[14]Mutabar Yuldosheva, one of the first dancers in the Bakhor Ensemble, quoted by Akhmadzhon Rakhimov, in *Mukarramkhonim "Tanovar"i*, Tashkent: Muharrir nashriyoti, 2018, p. 149.

[15]Ibid., p. 150.

new stage choreographies on the basis of traditional dances with staging that reflected "a modern conception of the world" that glorified "Uzbek woman set free by the revolution after centuries of slavery." Even though the 1917 revolution had taken place forty years earlier, the emancipation of Uzbek women unfolded slowly, especially in rural areas, and the experience of the *ichkari* was still vivid for some.

Mukarram recalled that after returning to Uzbekistan after the Uzbek artists' successful presentations at the 1930 Moscow *Olympiada* of Folk Arts, she was approached by an elderly woman who invited her to their quarters, and gave her a paranjah to wear while they went there together. She was met by women and children and asked many questions about her life as a dancer. How did she learn to dance? Who sewed the costumes? Did she have a husband? Mukarram learned that these women had tragic lives. Her hostess had a sister who was murdered because she went to work. Another woman had a sister who, when forced to marry, poured kerosene on herself and died by self-immolation.[16] From this experience, Mukarram realized that her personal example gave women hope for the possibility of a different life.

Mukarram Turgunbaeva sought to build a repertoire that represented the creativity of "the Uzbek people during many centuries of the highly developed Central Asian civilization, reflecting the interesting and complex history of the Uzbek people as well as their breathtaking energy in building a new life."[17] Bakhor presented a repertoire clearly divided into the three styles of the "dance zones"— Ferghana, Bukhara–Samarkand, and Khorezm—and also included dances drawn from Uzbekistan's Uyghur and Karakalpak populations. Mukarram felt that while she and other choreographers who created dances for Bakhor endeavored to reflect a modern and progressive spirit, "ethnographically precise movements are only the material from which we build a modern building."[18] The movement vocabulary may be traditional, but the themes were often contemporary.

From the beginning, *Bakhor* was an all-female dance ensemble, with a folk orchestra consisting of male musicians under the direction of Honored Artist of Uzbekistan Salakhutdin Tukhtasyanov. When Mukarram was asked why she made this decision to have only women in the company, she replied that the answer was "clear and simple."[19] Secluded in the *ichkari* for centuries and covered with a "bag" (*meshok*) whenever they ventured out into the street, Uzbek women still created songs and poems. "How many unique dances were created by Uzbek women— so how can you not show them to the world, not to sing this miracle! A miracle of the creativity of Central Asian women."[20] When the Bakhor Ensemble toured in the East, beyond the borders of Uzbekistan, the dance company became "a

---

[16]Mukarram Turgunbaeva, quoted in Avdeeva, *Tanets Mukarram Turganbaevoi*, p. 53.
[17]Text from *Gosudarstvennyy Ansambl' Tantsa UzSSR Bakhor*, an illustrated brochure. Pages are unnumbered.
[18]Mukarram Turgunbaeva, quoted in Avdeeva, *Tanets Mukarram Turganbaevoi*, p. 62.
[19]Ibid., p. 61.
[20]Ibid.

symbol of freedom" and "an example worthy of emulation."[21] Their art took on a political significance. For this reason, programming for touring concerts destined for countries of the East was selected "with special passion," choosing "such dances that most accurately and artistically reveal the character of a modern Uzbek woman."[22] Foreign press reviews described the "youth, joy, and love" in the dances, even the way that Bakhor had turned the concert hall into "a fairy-tale world." A writer for a Pakistani newspaper wrote that "if art is a reflection of the life of the people of a country, then obviously your country is as beautiful as your art."[23]

Mukarram was also keenly aware that for many audiences "there may not be a single person in the auditorium" who had a clear idea of who the Uzbeks were or where Uzbekistan was located. She noticed the foreign newspapers and concert posters advertised Bakhor as "Muslims from Russia."[24] While some audiences may have attended simply out of curiosity, they saw "completely unexpected dances" that "struck their imagination." The dancers themselves became more than touring artists and "they opened people's eyes to the very fact of the existence of our people."[25]

Influence of Ballet and Russian Folk Ensembles

The oft-repeated assertion by Western scholars that Uzbek women's stage dance is based on ballet and Russian folk dance reflects a misapprehension of the fundamental characteristics of ballet, Russian folk dance, and Uzbek dance. A comparative movement analysis of ballet and Uzbek women's dance, using the Laban *kinesphere*, reveals the legs in Uzbek dance are barely lifted off the ground. There is no "turn out"—the classic ballet rotation of the leg away from the front of the body, coming from the hip, knee, and ankle. There are no leaps, no arabesques, no *battements*. In Uzbek dance, feet stay relatively close together, and there is no intricate footwork.

Although Uzbek women's stage dance was not based on ballet or Russian folk dance, it did absorb a few elements of technique and staging. An investigation of how Mukarram Turgunbaeva constructed her choreographies provides a more precise understanding of the specific ways in which ballet impacted certain Uzbek stage techniques as well as the influence of Russian folk ensembles on the staging of *massovy* dances. Mukarram frequently found inspiration in the costuming, staging,

---

[21]Ibid.
[22]Ibid.
[23]Ibid., p. 62.
[24]Ibid.
[25]Ibid.

and themes of ballets and Soviet folk dance groups, but she reworked these ideas, making them truly Uzbek.

Bakhor made a significant contribution to the development of Uzbek women's dance by thoughtfully building upon tradition to create group choreographies, or *massovyi* dances. Some Soviet scholars insisted that many Central Asian ethnic groups "did not have dance" or at least not female *massovyi* dances, but most often were solo forms. They may have overlooked women's participation in the *zikr* ritual in which multiple participants in unison travel in a counterclockwise direction with a repetitive movement, perhaps because of the association of *zikr* with Islam and Sufism. However, like the other regions with ancient goddess cults, female solo dance was deeply rooted in Central Asia; traditional Uzbek women's dance is a solo improvisational form. As Si-Lan Chen recalled from her months in Uzbekistan in 1933, "the pure, untheatricalized Uzbek dance was the most satisfying folk form I had ever seen, rich and gay, spirited and the very essence of spontaneous dancing."[26]

Mukarram faced the challenge of molding *massovyi* choreographies from folkloric roots without destroying the original essence. From the successful Russian folk-dance groups of the USSR, Mukarram saw effective elements, such as an entrance used by the Beriozka Ensemble, in which girls sequentially appear from behind the curtain. She used this idea for the beginning of her choreography *Namangan Olmasi* (Apples of Namangan). At other times she found inspiration in choreographic themes and costume designs. In 1937, Igor Moiseyev (1906–2007), born the same year as Tamara Khanum, founded the celebrated Soviet folk-dance company that carries his name. He was a friend and inspiration to Mukarram, Tamara Khanum, and other Uzbek artists, all tackling the same challenge of translating village dances for the concert stage and creating a new dance genre of folkloric stage dance on an impressive scale.

Mukarram used some of the movement vocabulary from traditional Uzbek solo dances to create group choreographies.While she learned certain aspects of staging techniques from her Russian ballet teachers, she used discernment to determine which elements could be adapted without destroying the Uzbek essence. She recalled the precept of one of her professors, the experimental choreographer and influential pedagogue Fyodor Lopukhov (1886–1973), "to not overload the *massovyi* dance with a large number of different characteristic movements."[27] Following his advice, she usually used three or four basic movements in *massovyi* choreographies, but in regard to hand movements, she "disobeyed" her mentor to keep the expressiveness in the hands, otherwise "Uzbek dance will no longer be Uzbek."[28]

---

[26]Si-Lan Chen Leyda. *Footnote to History*, edited by Sally Banes. New York: Dance Horizons, 1984, p. 169.
[27]Mukarram Turgunbaeva in Avdeeva, *Tanets Mukarram Turganbaevoi*, p. 60.
[28]Ibid.

As she poetically expressed this sentiment: "the dancer's body is the vase and the hands are the flowers in it."[29]

As heirs to the Sogdian Whirl, Central Asians had long been known for the fast spins called *charkh*, and traveling turns *ailanash*, that are still part of the traditional movement vocabulary, but Mukarram added the ballet style *chaîné* turns—done with a slightly different foot placement—to some of her *massovyi* choreographies. She also found inspiration in certain aspects of costuming, such as the iconic white dresses from Mikhail Fokine's famous *ballet blanc*, *Les Sylphides* (1907), known in Russian as *Chopiniana*.[30] For her dance *Paxta* ("Cotton"), she imagined her dancers as fairies, living inside the fluffy cotton boll, and had them dressed in white, floor-length, long-sleeved Uzbek dresses with ruffled hems and sleeves. Still national in design, Mukarram adapted the ethereal enchantment of the Romantic tutu to the cotton fields of Central Asia. Likewise, she admired the poetic lyricism of *The Dying Swan* (1907)—another Fokine choreography—and decided to create an Uzbek woman's solo with similar deep expressiveness. The result was *Tanovar*, which Mukarram worked on for several years before bringing it to the stage in 1942, eventually adding it to the Bakhor repertoire. Performed to Uzbek music, in Uzbek costume, with Uzbek dancers, *Tanovar* shares no similarities with the *Dying Swan*, with the exception of deeply emotional qualities.

In addition to Uzbek dances, other choreographies in the Bakhor repertoire included Uyghur and Karakalpak dances. Soon other styles were added that reflected connections with the peoples of Central Asia and the Caucasus united with their "brothers"—Russian, Ukrainians, and Belarusians. The young ensemble performed in Uzbek cities and villages, but also presented concerts in Ukraine, Georgia, Armenia, Moscow, Leningrad, and the Baltic Republics.[31] The company's repertoire expanded to include *massovyi* choreographies of Uzbekistan's Korean and Crimean Tatar ethnic minorities, as well as the dances of the peoples of other Soviet republics: Azerbaijani, Kazakh, Kyrgyz, Turkmen, Tajik, Moldavian, Ukrainian, and, of course, Russian. Dances from other nations with political ties to the USSR, such as Cuba, Egypt, and Hungary, were also included. Adhering to the Soviet-endorsed theme of "internationalism," guest choreographers were invited to set dances of non-Uzbek ethnicities on the ensemble. For example, People's Artist of the USSR Galia Izmailova, who "had learned Arabian dances in their motherland, staged an Arabian dance."[32] A Bashkir dance was set by G. Askarov, who was a well-known Bashkir choreographer. People's Artist of Azerbaijan Amina Dilbazi (1919–2010), staged an Azerbaijani piece and Tajik dances were created by People's

---

[29]Ibid.
[30]Not to be confused with *La Sylphide* (1836).
[31]*Gosudarstvennyy Ansambl' Tantsa UzSSR Bakhor.* Illustrated brochure. No date or printing information.
[32]Although she did not specify, the solo performance and costume of Galia Izmailova that I saw was Egyptian.

Artist of the USSR Gafar Valamat-zade (1916–1976). Inclusion of these dances was intended to "acquaint the Uzbek audience with the folk dances of brotherly Republics [i.e. other Soviet Republics] and folk dances of Eastern countries."[33]

But while Mukarram and others committed themselves to retain traditional, characteristic Uzbek elements in their choreographies, there were political ramifications to this path. Stalin's policy of "nationalist in form, socialist in content" initially seemed to allow for national characteristics, but Russian cultural influence grew more dominant,[34] and Soviet artists wrestled with both the theory and praxis entangled with this issue. The central question focused on the "artificial acceleration of the process of creating a common culture, language, and traditions common to all the peoples of the country, while simultaneously there was an unspoken leveling of national characteristics in various folk cultures and national differences of a particular people" and the characteristics of certain folk cultures.[35] In the words of the prominent Belorussian folk choreographer and researcher Yu. M. Churko, the resulting disappearance of distinct ethnic features reduced stage versions of folk dance to a kind of "choreographic Esperanto."[36]

In spite of this pressure, Mukarram remained steadfast to her original vision, and the Thaw opened the way for her to continue on this path as she cultivated new dances for the repertoire of Bakhor.

Waltz Bakhor

The ensemble's signature choreography "Waltz Bakhor," traditionally opens every concert. It begins with the dancers center stage, standing in tight concentric circles. They hold branches with pink blossoms that at first tremble, anticipating the beginning of Spring. Wearing long pink dresses[37] and fitted green vests, the girls have flowers on their heads with their hair in six long braids. The dancers seemingly float from one formation to the next in a manner reminiscent of one of Beriozka's *khorovod* but accented by spins in the characteristic Ferghana third position and with one arm at the waist. The specially composed theme song *Bakhor* also includes bird calls in the opening and closing sections of the piece to further evoke the atmosphere of spring.

---

[33]*Gosudarstvennyy Ansambl' Tantsa UzSSR Bakhor.* Illustrated brochure. No date or printing information.

[34]For an examination of the complex issues surrounding this policy, see Yuri Slezkine, "The USSR as a Communal Apartment, or How a Socialist State Promoted Ethnic Particularism." *Slavic Review*, 53, no. 2 (1994): 414–52.

[35]Usman Karabaev, *Etnokul'tura: traditsionnaya narodnaya kul'tura.* Tashkent: Shark Publishing, 2005, p. 123.

[36]Yu. M. Churko,. "Khoreograficheskoye iskusstvo Belarusi (osnovnyye etapy i problemy razvitiya)." PhD diss. Moscow, 1972, p.51., cited by Khamraeva, Gulsum Rakhmedova. Obshchie zakony stsenicheskoy choreographii natsionalnaya obraz tantsa. Tashkent: Institute of Art Studies. Dissertation 1986., p. 10.

[37]Originally, the dresses were very pale pink, almost white, but the most recent set of costumes, debuted in late 2021, are a much deeper shade of pink.

However, Mukarram's deepest source of inspiration was that of music. She explained:

All my dances are born from music. Once I hear a melody, a song, rhythms, I begin to live them. Two, three years, and sometimes much more, music in my imagination seems to form itself movements, patterns, drawings, even the colors and lines of costumes ... Always, even in the most joyful melody there is some hidden pain that disturbs my soul and calls forth creativity.[38]

Namangan Olmasi

Some choreographies went beyond these major delineations of the dance zones to find inspiration in regional specifics. For example, *Namangan Olmasi*, which is a dance about the apples of Namangan. The costumes originally created for the piece reflected the traditional clothing of women from the Ferghana Valley—a long-sleeved, ankle-length white dress, worn over long pants (Figure 11.1). Adapted for stage, the relatively narrow chemise worn by women in the region became

FIGURE 11.1 Bakhor Ensemble in 1987, performing *"Dance with Doira*," accompanied by the ensemble's musicians. Choreography by Mukarram Turgunbaeva. Photo credit: Rustambek Sharipov.

[38]Mukarram quoted by Avdeeva, *Tanets Mukarram Turganbaevoi*, p. 60.

reimagined as a lightweight, full-skirted dress that created beautiful "delayed lines" during spins. The distinctive striped Ferghana fabric, known as *bekasam*, often made into coats for both men and women, was incorporated in long-sleeved, hip-length fitted jackets. Embroidered Ferghana-style skull-caps called *dupi*, partially covered by a scarf, topped the traditional long braids of Uzbek girls.[39] The entire spirit of the *Namangan Olmasi* reflects the playful folk games of unmarried girls, as the dancers pop out from behind the curtain one at a time—*a la Beriozka*—each with a squeal that is a distinctly feminine Uzbek vocalization of delight. The girls greet each other with a gentle Uzbek bow, or *salom*. The dance includes a pantomime section where the girls imitate the process of crushing *usma*[40] leaves with their hands to create a paste which Central Asian women use to darken their eyebrows, as thick, beautiful brows are considered a sign of beauty, often connecting them to create "the cherished charm of the united eye-brow."[41] At times, the dancers join hands to create small circles, leaning back with glee as these rings quickly rotate. The girls feign a shy demeanor, hiding from the gaze of young men but, of course, there are no male dancers on stage, leaving it to the audience to imagine their presence. The dancers line up in pairs to create a column, using their arms to make archways under which they run, before beginning their exit.

Katta O'yin

The ancient dance *Katta O'yin*, once performed by *bachas*, also became part of the Bakhor repertoire, but was modified by Mukarram working with Usta Olim Kamilov. Dancers wear a vibrant combination of bright red silk dresses with pants tucked into black boots. Over this, the dancers don a long-sleeved black velvet coat ornamented with trim down the center front and on the cuffs. On their heads they wear the distinctive Uzbek crown known as a *tillakosh* (golden eyebrows) with a red scarf attached. Danced solely to *doira* rhythms, *Katta O'yin* requires strict adherence to the beats that continually shift throughout the choreography. Two lines of dancers enter upstage from opposite sides. At first, they clap overhead in time with the rhythm, traveling downstage in mirrored diagonal lines, then move into a column, suddenly stopping when the rhythmic phrase ends. Based on Ferghana dance technique, the arms are frequently held in third position— one arm curved above the head, palm up, and the other extended to the side, palms outward, fingertips skyward, at the level of the shoulder. Dancers maintain

---

[39]For stage, Uzbek dancers usually have six long braids, while soloists may have as many as eight. They hang down below the hip and at times, some soloists wear even longer braids. Traditionally, unmarried girls could have as many as forty braids, or more—a rare sight today, even in remote villages.
[40]Most likely *Isatis tinctoria*.
[41]Charles MacFarlane, *Constantinople in 1828; A Residence of 16 Months in the Turkish-capital and Provinces*. London, Saunders & Otley, 1829, p. 206.

this pose as they travel to a new position, ending with a phrase punctuated by the characteristic *shokh* turn—a quick rotation in place, always done to the left. Big, sweeping side-to-side movements will abruptly end in a pose, followed by small movements, such as shoulder pushes or the *kigiir buyin* head slide. The juxtaposition of soft, lyrical moves with quick percussive gestures continues throughout the choreography as the dancers respond to the shifting rhythms. Originally set for eight, the dancers travel downstage, opening into a line across the front of the stage where they kneel, leaning forward and hiding their faces behind folded arms so only the tops of their heads show. Then they lower their arms revealing their faces, performing the *kigiir buyin* movement, only to playfully hide again. When at last they stand, the rhythm becomes faster and the dancers execute a series of spins, culminating in a dramatic final pose. The characteristic gestures, dramatic structure, and flirtatious elements all call to mind the original *Katta O'yin* of the Central Asian *bachas*, but in a shorter form and performed in unison.

Andijon Polka

In the Fergana Valley, Mukarram found inspiration for another kind of dance set to a specific rhythm that locals, rather surprisingly, called a "polka."[42] In a tribute to the horseback riding skills of the Uyghur *jigits*, she included masculine movements imitative of horseback riding. It begins with the female dancers tying the *belbok*—a men's scarf—around their waists in male fashion and adjusting their *dupi* to tilt at a rakish angle, then rolling up their sleeves. With hands clenched into fists, instead of delicate feminine positions, the dancers lean forward and alternately coil their arms in inward circles. At other moments, they alternate sharp shoulder pushes, as if challenging each other, using a hopping step to travel around the stage, brandishing a whip as if racing on horseback. This dance is so well-known that when played at weddings or other gatherings, both male and female guests perform some of the most characteristic steps.

Pakhta—"Cotton"

Uzbeks refer to cotton as *ok altyn*—"white gold"—a source of national wealth. When Mukarram first created this choreography, she—together with Usta Olim—diligently sought out the natural movements connected to the labor activities

---

[42]The origin of the mysterious appearance in the Ferghana Valley of the distinctive 2/4 polka rhythm with roots in a Bohemian dance originating in the 1830s—and used for an Uzbek dance—is as yet undetermined.

of cotton cultivation but had difficulty finding characteristic movements. The resulting "Cotton Holiday" is a dance suite originally set for thirty dancers in distinct teams and was created in 1930 for the Moscow Festival. Some dancers, dressed in white costumes with ruffled skirts and wide sleeves, depicted the cotton pickers, while the other dancers wore costumes that portrayed workers from different regions and ethnicities—Ferghana, Bukhara, Khorezm, Uyghur, and Karakalpakstan. At one point in the choreography, these five "teams" create a star, lining up in rows that radiate out from a central point, in a manner suggesting a five-pointed Soviet star, an emblem of the USSR. In the published details about the costuming, all of the different outfits have painted designs on them, a technique often used by designer Zinaida Kuryshch. The Karakalpak girls also wear "chak-chaki"—metal finger cymbals—on the middle finger and thumb.

Munojat

This dance and music comes from the Ferghana Valley, but *Munojat* shares a name with a prose piece written by the venerated Alisher Navoi (1441–1501), a lament to Allah, filled with regret and repentance. When music for the dance contains the poetic verses, it becomes even more commanding, as revealed in a description of a performance by singer Munadzhat Yulchieva and dancer Firuza Azatova: "Indeed the power of song and dance is so immense that together they elevate each individual to the heights of noble spirituality, re-opening the eyes to a childlike humanity, and gently softening the heart like white cotton."[43]

At least two different stage versions of this deeply emotional dance exist. One was created by Isaqar Aqilov for Kizlarkhon Dusmukhamedova and the other was choreographed by Mukarram Turgunbaeva for the opera *Ulugbek*, which premiered in 1942. She later set the dance on Mamura Ergasheva, bringing the piece into the Bakhor repertoire. In the opera, the dancer represents a snake sent to poison the eponymous hero. The undulating, serpentine arm movements, most dramatically performed in a deep backbend, depict an inner psychological struggle that is tearing apart the snake's soul because it was given this deadly mission.[44] The serpentine element is echoed by the costume, which is a long black lace coat with long fitted sleeves, worn over a white dress, echoing the tension between light and dark, good and evil. In one version, other dancers of Bakhor become a *corps de ballet*, framing the soloist.

---

[43]Rakhimov, *Mukarramkhonim 'Tanovar'i*, p. 99. Translation by Maksudakhon Ibragimova.
[44]Commentary by Gulnora Mavaeva and Mamura Ergasheva in the film, *Legends of Uzbek Dance* (2021).

Tanovar

Forever connected to Mukarram herself, this dance draws from a traditional genre from the Ferghana Valley expressing the deepest longings for love, happiness, and freedom, and the "tragedy of unfulfilled love."[45] There are dozens of songs called *Tanovar*, performed by unknown female poets, singers and dancers of the past from Ferghana and Margilan, verses filled with cries of suffering and a longing for happiness.[46] Mukarram advised every artist to find her own *Tanovar*, "to carry it in her own heart," but not in imitation of her own movements and gestures because the real measure is whether a dancer will be able "to reveal the inner pain, desires, cries of the heart, the secret of the woman, the spiritual world."[47] According to People's Artist of Uzbekistan Firuza Azatova, when *Tanovar* is performed the dancer must open the door of her heart.[48]

The beauty of the *Tanovar* is internal and timeless, as reflected in the simplicity of the costume, which is traditional Ferghana women's clothing. It consists of the characteristic striped *bekasam* coat worn over a long white shift, with a scarf tied across the dancer's brow, creating an iconic Uzbek image of "everywoman."

Mechanical Doll Dance

Another example of an idea inspired by ballet, this piece recalls the famous doll dance from the ballet *Coppelia* (1870), but as one of Mukarram's teachers, Fyodor Lopukhov, choreographed his own version of *Coppelia* in 1934, she may have seen his version. Bakhor's mechanical doll uses Uzbek dance movements. This solo is usually performed by a petite dancer who can be carried out on stage in a "frozen" position. The "doll" stands stiffly, bent forward from the waist, until wound up by a large key "inserted" in her back by a designated assistant. The dancer comes to life with crisp angular arm positions from the Ferghana dance style. Wearing a short but full-skirted dress of Uzbek *khan atlas* fabric, worn over traditional Uzbek pants, the "doll" has a huge bow on her head in the fashion of Soviet school girls. Makeup emphasizes a doll-like face with two round circles on her cheeks and exaggerated wide-eyed makeup. The dance begins slowly and the dancer steps stiffly with a straightened knee, lifting the foot much higher than would be normally done in Uzbek folk dance. At one point, the "doll" tilts forward into her original position, in need of "rewinding" with the key. The piece culminates in a flurry of fast *ailinash* or *chaîné* spins around the stage.

---

[45]Ibid.
[46]Avdeeva, *Tanets Mukarram Turganbaevoi*, p. 15.
[47]Mukarram Turgunbaeva cited by Rakhimov, Mukarramkhonim "Tanovar"i, p. 87.
[48]Feruza Azatova, cited by Rakhimov, ibid., p. 99.

All of the members of Bakhor were expected to participate in the group dances—the *massovyi* dances. If a dancer had a special individuality or talent that made her suitable for a particular role, she might be assigned a solo piece as well. By this policy, Mukarram set a standard of behavior that discouraged a prima donna attitude. As one company member learned under Mukarram's tutelage, "dance is a very complex and delicate art. It educates a person both spiritually and physically." It teaches proper stage conduct, such as "controlling one's temper, and behaving with politeness."[49] The spring bouquet that represented Bakhor should "consist of dancing girls with both external and internal beauty."[50]

Foreign Travel

The young ensemble performed in Uzbek cities and villages, also presenting concerts in Ukraine, Georgia, Armenia, Moscow, Leningrad, and the Baltic Republics, but with the goal of international travel they hoped to share Uzbek culture with a broader audience and raise the global prestige of Bakhor. Mukarram wanted the company to travel abroad, but that decision was something to ultimately be determined by the authorities in Moscow, in particular the Minister of Culture.

Costume Design

Bakhor's costuming created a powerful partnership with the choreography itself. Foreign audiences were enchanted not only by the unfamiliar and engaging dance forms, but also the "exotic" Eastern costumes and the unique, traditional jewelry worn by the dancers, such as the crown known as *tillakosh* (golden eyebrows) and elaborate pectoral called *zebigardon*, important elements because they also reflected national artistic creations.[51] As is traditional in Central Asian culture, something is always worn on the head, varying according to region and the rules for these special headdresses. Costume elements such as headscarves, *tillakosh*, *peshanabands*, and *dupi*, "were unswervingly observed."[52] Some choreographies called for costumes that were "ethnically specific," while other pieces had a more "generalized nature" that emphasized a theme rather than a regional distinction. For example, the signature choreography of the ensemble, *Waltz Bakhor*, featured

---

[49]Gulchekhra Jamilova, quoted by Rakhimov, Mukarramkhonim "Tanovar"i, ibid., p. 164.

[50]Jamilova quoted by Rakhimov, Mukarramkhonim "Tanovar"i, ibid., p. 165.

[51]Florida Nizomiddinova, quoted in Rakhimov, Mukarramkhonim "Tanovar"i, ibid., p. 166.

[52]Malakhat Makhmudova, "Stage Costume Features Ensemble 'Bakhor,' Lazgi Dance, Its Harmony with Traditional World Dances and Modern Stages of Development." Tashkent: Bookmany Print, 2022, p. 190.

light pink dresses, green vests, with apricot blossoms in the hair, conjuring a spring garden in the imagination of the viewer.[53] Costume designer Zinaida Kuryshch[54] worked with Mukarram Turgunbaeva in creating the dance garments for Bakhor, "preserving the principles of ethnic costumes, at the same time, using the method of free theatrical interpretation."[55] By maintaining this respect for regional differences, Bakhor set a standard which, according to some, has been slipping elsewhere in Uzbek stage costume design, marked by an increasingly eclectic, "non-observance of the local styles, excessive brightness … are widely observed."[56] As a result, stage costumes now sometimes "combine a gold embroidered Bukharan vest with a traditional Ferghana satin and a Namangan skullcap."[57] Mukarram Turgunbaeva felt that "Uzbek dance needs to be danced cleanly and academically—nothing extra is allowable, like mixing different characteristic elements, for example, only for Khorezm, Surkhandarya dance or Ferghana Valley. This begins with the shoes and headdress, and ends with the patterns of the movements—all should coordinate with the region which we present on stage."[58]

For performances of dances evocative of the Samarkand court of Tamerlane (1336–1405), costumes follow the lines of historical garments depicted in Central Asian and Persian miniatures. Mary Doi seemed somewhat dismissive when she wrote, "several scholars even told me to study Persian miniatures for understanding the dress and poses the dances used," commenting that "they seemed curiously encapsulated from change."[59] Yet clothing and movement impact each other; steps and gestures are enhanced or restricted by the dress of the dancer. As observed by professional dancer and scholar Gul'sum Khamraeva, the costume is "a very important integral part of the dance because it not only it reflects the artistic taste of the people but the costume creates a certain emotional atmosphere … the costume is inseparable from the movement as it both continues the movement and precedes it …"[60] The advice by scholars to "study Persian miniatures" reflects an awareness of the antiquity of certain gesture elements and their evolution with connection to clothing. Sir John Chardin, who traveled in Persia 1673–1677,

---

[53]Ibid., p. 191.
[54]Ibid. Zinaida Kuryshch also worked at the Uzbekistan State Academic Theatre of Opera and Ballet named for Alisher Navoi designing costuming for the ballet. She spent two years in Egypt creating designs for the Cairo Opera and Ballet Theatre.
[55]Ibid., p. 192.
[56]Ibid.
[57]Ibid.
[58]The words of Mukarram Turgunbaeva, recalled by Mamura Ergasheva, in Rakhimov, *Mukarramkhonim*, p. 191.
[59]Mary Masayo Doi, *Gesture, Gender, Nation: Dance and Social Change in Uzbekistan*. Westport, CT: Bergin & Garvey, 2002, p. 137.
[60]Gul'sum Rakhmedova Khamraeva, "Obshchie zakony stsenicheskoy choreographii natsionalnaya obraz tantsa." Dissertation, Institute of Art Studies, Tashkent, 1986, p. 54.

managed to view "some Cloaths that Tamerlain wore, which they keep in the Treasury at *Ispahan*; they are cut in the same Manner as those that are made at this time of Day, without the least difference,"[61] even though Tamerlane had lived more than two hundred years earlier. Today, gold-embroidered robes, similar to museum pieces from the court of the Emir of Bukhara, are still being produced in Uzbekistan. Costumes made from heavily embroidered velvet and brocade fabric impede movement while at the same time adding elegance and majesty. Floor-length, long-sleeved robes, sewn from faux *ikat* prints, have recently become fashionable among Uzbek women. As for "poses," Avdeeva has emphasized the fact that traditional Uzbek dance was performed almost entirely in place, often punctuated by stillness—a dance of "poses."[62] Dance phrases—accompanied by rhythm and music—will often begin or end with these poses, somewhat similar to the sculptural moments in Kathak and Bharatanatyam dance.

In 1978, the Bakhor Ensemble traveled to Moscow to perform in the Tchaikovsky Concert Hall. Mukarram planned to perform her signature piece, *Tanovar*, but backstage some of her dancers noticed her extreme pallor and tried to persuade her to rest instead. In reply, Mukarram insisted that she go on, asking when else will I have the chance to perform on such a stage? For someone who had experienced the most primitive conditions during performances at the Front during the Second World War, the beauty and prestige of the Tchaikovsky Concert Hall, where some of the world's greatest artists had performed, must have represented a great achievement. Mukarram went on as planned but apparently suffered a heart attack onstage, yet showed no outward sign, and finished her dance. When she came backstage she collapsed and lost consciousness.[63] Within a few days, on November 26, 1978, she passed away.

Less than a year later, in 1979, a touring group of dancers and musicians from Bakhor, along with soloists Kizlarkhon Dusmukhamedova and Nasreddin Shermatov, traveled to the United States, marking a significant achievement for the ensemble. *Bakhor* continued under new leadership, first under Kunduz Mirkarimova, then Ravshanoi Sharipova and, finally, Mamura Ergasheva. Bakhor survived even after the dissolution of the Soviet Union in 1991, but a

---

[61]Sir John Chardin, *Travels in Persia 1673–1677*. New York: Dover Publications, 1988, p. 212.
[62]People's Artist of Uzbekistan Kadir Muminov emphasized this during the 2020 Virtual Central Asian Dance Camp, when he taught Bukharan dance, distinguishing between "positions" and "poses."
[63]Ziyoda Madrakhimova, *Legends of Uzbek Dance*, 2021. See Filmography.

government reshuffling of the various regional dance ensembles, each with a distinct style and character, made them all part of a central organization named UzbekRaqs (Uzbek dance).[64] The once forty-member dance ensemble, with its own musicians and building that housed a concert hall and rehearsal space, was whittled away to perhaps a dozen dancers, then eliminated entirely. Uzbekistan's most beautiful and captivating "calling card" vanished.

Until 2020 …

---

[64]Decree of the President of the Republic of Uzbekistan, dated 08.01.1997 No. UP-1695:
ON THE DEVELOPMENT OF NATIONAL DANCE AND THE ART OF CHOREOGRAPHY IN UZBEKISTAN
"In order to further develop the national dance and the art of choreography, revive, preserve and enrich the historical traditions and methods of the art of Uzbek dance, create favorable conditions for promoting the original oriental attitude inherent in our nation, dances that carry high spirituality, prepare long-term targeted programs for the development of various directions of national dance, preserving the art of dance from superficiality, from imitation, which is manifested in inappropriate movements and costumes that contradict the high spirituality and subtlety of the taste of our people, improve the system of special education to better meet the needs for qualified personnel, as well as strengthen the material base of organizations of this areas."
https://lex.uz/docs/168854?ONDATE=30.04.2021.

12 CONSTRUCTING KARAKALPAK DANCE

Soviets and the Nomadic Heritage

When the Bolsheviks first came to power in 1917, they inherited a country with the world's largest land mass and over one hundred different nationalities. Spread out over eleven time zones, with climates ranging from humid continental to subarctic, these diverse ethnicities had distinct languages and spiritual traditions. Creating a new, shared Soviet identity presented an enormous challenge. One perceived solution was in the performing arts, with "all union" festivals held in Moscow to showcase the unique cultures of these nationalities, embodying the Soviet ideal of "friendship of the peoples"—*druzhba narodov*. Historian Yuri Slezkine characterized this approach as "the most extravagant celebration of ethnic diversity that any state had ever witnessed."[1]

During the early years of the USSR, the "nationalities question" shaped the formation of the political boundaries of the country, shifting several times. Only in 1924 did Uzbekistan officially become one of the Soviet Union's constituent republics. In 1925, the Karakalpak Autonomous Oblast was carved out from the Turkestan Autonomous Soviet Socialist Republic and the Khorezm People's Soviet Republic. In 1932, the region became the Karakalpak Autonomous Soviet Socialist Republic, and in 1936, merged with Uzbekistan. Initially the capital was Turtkul, but in 1939, moved to Nukus. The region where this large minority population lives, located on the coast of the Aral Sea and the lower reaches of the Amu Darya, accounts for almost forty percent of the territory of Uzbekistan. The very name, Karakalpak, means "black hat," a reference to the distinctive black karakul hats

---

[1]Yuri Slezkine, "The USSR as a Communal Apartment, or How a Socialist State Promoted Ethnic Particularism," in Sheila Fitzpatrick, ed., *Stalinism: New Directions*. London, New York: Routledge, 2000, p. 313.

worn by the men. Karakalpak is a Turkic language related to the Kipchak-Nogai, nomadic groups part of the Mongol horde.[2]

The Karakalpak are carriers of the ancient Central Asian bardic tradition of oral epics, known as *dastan*, presented by male bards called *zhirau* who both sing and recite the epics, accompanying themselves on the *kobyz*, a bowed, two-stringed fiddle. At times, the bard uses special gestures to convey the action.[3] The epic of *Alpamysh* goes back a thousand years, while the *dastan* of *Yedige* (also written as *Idige* and *Edige*) connects to the time of Tamerlane and also recounts the adventures of the "heroes of the Golden Horde."[4] The last known Karakalpak bard able to recite *Yedige* in its entirety was Jumabay *zhirau* Bazarov (1927–2006),[5] who trained with his master teacher for three years to memorize it.[6] In 1993, Bazarov's performance was recorded and transcribed by Karl Reichl in his book, *Edige: A Karakalpak Oral Epic as Performed by Jumabay Bazarov.*[7]

Keen to develop a sense of national unity between the different republics and autonomous regions, Moscow discovered that not all Soviet inhabitants could neatly fit into their new cultural paradigm. The three distinct pre-Soviet dance zones in what became Uzbekistan—Fergana, Bukhara/Samarkand, and Khorezm—provided fertile material for the development of stage dance, but the Karakalpak people presented a dilemma. Among the traditionally nomadic tribes, Moscow determined that not all had dance, specifically the Kazakh,[8] Turkmen,[9] and Karakalpaks. How Moscow interpreted "dance" was not clearly defined, but whatever movement patterns that may have existed among these people, they were not sufficient to be deemed "dance." These traditions were simply not "developed" enough to invite them to the state-sponsored, all-inclusive Soviet "dance party" of nationalities—they first needed to be "taught" to dance.

---

[2]On August 30, 1993, the Director of Karakalpak Ensemble, Polat Madreymov, told me the Karakalpaks were related to Pechenegs, one of the Turkic nomadic tribes mentioned in the *Russian Primary Chronicle*.

[3]E.A. Petrosova, *Karakalpakskii Tanets*. Tashkent: Literature and Art Press named for Gafur Gulyam, 1976.

[4]Mark Kirchner, "Edige: A Karakalpak Heroic Epic as Performed by Jumabay Bazarov (FF Communications, 293)," *Speculum*. Cambridge: Cambridge University Press, 2010.

[5]Theodore Levin, in *The Hundred Thousand Fools of God*, p. 183. Levin refers to Jumabay with his specific honorific. The term *zhirau* or *zhyrau* is the Kazakh word for a reciter of epics. See Gulnar Kendirbaeva, "Folklore and Folklorism in Kazakhstan." *Asian Folklore Studies*, 53, no. 1 (1994): 108. https://doi.org/10.2307/1178561.

[6]Levin's account of his search for, and meeting with, Jumabay provides detailed information about performance style and content. See p. 183 in his work.

[7]Karl Reichl, translator and editor of *Edige: A Karakalpak Oral Epic as Performed by Jumabay Bazarov*. Helsinki: Academia Scientiarum Fennica, 2007.

[8]See Rosa Vercoe and her interview with Anvara Sadykova, "Did the Kazakhs Have Their Own Dance Culture and What Are the Origins of Kara-Zhorga—The Nation's Favorite Dance?" *Voices on Central Asia*, September 17, 2021.

[9]"Kushtdepdi Rite of Singing and Dancing." *UNESCO Intangible Cultural Heritage*. 2017. https://Ich. Unesco.Org/En/RL/Kushtdepdi-Rite-Of-Singing-And-Dancing-01259.

Soviet scholar of Uzbek dance L. Avdeeva attempted to explain this lack of dance on the difficult realities of the semi-nomadic way of life,[10] perhaps not acknowledging ritualized movement as dance because of its association with spiritual traditions such as shamanism and Sufism, which the Soviets condemned as backward and superstitious. From one end of the Turkic World to the other, ritual dance brought communities together to heal and bless, as well as evoke a martial spirit in preparation for combat. Why was it dismissed? No mention was made of the Turkmen ritual *Kushtdepdi* in which the entire multi-generational community gathers to recite thanks to the earth and sky, blessing all gathered, with everyone moving together along a circular path, chanting "*hu hu*." One researcher believes that in "great likelihood" the origins of Kushtdepdi "lie in a Sufi healing ritual."[11] In 2017, UNESCO placed *Kushtdepdi* on the Representative list of the Intangible Cultural Heritage of Humanity.[12] Kazakh dance also shares shamanic traditions with the Karakalpaks and other Turkic people. Petroglyphs in Kazakhstan found at Tamgaly, located about one hundred and seventy kilometers northwest of Almaty, clearly depict humans dancing.[13] In her article on Kazakh dance for *The International Encyclopedia of Dance*, Lydia P. Sarynova wrote about several genres—hunting scenes, competition dances, humorous dances, imitations of animals, work dances, dance games, and rituals of folk healers—all reflecting everyday life. They were typified by "flexibility and sharp movements of the shoulders, tension and muscular concentration of the body, and an agility that enabled the dancer to perform intricate acrobatics."[14] She further asserted that "in the pastoral feudal society, each clan had its own professional master who was in the retinue of the khan."[15] Another ancient Turkic group, the Uyghurs, perform the *sama* in which men and women dance together in couples, rotating around each other while traveling within a larger circle. In 1988, Jean During recorded the powerful communal energy of an Uyghur men's *zikr*. At times, individuals break from the group to move into the center, spinning around themselves independently, turning to the left, recalling the "Sogdian Whirl."

---

[10]L. Avdeeva, introduction to E. A. Petrosova, *Karakalpakskii Tanets*, p. 3.

[11]Merjen Atayeva, "Kushtdepdi of the Turkmen and Its Origins." *Central Asia Forum*, January 15, 2020. https://centralasiaforum.org/2020/01/15/kushtdepdi-of-the-turkmen-and-its-origins/.

[12]The UNESCO decision on Kushtdepti as Intangible Heritage states that: "The Kushtdepdi rite of singing and dancing is a performing art involving creative poeticizing focused on good feelings and wishes. It involves singing with vocal improvisation and dancing with movements of the hands, gestures and footsteps in accordance with the tune of the song."https://ich.unesco.org/en/RL/kushtdepdi-rite-of-singing-and-dancing-01259.

[13]Petroglyphs of the Archaeological Landscape of Tanbaly—Gallery—UNESCO World Heritage Centre, which can be viewed at: https://whc.unesco.org/en/list/1145/gallery/&maxrows=27.

[14]Lydia P. Sarynova, "Kazakhstan", in *International Encyclopedia of Dance*, editor Jeanne Cohen, six volumes, Oxford University Press, New York, 1998. www-oxfordreference-com.proxygw.wrlc.org/display/10.1093/acref/9780195173697.001.0001/acref-9780195173697-e-0910?rskey=2f3rsr&result=1.

[15]Ibid.

Creating Dance for "A People Without a Dance"

While the Karakalpaks did not have dance traditions that met Moscow standards of what constitutes dance, legends from *dastan* were deeply woven into the fabric of Karakalpak life, so the first theatrical creations in Nukus drew on epic stories. Immediately after the Revolution, circles of theatrical and musical amateur activities were organized in Karakalpakstan, and in the late 1920s a professional theater was born. The attempt by the Soviets to create a Karakalpak dance tradition began in the late 1930s when "the first national ensemble of music, song and dance was organized under the local radio broadcasting committee,"[16] but was not successful. Theater and dance came when, in 1941, performing artists came to Nukus to present the musical dramas *Alpamysh* and *Black Hearts*. At one point, Mahmudjan Gafurov—the actor playing the title role of Alpamysh—rode onto the stage on horseback, to the delight and applause of the audience.[17]

Also in 1941, choreographer Isaqar Aqilov traveled to the region, assigned to help create a ten-day Festival of Art and Literature of the Autonomous Republic of Karakalpakstan. He gathered a group of two hundred and fifty young people to prepare new dances. He toured districts and villages, gathering "elements of dance needed for performances."[18] His initial work was based on the legend of the *Kyrk Kyz*, the "Forty Warrior Maidens"—a theme that would also inspire another choreographer in the future. Aqilov also created a dance based on the work movements of local fishermen, and another piece called *Chagallak*, the seagull. He taught these dances to members of the Karakalpak State Ensemble and to amateur dance teams. However, the outbreak of the Second World War put an end to these plans. All national energy now focused on "the desire to achieve a quick victory over the vicious enemy fascists."[19] Uzbekistan's artists launched into creating new works with patriotic themes, even performing for troops on the front.

In 1944, another attempt to create dances for the Karakalpaks brought Uzbek choreographer Ali Ardobus to the Autonomous Republic, but his pieces were not readily adopted by the local population.[20] They entered the repertoire of Uzbek professional and amateur groups, but the Karakalpaks did not dance these dances.

The very antiquity of Karakalpak epic *dastans* made them a target as "remnants" of feudalism. The successful musical drama based on the *dastan* of *Alpamysh* was removed from theater repertoires in 1952; even songs from this production were

---

[16] Avdeeva, introduction to Petrosova, *Karakalpakskii Tanets*, p. 4.
[17] Oltynoi Tadjibaeva, "'Alpamysh' is a Symbol of Youth." *San'at Journal of The Academy of Arts of Uzbekistan*, 2 (January 4, 2006). https://Sanat.Orexca.Com/2006/2006-2/Alpamish-2/.
[18] Makhmud Ahmedov, Isakhar Akilov. *Ocherki o zhizni i deyatel'nosti [baletmeystera]*: Tashkent: Izd-vo literatura i iskusstvo, 1975, p. 24
[19] Ibid., p. 25.
[20] Avdeeva, introduction to Petrosova, *Karakalpaksii Tanets*, p. 4.

forbidden and the actors who had played leading roles were dismissed from the theater.[21] The core message embedded in these *dastans* praising their national heroes made Moscow wary as they seemed to challenge the goal of developing patriotic allegiance to the new Soviet state. And there may have been an uncomfortable association with the centuries when Russia lived under "the Mongol yoke," because the Karakalpak share similar Central Asian ethnicity with the tribes who were part of the armies of Genghis Khan. Around the same time that recitation of *dastan* became forbidden, attempts were renewed to develop a national dance form for the Karakalpak people, perhaps as a cultural substitute. Moscow waged a political campaign against ancient traditions under the slogan of "struggle against the old" (*bor'ba protiv starovo*), that was "conducted with great excesses … " The result was "an artificial acceleration of the process of creating a common culture, language, and traditions for all the different nationalities of the country while at the same time there was an unspoken leveling" of the traditions and national differences.[22]

Oral traditions are highly portable and practical for semi-nomadic tribes for whom "Art" exists in actively creating the beauty that travels with them in their dwellings, clothing, music, and legends. Their art emerged in exquisitely crafted women's jewelry, portable "bank accounts" in silver that could be pawned or sold in emergency. Among the Turkmen nomads of the region, the abundance of jewelry "was probably occasioned by the need to insure against the risk of nomadic economy by the possession of readily saleable, valuable and easily transportable reserves of capital."[23] The jewelry, with deeply symbolic designs, along with the embroidery embellishing clothing and household items, such as the woven carpets decorating their yurts, created an everyday world steeped in artistic expression.

In 1951, Elizaveta Petrosova was "invited to create stage dance" for the Karakalpak people.[24] She was one of the remarkable family of Petrosian sisters that included Tamara Khanum and Gavkhar Rakhimova, all of whom contributed greatly to the development of Uzbek stage dance. Elizaveta immediately decided to "base the dance on some facet of ritual which is so rich in Karakalpak culture—a wedding" and here she was faced "with an unexpected difficulty" because the people "did not have dance" (*s nepredvidennymi trudnostyami—narod ne imel tantsa*).[25] She was astounded that these people with such an original culture, "rich applied arts, oral literature, countless songs and melodies, did not dance."[26] Instead of imposing elements from another culture, Petrosova sought inspiration in the everyday gestures and motions of the Karakalpak people, living in the community

---

[21]Tadjibaeva, "'Alpamysh' is a Symbol of Youth.
[22]Usman Karaboev, *Etnokul'tura:tradisionnaya kul'tura*. Tashkent: Shark, 2005, p. 123.
[23]Johannes Kalter in *The Arts and Crafts of Turkestan*. London: Thames and Hudson, 1983, p. 84.
[24]Petrosova, *Karakalpakskii Tanets*, p. 12.
[25]Ibid., p. 13.
[26]Ibid.

and closely observing their way of life, their means of livelihood, and their relationship with the natural world. A dance culture that normally would only emerge organically over time, had to be artificially developed in a short period. Noting "the presence of a developed complex of body movements, the love of the people for the plastic expression of thoughts and feelings," she felt "convinced that the Karakalpaks would be very receptive to the art of dance ... And indeed, the Karakalpak dance was born and took shape in a fantastically short time— the whole process of its birth took less than three years—from the summer of 1956 to the winter of 1959." According to Avdeeva, the inaugural performances of Karakalpak *massovyi* dances at 1957 Moscow World Festival of Youth and Students, "demonstrated the true originality of the Karakalpak choreography," winning success at the world dance competition.[27]

Petrosova's approach provides a fascinating exercise in "reverse engineering" folklore. Over a decade later, the American folklorist Alan Lomax, together with Forrestine Paulay and Irmgard Bartenieff, created Choreometrics, "a system of comparing performance style cross-culturally."[28] It was based on the theory that "danced movement is patterned reinforcement of the habitual movement patterns of each culture or cultural area."[29] The team developed an analytic coding system based on Laban Movement Analysis to compare movement across cultures, but this analysis began by looking at existing dance movements connected to everyday culture. Petrosova started in the opposite direction, looking at everyday cultural activities for potential dance movements. Avdeeva noted that the "principle of creating dance forms of Karakalpak dance is in many respects similar to the principle of creating Kazakh and Turkmen dance but the forms themselves, their imagery, are extremely individual."[30]

Petrosova decided to study the characteristic "plasticity of the people" and on this basis started creating an authentic Karakalpak dance that would be understandable to the people. "I needed to learn the language and everyday life to come into close contact with the life of the people." She lived in a Karakalpak family; "friendship with all its members and friends gave me the opportunity to understand the character of the people, to understand the nature of national music and songs."[31] Petrosova keenly observed Karakalpak clothing, noting the long dress of the women with sleeves that covered hands and the elaborate distinctive elaborate turban headdress "that obliges the woman to keep her head slightly to

---

[27]Avdeeva, Introduction to Petrosova, *Karakalpakskii tanets*, p. 11.
[28]Naowarat Buddee, "How Choreometrics Reflects Self-Identity and Self-Concept Through Cultural Dance: A Developing Method," *Expressive Therapies Capstone Theses* (2020), p. 333. https://Digitalcommons.Lesley.Edu/Expressive_Theses/333.
[29]Alan Lomax, *Folk Song Style and Culture*. New York: Routledge, 1968, p. xv.
[30]Avdeeva, Introduction to Petrosova, *Karakalpakskii Tanets*, p. 10. Turkmen, Kazakh, Kirgiz, and Mongol were frequently put into the category of "people without dance."
[31]Petrosova, *Karakalpakskii Tanets*, p. 15.

the side."[32] Even the measured, customary gait of the women and the manner they slowly drop to one knee helped to suggest dance movement. The natural world—the flight of the seagull, the neck of a swan, the antlers of a deer, the measured step of the camel—all provided choreographic material. Petrosova derived different hand and arm positions from ornaments in Karakalpak carpets and embroidery. She also took into consideration the distinctive jewelry of Karakalpak women by creating gestures that brought attention to the heavy necklaces and bracelets decorated with semi-precious stones. In addition to these elements, Petrosova primarily drew from three sources: (1) movements connected with everyday tasks and labor activities, (2) movements imitating local animals and nature, and (3) activities drawn from traditional games, rituals, and ceremonies.[33]

In her analysis of Petrosova's work, Avdeeva asserted that the new Karakalpak form exhibited a distinct character:

> Uzbek traditional choreography is primarily the dance of moving poses, a dance of hands, a dance of movement, but not movements of the legs. In the Ferghana school there are almost no leg movements, in the Bukharan school also almost none, but in Khorezm dance there are many.[34]

By contrast, in Karakalpak dance, the entire body dances, there are virtuoso movements of the legs, intricate movements of the hands and arms, and unusual movements of the shoulders and head.[35] The greater use of leg movements may reflect the active, transhumant quality of Karakalpak life, so different from that of the more sedentary oasis dwellers.

Petrosova derived different hand and arm positions from characteristic designs in Karakalpak embroidery; perhaps most distinctive was the *chagallak*, the seagull, in which the dancers' arms were extended outward at shoulder level, but rotated to turn the palms up, fingers extended skyward, and elbows lifted to mimic the wings of the seagull. Movements involved with work activities, like the actions of fishermen or the motions connected in making felt, became embedded in her dance creations. In addition, some choreographies were based on themes from everyday life, like the dances *"Fisherman"* and *"Shepherd."* *"White Gold"* (cotton) depicted cotton production and *"Wedding"* featured traditional rituals. The choreography *"Amu Darya"* took inspiration from the river itself.

Turning to the oral traditions of the Karakalpak people, Petrosova found inspiration in the famous legend of the *Kyrk Kyz*—the Forty Warrior Maidens. They are found in the epics of the Oghuz Turks and appear in the story of Lady

---

[32] Ibid.
[33] Avdeeva, Introduction to Petrosova, *Karakalpakskii Tanets*, p. 9.
[34] Ibid., pp. 10–11.
[35] Ibid., p. 11.

Burla the Tall in the *Book of Dede Korkut*.[36] In the Surkhandarya Region of Uzbekistan, near the city of Termez, the ancient fortress is called *Kyrk Kyz* after the forty young women, led by the sixteen-year-old Gulayim,[37] who defended the stronghold from invaders after all the men were killed. These female warriors may have been more than myth. Archeological discoveries of *kurgan* burial mounds contained women buried with weapons, armor, and sometimes even horses. "The bowed leg bones of one 13- or 14-year-old girl attest a life on horseback, and her array of arms included a dagger and dozens of arrowheads made of wood and leather."[38] Petrosova evoked the Turkic legends of the Central Asian Amazons when she choreographed *Kyrk Kyz*, a piece for forty female dancers, and a soloist in the role of the heroine Gulayim.

As she set about her creative work, Petrosova realized that there was "not enough completeness of the musical phrase" in Karakalpak tunes to support choreographic production. She contacted composers to create new compositions with enough of a national character "that people would accept and understand them as folk tunes for stage dance."[39] To create pieces in the *lapar* genre combining song and dance, she worked with poets to select poems for song lyrics. Reflecting on her efforts to attach dance to music, she concluded that it "firmly entered" the way of life of the people making it "difficult to imagine that for many centuries the music of this people existed without dance like a plant in the desert without water."[40]

The "invented tradition" of Karakalpak dance has taken root on the Uzbek stage. Several Tashkent professional ensembles include at least one Karakalpak piece in their repertoire; national festivals such as Mustaqillik (Independence) celebrations have featured dancers from the region. Led for many years by choreographer and People's Artist of Uzbekistan Polat Madreymov (b. 1942), the *"Aikulash"* State Song and Dance Ensemble of Karakalpakstan participates in all major festivals and holidays. The capital Nukus has increasingly attracted tourism, with its surprising and spectacular Savitsky Museum,[41] housing rescued Soviet era *avant-garde* art along with collections of stunning traditional Karakalpak folk art and jewelry, and archeological discoveries.

---

[36] *The Book of Dede Korkut*, translated by Geoffrey Lewis. London: Penguin Books, 1974.

[37] Elmira Gyul, "The Mystery of Kyrk Kyz, from 40 Women Warriors to the Warriors of Light." *Voices on Central Asia*, January 16, 2020. https://voicesoncentralasia.org/the-mystery-of-kyrk-kyz-from-40-women-warriors-to-the-warriors-of-light/.

[38] Jeanninee Davis-Kimball, "Warrior Women of The Eurasian Steppes." *Archeology*, January/February (1997), p. 47.

[39] Petrosova, *Karakalpakskii Tanets*, p. 17.

[40] Ibid.

[41] The official name of this museum is the *State Museum of Arts of the Republic of Karakalpakstan named after I. V. Savitsky*. The fascinating history of this museum is chronicled in the documentary film, *Desert of Forbidden Art*. https://desertofforbiddenart.com/.

Tragedy of the Aral Sea

Even a "created" folk dance derives from the connection between humans and their natural world. Everyday activities of the Karakalpak people, like fishing, from which Petrosova drew inspiration for her choreographic creations, have almost vanished with the desiccation of the Aral Sea, once the world's fourth largest lake. This ecological tragedy has an unexpected link going back to the trade disruption caused by the U.S. Civil War (1861–1865) when the American North blockaded Southern merchant ships carrying cotton across the Atlantic. Deprived of American cotton, Russia looked elsewhere for the raw materials for its textile mills. Around the same time, the Russian Empire conquered Turkestan and found the region ideal for the cotton production that already existed there. Even after the end of the American Civil War, Russia continued to import cotton from Central Asia. The establishment of the new, cash-poor Soviet Union also saw cotton as "white gold," despite the difficult work conditions it demanded of laborers. The tremendous communal labor effort of building the Ferghana Canal in 1939 also led to the desertification of the Aral Sea. In the 1960s, the Soviet government pushed to increase cotton production and more water from the Amu Darya and Syr Darya rivers was diverted from flowing into the Aral Sea. The once abundant fish species died off, destroying the fishing industry. As the sea evaporated, the pesticides and fertilizers used on crops were absorbed into the remaining salt, then picked up by increasing sand and dust storms with winds blowing it for miles, contaminating the soil. Local populations exhibit alarmingly high levels of throat cancer, anemia, and infant mortality.

> An evolving crisis, the Aral Sea disaster has a number of negative consequences, including land degradation and desertification, shortage of drinking water, malnutrition, and deterioration of health conditions and the livelihoods of the local population. The socio-economic and environmental consequences are further complicated by the rapid speed of its negative effects.[42]

Among the peoples of the Khorezm oasis, the pre-Islamic "cult of trees," identified individual tree species that were believed to have "supernatural" properties, even endowing fertility to women.[43] But now science, and not superstition, confirms the vital role of trees in continued human survival. In 2022, the EU launched a project,

---

[42]*European Union to Plant 27 Thousand Trees in Aral Sea Basin.* April 28, 2022, Delegation of the European Union to Uzbekistan European Union, External Action. https://www.eeas.europa.eu/delegations/uzbekistan/european-union-plant-27-thousand-trees-aral-sea-basin_en?s=233.

[43]Zaynab Abidova, "Worship of Trees in Cultural Practice of the Uzbeks of the Khorezm Oasis." *EPRA International Journal of Socio-Economic and Environmental Outlook (SEEO),* 10, no. 3 (March, 2023): 10.

"My Garden in the Aral Sea," to plant 27,000 trees in the Aral Sea basin in an effort to "strengthen the health of populations, reduce environmental degradation, and boost resilience of vulnerable populations affected by the Aral Sea disaster."[44]

For millennia, the Karakalpak people lived in harmony with Nature, but the dances created in the 1950s by Elizaveta Petrosova drew from a way of life that no longer exists. Across cultures and centuries, dance has nourished humans' resilience to change and disruption, but can an artificial dance legacy provide the strength needed to survive the ecological challenges that threaten Karakalpak existence?

---

[44]Ibid. See also Aral Sea Region: Zone of Environmental Innovations and Technologies. Government of Uzbekistan. 2023.

13 KIZLARKHON DUSMUKHAMEDOVA—"QUEEN OF ALL THE GIRLS"

Early Dance Lessons

The creation of the Choreographic Institute—now the Uzbekistan State Academy of Choreography—standardized and supported training for future professional dancers, but it was not the only path to the concert stage. Children with an interest in dance could receive free lessons through the *Dom Pionerov*, the "House of Young Pioneers," which were youth clubs offering free classes in a variety of subjects. Founded in 1922, this all-Soviet program imitated many aspects of the Boy Scout program that had been banned because it did not endorse socialist ideological content.[1] Programs were open to boys and girls aged nine to fourteen. Older children could move into the Komsomol ("Young Communist") program, with a recommendation. Classes were held in so-called "pioneer palaces," sometimes housed in buildings of the former Russian aristocracy.

One of Uzbekistan's most beloved dancers, Kizlarkhon Dusmukhamedova, received her first lessons at a *Dom Pionerov* in her hometown of Tashkent. Kizlarkhon's first teacher was an Armenian[2] woman, Bella Artyemovna Arutyunova from whom she learned basic elements of ballet and Uzbek folk dance. Arutyunova's young students included Dilyafruz Djabbarova and Kadir Muminov, both of whom later became People's Artists of Uzbekistan. As part of the Young Pioneer program, children enjoyed performance opportunities and were often included in public celebrations. Kadir Muminov recalled visiting the Tashkent Pioneer Palace,

---

The name Kizlarkhon literally translates from Uzbek as "queen—or ruler—of girls."

[1]Gabe Paoletti, "Life Inside The Young Pioneers: The Soviet Union's Answer To The Boy Scouts", August 18, 2017, https://allthatsinteresting.com/young-pioneers-soviet-union.

[2]In Uzbekistan and Iran, some of the earliest dance instructors in the twentieth century were of Armenian ethnicity.

which was originally the palace of Grand Duke Nikolai Konstantinovich Romanov (1850–1918), who was banished to Tashkent by the royal family as a result of his romance with an American dancer.[3]

Muminov recalled that "in addition to clubs, there were free attractions, and we often went there. One day my brothers and I happened to be at a festival that was held there. We were led into a round dance. I followed the guys and just repeated their movements."[4] He caught the eye of one of the teachers, who invited him to join a dance group, thus introducing Kadir to dance and soon involving him in performances.

Kizlarkhon's talent also caught the attention of another professional choreographer, Isaqar Aqilov, then director of the Uzbek Philharmonic, who in 1965 brought the teenage Kizlarkhon into the dance ensemble there. She was a few years younger than his daughter Viloyat and was treated like another member of his family. Isaqar recognized Kizlarkhon's subtle lyricism, a hallmark of the Ferghana style, and began to create solos for her. Mukarram Turgunbaeva also noticed the girl's grace and wanted to recruit her for the Bakhor Ensemble, saying "I need sixteen more like her."[5] But Kizlarkhon understood that Mukarram's style was quite different from her own and to fit into the ranks of Bakhor, she would have to dance in a new way. Instead, she decided to remain as a protégé of Isaqar Aqilov, who created unique choreographies for her and enabled her to actively participate in tailoring music, dances, and costuming to reflect her personal tastes. Kizlarkhon's steadfast, life-long connection with her mentor clearly reflects the traditional *Ustoz–Shagird* relationship, one which she would later enter into with her first American student.[6]

Role of Television

The late 1960s, 1970s, and 1980s were the era of many "dancing queens" who epitomized the Uzbek ideals of feminine beauty and grace, like Mamura

---

[3]Grand Duke Nikolai Konstaninovich Romanov was the grandson of Tsar Nikolai I. His relationship with American Fanny Lear, née Harriet Blackford, shocked the royal family and eventually resulted in charges of theft and madness against the Grand Duke, who would have been a possible claimant for the throne. He was eventually exiled to Tashkent, where he made genuine civic contributions. With his own funds he built canals, theaters, movie houses, and introduced cotton seed from the United States to improve the local cotton industry. He died shortly after the Bolsheviks came to power under contested circumstances. Igor' Zimin, "'Zabytii» velikiy knyaz'." *Voprosy istorii*, No. 10 (2002): 130–39.

[4]Khaydarov, Islom. "Balethmeister Activity of the People's Artist of Uzbekistan Gadir Muminov and his Pedogogic Skills." *Oriental Art and Cultur*, 4, no. 1 (February, 2023): 223–26. https://cyberleninka.ru/article/n/balethmeister-activity-of-the-peoples-artist-of-uzbekistan-gadir-muminov-and-his-pedogogic-skills/viewer.

[5]Author's interview with Kizlarkhon Dusmukhamedova in her home, Tashkent, May 13, 2022.

[6]The present author.

Ergasheva, Dilyafruz Djabbarova, Firuza Salikhova, Rushana Sultanova, and Malika Akhmedova. Dressed in elaborate dance costumes and jewelry, they graced the covers of magazines and even appeared on a special over-sized calendar. Each dancer had a unique style and often had their own television specials.

The dance that firmly established Kizlarkhon as a soloist and rising star was the 1968 televized performance of *Gozel* ("beauty") created by Isaqar Aqilov, on the 525th jubilee of poet Alisher Navoi. The piece began with Kizlarkhon facing away from the camera, her long black braids hanging down her back. *Gozel* unfolded gently, with Kizlarkhon gracefully undulating her arms until she turned toward the camera, continuing the dance in her lyrical Ferghana style. Her petite form and classical features made it seem as if she had emerged from an Eastern miniature painting. Not surprisingly, the celebrated Uzbek painter Chingiz Akhmarov (1912–1995) painted her portrait in this style. One of these paintings can be seen in Tashkent at the State Museum of Applied Arts of Uzbekistan.[7] When Uzbek dances moved out of the *ichkari*, the nuanced gestures and facial expressions of dance became less evident in the large *massovyi* dances of concert-stage performances. Television brought back that element of visual intimacy with the ability to use camera close-up to show subtle facial expressions. A glance of the eyes, the lift of a brow, a flutter of eyelashes—all of these are traditionally part of female dance and a reminder that the first professional dancers in Uzbekistan were initially known as actresses.

Kizlarkhon's unadorned elegance harkened back to this earlier style of personal introspection which characterized the original, improvised nature of women's dance. As she explained: "I danced from the soul. I listened to music. I understood the poetry and history."[8] This sensitivity won the hearts of Uzbek women, who saw in her dance the pain of their own lives as they struggled to balance their careers with the traditional domestic expectations of a wife and mother with a home and family. They admired and identified with her qualities—"reserved, humble, gracious, but still having internal strength, love for the beauty of life and women's unique experience."[9]

For *Gozel*, Kizlarkhon wore a simple corona on her head and not the more elaborate traditional *tillakosh*, meaning "golden brow" because it mirrors the curved shape of eyebrows. She wore a princess-line dress made from a soft shade of lemon-colored silk chiffon, which gradually flared out toward the hem. Because she disliked the way that full skirts often "lifted" during fast spins, sometimes exposing an unflattering gap between the top of the pants and the bodice of the dress, she wore a "combination" with the ankle-length pants sewn into the dress. Kizlarkhon maintained this style in her solo pieces and only when cast in group

---

[7]Official Uzbek name, *O'zbekiston Respublikasi Amaliy San'ati Muzeyi.*
[8]Author's personal interview with Kizlarkhon Dusmukhamedova in her home, Tashkent, May 13, 2022.
[9]Nilufar Rakhmanova, personal communication with author, October 6, 2022.

choreographies did she wear the dance dress developed by Tamara Khanum, which had a full skirt attached to a bodice that went to the waist, often topped with a short vest. Instead of the traditional Uzbek *dupi* skullcap, Kizlarkhon often wore a *tillakosh*, or sewed her own hats and headdresses.

The Uzbek musician Muhamadjon Mirzayev created several compositions for Kizlarkhon, including *Tong Malikasi*, "Dawn of the Princess." Her special quality led to her being cast in the film *Shashmaqom* (1972), which had a historical setting, innovatively using classical Uzbek music and the poetry of Alisher Navoi, and not dialogue, to tell the stories of the characters.[10]

Kizlarkhon danced with the Shodlik Ensemble when it was under the direction of Akbar Muminov and learned Uyghur dance from Diloram Sherova, who tutored the company. Kizlarkhon's solo repertoire included pieces in all three regional styles of Uzbek dance, as well as dances representative of Uzbekistan's other ethnic minorities, such as Uyghur and Tajik. Her dances of "foreign" nations— i.e., non-Soviet peoples—included Afghan, Cuban, Iranian, and Japanese pieces. Kizlarkhon's Korean dance solo was choreographed by Diana Kwon San.

Touring Beyond Uzbekistan

After the devastating Tashkent earthquake of April 26, 1966, which destroyed countless buildings and left hundreds of thousands homeless, Soviet workers from other regions, especially Russia and Ukraine, came into the area to help rebuild the city.[11] In a gesture of gratitude, artists from Uzbekistan's Philharmonic Society, including Kizlarkhon, were sent on a three-and-a-half-month tour through Russia and Ukraine, sharing traditional Uzbek music and dance. In 1968, Kizlarkhon was selected as the only dancer to accompany a group of Uzbek artists who performed in Cairo and Alexandria, Egypt. After this trip, she was frequently given the coveted opportunity to travel abroad, often with small groups of Uzbek performing artists that included singers and musicians. Decades of foreign travel followed, taking her to Afghanistan, Japan, Morocco, Tunisia, Mongolia, the UK, Australia, New Zealand, India, Czechoslovakia, Hungary, and Poland. Within the USSR, she performed in Armenia, Georgia, Kazakhstan, and the Baltic states, also traveling to the Siberian cities of Semipalatinsk, Archangel, Sakhalin, and Kamchatka. Within the USSR, she traveled with fellow artists by train, within their own designated wagon, staying in local hotels once they reached their performance destination.

---

[10]Verified through communication with Kizlarkhon, January 31, 2023.
[11]Many stayed on in Tashkent, making their homes there.

Uzbek Dance Comes to the United States

In 1979, Kizlarkhon traveled to the United States as a soloist with a group that included dancers from the Bakhor and Shodlik ensembles, along with male Nasreddin Shermatov, and leading musicians. The artists performed in cities that had an Uzbek diaspora population, including Philadelphia, New York City, and San Francisco.[12] Although Seattle had no significant Uzbek population at the time, it was included as a stop on the tour because Seattle had become Tashkent's Sister City in 1973, the first official Soviet–American Sister City relationship. The artists' visit included a reception at the office of Seattle's mayor Charles Royer and an evening concert at Seattle University that gave the American audience their first glimpse of Uzbek dances.[13] Kizlarkhon's solos included her signature piece

FIGURE 13.1 *Ustoz* Kizlarkhon Dusmukhamedova (right), People's Artist of Uzbekistan, with her *shagird*, Laurel Victoria Gray (left).
Photo source: Author's personal archive.

---

[12]Malika Khaidarova, one of the dancers in this tour, shared a poster from this tour and recalls that it was coordinated by a Soviet Uzbek organization, the Vatan Society for Cultural Relations with Countrymen Living Abroad, and the Soviet American Friendship Society. The twenty-three participants included dancers, musicians, an interpreter, and a cameraman. The tour director was Anvar Kasymov.

[13]In the 1980s, the Seattle–Tashkent Sister City Committee became increasingly involved in significant, ground-breaking cultural exchanges with Uzbekistan, including visits by Uzbek dancer Firuza Salikhova and singer Sherali Djuraev.

Munojat, which, before the tour, she had not wanted to perform because she felt "Europeans [i.e., 'Westerners,' including Americans] would not understand the music."[14] But the concert tour program had been approved, with the artistic council insisting that it be included because, "it is our Uzbek culture." It was this very dance, *Munojat*, which planted the seeds of Uzbek dance culture in Seattle that would later take root throughout the United States and beyond.[15]

During one of her subsequent sixteen trips to the United States, Kizlarkhon performed in Washington, DC, at the Smithsonian's Baird Auditorium in conjunction with the 1989 exhibition of *Timur and the Princely Vision*, featuring cultural achievements during the reign of Tamerlane (Figure 13.1). *Washington Post* dance critic Alexandra Tomalonis characterized Kizlarkhon as "a vivacious woman whose dancing changed from demure to robust, mournful to happy, in the blink of an eye."[16]

Marriage and Family

Even with her star status, Kizlarkhon was not free from the societal stigma still attached to dancers. While Uzbek girls most commonly marry early, rarely later than twenty-four years of age, Kizlarkhon instead focused on her career and was in her early thirties when she married in 1977. A young professor—a doctor of technical sciences—fell deeply in love with Kizlarkhon and begged his parents for permission to marry her, but they adamantly refused. Unwilling to give up, the son defiantly left his parental home, causing a scandal. In response, the groom's family did not attend the wedding. But the couple endured, creating a family with two successful sons and talented grandchildren. Kizlarkhon's husband allowed her to continue her career—not always a given for female dancers who often retired after marriage and the birth of children. His support enabled her to teach and perform in the United States sixteen times, with Kizlarkhon's mother tending their sons when they were still young children. Kizlarkhon's continued participation in the Central Asian Dance Camp, first held in Santa Fe, New Mexico in 1995[17] and later in the Washington, DC area, annually introduced American dancers to the

---

[14]Personal conversation, May 13, 2022. Uzbeks frequently use the term "European" to designate all Westerners, including Americans.

[15]It was Kizlarkhon's performance of *Munojat* that night that inspired this author to study and perform Uzbek dance.

[16]Alexandra Tomalinos, "Wonders of the Uzbek Silk Road," *Washington Post*, June 16, 1989. https://www.washingtonpost.com/archive/lifestyle/1989/06/16/wonders-of-the-uzbek-silk-road/d4514bd4-418b-49e2-bb04-4bd16fb8b28a/.

[17]The Central Asian Dance Camp, founded in 1995 by the Uzbek Dance and Culture Society, first took place in Santa Fe, New Mexico, but only in 1997 did Kizlarkhon begin to teach at the camp. www.uzbek-dance.org.

basic elements of Uzbek dance, as well as to specific choreographies which they learned to perform. Kizlarkhon also worked with the Silk Road Dance Company, adding to their repertoire the famous choreographies of Tamara Khanum, Mukarram Turgunbaeva, Isaqar Aqilov, Viktoria Viloyat Aqilova, and Kunduz Mirkarimova, as well as Kizlarkhon's own compositions.[18]

Creative Achievements

In 1999, Kizlarkhon established her own independent dance company, *Munojat*, which performed at the Kennedy Center Washington, DC, in 2001. In addition to the eponymous dance, the concert included the classics of Uzbek stage choreography, such as *Pilla*, *Chaban*, and *Lazgi*. The ensemble's Khorezm dresses— dark green coats worn over orange silk dresses—were based on Tamara Khanum's personal Khorezm costume, part of the collection now in the Tamara Khanum House Museum.

Kizlarkhon has received many medals and honors in recognition of her cultural contributions. In 1972, the Uzbekistan Ministry of Culture awarded Kizlarkhon the title of Honored Artist of Uzbekistan, followed by the Laureate of the Lenin Komsomol in 1976. She received the title of People's Artist of Uzbekistan in 1984. Kizlarkhon was also awarded a new honor in 1999—*El-Yurt Hurmati Ordeni* (Order of Respect of the Nation)—created after Uzbek Independence and given in recognition for promoting the growth of national spirit and culture. Her most recent recognition came in 2022 with the *Mehnat Faxriysi* (Veteran of Labor) medal for her years of artistic service.

At the 2019 Central Asian Dance Camp, held at the Embassy of Uzbekistan in Washington DC, Kizlarkhon was honored by the Silk Road Dance Company with a special award for her forty years of sharing Uzbek dance with Americans. Her legacy of selections from her solo repertoire, as well as some of her original *massovyi* choreographies, are still performed by the Silk Road Dance Company and other American students. Kizlarkhon's instruction marks the first and longest continual contribution in bringing Uzbek dance to U.S. soil.[19]

---

[18]Among these are *Pilla*, *Katta O'yin*, *Namangan Olmasi*, *Samarqand Ushoqi*, *Keling Gular*, *Mavrigi*, and *Guldasta*. People's Artist of Uzbekistan Kadir Muminov also directly worked with Silk Road Dance Company during a 2003 trip to Washington, DC, teaching his Surkhan Darya choreography.

[19]On May 25, 2023, Kizlarkhon Dusmukhamedova passed away. Her photo graces the cover of this book.

PART SIX

FROM RED STAR TO CRESCENT MOON

14
NEW CELEBRATIONS FOR A NEW NATION

On August 31, 1991, Uzbekistan became an independent country, no longer a part of the Soviet Union. The nation now had the opportunity to shape its image to reflect this new status, to assert its own identity. Even the national color scheme changed. The ubiquitous red of the Soviet era was replaced with hues that had deep symbolic value in Central Asia. Turquoise, long associated with the Turkic people, and green, sacred color of Islam,[1] promised growth and fresh beginnings, like the Khorezm Princess of the Green Dome in Nizami's *Haft Paykar*. White resonated on many levels as a color of purity and good luck. *Oq yol*, "white road," was a wish for a safe journey. *Oq altin*, "white gold," was the term for cotton, Uzbekistan's main crop and source of wealth. On the uppermost field of turquoise was the crescent moon, long a symbol of Islam, and before that, the emblem of the life-giving "lady of waters," the Goddess Anahita.

Two Soviet holidays, May Day and Revolution Day, quickly became replaced by new holidays—one very ancient, the spring holiday of *Navruz*; and the other, *Mustaqqilk* ("Independence"), quite new. *Navruz* with its deep connection to Nature and agrarian patterns had long been observed in the Persianate and Turkic worlds. As a pre-Islamic practice it was discouraged in Iran and, "in the former Soviet system ... our holiday was banned—added to the category of reactionary ceremonies—*k'atopuga reaktison mapocimlariga*."[2] Only after the independence

---

[1]For an analysis of the color green in Islam, see Kazan Danesh and Mohammad Khazaie, "The Symbolism of Green Color in Iranian-Islamic Culture and Art."*PAYKAREAH*, 9, no.19 (2020): 18–29. DOI: 10.22055/pyk.2020.15725.

[2]Gafkhar Matyokubova, Shukhrat Tokhtasimov, and Khulkar Khamroeva, *Khorazm "Lazgi" Tarikhi va Tavsifi*. Tashkent: Zamon Poligraf, 2022, p. 26.

of Uzbekistan did *Navruz* gain status as a national holiday celebrated on an unprecedented level, blending new ideas while attempting to preserve traditions.[3]

In the following year of 1992, the nation prepared its first Independence Day celebration, crafting a program slated to take place in the former Lenin Square, now renamed Mustaqillik Maidoni. Dance rehearsals took place in the Dvorets *Druzhba Narodov* Palace of (People's Friendship) – now Xalqlar Do'stligi Saroyi – with members of all of Tashkent's professional dance ensemble participating in a *massovyi* performance piece. Choreography by People's Artist of Uzbekistan Kadir Muminov built on a theme of creation, with humanity emerging from beneath a huge canvas circle that was planned to be painted like the planet Earth. As the date of the concert drew nearer, the rehearsals moved from Druzhba Narodov to the Mustaqillik Maidoni itself, with run-throughs of all the different components in the celebration. But in the second half of August, when temperatures soared to 104 degrees or higher, conditions proved challenging. The surface of the stage, uncovered and exposed to the intense Central Asian sun, became too hot to touch or kneel upon.

Every spoken or musical element was pre-recorded, even the recitations of poetry of Alisher Navoi.[4] There were apparently no live microphones, with the exception of the one used for the speech by President Karimov. Uzbek folk entertainers performed, even tightrope walkers, a tradition that the Soviets had once tried to eliminate. Young men dressed in costumes and armor of medieval Central Asian warriors were also part of the pageant, a reminder of the region's history of conquest. Modern-day military was represented by tanks that rolled onto the square in the space behind the stage; the hatches popped open for soldiers who ran onto the stage to perform a rifle drill. A parachutist jumped from a plane to land on stage as part of the display.

Dance groups from the provinces also participated, wearing costumes of Uzbekistan's various ethnic minorities, including Tatar and Karakalpak communities. While the general approach resembled past programs of Soviet-era May Day celebrations, the content now was clearly a celebration of Uzbekistan's history and culture. The second anniversary of Independence was similar, except the unifying theme of the dance program was Motherhood. At one point, women holding their young children in their arms marched across the stage. Perhaps unconsciously, the ancient fertility cult of Anahita had returned.

Eventually the Mustaqillik celebration was moved to a new location,[5] the large plaza behind the *Xalqlar D'ostligi* (People's Friendship) concert hall. The previous

---

[3]Ibid.

[4]This practice of not allowing live microphones was similar to the practice at that time at Radio Tashkent. All announcers read from scripts and broadcasts were recorded. Only a few specially designated persons were allowed to speak at a live microphone and then only in cases of emergency.

[5]I have attempted to determine whether this happened after the 2011 Arab Spring uprising which centered around Cairo's Tahrir Square.

site of celebrations, *Mustaqillik Maydoni* (Independence Square) was redesigned, with regular rows of evergreens planted throughout the plaza, leaving no room for large public gatherings, a dance stage, or, perhaps most importantly, tanks.

The nature of the celebrations evolved as well, with an even more extensive program of dance and music and a move away from military displays. Selections from well-known European operas and ballets were performed by representatives from Uzbekistan's State Academic Bolshoi Theater of Opera and Ballet named for Alisher Navoi. Children's groups performed songs and dances and Uzbekistan's most beloved pop stars also appeared. Organized in "blocs," traditional elements occurred earlier in the program with contemporary offerings coming later in the evening. The grand finale of music and dance almost always featured the Khorezm *Lazgi*, with its lively and infectious energy with the humorous and vigorous elements of Khorezm men's dances featured in the piece. Karakalpak dance, having developed from the research and creativity of Elizaveta Petrosova, was also included, allowing for male and female pairing on stage. As in Soviet times, the holiday program still carried themes of patriotism, but now it was channeled toward Uzbekistan and focused on the creative achievements of the Uzbek people.

Just as the *Mustaqillik Bayram* quickly took the place of the Soviet-era October Revolution festivities, Uzbekistan replaced the Soviet observance of May Day with an ancient, pre-Islamic holiday throughout Central Asia and the Persianate world, uniting many nations and ethnicities. *Navruz, Nooruz, Nevruz, Nauryz*—these are all names derived from the Persian words "now ruz," or "new day," marking the Vernal Equinox and the astronomical beginning of spring.

Uzbekistan lost no time in reclaiming this traditional holiday, which had been unofficially observed in the cities and countryside, even if limited to the preparation of the traditional *sumalak* dish.[6] Curiously, Soviets had banned Navruz, perhaps because of its perceived connections to Islam, or to "old" superstitions, but the holiday was not based on any political occurrence like a revolution, or the birthday of a religious figure, but centered instead on the natural phenomenon of the spring equinox, the awakening of Nature after the darkness of winter. And for a region with primarily agrarian roots, this marked the beginning of the growing season.

Cultural Festivals

Dance played a central role in the opening and closing ceremonies of a new event, *Sharq Taronalari* (Melodies of the East), a biannual international UNESCO-sponsored music festival launched in 1997 and held in Samarkand's historic

---

[6]In Persian, this same wheat pudding is called *samanu* and is one of the seven elements, the *Haft Sin*, associated with the Nowruz holiday.

Registan. Singers and musicians were invited to compete in this juried event, although the focus was intended to be on song, as suggested by the word *tarona*. Contestants were drawn primarily from Asian countries, but also included a few participants from European nations. The jury, too, was international, with adjudicators from Egypt, Turkey, India, Germany, Korea, and the USA.[7] The Uzbek musician Diloram Amanullaeva, People's Creative Worker of Uzbekistan, composed the festival's anthem, which was recorded in five languages—Uzbek, English, French, Arabic, and Persian—and played for the opening and closing ceremonies.[8] The opening pageant in Samarkand's Registan depicted the ancient city's past as an important center on the Great Silk Road. The Executive Director for the festival's opening and closing pageants was the theater director and People's Artist of Uzbekistan Bakhodir Yuldashev. In addition to choreographies performed by Uzbekistan's professional dance companies and favorite dance soloists, teams of young girls were positioned throughout the venue to perform simple unison movements, recalling the legacy of Meyerhold and those early mass spectacles of the years immediately following the Bolshevik Revolution. Out of view of the audience, a special dance coach conducted this "movement choir," suggesting continued influences of those early theater experiments. Scores of young girls, all in simple matching costumes, waved their arms in unison, not only for the opening number, but also during the performances of the musicians, while smoke from fog machines rolled across the stage.[9]

Sharq Taronalari proved the first in a series of themed festivals in different Uzbek cities, designed to showcase the historic legacy and character of each place, along with the regional cultural specialties. At every festival, dance performances took center stage, emphasizing the specific style, folk costume, and traditions of the area. First was the *Silk and Spices Festival*, initiated in 2015 and held in Bukhara. In 2018, the *Maqom Festival* was launched in Shahrisabz, the birthplace of Tamerlane and devoted to this ancient musical genre. The *Raqs Sehri* (Magic of Dance) *Festival* was held in Khiva in 2018 and 2019 but was suspended during the global COVID-19 pandemic. In 2022, the event was reborn as the Lazgi International Dance Festival in Khiva, with participants from thirty different countries and a panel of several international judges, including representatives from Korea, France, Germany, and the USA. In 2019, the ancient city of Kokand hosted the first International Festival of Handicrafts with a grand opening ceremony in front

---

[7]The author represented the USA as a member of the Festival Jury.
[8]Confirmed by communication with the composer.
[9]For that first Sharq Taronalari Festival in 1997, I served as a member of the jury. I expressed concern for the deleterious effect that chemicals from the fog machine might have on the vocalists and also suggested that as the event was not an *estrada* (pop) concert but an international music competition, the extraneous movement distracted from the performances that were being considered in competition, especially the serious classical forms, like Indian *raga*. The fog machine and "movement chorus" were not used during the competitive musical performances for the rest of the festival that year.

of the palace that was once the residence of the Khan. The program boldly—and rather unexpectedly—opened with an elderly woman, alone on stage, singing a traditional song of welcome *a cappella* a beautiful embrace of genuine folk culture. Regional folklore, music, and dance showcased traditions while, amazingly, carpenters constructed two traditional pavilions in full view of the audience during the stage presentations. At the beginning of 2020, with changes easing visa procedures and the creation of new hotels, Uzbekistan seemed poised on the verge of a surge in international tourism, which had to pause when the planet faced the coronavirus pandemic.

On television, inspired by the worldwide popularity of programs like *So You Think You Can Dance, Dancing with the Stars, American Idol,* and other contests, Uzbekistan's Z'or TV launched its own competition, *Joziba.* Beginning in 2018, the program featured dance groups and soloists who performed in front of a jury of renowned dancers and choreographers. Most presented Uzbek regional styles, but Tajik, Russian, Turkish, Bollywood, and other styles were also included. The *Joziba* KIDS edition featured dance solos by children from eleven to sixteen years of age.

Unlike some of the Western talent shows where judges often cruelly mock contestants, the adjudicators on *Joziba* offered helpful and constructive criticism, advising the artists on the fine points of dance, encouraging them. Winners received prizes and the popular program ran until 2020 when COVID-19 made filming unsafe.

The Power of Pop

Known as *estrada*, popular music concerts often include dancers. The beloved and long-lived music group Yalla consistently worked for many years with one soloist, Roza Abdulkhairova, who beautifully performed Uzbek dances as well as an Arabic piece to the hit song *Jinuni*, modestly attired in a sparkling, long-sleeved, golden gown. Many pop singers include dancers in their performances, but not always as successfully as Yalla. Alina Magdiyeva, a senior teacher of the Uzbek State Academy of Choreography, believes that dance is an "expressive means used by a pop singer only when it helps to reveal the idea of a song" and "illustrates it with the language of choreographic expressiveness. The dancer embodies on stage the image of the character about which the vocalist sings. For this, of course, she must possess the skills of acting."[10] And a professional choreographer is needed. The deep-rooted connection between song and movement goes to the heart of Uzbek dance. Pop music is no exception, and "in turn, dance can

---

[10]Alina Aripovna Magdeiyeva, "Uzbek Dance: The Way to Renewal and Revival." *International Journal of Innovations in Engineering Research and Technology*, 7, no.8 (2021): 82. https://repo.ijiert.org/index.php/ijiert/article/view/169.

greatly contribute to the popularization of pop songs."[11] Instead "you can often see dancers performing not so much a dance as certain rhythmic movements to the beat of a sounding song. They only serve as a background for the song, and nothing more."[12] Magdiyeva asserts that all too often "poor choreographic training of performers is hidden behind the splendor or extravagance of the costume."[13]

Reclaiming the Legacy

In the early years of Uzbek independence, some changes had a deleterious impact on dance groups. In 1997, a presidential decree creating the UzbekRaqs organization, named for Mukarram Turgunbaeva, had the result of ending the sovereignty of individual ensembles like *Shodlik, Zarafshan, Lazgi, Tanovar*, and *Bakhor*, bringing them all under the official umbrella of this new entity. These original ensembles, each with their unique character reflecting a particular regional emphasis and the unique vision of their directors and choreographers, promoted diversity and creativity in the further development of Uzbek stage dance. While some ensembles like Bakhor were all-female, other companies such as Shodlik, Zarafshan, and Lazgi included male dancers. Bakhor Ensemble also lost its home building on the former Lenin Square—now *Mustaqullk Maydonai*—which housed rehearsal space and a performance hall. By 1997, the ensemble consisted of only about a dozen dancers. The signature *massovyi* choreographies of Bakhor were no longer possible. For nearly twenty years the ensemble ceased to exist.

Renaissance of Dance

Islam Karimov served as president of Uzbekistan for twenty-five years; an entire generation had grown up under him. His passing on September 2, 2016, and the inauguration of Shavkat Mirziyoyev president on December 14, 2016, marked the beginning of a new era of reforms which touched all aspects of Uzbek life.

The attention and support given to Uzbekistan's dance heritage stimulated the dawn of a renaissance. One major contribution came when the Choreographic Institute, a dance school for training children in Uzbek dance, folk dance, character dance, and ballet, along with academic courses, was augmented and elevated to a new status as the Uzbekistan State Academy of Choreography. On February 4, 2020, a presidential decree was adopted on measures to "radically improve the system for training highly qualified personnel and further develop scientific potential

---

[11]Ibid.
[12]Ibid.
[13]Ibid.

in the field of dance art (No. PP-4585, 04.02.2020)."[14] This encouraged not only dance training in national and world dance as a performance art, but also as a field of academic research and study. Significantly, the decree referenced the "*ustoz-shogird*" tradition as a foundation for creating dance schools and "training of specialists and personnel of high qualification according to international standards."

The Rebirth of Bakhor

Most significant for the future development of Uzbek stage dance was the rebirth of the Bakhor Ensemble as a result of the February 4, 2020 presidential decree, giving the ensemble a new birthday. Even though the announcement of Bakhor's restoration was soon followed by the difficult circumstances which emerged during the world-wide COVID-19 pandemic, plans went forward with rebuilding the company, holding online auditions, and eventually rehearsing under quarantine conditions. The first efforts were to train a new generation of dancers and revive the classic choreographies of Mukarram Turgunbaeva. New costumes were sewn, based on the traditional dresses of the original company. In a very short time, especially given the circumstances, the ensemble first premiered in late 2021 and by the spring of 2022, began to perform at local and international festivals, resuming the work of Mukarram Turgunbaeva of sharing Uzbek dance on a global scale.

In 2023, the Bakhor Ensemble performed in Dubai as well as in several cities in Russia. Most importantly, the 110th anniversary of Mukarram Turgunabeva on her "adopted" birth date of May 31 was celebrated in Tashkent with a gala concert held at the newly refurbished Sverdlov Theatre where she began her dance career after running away from home to her fate as one of the most influential creators of Uzbek stage dance.

Emerging Global Presence

The onset of the world-wide COVID-19 pandemic moved planned international conferences to the Zoom format, as in the case of the *Colors of Bukhara: National Dance in the 21st Century*, which was hosted in Tashkent and held in a virtual format on September 30, 2020. By 2022, in-person dance events were held and the First International Scientific–Practical Conference took place in Khiva, Uzbekistan in April 2022, with the theme of "Khorezm Dance Lazgi: Development of National Dances and Their Significance at the Present Time."

---

[14]Resolution of the President of the Republic of Uzbekistan, February 4, 2020, No. PP-4585, https://cis-legislation.com/document.fwx?rgn=122372.

The question of maintaining Uzbek identity in the age of globalization presents challenges. Alina Magdiyeva, senior teacher at the Uzbek State Academy of Choreography, noted that with independence, "art workers of Uzbekistan, including dance, got the opportunity to freely enter the world stage."[15] However, as Magdiyeva noted, with widening contact comes a responsibility to "carefully preserve the national identity of Uzbek dance schools in the context of globalization from the negative impact of 'mass culture.'"[16] In answer to the question of how "to preserve the original 'purity' of the Uzbek national dance," Magdiyeva cited the legacy of the "outstanding figures of the Uzbek national dance art of the 20th century"—specifically Yusufjon-Kyzyk Shakarjanov, Tamara Khanum, Usta Olim Kamilov, Isaqar Aqilov, Mukarram Turgunbaeva, Gavkhar Rakhimova, Kunduz Mirkarimova, Yulduz Ismatova, "and many other masters," crediting them with the fame that Uzbek dance has achieved worldwide "not only among fans of the art"[17] but that has also inspired and trained many future dancers.

An emerging trend in Uzbek dance presentations threatens the integrity of stage performances when choreographies are placed in front of huge LED screens showing videos of popular tourism sites. The moving images do not connect directly to the regional origins of the dances being performed, nor do they enhance thematic content of the piece. They are clearly videos made to promote tourism. They distract the viewer and literally "upstage" the dancers, with movements and colors that compete for attention. The constantly changing light levels from the screen also impact the eyes of audience members, whose pupils continually expand and contract in response. At times the dancers become underlit, their facial expressions disappearing into shadows as the screen behind them fills with bright light. Instead of projecting images that artistically interact with choreography, music, and movement (as has been done so skillfully in Chinese contemporary dance and also in certain BTS K-Pop performances),[18] the visual disruption sends a disrespectful message that the dance by itself is not sufficient entertainment. It is a painful irony that the very dance form that was hidden away for centuries in the *ichkari* is now being overshadowed by technology that fights with the architecture of the choreography and obscures the emotional expressiveness of the performers.

As Mukarram Turgunbaeva observed, Uzbek dance traditions were thousands of years old but not deeply studied and written about, in contrast to ballet which is only a few centuries old, yet well-known to the world. She hoped Bakhor would

---

[15]Magdiyeva, "Uzbek Dance," p. 83.
[16]Ibid., p. 84.
[17]Ibid., p. 83.
[18]For Chinese contemporary choreography, see: "Romantic Peacock Duo on CCTV," https://youtu.be/EB8RmZoiKGE?si=yj2MUC-9zE-j6pA7. For BTS K-Pop, the choreography "Black Swan" exemplifies the use of projections on an LED surface that harmoniously merge with the choreography instead of detracting from it: https://youtu.be/0bgL7juKY6Q?si=Cl_pUyNFYQKOoiWq.

FIGURE 14.1 Kadir Muminov performing "*Lagan*," the platter dance created by Isaqar Aqilov. Muminov performs with dancers from his Shodlik Ensemble at Pakhtakor Stadium at the opening of the football season, 1987. After Independence, public performances of dance continued at community celebrations.
Photo credit: Rustambek Sharipov.

increase global awareness of these Central Asian dance traditions, but it was only after her passing that members of the Bakhor Ensemble performed in the United States, when in 1979 a smaller group of dancers and musicians toured along with guest soloists. In 1990, Ensemble Uzbekistan, directed by Kadir Muminov and with both male and female dancers, performed to enthusiastic, sold-out audiences in Seattle and Berkeley (Figure 14.1).[19] In 2000, Ensemble Munojat, with female dancers and their musicians, led by Kizlarkhon Dusmukhamedova, performed to an enraptured crowd at the Kennedy Center in Washington, DC, but no sizeable Uzbek dance and music group appeared in the United States after that. Since then, the world has changed and popular dance world-wide is more sexualized with costuming more revealing, while just across Uzbekistan's southern border, on the other side of the Amu Darya, women in Afghanistan are being excluded from the public sphere, denied education and the opportunity to work, conditions that mark a return to the conditions of the *ichkari* from more than a hundred years ago. The original impetus of the dance pioneers to share their dances in public motivated courageous women to defy tradition, facing harassment and even death simply to leave their homes with an open face. These artists found common cause with the new socialist goal of female emancipation, opening up opportunities for education and travel, and the chance to learn and develop their art. Their striving resonated with world developments in dance. The original pioneers of modern dance in the West were all female. Were the women of Uzbekistan so very different?

---

[19]In Seattle, at Meany Hall at the University of Washington in Berkeley, at Zellerbach.

15 CONCLUSION: LESSONS OF RESILIENCE

Shaped by the continuing legacy of cultural interaction and exchange, Uzbek stage dance grew from the important role of dance in the lives of Central Asian women. It developed from the ancient spiritual elements and regional roots of various folk dance styles, such as the *yallachi* of the Ferghana Valley, the *sozanda* of Bukhara and Samarkand, and the *khalfa* of Khorezm. The distinct geography and history of these dance zones led to recognizable qualities of movement, music, and clothing. The early innovators themselves reflected these diverse demographics. As elsewhere in Muslim cultures, Christians, Jews, and Roma-Sinti people often filled the role of public performers. Non-Uzbek individuals like the ethnic Armenian Tamara Khanum, and the Bukharan Jew Isaqar Aqilov, were both born on the territory of present-day Uzbekistan and were deeply connected to local culture. The unique elements of different Uzbek dance zones reveal connections to ancient origins and links to other Turkic, Central Asian and Persianate dance forms, and hints at the more difficult to trace elusive yet continual influences of Romani populations who make mercurial appearances over the centuries.

The foundation beneath Uzbek dance is rhythm, upon which all other elements are built. Even without vocal or instrumental accompaniment, rhythm dictates movement, constantly shifting patterns and adding sharp accents for dramatic poses that finish movement phrases. Highly gendered roles led to the development of different spheres of work and leisure activities. Removed from active participation in public life and sequestered within the *ichkari*, women's vestigial links to the Divine Feminine remained. Their house-bound dances now became part of the repertoire of those sons who took them into the public sphere as professional entertainers and artists.

The struggle to win the right to appear in public with "an open face" took the lives of many women who cast aside the *paranjah*. It took courage, not just for one day, but continual valor. The girls who first stepped onto the stage and risked their lives were genuine fighters and not passive creatures mindlessly shaped by Soviet policy. They expressed their innermost sentiments as new possibilities opened to them. After these first steps, they established institutions to develop and disseminate systematic dance education. The significant role of women as dance innovators was a global phenomenon at the beginning of the twentieth century. Uzbekistan's female dance makers should be recognized as part of this feminist movement in the arts.

Archeological excavations on the territory of present-day Uzbekistan have uncovered multilayered sites bearing witness to the endless and nameless waves of humans who have swept over this land with their own languages, traditions, and histories. The details of many past floods of invasion and immigration are lost, but the more recent forced resettlements of entire populations such as the Koryo-saram and Crimean Tatars provide insight into how these people, with their own rich and long-established traditions of music and dance, managed to preserve their cultural heritage and find a place in their new home.

Invasion and war—all too familiar on the lands that now comprise Uzbekistan—met with an immediate response from Uzbekistan's performing artists. Many of them were the same dancers who had endured the dangers and hardships of the AgitProp brigades during the Russian Civil War (1917–1923), facing attacks from family members, conservative elements of society, and the Basmachi. Ever resilient, this experience of creating and performing dances that had ideological content, and often in the simplest physical conditions, prepared them to restore past pieces and create new works to encourage those on the war Front. These activities took dancers into new lands as the front opened up in Europe. Performances in Iran by Tamara Khanum's group brought them into direct contact with a culture with which they shared many common roots.

Displaced by the Second World War, those Soviet artists sent from Moscow and Leningrad to Uzbekistan found themselves suddenly immersed in Central Asian culture—the land, the people, the food—and the traditions of music and dance. This cross-cultural experience, similar to that of Central Asian artists in Moscow during the 1920s and 1930s, was just one of many over millennia, but the Central Asian impact on the art of these uprooted artists deserves greater examination rather than an assumption of a one-sided influence of Russian culture upon the local inhabitants.

The Soviet government's insistence that all ethnic groups have a developed national stage dance required that the traditionally nomadic Karakalpak people be included in the Great Soviet "dance party." While earlier attempts to create a Karakalpak folk dance did not meet with great success, Elizaveta Petrosova took on the challenge with "reverse engineering," looking at the customary movement patterns of daily activities and turning them into dance vocabulary. She approached the project with respect for the people, living with them and studying their traditional legacy which was stored in highly portable culture—epic poetry and stories, intricate carpet and embroidery designs, and remarkable jewelry. As descendants of the armies of Genghis Khan, the Karakalpak's link to the nomadic ancestors of many in present-day Uzbekistan appeared in movement patterns, especially elements connected to the important role of the horse in their society. In this singular case of "invented tradition," the Karakalpaks now had the requisite "dance card" that has continued to secure them inclusion and recognition in celebrations of independent Uzbekistan.

Recovering from the war with its disruptions and privations—truly a psychological winter—led to the hope of a better world, and a commitment to international understanding that could lead to World Peace. Concert programs that had previously focused on Uzbek regional dances as well as those from the various republics of the USSR now expanded to include non-Soviet nationalities. For Tamara Khanum, her all-too-personal experience with death and violence, as well as a deep commitment to social justice and world peace, motivated her to further develop the *lapar* genre she had used at the very beginning of her days as a performing artist. True to the syncretic roots of Central Asian performing arts, she incorporated song, dance, and theater into vignettes depicting elements from the various cultures she encountered. Her genuine embrace of other peoples and their arts made her an ideal representative of the post-war USSR.

Another development in Uzbekistan's dance scene furthered international contact beyond the borders of the USSR. Mukarram Turgunbaeva, who had stepped onto the Uzbek stage in the early, perilous years following the Bolshevik Revolution, had long been performing in ensembles and creating choreographies. But she wanted to create a permanent, all-female collective with a repertoire dedicated to bringing Central Asian dance traditions to the concert stage. The powerful impact of the 1957 World Exhibition of Youth and Students, held in Moscow, proved the perfect showcase for the fledgling Bakhor Ensemble. The development of the Bakhor Ensemble became the zenith of Mukarram's creative work into which she poured all her knowledge and experience. Bakhor toured throughout the USSR and performed in dozens of foreign countries. After the passing of Mukarram Turgunbaeva in 1978, the ensemble continued for almost two decades under various leadership until 1997 when Bakhor, along with the other professional folkloric dance ensembles, was absorbed into the UzbekRaqs organization, ironically named for Mukarram Turgunbaeva.

In 1979, members of the Bakhor Ensemble for the first time toured the United States along with guest dance artists Kizlarkhon Dusmukhamedova and Nasreddin Shermatov. Here was the flowering of a new era of Uzbek dance, when leading soloists became the nation's "dancing queens." Their performances were aired regularly on Uzbek television. They appeared on magazine covers and even graced oversized calendars featuring them in beautiful costumes. Mamura Ergasheva,

Dilyafruz Djabbarova, Kizlarkhon Dusmukhamedova, Firuza Salikhova, Malika Akhmedova, Lola Aqilova, Rushana Sultanova, and several others became cultural icons embodying the beauty and grace of Uzbek femininity. While most had graduated from the Choreographic Institute and went on to join professional ensembles, Kizlarkhon followed a different path, first learning dance at the House of Young Pioneers, then being selected by Isaqar Aqilov to join the dance group at the Uzbek Philharmonic. Although she participated in ensembles, Kizlarkhon exerted considerable control over her solo career, performing choreographies specifically created for her by Aqilov. She actively participated in shaping musical accompaniment and the design of her costumes. It was through Kizlarkhon's repeated trips to the USA as a guest instructor at the Central Asian Dance Camp that Uzbek dance traditions began to gain a permanent foothold with Americans.

Independence for Uzbekistan opened many possibilities to shape national character, but the dissolution of the USSR also created economic and social challenges, including questions of identity. The dance arts struggled but continued to be featured in the celebrations that replaced former Soviet holidays. The official recognition of the ancient pre-Islamic holiday of Navruz marked a return to native traditions, and the observance of Mustaqillik Bayram celebrated the new independence of Uzbekistan. Dance also played a role in new events, like the international music festival *Sharq Taronalari* (Melodies of the East), which takes place biennially in Samarkand's historic Registan.

The uncertainty of those years of building Uzbek nationhood have been studied elsewhere, but significant governmental support for the dance arts came in 2019 by decree of President Shavkat Mirziyoyev, who created a new physical home for the Choreographic Institute, making it the basis for the new Uzbekistan State Academy of Choreography offering, in addition to early dance training and advanced degrees in dance. In a remarkable testament to resilience, after decades of dormancy, the Bakhor Ensemble was granted new life in the same 2019 decree. Even when the worldwide COVID-19 epidemic placed much of the world in quarantine, organizers continued to audition and train new dancers to revive the repertoire, enabling the Bakhor Ensemble to return to the world stage in 2022.

The isolation of the pandemic also brought Uzbek dance training to a world audience through the technology of Zoom. While remote teaching has definite drawbacks because of the less-than-ideal spatial conditions of home settings and the students' need to constantly direct their gaze to the screen, it did allow a rudimentary exposure to the elements of Uzbek dance to new enthusiasts.

As cited earlier, ethnomusicologist Jean During, reflecting on the nomadic heritage of Central Asians, observed that "they adapt, they make do, they borrow from others."[1] This flexibility, this resilience, allowed them to absorb many

---

[1]Jean During, "Power, Authority and Music in the Cultures of Inner Asia." *Ethnomusicology Forum*, 14, no. 2 (2005): 160.

influences, shaping them to their needs and aesthetics. The Russian and Soviet cultural influences that followed in the wake of the Bolshevik Revolution were yet another set of possibilities to enhance the development of traditional Central Asian women's dance, another episode in the ongoing conversation between East and West. The Uzbeks did not "lose" their dance as a result of exposure to Russian and Soviet ballet and folk ensembles. Instead, they absorbed elements that they could adapt to their goal of bringing Uzbek women's dance to the concert stage on a professional level.

Improvisation is long established as one of the hallmarks of Central Asian music and dance. If Uzbek dance looks different today than as described in some earlier accounts or preserved on archival film footage, it should be remembered that the women themselves have changed. Access to education and greater social freedom, along with systematic dance education, has changed them, just as earlier generations had to adapt to gender separation. Although new choreography has emerged from fresh improvisation, the dance has kept the flavor of its characteristic roots.

The central importance of dance as a form of expression, whether in the private setting of a home, as a communal celebration, or on the concert stage, continues to develop. Traditional dance always evolves to fulfill new needs and functions. But perhaps most importantly, the persistence of traditional dance elements reflects cultural resilience. Although women's participation in the public sphere diminished under Islam, *dance did not disappear*. Women's artistic expression simply moved to the *ichkari*, where it adapted and developed. And when the Soviet emancipation of women offered a "bigger stage" for Uzbek artists, the dance evolved to fill this exciting new venue. The cultural roots and spiritual outlook embodied in Uzbek dance remain, a powerful and enchanting gestural legacy of their unique and enduring heritage.

More can, and should, be written about the women's dance traditions of Uzbekistan and their deeper connections with the diverse cultures of the Silk Road, both past and present. Scholarship must confront oppressive ideologies that blur understanding of the dance, from the Orientalism of the Russian Imperial era to the political dogma of the Soviet era and to the neo-colonial assertions of Western scholars focusing on paradigms of power.

Scholarship should move forward with greater cultural sensitivity from a non-colonialist perspective. Collaborative research with Uzbekistan's scholars, combined with embodied knowledge, will facilitate a deeper understanding of Central Asian dance and culture. Most importantly, Western scholars must lift their self-imposed *paranjah* of gender bias and acknowledge women's seminal role as culture bearers. Through the resilient creativity of Central Asian dance pioneers, innovators, practitioners, and archivists, one of humanity's most engaging art forms continues to thrive and evolve.

GLOSSARY OF DANCE-RELATED TERMS[1]

Ailanish "turn," a traveling spin, known to have been done by the *bachas*.

Aka "elder brother," respectful form of address for a man who is older than the person addressing him.

Askia from Arabic "aqeel" for the traditional Uzbek folk humor competition.

Auch in music, the emotional highpoint and often expressed in dance with fast spins.

Bacha from Persian for "child," a Central Asian dancing boy.

Bakbaka Silash "stroking the chin," movement when the hand top of one hand gently passes under the chin.

Barmoq qirsillatish snapping with one or both hands, using first and third fingers of hand.

Belkuchlar "waist" embrace, when arms encircle the waist.

Chagalak balikh tutushi "seagull catching fish," from Khorezm men's dance, performed with widespread legs, torso bent forward, arms behind like wings with palms open, in imitation of seagull diving for fish.

Chang Central Asian hammer dulcimer, often used in folk orchestras

Charkh from Persian for "wheel," Central Asian classical turn in which the upper body moves in the sagittal plane, performed in place or while traveling in a circular path.

Childirma another term for *doira,* the Central Asian frame drum.

Chuchvah face screen woven from horse hair, traditionally made by the Luli population.

Doira the circular Central Asian hand drum with metal rings set into the inner frame.

Dutar also **dutor** the long-necked string instrument found throughout Central Asia, often played by women in the *ichkari.*

Gap from Uzbek "word" or "conversation," an informal social group that gathers regularly.

Garmon from Russian "garmon," a term for a button accordion used in Khorezm music.

Gavda Irgitish Khorezm dance, when the dancer lifts ribs in final pose.

Guncha "flower bud." Gesture in which in fingertips are brought together like a closed blossom.

Gulbargi from Persian "flower" "leaf," performed with arms crossed in front of body and can be done with palms turned inward o routward.

Gul oyin "flower dance," begin with arms in first position, bring hands together to clap in sixth, then left hugs waist right opens between first and third.

---

[1]Uzbek dance terms reflect the multi-ethnic heritage of Turkic and Persianate cultures, especially in bilingual areas. R. Sayfullaeva, H. Hamroeva, and T. A. Butunbaeva (2021). "Language of Uzbek National Dance Art Movements: Interpretation of National Values." *Linguistics and Culture Review,* 5(S4): 2429. https://doi.org/10.21744/lingcure.v5nS4.1992.

Harakat from Arabic meaning "action," category of specific movements and gestures.

Ichkari the inner area, female portion of a traditional Central Asian house.

Ilon "snake," the coiling movement of arms led by hands with fingers brought together to form the shape of a snake head.

Iyak harakati movements accented with a small, quick chin lift.

Jayron Shohi "gazelle antlers," performed with arms held above head, palms outward, fingers extended upward.

Jigit from Turkic for daring and skillful horseman.

Kaichi "scissors," a traveling step executed with alternating toes turned inward, then rotating so the heels touch.

Kairoki a pair of stone "castanets" often used in Khorezm and Bukharan dance.

Kari Also written as **Qori** honorific given to a reciter of the Quran.

Katta O'yin "Great Dance," a cycle of dances and rhythms central to the traditional KISHLAK bacha repertoire.

Kigiir buyin "bird neck," the isolated lateral head slide imitating the movement of a bird's head, often accompanies movements for women.

Kliuch a short movement combination that ends a dance phrase.

Khalfa professional female entertainers in the Khorezm region.

Khanum also written as **Khonum**. "Lady" or "Madam," honorific title for a respected woman.

Kyzyk honorific title given to Uzbek folk comedian, jester, or humorist.

Koryo-saram from Korean for "Korean People," term used to signify Korean population in Russia and Central Asia.

Labi shakar from Persian "labi" lips, and "shakar" meaning sugar. It refers to a gesture indicating the lips.

Lazgi genre of dances specific to the Khorezm dance zone.

Luli distinct historic Central Asian population also found in Iran and Azerbaijan, possibly of Roma-Sinti origin.

Main sabo "gentle breeze," a movement of wrists with hands above the head.

Maskaraboz traditional clowns in Uzbek folk theater.

Massovyi from Russian for large group choreography.

Mukomlar decorative movement in dance.

Munojat from Arabic for a prayer or entreaty, a traditional song.

Mushak fireworks.

Oizhamol from Uzbek "oi" for mirror and moon, and Arabic "jamaal" meaning "beautiful." In Ferghana dance, the right hand is lifted out from the side of face to reveal and hide.

Oinaga karash "looking in mirror," gesture down with palm of one hand flattened, fingers held tightly together, and held out from face.

Opa "elder sister," respectful form of address added to an individual's first name.

Oyok harakatlari category of leg actions or movements.

Peshanaband from Persian "peshani" for forehead and "band" for something which ties. In Bukhara, this is the name of the cylindrical headdress worn by women.

Peshkurta from Persian, the "Y"-shaped piece of embroidery attached to the front of a Bukharan woman's dress.

Qo'ldasta ailanishi rotation of the hands, wrist circles.

Qo'ldasta xarakatlari movements of wrists and hands clapping.

Qo'lband in Ferghana dance, arms crossed at chest level with right hand under left, with hands palms resting on top arms just above elbows.

Qosh uchirish eyebrow movement done with one eyebrow or both or alternately.

Raqs from Arabic, "dance." Uzbeks also use "oyin" for dance.

Raqqosi from Arabic, "dancer."

Rumol uyin dance or dance movements done with scarf.

Sadr the *usul* and ritual dance associated with a funeral dance of mourning.

Salom the formal bow done at the beginning and end of dance to acknowledge the audience.

Sart term used to distinguish between the settled populations of Turkestan and the nomadic peoples.

Shokh or shox the characteristic 360-degree turn, similar to pirouette, but always done to the left.

Sildirma movement of body from waist, a rib "break" accent.

Soch silash "hair brushing," a movement in which the hands alternately stroke the hair.

Sozanda professional female entertainers from Bukhara and Samarkand dance zone who originally performed only for women.

Suzish "swimming," a turn with both hands placed in the small of back, palms turned outward.

Tajik a recent ethnonym for an ancient Persianate population and language of Central Asia. Tajik population can be found throughout Uzbekistan, especially Bukhara and Samarkand. Within Tajikstan, numerous distinct regional dances can be found.

Tanovar traditional Ferghana women's dance and song, often expressing longing.

Tashkari male area of the Central Asian home, also where male guests are received.

Tatar a historic term once used to identify any Turkic-speaking population in Central Asia and the Caucasus. Now signifies specific Tatar populations, such as the Crimean Tatars and Kazan Tatars.

Tebranish swaying of the upper body, with head leaning to the opposite side and gently pulled along by the torso movement.

Titratma trembling, vibration, quiver, done with hands and upper body, especially characteristic of Khorezm dance.

Tumor traditional amulet made from fabric or metal, often worn by women in traditional dances.

Usul from Arabic "asl" for "origin or base", the general term for rhythm, although specific rhythms have individual names.

Uyghur ancient Turkic people with close linguistic and cultural ties to Uzbeks. They have distinct dance traditions including traditional group and ritual dances.

Uyin dance, entertainment, play, also spelled *oyin*.

Yallachi professional female entertainers in the Ferghana dance zone who performed exclusively for women's gatherings.

Yolka kokish isolated shoulder movements, sometimes layered with small vibrations.

Zang small metal bells worn on the wrists, formerly also worn on dancers' ankles.

Zebigardon traditional pectoral jewelry worn by Uzbek women.

Zhiyak woven trim used as a border of coats and hems of pants.

BIBLIOGRAPHY

Abazov, Rafi. *Culture and Customs of the Central Asian Republics*. Westport, CT: Greenwood Press, 2007.

Abbott, Nabia. "Pre-Islamic Arab Queens." *The American Journal of Semitic Languages and Literatures* 58, no. 1 (1941): 1–22.

Abidova, Zaynab. "Worship of Trees in Cultural Practice of the Uzbeks of the Khorezm Oasis," *EPRA International Journal of Socio-Economic and Environmental Outlook (SEEO)*, Vol. 10, Issue 3, March 2023, pp. 10–12.

Abdi, Ali. "The Afghan Bachah and Its Discontents: An Introductory History." *Iranian Studies*, 56, no. 1 (2023): 161–80. doi:10.1017/irn.2022.42.

Abdukhalimov, Bakhrom, and Natalia Karimova. "Central Asia and the Republic of Korea: A Sketch on Historical Relations." *Acta Via Serica*, 4, no. 2 (2019): 119–28.

Abraikulova, N. Ye. Khoreograficheskaya interpretatsiya obshchechelovecheskikh tsennostey. *Molodoy uchenyi*, No. 10 (144), 2017, pp. 462–64. https://moluch.ru/archive/144/40506/.

Adams, Laura L. "Globalization, Universalism, and Cultural Form." *Comparative Studies in Society and History*, 50, no. 3 (2010): 614 –40. Doi:10.1017/S0010417508000273.

Adams, Laura L. "Invention, Institutionalization and Renewal in Uzbekistan's National Culture." *European Journal of Cultural Studies*, 2, no.3 (1999): 355–73. https://doi-org.proxygw.wrlc.org/10.1177/136754949900200304.

Adams, Laura L. *The Spectacular State: Culture and National Identity in Uzbekistan*. Durham, NC: Duke University Press, 2010.

Ahmed, Shahab. *Before Orthodoxy: The Satanic Verses in Early Islam*. Cambridge, MA: Harvard University Press, 2017.

Akhmedov, Makhmud. *Isakhar Akilov, Ocherki o zhizni i deyatel'nosti [baletmeystera]*. Tashkent: Gosudarstvennoe Izdatel'stvo Khudozhestvennoi Literatura, 1975.

Aini, Sadriddin. *Bukhara: Reminiscences*. Moscow: Raduga Publishers, 1986.

al-Narshakhī, Abu Bakr Muhammad ibn Jaʻfar. *The History of Bukhara; Translated from a Persian Abridgement of the Arabic Original by Narshakhī*. Ed. and transl. by Richard N. Frye. Princeton, NJ: Markus Wiener Publications, 2011.

Allworth, Edward, editor. *The Tatars of Crimea: Return to the Homeland*. Durham, NC: Duke University Press, 1998.

Ameri, Azardokht. "Iranian Urban Popular Social Dance and So-Called Classical Dance: A Comparative Investigation in the District of Tehran." *Dance Research Journal*, 38, no. 1/2 (2006): 163–79. Accessed September 1, 2020. http://www.jstor.org/stable/20444669.

Aminova, R. KH. *The October Revolution and Women's Liberation in Uzbekistan*. Moscow: Nauka Publishers, 1985.

Amir-Mokri, Mahvash. *Noerooz & Other Iranian Celebrations: A Mythological and Historical Study*. Mahvash Amir-Mokri, 2015.

And, Metin. *Turkish Dancing*. Ankara: Dost Yayinlari, 1976.

Andreev, Boris. *Povest' o tantsovshchitse*. Tashkent: Gafur Gulyam, 1987.

Anthony, David W. *The Horse, the Wheel, and Language; How Bronze-Age Riders from the Eurasian Steppes Shaped the Modern World*. Princeton, NJ: Princeton University Press, 2007.

Aschenbenner, Joyce. *Katherine Dunham: Dancing A Life*. Urbana, IL: University if Illinois Press, 2002.

Ashirov, Adkham. "Traces of Shamanistic Beliefs in Life Patterns of The Uzbeks in the Fergana Valley." www.Academia.Edu/9761920/Traces_Of_Shamanistic_Beliefs_In_Life_Patterns_Of_The_Uzbeks_In_The_Fergana_Valley.

Ashirov, Adkhamjon. "Thoughts Related to the Cult of Water in Zoroastrianism." *EPRA International Journal of Multidisciplinary Research (IJMR)*, 6, no. 5, May 2020, DOI:10.36713/epra2013.

Atamukhamedov, Akbar. "Forms of a Mass Holiday in Uzbekistan: The Content of the Spectacle, Game Models, Rules for Staging." *International Journal of Social Science and Human Research*, 5, no. 12 (2022): 5371–76. DOI:10.47191/ijsshr/v5-i12–18.

Atayeva, Merjen. "Kushtdepdi of the Turkmen and Its Origins." *Central Asia Forum*, January 15, 2020. https://centralasiaforum.org/2020/01/15/kushtdepdi-of-the-turkmen-and-its-origins/.

Avdeeva, L. *Galia Izmailova*. Tashkent: Gafur Gulyam, 1975.

Avdeeva, L. *Narodnaya Artistka SSSR Tamara Khanum*. Ministry of Culture of UzSSR, 1959.

Avdeeva, L. *Tanets Mukarram Turganbaevoi*. Tashkent: Gafur Gulyam, 1989.

Avdeeva, L. *Tantseval'noe Iskusstvo Uzbekistana*. Tashkent: Gosudarstvennoe Izdatel'stvo Khudozhestvennoi Literatury, 1963.

Avesta: Khorda Avesta, *Aban Yasht* ("Hymn to the Waters"). Trans. James Darmesteter. Digital version copyright 1995, Joseph H. Peterson. www.avesta.org/ka/yt5sbe.htm

Ayubdjanova, F. Traditsionnye tadzhikskiye tantsy. Khudzhand: Fakul'tet iskusstva, 2000.

Babur. *Babur Nama: Journal of Emperor Babur*. Transl. Annette Susannah Beveridge. London: Penguin Books, 2006.

Bagdasarova, Guarik. "Magiya tantsa: balet 'Lazgi' na stsene GABT im. A. Navoi." www.kultura.uz http://www.kultura.uz/view_4_r_16923.html.

«Bakhor» – put' k vozrozhdeniyu. Dec. 12, 2022. https://silkway.uz/news/bahor-put-k-vozrozhdeniyu/.

Baldwin, Kate A. *Beyond the Color Line and The Iron Curtain*. Durham, NC: Duke University Press, 2002.

Balet: Entsiklopediya, ed. Iu. N. Grigorovich. Moscow: Order of the Red Banner of Labor, publishing house Sovetskaya Entsikloediya, 1981.

Balzer, Marjorie Mandlestam. *The Tenacity of Ethnicity*. Princeton, NJ: Princeton University Press, 1999.

Barber, E. J. W. *The Dancing Goddesses: Folklore, Archaeology, and the Origins of European Dance*. New York, NY: W.W. Norton & Company, 2013.

Barber, E. J. W. *The Mummies of Ürümchi*. New York, NY: W.W. Norton & Company, 1999.

Baron, Samuel H. *Plekhanov: The Father of Russian Marxism*. Stanford, CT: Stanford University, 1966.

Barthold, W. *Turkestan. Down to the Mongol Invasion*. London: Messrs, Luzac and Company, Ltd., 1968.

Beauchamp, Fay. "Tang Dynasty Revolution and Poetry: Bai Juyi's 'Construction' of Yang Guifei," *Education About Asia*, 14, no.1 (Spring 2009). www.asianstudies.org/publications/eaa/archives/tang-dynasty-revolution-and-poetry-bai-juyis-construction-of-yang-guifei/.

Beckwith, Christopher I. *Empires of the Silk Road; A History of Central Eurasia from the Bronze Age to the Present*. Princeton, NJ: Princeton University Press, 2009.

Beeman, William O. "Music at The Margins: Performance and Ideology in the Persianate World." In *Music and Conflict*, edited by John Morgan O'Connell and Salwa El-Shawan Castelo-Branco, 141–54. Champaign, IL: University of Illinois Press, 2010: 141–54.

Berg, Hetty, ed. *Facing West. Oriental Jews of Central Asia and the Caucasus*. Zwolle, Netherlands: Waanders Publishers, 1999.

Bettelheim, Bruno. *Symbolic Wounds*. New York, NY: Collier Book, 1962 edition.

Bibish. *The Dancer from Khiva*. New York, NY: Grove/Atlantic, Inc., 2008.

Biography of An Lu-Shan. Translated and annotated by Howard S. Levy. Berkley and Los Angeles: University of California Press, 1960.

Boba, Imre. *Nomads, Northmen and Slavs; Eastern Europe in the Ninth Century*. The Hague: Mouton, 1967.

The Book of Dede Korkut, translated by Geoffrey Lewis London: Penguin Books, 1974.

Borroni, Massimiliano. "Samāǧa Performances in Third/ Ninth-Century Abbasid Courts." *Bulletin of the School of Oriental and African Studies*, 82, no. 2 (2019): 289–302. doi:10.1017/S0041977X19000351.

Brosius, Maria. *Women in Ancient Persia 559–331 BC*. Oxford: Clarendon Press, 1996.

Buddee, Naowarat, "How Choreometrics Reflects Self-Identity and Self-Concept Through Cultural Dance: A Developing Method." *Expressive Therapies Capstone Theses* (May 16, 2020). 333. Https://Digitalcommons.Lesley.Edu/Expressive_Theses/333.

Bulliet, Richard W. *Cotton, Climate, and Camels in Early Islamic Iran; A Moment in World History*. New York, NY: Columbia University Press, 2009.

Burnaby, Fred. *A Ride to Khiva: Travels and Adventures in Central Asia*. New edition. London: Cassell and Company, Limited, 1895.

Cameron, Catherine M. *Invisible Citizens: Captives and Their Consequences*. Salt Lake City, UT: University of Utah Press, 2008.

Cho'lpon, Abdulhamid Sulyamon o'g'li. *Night and Day*, translated by Christopher Fort. Boston: Academic Studies Press, 2019.

Compareti, Matteo. "The Last Sasanians in China." *Eurasian Studies*, 2, no. 2 (2003): 197–213.

Chakravorty, Pallabi. *Bells of Change: Kathak Dance, Women, and Modernity in India*. Kolkata: Seagull Books, 2008.

Chamney, Lee. *The An Shi Rebellion and Rejection of the Other in Tang China, 618–763*. Masters Thesis, University of Alberta, 2012.

Chanana, Dev Raj. *Slavery in Ancient India as Depicted in Pali and Sanskrit Texts*. New Delhi: People's Publishing House, 1990.

Chang, Jon K. *Burnt by the Sun: The Koreans of the Russian Far East*. Honolulu: University of Hawai'i Press, 2016.

Chang, Jon K. "A Forgotten Diaspora: Russian-Koreans Negotiating Life, Education, and Social Mobility." In *Education, Ethnicity and Equity in the Multilingual Asian Context*, edited by Jan Gube and Fang Gao. Singapore: Springer, 2019: 141–159.

Chapple, Amos. "Boom! The Great Baku Oil Rush." Radio Free Europe Radio Liberty, June 15, 2021. www.rferl.org/a/baku-oil-fields-historical-photos-nobel/31309153.html.

Chardin, Sir John. *Travels in Persia 1673–1677*. New York, NY: Dover Publications, 1988.

Chen, Da-Sheng. "Chinese–Iranian Relations VII. Persian Settlements in Southeastern China during the Tang, Sung, and Yuan Dynasties." *Encyclopedia Iranica*. December 15, 1991. www.iranicaonline.org/articles/chinese-iranian-vii.

Choksy, Jamsheed K. "Women During the Transition from Sasanian to Early Islamic Times." In *Women in Iran from the Rise of Islam to 1800*, edited by Guity Nashat and Lois Beck. Urbana, IL: University of Illinois Press, 2003: 48–67.

Chung, Y. David and Matt Dibble. *Koryo Saram—The Unreliable People*. Documentary film (2007). www.koryosaram.net/about_film.html.

Clavijo, Ruy Gonzalez de. *Embassy to Tamerlane 1403–1406*. Translated by Guy Le Strange. London: Routledge, 1928.

Cohen, Edward E. "Slaves' Erotic Experience at Athens and Rome." In *Blackwell Companions to the Ancient World: Companion to Greek and Roman Sexualities*, edited by Thomas K. Hubbard. Somerset: John Wiley & Sons, Inc., 2013: 184–98.

Craine, Debra, and Judith Mackrell. "Fountain of Bakhchisarai, The." In *The Oxford Dictionary of Dance*. Oxford: Oxford University Press, 2010. www-Oxfordreference-Com.Proxygw.Wrlc.Org/View/10.1093/Acref/9780199563449.001.0001/Acref-9780199563449-E-984.

Crane, Robert F. "From Kamchatka to Georgia, The Blue Blouse Movement and Early Soviet Spatial Practice." PhD diss. University of Pittsburgh, 2013.

Danesh, Kazem and Mohammad Khazaie, "The Symbolism of Green Color in Iranian–Islamic Culture and Art," *PAYKAREAH*, 9, no. 19 (2020): 24–32. DOI: 10.22055/pyk.2020.15725.

Daryaee, Touraj, and Nina Mazhjoo. "Dancing in Middle & Classical Persian." *Digital Archive of Brief Notes & Iran Review*, 1, no. 2 (2016): 10–14.

Davidov, Allan. "World of Song and Dance." *Soviet Uzbekistan*, 9, no. 287 (1986): 20.

Davis-Kimball, Jeannine. "Warrior Women of The Eurasian Steppes." *Archeology*, January/February (1997): s44–48.

Davis-Kimball, Jeannine. *Warrior Women*. New York, NY: Warner Books, 2002.

Deák, František. "'Blue Blouse' (1923–1928)." *The Drama Review: TDR*, 17, no. 1 (1973): 35–46. https://doi.org/10.2307/1144790.

Dee, Katerina. "Repeating History: Russia Inflicting Crimes Against Humanity Upon the Crimean Tatars." *American University International Law Review*, 36, no. 2 (2021): 287–336.

Djumaev, A. "Musical Traditions and Ceremonies of Bukhara." *Anthropology of the Middle East*, 3, no.1 (2008): 52–66. doi:10.3167/ame.2008.030106.

Doi, Mary Masayo. *Gesture, Gender, Nation: Dance and Social Change in Uzbekistan*. Westport, CT: Bergin & Garvey, 2002.

During, Jean. "Power, Authority and Music in the Cultures of Inner Asia." *Ethnomusicology Forum* 14, no. 2 (2005): 143–64.

During, Jean. "Uyghur Sufi Zikr. Xinjiang.1988." Uyghur Sufi Zikr in South Xin. 1988. Youtube Video. www.Youtube.Com/Watch?V=N6Nv02YZtTQ.

Eden, Jeff. "Slavery in Islamic Central Asia." *Oxford Research Encyclopedia of Asian History*. New York, NY: Oxford University Press, 2019.

Eickelman, Dale F. *The Middle East and Central Asia: An Anthropological Approach*. New York, NY: Simon & Schuster, 1988.

El-Cheikh, Nadia Maria. "Courts and Courtiers; a preliminary investigation of Abbasid Terminology." In *Court Cultures in the Muslim World; Seventh to Nineteenth Centuries*, edited by Albrecht Fuess and Jan-Peter Hartung. London: Routledge, 2011: 89–90.

Eliade, Mircea. *Shamanism: Archaic Techniques of Ecstasy*. Translated by Willard R. Trask. Princeton, NJ: Princeton University Press, 1964.

Elmuratova, Shokhista. "The Issues of Perpetuation of the Memory of the Famous Artist of Tashkent, Tamarakhonim." *Emergent: Journal of Educational Discoveries and Lifelong Learning*, 3, no. 1 (Jan 2022): 117–20. https://ejedl.academiascience.org.

Emelyanenko, Tatjana, and Hetty Berg ed."Central Asian Jewish Costume." In *Facing West: Oriental Jews of Central Asia and the Caucasus*. Zwolle: Waanders Publishers, 2nd edition, 1999.

"European Union to Plant 27 Thousand Trees in Aral Sea Basin." Press and Information Team of The Delegation to Uzbekistan. April 28, 2022. www.Eeas.Europa.Eu/ Delegations/Uzbekistan/European-Union-Plant-27-Thousand-Trees-Aral-Sea-Basin_ En?S=233.

Fakhretdinova, Delyara A., *Yuvelirnoye Iskusstvo Uzbekistana*. Tashkent: Gafur Gulyam, 1988.

"Fantasy Rules As 'Le Coq D'or' Gitters Again at Metropolitan." Review By P.C.R. of the Metropolitan Opera. January 21, 1924. Performance cited in www.Sarasotaopera.Org/ Sites/Default/Files/Inline-Files/Sarasota_Opera_Teacher_Resource_Guide_Cockerel. Pdf.

Farmer, Henry George. *A History of Arabian Music to the XIIIth Century*. London: Luzac & Co., Ltd., 1967.

Fay, Mary Ann. *Unveiling the Harem: Elite Women and the Paradox of Seclusion in Eighteenth-Century Cairo (Middle East Studies Beyond Dominant Paradigms)*. Syracuse, NY: Syracuse University Press, 2012.

Fletcher, James Elroy. *Hassan: The Story of Hassan of Bagdad and how he came to Make the Golden Journey to Samarkand*. London: William Heinemann, 1922.

Foltz, Richard. "Cultural Contacts Between Central Asia and Mughal India." *Central Asiatic Journal* 42, no. 1 (1998): 44–65. Accessed September 25, 2020. www.jstor.org/ stable/41928135.

Fort, Christopher. "Uzbek author Cho'lpon's Equivocal Legacy and Its Importance in Post-Soviet Uzbekistan." *Academic Studies Press*. August 29, 2019. www. academicstudiespress.com/asp-blog/uzbek-author-cholpon-night-and-day.

Frolova-Walker, Marina. "National in Form, Socialist in Content: Musical Nation-Building in the Soviet Republics," *Journal of the American Musicological Society*, 51, no. 2 (Summer, 1998): 331–71.

Fuess, Albrecht, and Jan-Peter Hartung. *Court Cultures in the Muslim World; Seventh to Nineteenth Centuries*. London: Routledge, 2011.

Gabitov, Tursun, Zukhra Ismagambetova, Aliya Karabayeva, Saltanat Aubakirova, and Zarina Mukanova. "Circle Dance as a Symbolic Form of Culture." *International Journal of Advanced Research*, 4 (May 2016): 75–84. www.Journalijar.Com

Gaca, Kathy L. "Girls, Women, and the Significance of Sexual Violence in Ancient Warfare." In *Sexual Violence in Conflict Zones: From the Ancient World to the Era of Human Rights*, edited by Elizabeth D. Heineman. Philadelphia, PA: University of Pennsylvania Press, 2011: 73–88. http://www.jstor.org/stable/j.ctt3fhfgp.7.

Ganiev, Mukhtar. "Shut Margilanskiy." *Pis'ma o Tashkente*, Dec. 31, 2020. https:// mytashkent.uz/2020/12/31/shut-margilanskij/.

Gaster, Theodore. *Myth, Legend and Custom in the Old Testament*. New York, NY: Harper and Row, 1969.

Gaziev, Saidolimkhon. "Dancing Boys and Gay Escapades in Fin-de-siècle Tashkent: A Sketch from a Queer History of Central Asia." Blogpost on site of the Commission for the Study of Islam in Central Eurasia. www.oeaw.ac.at/sice/sice-blog/dancing-boys-and-gay-escapades-in-fin-de-siecle-tashkent-a-sketch-from-a-queer-history-of-central-asia.

Gaziev, Saidolimkhon."Regulating the Intimate: Prostitution in Russian Turkestan." 2018 CESS conference paper abstract. https://nomadit.co.uk/conference/cess2018/paper/43874.

Genocchio, Benjamin. "Russia, Before Art Became Mere Ideology." Review of *Mir Iskusstva: Russia's Age of Elegance. New York Times*, March 5, 2006. Http://Proxygw.Wrlc.Org/Login?Url=Https://Www-Proquest-Com.Proxygw.Wrlc.Org/Newspapers/Russia-Before-Art-Became-Mere-Ideology/Docview/433310857/Se-2?Accountid=11243

Goncharova, P. A. *Buxoro zarduzlik san'ati*. Tashkent: Gafur Gulyam, 1986.

Gosudarstvennyy Ansambl' Tantsa UzSSR Bakhor. Illustrated brochure. No date or printing information.

Gosudarstvennyi muzei etnografii narodov SSSR. *Jewellery: Museum of the Ethnography of the Peoples of the USSR*. Leningrad: Aurora Art Publishers, 1988.

Government of Uzbekistan. *Aral Sea Region: Zone of Environmental Innovations and Technologies*. 2023.

Gray, Laurel Victoria. "A Living Legacy: Women's Dances of Uzbekistan." *Arabesque*, VII, no. 5 (January–February 1983): 6–7, 24–25.

Gray, Laurel Victoria. "Arts: Folk Dancers and Folk Singers: Caucasus." In *Encyclopedia of Women & Islamic Cultures*, general editor Suad Joseph. Consulted online on 21 May 2023. http://dx.doi.org.proxygw.wrlc.org/10.1163/1872-5309_ewic_EWICCOM_0291b>.

Gray, Laurel Victoria. "Dancing Boys." *Arabesque*, XII, no. 1 (May–June 1986): 8–11.

Gray, Laurel Victoria. "Dancing into the Future with Ancient Steps: Lessons on Healing and Restoration from Khorezm Traditions." Paper presented at International Cultural Forum "Central Asia at the Crossroads of World Civilizations," 2021.

Gray, Laurel Victoria. "Envisioning the East: Russian Orientalism and the Ballet Russe." *Habibi*, 19, no. 1 (2002): 44–47.

Gray, Laurel Victoria. "The Goddess Dances: Women's Dance of Georgia." *Habibi* 14, no. 4 (Fall 1995): 17, 39. thebestofhabibi.net/vol-14-no-4-fall-1995/the-goddess-dancing/.

Gray, Laurel Victoria. "Tamara Khanum, Uzbekistan's Heroine of Dance." *Arabesque*, X, no. V (January–February 1985): 14–15.

Gray, Laurel Victoria. "Music and Dance within the Islamic Context." *Arabesque*, X, no. 1 (May–June 1984): 24–25, 34–35.

Gray, Laurel Victoria. "Mystique of the Veil." *Arabesque*, XI, no. 4 (November–December 1983): 8–9, 17, 25.

Gray, Laurel Victoria. "New Stop on the Ancient Silk Route." *Soviet Uzbekistan*, 6, no. 308 (1988): 12.

Gray, Laurel Victoria. "Silk Road: Commerce, Conquest, and College." In *Milestones in Dance History*, ed. Dana Tai Soon Burgess. London: Routledge, 2023.

Gray, Laurel Victoria. "The Splendor of UzbekDance. Part One: Khorezm." *Habibi*, 14, no. 2 (Spring 1995).

Gray, Laurel Victoria. "The Splendor of Uzbek Dance. Part Two: Ferghana." *Habibi*, 14, no. 3 (Fall 1995).

Gray, Laurel Victoria. "The Splendor of Uzbek Dance. Part Three: Bukhara." *Habibi*, 16, no. 3 (Fall 1997).

Gray, Laurel Victoria. "Sozanda: Women's Professional Dance Traditions in Bukhara before the Soviets." Conference presentation, Middle Eastern North African Central Asian (MENACA) Dance Symposium, Pomona College, April 13–16, 2023.

Gray, Laurel Victoria. "Uzbek Women Dance Through Time." *Middle Eastern Dancer*, 6, no. 7 (April 1985): 17–20.

Gray, Laurel Victoria. "Uzbek Women's Dances, Past and Present." *Viltis*, 43, no. 6 (March–April 1985): 7–9.

Gray, Laurel Victoria, and Elena Gvaramadze. "Georgia." *The International Encyclopedia of Dance*. Oxford: Oxford University Press, 1998.

Gray, Laurel Victoria, and Natasha Rapoport. "Uzbekistan." In *The World Encyclopedia of Contemporary Theatre: Asia/Pacific. Vol. 5*, edited by Don Rubin et al. London: Routledge, 2001: 450–65.

Gray, Laurel Victoria, and Liubov Avdeeva. "Uzbekistan." *International Encyclopedia of Dance*, edited by S. J. Cohen: New York, NY: Oxford University Press, 1998: Vol. 6, 304–07.

Grytsenko, Oksana."'Haytarma', The First Crimean Tatar Movie, is a Must-See For History Enthusiasts." *Kyivpost*. July 8, 2013, https://www.kyivpost.com/post/9269.

Guran, Letitia. "Insurgent Hughes: Negotiating Multiple Narratives Digitally." *Melus* 42, no. 4 (2017): 136–63. www.Jstor.org/Stable/26566093.

Gurdjieff, G. I. *Meetings with Remarkable Men*. Routledge: 1960; Arkan: 1985; London: Penguin Classics, 2015.

Gyul, Elmira. "The Mystery of Kyrk-Kyz: From 40 Women-Warriors to the Warriors of Light." *Voices of Central Asia*. January 16, 2020. https://voicesoncentralasia.org/the-mystery-of-kyrk-kyz-from-40-women-warriors-to-the-warriors-of-light/.

Hahn, Emanuel. "Koryo-Saram in American: Meet the Korean-Uzbeks who Fled Prejudice in Russia and Made Brooklyn Their Home." *The Calvert Journal*, January 17, 2020. www.calvertjournal.com/features/show/11570/korean-uzbek-photography-koryo-saram-brooklyn-new-york.

Hain, Kathryn A., 'Epilogue: Avenues to Social Mobility Available to Courtesans and Concubines', in Matthew S. Gordon, and Kathryn A. Hain (eds), *Concubines and Courtesans: Women and Slavery in Islamic History* (New York, 2017; pp. 324–340, online edn, Oxford Academic, 19 Oct. 2017), https://doi.org/10.1093/oso/9780190622183.003.0017, accessed 16 Oct. 2023.

Hale, Andy and Kate Fitz Gibbon, "Introduction." In *Ikats, Woven Silks from Central Asia: The Rau Collection*. Oxford: Basil Blackwell, 1988.

Hambly, Gavin R. G., ed. *Women in the Medieval Islamic World: Power, Patronage, and Piety*. New York, NY: St. Martin's Press, 1988.

Hamza Khakimzade Niyazi. Wayback Machine (archived March 25, 2008). https://web.archive.org/web/20080325040811/http://www.geocities.com/marxistes_lb/khamza_khakimzade_niyazi.htm.

Hamza. *Paranji sirlaridan bir lavha Yoki yallachilar ishi* (*One Episode from the Secrets of the Veil or the Case of Yalla Singers*) (1922).

Hansen, Valerie. *The Silk Road: A New History*. New York, NY: Oxford University Press, 2012.

Hasanova, Nargiza. "Ladies of Andijan Receive a Dignified Place in the History of State and Public Governance." *Eurasian Journal of History, Geography and Economics*, 7 (April 2022): 64–69. https://www.geniusjournals.org/index.php/ejhge/article/download/1235/1092.

Hedin, Sven. *My Life as an Explorer*. Translated by Alfhild Huebsch. New York, NY: Kondasha International, 1996.

Heyman, Alan, editor. *The Traditional Music and Dance of Korea*. Seoul: Song Lim Printing Co., Ltd., 1993.

The History of Herodotus. Translated by George Rawlinson. New York, NY: Dutton & Co., 1862.

History of the Zurkhaneh and the story of Hossein e Golzar Kermanshahi. Documentary film. www.youtube.com/watch?v=mOmY2ljQ_Ws.

Hitti, Philip K. *History of the Arabs.* New York, NY: St. Martin's Press, 1953.

Homans, Jennifer. *Mr. B: George Balanchine's 20th Century.* New York, NY: Random House, 2022.

Hopkirk, Kathleen. *Central Asia through Writers' Eyes.* London: Eland, 1993.

Hopkirk, Peter. *Foreign Devils on the Silk Road; The Search for the Lost Cities and Treasures of Chinese Central Asia.* Amherst, MA: University of Massachusetts Press, 1980.

"House Of Korean Culture & Art, Symbol of Korean-Uzbek Future." Korea.Net. May 23, 2016. www.Korea.Net/Newsfocus/Policies/View?Articleid=136474.

Houseal, J. (2016). "Dance at Dunhuang: Part Three—The Sogdian Whirl." Buddhistdoor Global. www.buddhistdoor.net/features/dance-at-dunhuang-part-three-the-sogdian-whirl.

Hughes, Langston. "Dances and Music of Uzbekistan," *A Negro Looks at Soviet Central Asia.* Moscow-Leningrad: Co-operative Publishing Society of Foreign Workers in the U.S.S.R., 1934. pp.32–38. Reprint by Red Star Publishing. www.redstarpublishers.org/HughesSovietCentralAsia.pdf.

Hughes, Langston. "In An Emir's Harem." In *Women's Home Companion.* Springfield, OH: Crowell Publishing Company, 1934.

Hughes, Langston. "Tamara Khanum, Soviet Asia's Greatest Dancer." In *Theatre Arts Monthly,* 1934, pp. 828–35.

Ingenito, Domenico. "Hafez's 'Shirāzi Turk': A Geopoetical Approach." *Iranian Studies* 51, no. 6 (2018): 851–87. doi:10.1080/00210862.2018.1511507.

"Immigration Policy." *International Journal of Korean History,* no. 12 (2008): 157–91. https://Ijkh.Khistory.Org/Upload/Pdf/12-07_Alexander%20i.%20petrov.Pdf.

"International Dance Day—Kazakh Folk Dances." *Info Shymkent.* April 29, 2021. www.Shymkent.Info/2021/04/29/International-Dance-Day-Kazakh-Folk-Dances/

Iovchuk, Mikhail Trifonovich, and Irina Nikolaevna Kurbatova. *Plekhanov.* Moscow: Molodaiā gvardiiā, 1977.

"Isadora Duncan: A Revolutionary Dancer in Revolutionary Russia." Wilson Center. Published January 29, 2008. www.wilsoncenter.Org/Event/Isadora-Duncan-Revolutionary-Dancer-Revolutionary-Russia.

Ismailov, Hamid. *The Devils' Dance,* translated by Donald Rayfield. London: Tilted Axis, 2018.

Israeli, Raphael. "Medieval Muslim Travelers to China." *Journal of Muslim Minority Affairs* 20, no. 2 (2000): 313–21.

Jaiswal, Suvira. "Female Images in the Arthasastra of Kautilya." *Social Scientist* 29, nos. 3–4 (2001): 51–59.

Jeon, Bongsu. "The Koryo Saram Dance Troupes of Uzbekistan." *ICH Courier,* no. 28. Ichcourier.ichcap.org

Jeschke, Claudia and Cary Rick. "Review of Diaghilev's Ballets Russes, by Lynn Garafola." *Dance Research Journal,* 22, no. 2 (Autumn 1990): 29–31. https://Doi.Org/10.2307/1477782.

Jones, Janet. "Horse–Human Cooperation is a Neurobiological Miracle: Aeon Essays." Edited by Pam Weintraub. *Aeon Magazine,* January 14, 2022. https://aeon.co/essays/horse-human-cooperation-is-a-neurobiological-miracle?utm_source=pocket-newtab.

Juliano, Annette L., Michael Alram, and Judith A. Lerner. *Monks and Merchants: Silk Road Treasures from Northwest China Gansu and Ningxia 4th–7th Century.* New York, NY: Harry N. Abrams with the Asia Society, 2001.

Kalter, Johannes. *The Arts and Crafts of Turkestan.* London: Thames and Hudson, 1983.

Kamp, Marianne. "Femicide as Terrorism: The Case of Uzbekistan's Unveiling Murders." In *Sexual Violence in Conflict Zones: From the Ancient World to the Era of Human Rights,* edited by Elizabeth D. Heineman. Philadelphia, PA: University of Pennsylvania Press, 2011: 56–70. http://www.jstor.org/stable/j.ctt3fhfgp.6.

Kamp, Marianne. *The New Woman in Uzbekistan: Islam, Modernity, and Unveiling under Communism.* Seattle, WA: University of Washington Press, 2008.

Kamp, Marianne. "Pilgrimage and Performance: Uzbek Women and the Imagining of Uzbekistan in the 1920s." *International Journal of Middle East Studies* 34, no. 2 (2002): 263–78. http://www.jstor.org/stable/3879827.

Kang, Xiaofel. "The Fox [hu] and the Barbarian [hu]: Unraveling Representation of the Other in Late Tang Tales." *Journal of Chinese Religions,* 27, no. 1 (1999): 35–67.

Kaptan, Remzi. *Alevi Teaching.* Stuttgart. www.alevitentum.de.

Karabaev, Usman. *Etnokul'tura: traditsionnaya narodnaya kul'tura.* Tashkent: Shark Publishing, 2005.

Karimova, Rozia. *Bukharskii Tanets.* Tashkent: Literatura i Isskustvo, 1977.

Karimova, Rozia. *Ferganskii Tanets.* Tashkent: Literatura i Isskustvo, 1973.

Karimova, Rozia. *Khorezemskii Tanets.* Tashkent: Literatura i Isskustvo, 1975.

Karimova, Rozia and D. I. Sayfullayeva. *Ozbek Ayollar Yakka Raqslari.* Edited by Azimova Ra'no. Tashkent: Cho'lpan Publishing House, 2007.

Karimova, Roziakhanum. "Tanovar—an Uzbek dance." *Soviet Uzbekistan,* no. 1 (291), (1987): 18–19.

Karimova, Roziakhanum. *Urok uzbeksyaya tantsa.* Tashkent: O'qituvchi Publishing, 1987.

Karimova, Roziakhanum. *Uzbekskie Tantsyi v Postanovke Isakhara Akilova.* Tashkent: Gafur Gulyam, 1977.

Karimova, Roziakhanum. *Tantsy Ansambl'a Bakhor v Postanovke Mukarram Turgunbaevoi.* Tashkent: Literatura i Isskustvo, 1979.

Kari-Yakubova, Elena. "Tanets Cherez Prizmu Voinu." *Iskusstvo i Khoreograficheskoi Obrazovaniye v Godu Velikoi Otechestvennoi Voiny.* Moscow: Moscow State Academy of Choreography (МГАХ), special issue IV, no. 2 (50), (2020): 62–67.

Kari-Yakubova, Elena. "Vo Dvortse iskusstv 'Turkiston' sostoyalsya bol'shoy vecher natsional'nogo tantsa, posvyashchennyi pamyati Narodnoy artistki Uzbekistana Viloyat Akilovoi." Kultura.uz. October 19, 2022. http://kultura.uz/view_4_r_18570.html.

Karpova, Ksenia. "Art in Evacuation." *The Tretyakov Gallery Magazine,* no. 2 (2015): 47.

Keddie, Nikki R. "Review of *Women in the Medieval Islamic World: Power, Patronage, and Piety* by Gavin R. G." *Iranian Studies,* 33, nos. 1/2 (2000): 242–45. www.jstor.org/stable/4311359.

Kendirbaeva, Gulnar. "Folklore and Folklorism in Kazakhstan." *Asian Folklore Studies,* 53, no. 1 (1994): 97–123. https://doi.org/10.2307/1178561.

Khalid, Adeeb. *Central Asia: A New History from the Imperial Conquests to the Present.* Princeton, NJ: Princeton University Press, 2021.

Khalid, Adeeb. *Making Uzbekistan: Nation, Empire, and Revolution in the Early USSR.* 1st ed. Ithaca, NY: Cornell University Press, 2016. www.jstor.org/stable/10.7591/j.ctt20fw5rf.

Khamidova, M. A. *Akterskoye iskusstvo uzbekskogo muzykal'nogo teatra.* Tashkent: Fan Publishing, 1987.

Khamraeva, Gul'sum Rakhmedova. *Obshchie zakony stsenicheskoy choreographii natsionalnaya obraz tantsa.* Tashkent: Institute of Art Studies. Dissertation 1986.

Khamroeva, Khulkar. *Gavkhar Matyokubova Izhod va Ilm Integratsiyasi.* Tashkent: Monografiya, 2022.

Khaydarov, Islom. "Balethmeister Activity of the People's Artist of Uzbekistan Gadir Muminov and his Pedogogic Skills." *Oriental Art and Culture,* 4, no. 1 (February 2023): 223–26. https://cyberleninka.ru/article/n/balethmeister-activity-of-the-peoples-artist-of-uzbekistan-gadir-muminov-and-his-pedogogic-skills/viewer.

Khitrova, Daria. "'This Is No Longer Dance:' Media Boundaries and the Politics of Choreography in The Steel Step." *Critical Inquiry,* 40, no. 3, Comics & Media, edited by Hillary Chute and Patrick Jagoda (Spring 2014): 134–49.

Khorezmskii tanets lazgi: razvitiye natsional'nykh tantsev i ikh znacheniye na sovremennom etape. Materials of the 1st International Scientific–Practical Conference. Tashkent: Bookmany Print, 2022.

Khudoev, G. M. "Peering into Culture of Ancient Bukhara." *Journal Of Literature and Art Studies,* 5, no. 8 (Aug. 2015): 630–33. Doi: 10.17265/2159-5836/2015.08.007.

Kim, German. "Dances of Divided Korea on The Central Asian Soil." *S/N Korean Humanities,* 7, no. 1 (2021).

Kim, Viktoria. "Lost and Found in Uzbekistan: The Korean Story." Copyright 2015. https://centralasiaprogram.org/initiatives/cultures-and-societies-initiative/lost-and-found-in-uzbekistan-the-korean-story.

Kirchner, Mark. "Review of 'Edige: A Karakalpak Heroic Epic as Performed by Jumabay Bazarov,' By Karl Reichl." *Speculum,* 85, no. 4 (October 2010): 1016–17.

Koulabadi, Rahele, Seyyed Mehdi Mousavi Kouhpar, Javad Neyestani, and Seyyed Rasool MousaviHaji. "An Overview of Goddess Anahita and Her Iconography in Ancient Iran." *Central Asiatic Journal,* 62, no. 2 (2019): 203–26. Accessed August 27, 2021. doi:10.13173/centasiaj.62.2.0203.

Kraff, Jonathan Karam. *Sui-Tang China and its Turko-Mongol Neighbors: Culture, Power, and Connections.* New York, NY: Oxford University Press, 2012.

"Kushtdepdi Rite of Singing and Dancing." *UNESCO Intangible Cultural Heritage.* 2017. https://Ich.Unesco.Org/En/RL/Kushtdepdi-Rite-Of-Singing-And-Dancing-01259.

Kuzmina, E. E. *The Prehistory of the Silk Road.* Philadelphia, PA: University of Pennsylvania Press, 2008.

Lane, Edward. *The Manners and Customs of the Modern Egyptians.* New York, NY: E.P. Dutton and Co., Ltd. 1908.

Laruelle, Marlene. "The Nation Narrated: Uzbekistan's Political and Cultural Nationalism." In *Constructing the Uzbek State.* Lanham, MD: Lexington Books, 2017: 261–282.

Laufer, Berthold. *Sino-Iranica: Chinese Contributions to the History of Civilization in Ancient Iran, with Special Reference to the History of Cultivated Plants and Products.* Chicago, IL: Field Museum of Natural History, 1919.

Lee, Hana. "House of Korean Culture & Art, Symbol of Korean-Uzbek Future." May 23, 2016. www.korea.net/NewsFocus/policies/view?articleId=136474

Lee, Joo-Yup. "The Sogdian Descendants in Mongol and post-Mongol Central Asia: The Tajiks and Sarts." *Acta Via Serica,* 5, no. 1 (June 2020): 187–98.

Lee, Kyung-Sik. "Korea, Uzbekistan Agree to Build House of Korean Culture and Art in Uzbekistan." *The Korea Post.* August 11, 2014. www.koreapost.com/news/articleView.html?idxno=607.

Lee, Woosung. "The Korean's Migration to the Russian Far East and their Deportation to Central Asia: from the 1860s to 1937." MA Dissertation, University of Oregon, June 2012.

Leoni, Erica. "Traditional Dances from Kazakhstan. The Nomadic Khara-Zhorgha." *Erica Leoni* (Blog). May 24, 2018. https://Ericaleoni.Com/2018/05/24/1588-2/.

Leslie, Donald Daniel. "Persian Temples in T'ang China." *Monumenta Serica*, 35 (1981): 275–303. Accessed September 24, 2020. www.jstor.org.proxygw.wrlc.org/stable/40726510.

Levin, Theodore. *The Hundred Thousand Fools of God: musical travels in Central Asia (and Queens, New York)*. Bloomington, IN: Indiana University Press, 1996.

Levy, Scott C. *The Rise and Fall of Khoqand 1709–1976*. Pittsburgh, PA: University of Pittsburgh Press, 2017.

Leyda, Si-Lan Chen. *Footnote to History*. Edited by Sally Banes. New York, NY: Dance Horizons, 1984.

Liu, Xinru. "A Silk Road Legacy: The Spread of Buddhism and Islam." *Journal of World History*, 22, no. 1 (2011): 55–81. www.Jstor.Org/Stable/23011678.

Lonsdale, Steven. *Animals and the Origins of Dance*. New York, NY: Thames and Hudson, 1982.

Losey, Steve, "Top General Pressed on Biden Remark About Climate Change's Threat to US." www.military.com/daily-news/2021/06/10/top-general-pressed-biden-remark-about-climate-changes-threat-us.html.

MacFadyen, David. *Russian Culture in Uzbekistan: One Language in the Middle of Nowhere*. Central Asian Studies Series. New York, NY: Routledge, 2006.

Macfarlane, Charles. *Constantinople In 1828; A Residence Of 16 Months in The Turkish-Capital and Provinces*. London: Saunders & Otley, 1829.

Mackerras, Colin. "The 'New Tang History' (Hsin Tang-shu) on the History of the Uighurs." The Uighur Empire According to the Tang Dynastic Histories. 2004. Accessed February 25, 2016. www.coursehero.com/file/18884055/The-New-Tang-History/

Magdiyeva, Alina Aripovna. "Uzbek Dance: The Way to Renewal and Revival." *International Journal of Innovations in Engineering Research and Technology*, 7, no. 8 (2021): 81–84. https://repo.ijiert.org/index.php/ijiert/article/view/169.

Mahdavian, Emelie. "Gendered Nostalgia: Tajik Traditional Dance and The Logic of Nationalism." *Asian Theatre Journal* 35, no. 2 (Fall 2018): 329–53.

Maillart, Ellie. *Turkestan Solo: A Journey Through Central Asia*. New York, NY: Tauris Parke Paperbacks, 2005.

Mair, Victor H. "Kinesis Versus Stasis, Interaction Versus Independent Invention." In *Contact and Exchange in the Ancient World*, edited by Victor H. Mair. Honolulu: University of Hawai'i Press, 2006, pp.1–16.

Mair, Victor H. "Mummies of the Tarim Basin." *Archaeology*, March/April (1995): 28–35.

Makaryk, Irena R. *April in Paris: Theatricality, Modernism, and Politics at the 1925 Art Deco Expo*. Toronto: University of Toronto Press, 2018: 328. www.Jstor.Org/Stable/10.3138/J.Ctv2fjwwjz.

Manley, Rebecca. "Escape to Tashkent: Fleeing Operation Barbarossa." *War History Network*. Summer 2011. https://warfarehistorynetwork.com/article/escape-to-tashkent-fleeing-operation-barbarossa/.

Marinova, Maria. (2021). Status of Women in Ancient Sogdian Society 古代粟特社会中女性的地位. 10.13140/RG.2.2.31477.29922.

Marushiakova, Elena, and Vesselin Popov. *Gypsies in Central Asia and the Caucasus*. Palgrave Macmillan, 2016. doi:10.1007/978-3-319-41057-9.

Marozzi, Justin. *Tamerlane: Sword of Islam, Conqueror of the World*. Cambridge, MA: Da Capo Press, 2004.

Matiossian, Vartan, and Artsvi Bakshinyan. *A Woman of the World: Armen Ohanian, The Dancer of Shamakha*. Fresno, CA: California State University, 2022.

Matyokubova, Gavkhar. "Khorazm 'Lazgi' raqsining 'Avestot'ga Tutash Ildizlari." *Materials of the First International Scientific–Practical Conference*. Tashkent: Bookmany Print, 2022: 14–20.

Gavkhar Matyokubova, Gavkhar, Shukhrat Tokhtasimov, and Khulkar Khamroeva. *Khorazm "Lazgi" Raksi: Tarikhi va Tavsifi*. Tashkent: Monografiya, 2022.

Mayor, Adrienne. *The Amazons: Lives and Legends of Warrior Women Across the Ancient World*. Princeton, NJ: Princeton University Press, 2014. Https://Doi.Org/10.2307/J. Ctt7zvndm.15.

Meakin, Annette M. B. *In Russian Turkestan: a Garden of Asia and Its People*. London: G. Allen, 1903.

Merchant, Tanya. *Women Musicians of Uzbekistan: From Courtyard to Conservatory*. Urbana, IL: University of Illinois Press, 2015.

Mernissi, Fatima. *Beyond the Veil: Male-Female Dynamics in a Modern Muslim Society*. New York, NY: Schenkman Publishing, 1975.

Mernissi, Fatima. *The Forgotten Queens of Islam*. Minneapolis, MN: University of Minnesota Press, 1993.

Mernissi, Fatima. *The Veil and the Male Elite*. New York: Addison-Wesley Publishing Company, Inc., 1991.

Michell, Stephen. *Gilgamesh/a new English version*. New York, NY: Free Press, 2004.

Minahan, James B. *Encyclopedia of Stateless Nations: Ethnic and National Groups Around the World*, 2nd Edition. Westport, CT: ABC-CLIO, LLC, 2016. Accessed July 10, 2022. Proquest Ebook Central.

Mirza, Younus Y. "Remembering the Umm al-Walad: Ibn Kathir's Treatise on the Sale of the Concubine." In *Concubines and Courtesans: Women and Slavery in Islamic History*, edited by Matthew S. Gordon and Kathryn A. Hain. New York, NY: Oxford University Press, 2017, pp. 297–323.

Mirzayeva, Shakhrinsa Komiljonkiz. "Lapar is the Treasury of Uzbek Folklore." *Journal of Advanced Research and Stability*, 2022. https://sciencebox.uz/index.php/jars/article/view/3491/3174.

Moore, David Chioni. "Colored Dispatches from the Uzbek Border: Langston Hughes' Relevance, 1933–2002." *Callaloo*, 25, no. 4 (Autumn, 2002): 1114–35. www.jstor.org/stable/3300273.

Mukhtarov, Ildar. "A Little About Women … and Theatre." *Sanat Magazine*, 1 (2005). https://Sanat.Orexca.Com/2005/2005-1/Title_About_Woman/

Muratova, S. C. "The History of Uzbek National Dance, its Types and Schools." *ISJ Theoretical & Applied Science*, 12, no.80 (2019): 88–92.

Najmabadi, Afsaneh. *Women with Mustaches and Men Without Beards Gender and Sexual Anxieties of Iranian Modernity*. Berkeley, CA: University of California Press, 2005.

Nalivkin, Maria, and Vladimir. *Muslim Women of the Fergana Valley*. Edited by Marianne Kamp. Translated by Mariana Markova. 2nd ed. Bloomington, IN: Indiana University Press, 2016.

Nedvetsky, Andrei G. *Bukhara: Caught in Time: Great Photographic Archives*. Edited By Vitaly Naumkin. Reading, UK: Garnet Publishing Limited, 1993.

Neher, Andrew. "A Physiological Explanation of Unusual Behavior in Ceremonies Involving Drums." *Human Biology*, 34, no. 2 (1962): 151–60. https://Doi.Org/10.1177/136346156400100204.

Neogi, Haran Chandra. "The Dancing Girl of Mohenjo-Dara." *Journal of Indian History*, 48, no. 3 (December 1970): 559–64.

Neserve, Ruth. "Barbarian Entertainments." *Journal of Popular Culture*, 16, no. 1 (Summer 1982).

Nevile, Pran. *Nautch Girls of the Raj*. London: Penguin Books, 2009.

Nikonorov, Valerii P. "The Use of Musical Percussions in Ancient Eastern Warfare: Parthian and Central Asian Evidence." In *Music Archaeology of Early Metal Ages: papers from the 1st Symposium of the International Study Group on Music Archaeology at Monastery Michaelstein*, 18–24 May, 1998 (Blankenburg, Germany), edited by Ellen Hickmann, Ingo Laufs, and Ricardo Eichmann. *Orient-ArchŠologie, 7; Studien zur MusikarchŠologie II*. Rahden/Westf: Verlag Marie Leidorfe, 2000, pp. 71–82.

Niyazi, Hamza Hakimzade. *Paranji sirlaridan bir lavha Yoki yallachilar ishi* (*One Episode from the Secrets of the Veil or the Case of Yalla Singers*) (1922).

Niyazi, Khamza Khakimzade. "A Song of Emancipated Women." In *A New Life Begun: Prose Poetry and Essays of the 1920s–1930s*. Moscow: Progress Publishers, 1987. www.marxists.org/subject/women/poetry/song.html.

Nizami Ganjavi, *The Haft Piakar: Containing the Life and Adventures of King Bahrām Gūr, and the Seven Stories Told Him by his Seven Queens*, translated by C. E. Wilson. London: Pronbsthain & Co., 1924.

Nizami Ganjavi. *The Haft Paykar, A Medieval Persian Romance*. Translated by Julie Scott Meisami.Oxford: Oxford University Press, 1995.

"NPCA Sponsors Uzbekistan Program on July 2." *Peace Corps Online*. July 2, 2003. http://Peacecorpsonline.Org/Messages/Messages/2629/2014486.Html

Northrop, Douglas. *Veiled Empire: Gender and Power in Stalinist Central Asia*. Ithaca, NY: Cornell University Press, 2004.

Nurdzhanov, Nizam. *Traditsionnyi teatr tadzhikov*. Vols. I and II. Published with the support of the Aga Khan Humanities Project in Dushanbe, Tajikistan, 2003.

Oberhänsli, Hedi, Nikolaus Boroffka, Philippe Sorrel, and Sergey Krivonogov. "Climate Variability During the Past 2,000 Years and Past Economic and Irrigation Activities in the Aral Sea Basin." *Irrigation and Drainage Systems*, Vol 21, nos. 3–4 (December 2007): 167–83. DOI:10.1007/s10795-007-9031-5.

Ohanian, Armen. *The Dancer of Shamakha*. London: J. Cape, 1922.

Olufsen, O. *The Emir of Bukhara and his Country*. London: William Heinemann, 1911.

"О Народном Танце Узбекистана Сняли Документальный Фильм." *Tafsilar*. https://Tafsilar.Info/Obshhestvo/O-Narodnom-Tance-Uzbekistana-Snjali-Dokumentalnyj-Film/.

Pahlen, Konstantin Konstanovich, N. J. Couriss, and Richard A. Pierce. *Mission to Turkestan, Being the Memoirs of Count K. K. Pahlen, 1908–1909*. London: Oxford University Press, 1964.

Paoletti, Gabe. "Life Inside The Young Pioneers: The Soviet Union's Answer To The Boy Scouts." August 18, 2017. https://allthatsinteresting.com/young-pioneers-soviet-union.

Penzer, N. M. *The Harem: An Account of the Institution as it Existed in the Palace of the Turkish Sultans with a History of the Grand Seraglio from its Foundation to the Present Time*. Philadelphia, PA: J. B. Lippincott Co., n.d.

Peshkova, Svetlana, Ruthia Jenrbekova, and Maria Vilkovisky. "Prevrashenie (Transformation) of Bacha: Cracks and Ghostly Matters in the National/ist Heritage of Central Asia." *Central Asian Affairs*, 9 (2022): 177–207. https://doi.org/10.30965/22142290-12340020.

Petrosova, E. A. *Karakalpakskii Tanets*. Tashkent: Literature and Art Press named for Gafur Gulyam, 1976.

Pickett, James. *Polymaths of Islam: Power and Networks of Knowledge in Central Asia*. Ithaca, NY: Cornell University Press, 2020.

Potter, David S. "Entertainers in the Roman Empire." In *Life, Death, and Entertainment in the Roman Empire*. Edited by D. S. Potter and D. J. Mattingly. Ann Arbor, MI: University of Michigan Press, 1999: 256–326.

Prasad, Pushpa. "Female Slavery in Thirteenth-Century Gujarat: Documents in the Lekhapaddhati." *Indian Historical Review*, XV, nos. 1–2 (1988–1989): 269–75.

Pulatov, Timur. *The Life Story of a Naughty Boy from Bukhara*. Moscow: Raduga Publishers, 1983.

Qingje, Zhang. "Studies of Sogdian Dancing Images in China." *Circle of Inner Asia Art*, Issue 17 (June2003): 3–9.

Qodiriy, Abdullah. *Bygone Days: O'tkan Kunlar*, translated by Mark Reese. Nashville, TN: Bowker, 2019.

Qorabaev, Usmon. *O'zbek Xalqi Bairamlari*. Tashkent: Sharq Publishing, 2002.

Rakhimov, Akhmazhon. *Mukarramkhonim "Tanovar"i*. Tashkent: Muharrir nashriyoti, 2018.

Rakhimova, Gulmira. *Tuhfakhon, The Greatest Sozanda*. Published by Gulmira Rakhimova, 2013.

Ramazani, Nesta. *The Dance of the Rose and the Nightingale*. Syracuse, NY: Syracuse University Press, 2002.

Redmond, Layne. *When the Drummers Were Women: A Spiritual History of Rhythm*. 1st ed. New York, NY: Three Rivers Press, 1997.

Reikher, Elena (Temin). "The Female 'Sozanda' Art from the Viewpoint of Professionalism in the Musical Tradition: A Preliminary Survey." *Musica Judaica*, 18 (2005): 70–86.

"Revolution and Fire Are Devastating Baku: It Is Feared the Whole Oil Industry Will Be Wiped Out. The Troops Are Helpless Tarters Massacring Villagers—Rioters Robbing and Murdering Jews at Kishineff." 1905. *New York Times* (1857–1922), Sep 07, 1905. Accessed June 3, 2022. http://Proxygw.Wrlc.Org/Login?Url=Https://Www-Proquest-Com.Proxygw.Wrlc.Org/Historical-Newspapers/Revolution-Fire-Are-Devastating-Baku/Docview/96537310/Se-2?Accountid=11243.

Robeson, Paul. *Here I Stand*. Boston: Beacon Press, 1958/1988. Preface by Lloyd L. Brown, 1971.

Robeson, Paul. "To You Beloved Comrade." Originally published in *New World Review*, April, 1953. Public domain: Marxists Internet Archive (2008).

Robinson, Harlow. "Love For Three Operas: The Collaboration of Vsevolod Meyerhold and Sergei Prokofiev." *The Russian Review*, 45, no. 3 (1986): 287–304. Https://Doi.Org/10.2307/130112.

Ro'ziyeva, Mohichehra. "Color Symbolism in Uzbek Folklore." *International Scientific Journal Theoretical & Applied Science*, 85, no. 5 (2020): 277–84.

Roy, M. N. *Roy's Memoirs*. New York, NY: Allied Publishers, 1964.

Rozwadowski, Andrzej, and Maria M. Kosko, editors. *Spirits and Stones: Shamanism and Rock Art in Central Asia and Siberia*. Poznan: Instytut Wschodni UAM, 2002.

Rubin, Gayle. "The Traffic in Women: Notes on the 'Political Economy' of Sex." In *Toward an Anthropology of Women*, edited by Rayna R. Reiter. New York, NY: Monthly Review Press, 1975: 157–210.

Rudnitsky, Konstantin. *Meyerhold, The Director*. Ann Arbor, MI: Ardis, 1981.

Rustomji, Nerina. "Are Houris Heavenly Concubines?" In *Concubines and Courtesans: Women and Slavery in the Islamic World*, edited by Matthew S. Gordon and Kathryn A. Hain. Oxford: Oxford Scholarship Online, 2017.

Saadi-Nejad, Manya. "Anāhitā: Transformations of An Iranian Goddess." Proquest Dissertations Publishing, 2019. Accessed February 23, 2022.

Sabet, Zarifa. "Behind The Shame and Silence: A Story Shrouded in a Miasma of Shame." *Eurasia Review*, April 28, 2020. https://www.eurasiareview.com

Sadikova, Nafisa and Yulduz Gaibullaeva. *Uzbek millii kiiimlari XIX-XX asrlar*. Tashkent: Sharq, 2014.

Sadykova, Anvara. "Did The Kazakhs Have Their Own Dance Culture and What Are the Origins of Kara-Zhorga—The Nation's Favorite Dance?" *Voices On Central Asia*, September 17, 2021. https://voicesoncentralasia.org/did-the-kazakhs-have-their-own-dance-culture-and-what-are-the-origins-of-kara-zhorga-the-nations-favorite-dance/.

Safarova, Z. S. "Art by Tamara Khanum and Roza Karimova." *Middle European Scientific Bulletin* 7, (Dec. 2020): 34–9. https://doi.org/10.47494/mesb.2020.1.137.

Safarova, Zilola. "Deyatel'nost' Intelligentsii Uzbekistana V Gody Vtoroy Mirovoy Voyny." *Mirovaya nauka*, vol. 5, no. 2, 2016: 8–12.

Sagatov, Qo'rqmas Sagatovich. "Uzbek Dance National Heritage," *European Journal of Research and Reflection in Educational Sciences* Vol. 8 No. 11, 2020 Part II ISSN 2056–5852

Sahni, Kalpana. *Crucifying the Orient: Russian Orientalism and the Colonization of Caucasus and Central Asia*. Bangkok: White Orchid Press, 1997.

Said, Edward. *Orientalism: Western Concepts of the Orient*. Harmondsworth: Penguin, 1991.

Saidov Abdukakhor, Abdulkhamid Anarbaev, and Valentina Goriyacheva. "The Ferghana Valley: The Pre-Colonial Legacy." In *Ferghana Valley: The Heart of Central Asia*, Edited by F. Starr. London: Armonk, 2011: 3–28.

Saitova, G. Y., A. S. Tskhay, and R. V. Kenzikeyev. "Korean Stage Dance as A New Trend in Kazakhstan Choreography." *Global Media Journal* 14, No. 26 (06, 2016): 1–11, http://Proxygw.Wrlc.Org/Login (Accessed July 17, 2022).

Sakalis, Alex. "Arseny Avraamov: The forgotten Soviet genius of modern music." BBC www.bbc.com/culture/article/20221103-arseny-avraamov-the-man-who-conducted-a-city.

Sankir, Hasan. "Construction of Gender Roles in 17th-Century Ottoman Dancing Boys (Köçeks): Habitus, Body, and Dance." *Asian Journal of Social Science* 48, no. 1-2 (2020): 44–68.

Saylor, Nicole. "Dance Heritage Coalition Intern Helps Expand Access to Lomax Choreometrics Materials." *Library Of Congress* (Blog). July 21, 2014. https://Blogs.Loc.Gov/Folklife/2014/07/Lomax-Choreometrics-Collection//.

Schafer, Edward H. *The Golden Peaches of Samarkand: a study of T'ang Exotics*. Berkeley: University of California Press, 1963.

Schroeder, Eric. *Muhammad's People*, trans. Portland, Maine: The Bond Wheelwright Company, 1955.

Schuyler, Eugene. *Turkistan; Notes of a Journey in Russian Turkistan, Khokand, Bukhara, and Kuldja*. 2nd ed. London: S. Low, Marston, Searle & Rivington, 1876.

Scott, Erik R. "Dances of Difference," *Familiar Strangers: The Georgian Diaspora and the Evolution of Soviet Empire*. New York; online edition Oxford Academic, 2016. https://doi.org/10.1093/acprof:oso/9780199396375.003.0005, accessed 17 Sept. 2022.

Shadyev, Boltabai. "The Issue of Artistic Integrity of Mass Performances." *Sanat*, no. 2 (April 1, 2005).

Shagidullina, Adelya. (2019) Tatar Folk Music and Its Influence in the First National Ballet. (PhD Diss.) Temple University.

Shahbazi, A. Shapur. "Harem in Ancient Iran." *Iranica Online*. December 15, 2003. Accessed March 3, 2016. www.iranicaonline.org/articles/harem-i.

Shakarjanov, Yusuf Qiziq. "On The Example of People's Artist of Uzbekistan." *IJIEMR Transactions*, published online May 12, 2021. https://ijiemr.org/downloads/volume-10/issue-5.

Sharifzadeh, Afsheen. "The Origin of Khorezmian 'Lazgi'." *Borderless Blogger* (Blog). December 5, 2021. https://borderlessblogger.wordpress.com/2021/12/05/the-origin-of-khorezmian-lazgi/.

Sharifzadeh, Afsheen. "The Persian Vernacular of Samarkand and Bukhara: A Primer." *Borderless Blogger* (Blog). May 24, 2019. https://borderlessblogger.wordpress.com/2019/05/24/on-the-persian-vernacular-of-samarkand-and-bukhara/.

Shay, Anthony. *Dance and Authoritarianism: These Boots Are Made for Dancing*. Bristol, UK: Intellect Books Ltd, 2020. http://ebookcentral.proquest.com/lib/gwu/detail.action?docid=6425280.

Shirokaya, O. I. *Tamara Xonim (Tamara Artemovna Petrosian)*. Tashkent: Gafur Gulyam, 1973.

Sicotte, Jonathan H. *Baku: Violence, Identity, and Oil, 1905–1927*. Dissertation. Georgetown University, Washington, DC (2017).

Siderenko, A. I., A. R. Arykob, and R. R. Radjabov. *Zolotoe Shitye Bukharyi*. Tashkent: Gafur Gulyam, 1981.

Simbirsteva, Tatiana. «Муза Востока» Тамара Ханум и ее корейские песни, *Koryo-Saram*, Dec 11, 2014. https://koryo-saram.site/muza-vostoka-tamara-hanum-i-ee-korejskie-pesni/.

Sine, Elizabeth E. "The Radical Vision of Si-lan Chen: The Politics of Dance in an Age of Global Crisis." *Small Axe*, 20, no. 2 (2016): 28–43. muse.jhu.edu/article/622467.

Sirotkina, Irina. "Dance-plyaska in Russia of the Silver Age." *Dance Research*, 28 (November 2010): 135–52.

Sirotkina, Irina. "Reforming Early Twentieth Century Dance Theatre: Mikhail Fokin and Isadora Duncan." *Russian Literature*, 135–137 (2023): 349–64. https://doi.org/10.1016/j.ruslit.2022.11.014.

Slezkine, Yuri. "The USSR as a Communal Apartment, or How a Socialist State Promoted Ethnic Particularism." *Slavic Review* 53, no. 2 (1994): 414–52.

Snesarev, G. P. "Remnants of Pre-Islamic Beliefs and Rituals Among the Khorezm Uzbeks [Part XI]." *Soviet Anthropology and Archeology*, 15, no.4 (1977): 3–49.

Soo, Lee Hee. "Evaluation of Kŭshnāma as a Historical Source in Regard to Descriptions of Basīlā." *Acta Koreana*, 21, no. 1 (2018): 15–36. Muse.Jhu.Edu/Article/756449.

Sosnovskaya, A. G. *Put' razvitiya teatral'no-dekoratsionnogo iskusstva uzbekistana*. Tashkent: Fan Publishing, 1989.

Souritz, Elizabeth. "Isadora Duncan's Influence on Dance in Russia." *Dance Chronicle* 18, no. 2 (1995): 281–91.

Spector, Johanna. "Musical Tradition and Innovation." In *Central Asia, 120 Years of Russia Rule,* edited by Edward Allworth. Durham, NC: Duke University Press, 1989: 434-84.

Starr, S. Frederick. *Lost Enlightenment; Central Asia's Golden Age from the Arab Conquest to Tamerlane.* Princeton, NJ: Princeton University Press, 2013.

Staviskii, B. Ya. *Iskusstvo Srednei Azii.* Moscow: Iskusstvo, 1974.

Straus, Rachel. "Leonid Massine." In *Routledge Encyclopedia of Modernism.* 2016. www. Academia.Edu/11354500/L%C3%A9onide_Massine?Email_Work_Card=View-Paper.

Strong, Anna Louise. "Red Rule in Golden Samarkand." *The North American Review,* 228, no. 3 (1929): 309–15.

Strong, Anna Louise. *Red Star in Samarkand.* New York, NY: Coward-McCann, Inc., 1929.

Suhrawardi, Sheikh Shahabuddin. *A Dervish Textbook,* translate by Lt. Col. H. Wilberforce Clarke. London: The Octagon Press, 1980.

Sukhareva, O. A. *Istoriya sredneaziatskogo kostyuma.* Moscow: Nauka Publishing, 1982.

Sultangirova, Irina Radikovna. "Musical Dramaturgy of U. Musaev's Ballet 'Tomiris.'" *Oriental Art and Culture,* 3, no. 1 (2022). https://Cyberleninka.Ru/Article/N/Musical-Dramaturgy-Of-U-Musaevs-Ballet-Tomiris.

Sultanova, Razia. "Female Celebrations in Uzbekistan and Afghanistan: The Power of Cosmology in Musical Rites." *Yearbook for Traditional Music,* ICTM, 40 (2008): 8–20.

Sultanova, Razia. *From Shamanism to Sufism: Women, Islam and Culture in Central Asia.* London; New York: I.B. Tauris, 2011.

Sultanova, Razia. "Islamic and Sufi Soundscape in Central Asia: Genres, Rituals, and Lament." *Kyoto Bulletin of Islamic Area Studies,* 16 (March 2023): 32–34.

Sultanova, Razia, editor. *Turkic Soundscapes: From Shamanic Voices to Hip-Hop.* New York, NY: Routledge, 2018.

Suhrawardi, Sheikh Shahabbudin, Lieut.-Colonel H. Wilberforce Clarke. *A Dervish Textbook.* London: Octagon Press, 1980.

Sutil, N. S. "Rudolf Laban and Topological Movement: A Videographic Analysis." *Space and Culture,* 16, no. 2, (2013): 173–93. https://doi.org/10.1177/1206331213475776.

Svetkova, O. S., ed. *Dusha Russkogo Tantsa.* Kalinin: Regional Printing House, 1979.

Swift, Mary Grace. *The Art of the Dance in the USSR.* Notre Dame, IN: University of Notre Dame Press, 1968.

Sykes, Ella C. and Sir Percy Sykes, *Through deserts and oases of central Asia,* London, Macmillan and Co., limited, 1920, p. 314.

Tadjibaeva, Oltynoi. "'Alpamysh' Is A Symbol of Youth." *San'at Journal of The Academy of Arts of Uzbekistan,* 2 (January 4, 2006). https://Sanat.Orexca.Com/2006/2006-2/Alpamish-2/.

Taj al-Saltana, Zahra Khanom. *Crowning Anguish: The Memoirs of a Persian Princess from the Harem to Modernity, 1884–1914,* edited by A. Amanat, translated by A. Vanzan and A. Neshati. Washington, DC: Mage, 1993.

Театр имени Алишера Навои—культурное сердце Ташкента. *Sputnik Uzbekistan,* October 8, 2015. https://uz.sputniknews.ru/20151008/676086.html.

«То ли бомбят, то ли что-то другое»: как Ташкент пережил землетрясение. *gazeta.ru,* April 26, 2021.https://www.gazeta.ru/science/2021/04/25_a_13572272.shtml

(Temin), Elena Reikher. "Bukharan Jews in the Art Music of Central Asia." *Musica Judaica* 19 (2009): 131–64. http://www.jstor.org/stable/26454530

(Temin), Elena Reikher. "The Female 'Sozanda' Art from the Viewpoint of Professionalism in the Musical Tradition: A Preliminary Survey." *Musica Judaica,* 18 (2005): 70–86. Accessed October 5, 2020. http://www.jstor.org/stable/44511391.

Thesiger, Wilfred. *Arabian Sands.* New York, NY: E.P. Dutton and Company, 1959.

Thompson, Nevin. "Tashkent theatre offers window into Japanese internment after World War II." *Global Voices*, November 18, 2019. https://globalvoices.org/2019/11/18/tashkent-theatre-offers-window-into-japanese-internment-after-second-world-war/.

Thurbon, Colin. *The Silk Road, Beyond the Celestial Kingdom.* London: Simon and Schuster, 1989.

Tiurikov, A. *Istoriya o Tashkente: Ocherki.* Tashkent: Yosh Gvardiya, 1983.

Tkachenko, T. *Narodnyi Tanets.* Moscow: Gosudarstvennoe Izdatel'stvo, 1954.

Tomoff, Kiril. "Uzbek Music's Separate Path: Interpreting 'Anticosmopolitanism' in Stalinist Central Asia, 1949–52." *The Russian Review (Stanford)*, 63, no. 2 (2004): 212–40.

Tuhfakhon: Sanat ba Sanatkoroni Musikikai Nananavia Bukhori. Tel Aviv: Studio Shalom, 2000.

Tukliev, Nurislom, editor. *Toshkent: Entsiklopediya.* Tashkent: Press of the Republic of Uzbekistan State Committee, 1992.

Turgunova, Nasiba. "The Traditions of the Women's Art 'Yalla' of Central Asia." *Journal of Literature and Art Studies*, 5, no. 3 (March 2015): 217–21. doi: 10.17265/2159-5836/2015.03.008.

Ubiria, Grigol. *From Tribes to Modern Nations: Soviet Nation-Building in Kazakhstan and Uzbekistan.* PhD dissertation. The Australian National University, 2012.

"Uzbek, South Korean Presidents Open House of Korean Culture and Art." *Uzdaily.Com.* April 20, 2019. Http://Www.Uzdaily.Com/En/Post/49301.

Valyanskaya, O. *Zhenshchina v mifakh i legendakh: entsiklopedicheskiy slovar'.* Tashkent: Sharq Publishing, 1992.

Van Zile, Judy. *Perspectives on Korean Dance.* Middletown, CT: Wesleyan University Press, 2001.

Vercoe, Rosa. "How they met Tamara Khanum in London and the secret of Usto Olim Komilov's turban." *Voices on Central Asia* online, October 22, 2019.

Vershchagin, V. V. *Povesti, Ocherki, Vosnominaniya.* Moscow: Sovetskaya Rossia, 1990.

Vollmer, John, E. J. Keall, E. Nagai-Berthrong. *Silk Roads, China Ships.* Toronto: Royal Ontario Museum, 1983.

Wade, Bonnie C. *Imaging Sound: An Ethnomusicological Study of Music, Art, and Culture in Mughal.* Chicago, IL: University of Chicago, 1998.

Walker, Barbara G. *The Women's Encyclopedia of Myths and Secrets.* San Francisco, CA: Harper &Row, 1983.

Walker, Margaret E. *India's Kathak Dance in Historical Perspective.* Farnham: Ashgate, 2014.

Weil, Martin. "One of the 20th Century's Great Ballerinas." *The Washington Post.* 2015.

Wheeler, William. "The USSR As a Hydraulic Society: Wittfogel, The Aral Sea and the (Post-) Soviet State." *Environment and Planning C: Politics and Space*, 37, no. 7 (November 2019): 1217–34. https://Doi.Org/10.1177/2399654418816700.

Whitfield, Susan. *Life Along the Silk Road.* Berkeley, CA: University of California Press, 1999.

Wilcox, Emily. *Revolutionary Bodies: Chinese Dance and the Socialist Legacy.* Oakland, CA: University of California Press, 2018

Wilcox, Emily. "When Folk Dance Was Radical: Cold War Yangge, World Youth Festivals, and Overseas Chinese Leftist Culture in the 1950s and 1960s." *China Perspectives*, no. 1 (2020): 33–42. www.Jstor.Org/Stable/26902754.

Williams, Brian Glyn. "The Crimean Tatar Exile in Central Asia: A Case Study in Group Destruction and Survival." *Central Asian Survey*, 17, no. 2 (1998): 285–317. DOI: 10.1080/02634939808401038.

Williams, Maynard Owens. "First Over the Roof of the World by Motor." *National Geographic*, March 1932.

Wilson, Jennifer. "Overlooked No More: Si-Lan Chen, Whose Dances Encompassed Worlds." *New York Times*, May 27, 2021. www.Nytimes.Com/2021/05/27/Obituaries/Si-Lan-Chen-Overlooked.Html.

Wong, Peter Kim-Hung. "Cultural Influences on Dance in the T'ang Dynasty and the Movement Characteristics of a Dance of the Period." PhD. Dissertation, University of Wisconsin, Madison, 1989.

Wright, Louise E. "Touring Russia with Isadora: Maurice Magnus' Account." *Dance Chronicle*, 23, no. 3 (2000): 233–61.

"Xorazm Lazgi Raqsi: Milliy Raqslaring Rivojlanishi Va Ularing Hozirigi Davrdagi Ahamiyati (Khorezm Lazgi Dance: Development of National Dances and Their Contemporary Importance)." In *Materials of The 1st International Scientific and Practical Conference*. Tashkent: Bookmany Print LLC, 2022.

Yuldashev, Ilkhom Ibrokhimovich. "National Features of Estrada Acting Skills." *International Journal for Innovative Engineering and Management*, 10, no. 5 (2021): 43–45.

Yushkova, Elena. "Isadora Duncan's Dance in Russia: First Impressions and Discussions, 1904–1909." *Journal of Russian American Studies*, 2, no. 1 (May 2018): 15–43.

Zhang, He. "A Study of the Sogdian Whirl Dance and Shaman's Performance," presented at Asian Studies Development Program National Conference, March 2009.

Zimin, I. V. "Zabytyy" velikiy knyaz': Romanov Nikolay Konstantinovich." *Voprosy istorii*, no. 10 (2002): 131–39.

INDEX

Nizami 199
Nizamova, Rano 163
nongak (farmer dance) 140–1
nosi-gardon 87
Nurdzhanov, Nizam 68

Obukhova, Yevgeniya 128, 151
Ohanian, Armen: *Dancer of Shamahka,
  The* 118
Ohundi, Nasrullo 152
Olympics, Moscow (1980) 146
Operation Barbarossa 153
Otaniyozov, Komiljon 93

Pahlavan 61
Pahlen, Count K. K. 91, 100
Pai-Kabak 30
pakapak 91
Pakhta "Cotton" 171–72
Palace of Young Pioneers in Tashkent
  156
paranjah 46, 52, 105–6, 107, 209, 213
Paris, Performance in 1925 118–20
Parsees 6
Parvoz Folk Song and Dance Ensemble
  131
Paulay, Forrestine 184
Paxta ("Cotton"), 167
Penjikent in Tajikistan 4, 62–3
Peroz III 6
peshanaband 77, 174
Petrosova, Elizaveta 150, 183, 184, 185,
  186, 187, 189, 201, 210
Pilla ("Silkworm") 35, 117, 124, 195
Pinkhasova, Tufakhon 23, 65, 71, 72, 79,
  109
pishek kum 91
Plekhanov, Georgi 120
Plekhanova, Rosalie 120
Polo, Marco 28
Polovtsian Dances 113, 115, 144
popak 53
popkoch'um drum dance 140, 143
popular music 203–4
poyamol 34
Poznyakov, Nikolai 116
Prince Igor (opera) 113
Prokofiev, Sergei 112, 113
proletkult 112

Pulatov, Timur: *Life Story of a Naughty
  Boy from Bukhara, The* 65
Pushkin, Alexander 143
  Tale of the Golden Cockerel, The
  (*Zolotoy Pyetushok.* 118
Putin, Vladimir 148
Pyongyang 141

Qadriy, Abdullah
  Mehrobdan Chayon ("Scorpion from
  the Altar") 23
  O'tkan Kunlar (Bygone Days) 24
qala 86
Qalandars 23
qarsak 31
Qingje, Zhang 64
izlar majlisi 24
Qo'shiqlar Uchadi (Songs Fly) (film) 102
Qodiriyi, Abdullah *see* Qadriy, Abdullah
qoghirchoqbozlik (puppetry) 101
qoshiq 30
Qyrq Qyz, the "Forty Warrior Maidens"
  182, 185–6
  See also Kyrk Kyz

Radek, Karl 43
Rajasthani Roma folk dances 79
Rakhimov, Pulatjon 151
Rakhimova, Gavkhar 108, 109, 150, 183
Rapo 62
Rapoport, Yuri 86
Raqs Sehri (Magic of Dance) *Festival* 202
raqs sharqi dance 96
Rasulmatova, Kuydiniso 23
Razikova, Zevar 70–1
Rebeck, Raymondo 94
Reichl, Karl: *Edige: A Karakalpak Oral
  Epic as Performed by Jumabay
  Bazarov* 180
Representative list of the Intangible
  Cultural Heritage of Humanity 181
rhythm 27–39
Rimsky-Korsakov, Nikolai 118, 143
Rizo 100
Robeson, Paul 122
Rodchenko, Alexander 119
Romanov, Grand Duke Nikolai
  Konstantinovich 190
Roosevelt 130, 153

Roy, M. N. 70
Royer, Charles 193
rubais 68
Rumi, Jaladdin 62
Russian Civil War 210
Russian Orientalism 112–16
Russian State Academic Choreographic
  Ensemble *Beriozka*, 162–3

Saadi Mahdi, Usta 101
sadra 34, 39
saekdong 140
Said Kissach 101
Said Mir Muhammad Olimxon, Emir 69,
  70, 71
Saidazimova, Tursunoi 106
Salikhova, Firuza 191, 212
Salomat 35
Salomat-khola 35
Salomlar 81
salp'uri 140
sama 89, 181
Samāğa performances 10
salomlar 81
Samarkand 55–81
  bells, *mudras*, and spins 62–6
  costuming and movement 75–6
  dance characteristics 76–8
  Indian and Sogdian connections 78–80
  movements on the floor 81
  salomlar 81
  sozanda 66–73
Samaya (Georgian dance) 5
Samguk Sagi (*The History of the Three
  Kingdoms*) 8
samyukta hastas ("double hand" gestures)
  63
sangmo 141
Sanin, Rimma 156
Sarasvati (Indian goddess) 63
Sarbozi 34
Saroy lazgi 92
Sarynova, Lydia P. 181
Sasanian Empire 6
Satanic verses 5
Savitsky Museum 186
sayil 49
Scheherazade 113, 144
Schuyler, Eugene 20, 21, 122

Sejong, King 142
setara 30
Shahnameh 32
Shakarjanov, Yusufjon Kyzyk (Yusuf-
  Kyzyk) 24–5, 31, 32, 34, 48, 49, 54,
  99–104, 110, 126, 127, 131, 206
Shamakhmudov, Shaahkmed 154
Shamanism 38, 39, 140
Sharipova, Ravshanoi 176
Sharq Taronalari (Melodies of the East)
  201–202, 212
Shashmaqom (1972) (film) 192
Shaybanids 56
Shchusev, Alexey 157
Shermatov, Nasreddin 176, 211
Sherova, Diloram 192
Shia Alevi sect 62
Shiva, Lord 63
Shodlik 204
Shodlik Ensemble 192
shokh turn 33, 101, 132, 171
Shukufa 7
Silk and Spices Festival (Bukhara) 202
Silk Road Dance Company 195
Siniaya Bluza 73
Sitara, Samara 147
Siyavash, Prince 32, 33, 56
sleeve dance traditions 140
Slezkine, Yuri 179
Sobirova, Anabibi 92
Sogdian Whirl 17, 34, 44, 50, 59–62, 64,
  77, 140, 181
Sogdiana 43
Sogdians 44, 59
song lyrics 15
sozanda 22, 23, 24, 31, 63, 65, 66–73, 121,
  209
sozanda bozinga 68
Stalin, Josef 113, 130, 144, 153, 161, 168
  "cult of personality." 139
Stanislavsky, Konstantin 113
Star of Bukhara 65
Stein, Aurel 85
Strong, Anna Louise 43, 73, 106, 121
Sufism 38, 39
  Naqshbandi 63
Suidieva, Zulfi 23
Sultanov, Jalal 157
Sultanova, Rushana 191, 212